Immigration and Ethnicity

The Integration of America's Newest Arrivals

THE URBAN INSTITUTE PRESS
Washington, D.C.

THE URBAN INSTITUTE PRESS
2100 M Street, N.W.
Washington, D.C. 20037

Library of Congress Cataloging in Publication Data

Immigration and Ethnicity : The Integration of America's Newest Arrivals
Barry Edmonston and Jeffrey S. Passel, editors.

1. Immigrants—United States. 2. Ethnicity—United States. 3. United States— Emigration and Immigration—Government Policy. I. Edmonston, Barry. II. Passel, Jeffrey S.

JV6455.I556	1994	93-41406
304.8′73—dc20		CIP

ISBN 0-87766-579-6 (paper, alk. paper)
ISBN 0-87766-578-8 (cloth, alk. paper)

Printed in the United States of America

Distributed by University Press of America

4720 Boston Way
Lanham, MD 20706

3 Henrietta Street
London WC2E 8LU ENGLAND

THE URBAN INSTITUTE is a nonprofit policy research and educational organization established in Washington, D.C., in 1968. Its staff investigates the social and economic problems confronting the nation and public and private means to alleviate them. The Institute disseminates significant findings of its research through the publications program of its Press. The goals of the Institute are to sharpen thinking about societal problems and efforts to solve them, improve government decisions and performance, and increase citizen awareness of important policy choices.

Through work that ranges from broad conceptual studies to administrative and technical assistance, Institute researchers contribute to the stock of knowledge available to guide decision making in the public interest.

Conclusions or opinions expressed in Institute publications are those of the authors and do not necessarily reflect the views of staff members, officers or trustees of the Institute, advisory groups, or any organizations that provide financial support to the Institute.

ACKNOWLEDGMENTS

This volume results from the efforts of many people. The authors of the papers in this volume originally presented their work at a conference held at the Urban Institute, with the sponsorship of the Ford Foundation. William Diaz at the Ford Foundation provided good-natured encouragement and support for the conference. William Gorham, President of the Urban Institute, devoted his attention to the organization of the conference and provided thoughtful comments at the opening of the conference.

No editors can perform their duties well without an excellent staff. Sheila Lopez, Sonja Drumgoole, and Lavonia Proctor helped organize the conference, nudged us on to meet our deadlines, and assisted in the administrative tasks of preparing this volume.

Finally, we wish to express our profound appreciation to our fellow colleagues for their willingness to devote time and their special knowledge to the development and writing of the chapters of this volume. They worked well together at a stimulating conference. And they cooperated willingly, a critical element in a multidisciplinary enterprise, in revising their papers for publication here.

CONTENTS

Tables

Figures

FOREWORD

Immigration has been a major focus of Urban Institute research for more than a decade. Our first major study in this area was begun in the early 1980s—a period, like the current one, when there was intense interest in changing U.S. immigration policy. The Simpson-Mazzoli and other bills were being vigorously discussed within a context of widespread concern about the impacts that immigration was having, particularly on the job and earnings prospects of U.S. workers, among other concerns.

The Institute brought together a group of demographers, economists, political scientists, sociologists, education specialists, and lawyers to participate in that first major study—a foundation of expertise upon which we have continued to build.

The subject of immigration is again high on the political and legislative agenda, with the focus widening to include not only the economic effects of immigration but also the role of immigrants in U.S. society more generally. It is the Institute's intent now, as it was when we began our immigration work, to produce reliable information on immigration and its effects, in an effort to inform the public debate, which has as often misled as it has clarified the issues before the nation.

This book focuses on key trends relating to the integration of immigrants who have entered the United States since 1980. Contributing authors examine the changing ethnic origins of immigrants; adjustments of the "new ethnic" immigrants in the United States; special issues in immigrant adjustment (earnings, language, secondary migration, and political change); the components of U.S. policy toward immigrants once they are here; and the projected impact of immigrants on the future racial-ethnic composition of this country.

Although U.S. policy toward immigration is a federal responsibility, policy toward immigrant integration has been left in the hands of states and localities and, thus, varies widely by region. The time may be ripe to reconsider the wisdom of this approach to immigrants and their integration into American society. It is my hope that the information presented here will encourage and help inform such a debate.

William Gorham
President

Chapter One

ETHNIC DEMOGRAPHY: U.S. IMMIGRATION AND ETHNIC VARIATIONS

Barry Edmonston and Jeffrey S. Passel

The United States has experienced a large volume of immigration during the past century, with a wave of "new" immigrants beginning in the late 1960s as a result of the Immigration Act of 1965. Prior to the 1965 legislation, U.S. immigration policy had been based on nationality quotas that favored immigrants from Canada and Europe and restricted immigrants from Africa, Asia, Latin America, and the Caribbean. The 1965 legislation opened the doors to immigrants from "new" nations by eliminating restrictions on national groups. The total volume of immigration (legal and illegal, as well as refugees) to the United States during the past three decades has come increasingly from Asia and Latin America.

The subject of immigration continues to arouse controversy in the United States, with considerable public debate about immigrants in U.S. society and their future role. Current debate centers around a number of trends in U.S. immigration. First, the resident population is aging and will eventually decline without substantial immigration. Current immigration implies dramatic growth in new ethnic communities and raises new concerns about large, relatively young Asian and Hispanic immigrant populations. Second, the shift in new ethnic communities will not be felt evenly throughout the United States. It will be concentrated in a few large metropolitan areas (Los Angeles, Miami, New York, and the large cities of the Southwest and Mexican-border region) and in selected areas (the Pacific Coast area and along the Mexican border). Areas with most of the "new" immigrants are also the places where ethnic relations will be challenging and where social disturbances are most likely to arise from, for example, perceived resident unemployment. Third, the demographic consequences of current immigration are difficult to assess because demographic growth depends upon the future level and composition of immigration, fertility levels, and emigration from the United States. Current levels of fertility, mortality, and immigration indicate a sustained increase in numbers and the relative proportion of "new" immigrants in the U.S. population, and an amplification of the size and growth of new ethnic minorities in schools, politics, and the labor force.

The year 1992 was the centennial of Ellis Island, entrance site for millions of immigrants into the United States. The celebration of the centennial of Ellis Island is, in a broad sense, the celebration of the ordinary immigrant seeking a better life. It should be remembered that most immigrants are noteworthy for their "ordinary" status and are generally neither peasants nor Nobel prize winners. The story of ethnic variations in immigrants is composed of millions of people seeking to improve their lives and attempting to fulfill their dreams through immigration to the United States. The chapters in this volume, therefore, emphasize the social, political, and economic adjustments—the successes and failures—of these new immigrants.

This volume brings together work that examines a broad scope of immigration issues including political, social, demographic, and economic change. Well-known immigration specialists from several fields were invited to prepare essays on key trends relating to the integration of America's newest immigrants. They were asked to examine the latest data available on integration issues, focusing on immigrant groups that have recently entered the United States. Preliminary versions of the chapters that follow were presented at a conference sponsored by the Urban Institute's Program for Research on Immigration Policy in June 1991 (in Washington, D.C., at the Urban Institute). The contributing authors then made extensive revisions in response to both the conference discussion and outside reviewers' comments.

The resulting book assesses the integration of America's recent "new" immigrants. It presents essential facts about current immigration and the progress of America's newest immigrants. The chapters in the volume discuss problems, policies, and recent research on new immigrants in order to offer a better understanding of U.S. immigration policies. The time seems ripe for such an evaluation of the adjustment of recent immigrants, particularly within the context of the variety of different ethnic backgrounds of these immigrants. This evaluation extends to a discussion about how the success of their adjustment informs U.S. immigration policy. Toward this end, the chapters emphasize five themes:

☐ a description of recent immigration trends, stressing the changing

ethnic origins of immigrants and the influence of past trends on the current generational composition of major racial/ethnic groups;
□ adjustment of the "new ethnic" immigrants in the United States, focusing on evaluation using the latest available data;
□ special issues in immigrant adjustment (earnings, language, secondary migration, and political change);
□ the components of U.S. policy toward newcomers (both express and de facto) and the implementation of such policies at different levels of government; and
□ future trends in immigration and the impact of immigrants on the future racial/ethnic composition of the U.S. population.

This introductory chapter reviews the policy issues and available research on the integration of ethnic groups into U.S. society. It discusses the lessons learned from historical studies and contrasts the past situation with the current one. The other chapters of this volume cover broad social, political, and economic topics. The intended audience for the book includes those in the policy-making, business, and academic communities with an interest in immigration and immigrant integration. Although several chapters include technical materials, the discussion should be readable for the general audience. With its up-to-date analysis, fairly comprehensive coverage of substantive topics, and current immigration policy discussion, we hope that the book will find interest among legislators, policymakers, libraries, and researchers in immigration studies and policy.

U.S. IMMIGRATION POLICY: AN HISTORICAL SYNOPSIS

Until the latter half of the 1800s, immigrants to the United States entered freely and without federal controls. The federal government, in the first century after independence, allowed unrestricted admission of aliens and the automatic qualification of immigrants and their children as citizens. The first restrictive immigration law, passed in 1875, prohibited "obnoxious" immigrants (persons who were destitute, active in immoral activities, or physically handicapped). The 1875 Immigration Act was followed by additional acts in 1882, 1891, 1903, and 1917, which excluded immigrants on a variety of moral, economic, and physical grounds (U.S. Immigration and Naturalization Service [INS] 1991a).

Until 1860, virtually all immigrants to the United States were from

Germany, Ireland, and the United Kingdom. After 1860, growing numbers came from Scandinavia, China, and South America. The expanding American West required immigrant labor for the mines and railroads, two industries that hired large numbers of Chinese and others as contract laborers. In the 1860s, for instance, about one-third of western miners were Chinese. Many other miners came from Chile, Peru, and Mexico. As the numbers of immigrant laborers increased, they faced growing opposition from native labor groups. American anxiety over economic threats from cheaper immigrant labor, as well as racism, was, in large part, behind the passage of the Chinese Exclusion Act of 1882. This law limited the number of Chinese allowed to enter the United States. Later amendments to the 1882 Act ultimately prohibited immigration of all Chinese.

Late nineteenth century immigration law increased the role of the federal government in monitoring and regulating immigration. The Immigration Act of 1891 created the Office of Immigration, the precursor to the current Immigration and Naturalization Service. The 1891 Act directed the Superintendent of Immigration to enforce immigration law under the supervision of the Secretary of the Treasury.

Continued concern about Asian immigration, originally only specific to Chinese, was expanded to deal with Japanese immigration in the early 1900s. The 1907 Gentleman's Agreement with Japan restricted Japanese immigration, with the agreement of the Japanese government. Japanese immigration was formally and unilaterally prohibited by the United States government in the Japanese Exclusion Act of 1924.

Another shift in the origins of European immigrants began in the 1880s with sharp increases from countries in the southern and eastern portion of Europe. This development—large numbers of immigrants from Austria-Hungary, Italy, Greece, Poland, and Russia—provoked a strong reaction in the United States to the "new" immigrants. As noted in chapter two, the nation witnessed a dramatic increase in the numbers of immigrants in the first two decades of the 1900s—more than a million immigrants per year for several years—and over half of the new immigrants were from Italy, Russia, and Austria-Hungary.

The rise in immigration overlapped, for some years, with periods of economic weakness and high unemployment in the United States. Several federal commissions in the 1910s suggested that the nation needed to restrict immigration and add qualifications for admission. The Dillingham Commission, for example, recommended in 1917 that immigrants should be literate and that no immigrants should be from "barred zones" in Asia.

Immigration lessened during World War I but resumed at a high level after the war, despite the existing employment and housing shortage. Public opinion, which had previously regarded free immigration as important and healthy for the nation, shifted. In response to the economic situation and with widespread public support, Congress enacted the 1921 Quota Act. That Act limited immigration to only 3 percent of the foreign-born population, by national origin, already in the United States and based the limit on the 1910 Census. The Immigration Act of 1924 made national origin quotas permanent and further limited immigration to 2 percent of the national origin groups in the U.S. population according to the 1890 Census. Thus, the 1924 restrictions accorded the largest quotas to Northern and Western Europe—because these were the dominant national origin groups in the 1890 population—and sharply diminished immigration from Southern and Eastern Europe. The 1924 Act also barred completely aliens who were ineligible for citizenship—i.e., Asians who, as a group, had been declared as not eligible for U.S. citizenship in previous naturalization legislation.

The 1924 Act also made one important change in the administration of immigration law. The 1924 legislation provided funds to form a larger Border Patrol from the existing mounted inspectors. By the 1930s, the work of the Immigration Bureau had shifted to reliance on the Border Patrol for apprehension, exclusion, and deportation and to application review of immigrants at major ports of entry. An Executive Order by President Roosevelt in 1933 created the Immigration and Naturalization Service.

Major changes were made in the compilation of immigration laws after World War II. The Immigration and Nationality Act, passed in June 1952, codified many previous immigration and naturalization laws. The 1952 Act also introduced a preference structure, with separate categories for types of relatives and worker skills. The Act removed racial barriers to naturalization, although it retained the national origin restrictions that had been in place since 1924. President Harry Truman vetoed the Act because it did not remove the national origin restrictions. Congress overrode his veto, however, and the law went into effect in December 1952. President Truman subsequently named a commission to study the weaknesses of the 1952 Act. The commission reported in 1953 that the national origins system should be replaced with immigration selection based on family reunification and employment skills.

Like President Truman, President Eisenhower called for changes in the national-origin restrictions of immigration law in order to eliminate its injustices. Reforms finally occurred when, in 1963, President Kennedy proposed a revision and update of national immigration policy. The reforms were enacted in 1965 as amendments to the 1952 Act. The 1965 amendments eliminated the old national origins system. In particular, the 1965 amendments abandoned country-specific quotas (including the "zero" quotas for Asian countries), gave special preferences for relatives of U.S. citizens and legal residents, and added parents to immediate family members who are exempt from numerical quotas. At about the same time as the 1965 amendments, Congress also terminated the Bracero Program, which had funnelled temporary Mexican workers into agriculture in the southwestern United States for more than two decades. These legal changes set the stage for two of the major shifts in the character of immigration that were to occur in subsequent decades. Economic incentives for Mexican workers in agriculture continued but now became the major magnet for heavy illegal immigration. Greater access to legal immigration slots led to substantial increases in immigration from Asia and Latin America.

Immigration reform in the 1980s produced three major pieces of new legislation. The Refugee Act of 1980, the Immigration Reform and Control Act of 1986 (IRCA), and the Immigration Act of 1990 together offered an overhaul of U.S. immigration policy. The Refugee Act of 1980 modernized refugee policy and provided categories of refugee admission for handling aliens who declare themselves to be refugees.

The primary purpose of IRCA was to decrease the number of illegal immigrants by limiting the flow of illegal immigrants and by legalizing the status of illegal aliens already residing in the United States. To reduce the flow of illegal immigrants, IRCA strengthened the Border Patrol and established penalties for employers who knowingly hire illegal aliens. IRCA also established a program of admission of agricultural workers should an insufficient number of native farmworkers be available. The result of IRCA was the legalization of almost three million persons who were residing in the United States prior to 1986 as illegal aliens. The role of employer sanctions has been widely debated (Fix 1991), although employer sanctions, even in combination with a strengthened Border Patrol, have not apparently diminished the flow of illegal immigrants (Bean, Edmonston, and Passel 1990).

The Immigration Act of 1990 substantially revised immigration law for the first time in 25 years. The 1990 Act dealt with family reunification (allowing for an unlimited number of visas for immediate relatives of U.S. citizens), labor shortages (restricting the number of visas for unskilled workers and increasing the number of visas for priority workers and professionals with U.S. job offers), entrepreneurial immigrants (offering 10,000 visas for investors with $1 million or more to create employment for at least ten U.S. residents), and a more diverse immigrant stream (opening immigrant visas for "underrepresented" countries, with 40 percent of new "diversity" visas reserved for Irish applicants for 1992 to 1994). The 1990 Act also includes specific provisions legalizing some Central American refugees who were residing in the United States and offering naturalization to certain Filipino veterans of World War II (see Fix and Passel 1991).

NEW IMMIGRANTS TO THE UNITED STATES

The United States has experienced a large volume of immigration of diverse peoples. The United States is a country of relatively recent large-scale settlement and, correspondingly, the number of immigrants arriving over the past 100 years has been high relative to other industrialized nations. The number of immigrants has also been high in terms of demographic impact, particularly in the nineteenth and early twentieth centuries, when the U.S. population was substantially smaller than it is today. Immigration flows into the United States during the twentieth century have averaged around 500,000 arrivals annually, with very wide fluctuations from one year and decade to the next.

As table 1.1 shows, there was a boom in immigration in the early years of the twentieth century, prior to World War I. In dramatic contrast, few immigrants came during the Depression in the 1930s. After World War II, immigration levels increased, with about 250,000 to 300,000 immigrants arriving annually. The relative prosperity of the United States and its labor shortage compared with Europe provided the incentive. These higher immigration levels continued into the 1960s, but the source of immigrants shifted steadily to Asian and Latin American countries. The 1970s and 1980s were characterized by increasing numbers of immigrants—legal, illegal, and refugees.

With growth of the population of the United States, the ratio of immigrants to population is lower now than at the turn of the century,

Table 1.1 IMMIGRATION AND U.S. POPULATION GROWTH: 1820 TO 1990

Period	Population at End of Period	Population Growth over Period	Immigration over Period	Annual Immigration as a Percentage of Average Population
1980–1990	248,712,000	22,087,000	9,972,000	0.4
1970–1980	226,625,000	21,058,000	7,726,000	0.4
1960–1970	205,567,000	23,512,000	3,738,000	0.2
1950–1960	182,055,000	26,899,000	3,011,000	0.2
1940–1950	155,156,000	18,228,000	1,849,000	0.1
1930–1940	136,928,000	9,343,000	750,000	0.1
1920–1930	127,585,000	16,838,000	4,185,000	0.4
1910–1920	110,747,000	16,868,000	5,906,000	0.6
1900–1910	93,879,000	17,684,000	8,024,000	0.9
1890–1900	76,195,000	13,247,000	3,688,000	0.5
1880–1890	62,948,000	12,792,000	5,247,000	0.9
1870–1880	50,156,000	10,338,000	2,812,000	0.6
1860–1870	39,818,000	8,375,000	2,315,000	0.6
1850–1860	31,443,000	8,251,000	2,599,000	1.0
1840–1850	23,192,000	6,123,000	1,713,000	0.9
1830–1840	17,069,000	4,203,000	599,000	0.4
1820–1830	12,866,000	3,228,000	152,000	0.2

Total Immigration 1900 to 1990 = 45,161,000

Sources: U.S. Bureau of the Census 1991, Tables 1 and 5. (Data for 1820 through 1900.) Passel and Edmonston 1992, table 2.1 in this volume. (Data for 1900 through 1990.)

even though the number of immigrants is high. Whereas annual arrivals represented 0.9 percent of the population in the early 1900s, this ratio fell to levels of about 0.4 percent in the recent decades. More detailed data on annual immigration numbers reveal wide fluctuations each year. These fluctuations stem from several policy considerations. First, the general upward shift in legal immigration reflects changes from simply admitting larger numbers of immigrants. Second, inflows arise in part as a response to the changing world refugee situation. When large numbers of refugees occur, particularly if from countries where the United States feels a special responsibility (Cuba and Vietnam, for instance), U.S. immigration policy often permits admission of these individuals. Third, the 1980s witnessed the first large-scale legalization of immigrants—over three million previously illegal aliens. Illegal immigration to the United States continues, however, unabated (Bean et al. 1990), and future programs may occur in the United States to legalize its illegal resident population.

As a result of large-scale immigration from many countries into the United States, the present U.S. population is now one of the world's largest multiethnic societies. The proportion of foreign-born in the total U.S. population was almost 9 percent in 1990. Among the large immigrant-receiving countries, only Canada has a larger proportion of foreign-born, with an estimated 16 percent in the late 1980s. The main immigrant-receiving countries of Europe have relatively low levels of foreign-born population. For example, within the European Community, Belgium has 3 percent foreign-born of its total population; France has 4 percent; Germany has 6 percent; the Netherlands has 3 percent; and the United Kingdom has 2 percent. Most European countries have less than one-half the foreign-born population, as a proportion of their total population, as the United States.

The immigrant groups of the United States are also comparatively diverse. The largest ethnic group of immigrants in the United States is from Mexico, comprising over one-fifth of the foreign-born population. Chinese are the next largest immigrant group, with about 5 percent of the immigrant population. Filipinos are the third largest immigrant group, with an estimated 4 percent. Overall, the three largest immigrant groups comprise slightly over one-fourth, 27 percent, of the total foreign-born population. Canada has a higher proportion of foreign-born in its population, but the immigrants are less diverse, with 47 percent of its immigrants from the United Kingdom, Chinese countries and areas, and Italy. Immigrants in European countries are more likely to be from only a few countries of origin. In Belgium, two-thirds of the immigrants are from only three countries (Morocco, Turkey, and Algeria), and about 40 percent are from one country, Morocco. In France, 65 percent are from three North African countries (Algeria, Morocco, and Tunisia). In Germany, 71 percent of immigrants are from three countries (Turkey, Yugoslavia, and Austria), and 46 percent of its immigrants are from Turkey alone. In the Netherlands, 73 percent of immigrants are from three countries (Turkey, Morocco, and the former Yugoslavia). Only the United Kingdom, which has permitted very few immigrants in the past decade, derives less than one-half (39 percent) of its foreign-born from three places (South Asia, West Indies, and Middle East).

REALITY OF CURRENT IMMIGRATION

The major challenge of immigration is the adaptation of immigrants. Since the new waves of immigrants are different in some ways from those in the past, different problems of adaptation—whether economic, social, cultural, or political—will arise. The question that requires attention is: Will the adaptation and integration of these new immigrants take longer or proceed in different ways than before? Will increased labor market discrimination occur against them, for instance? The first generation (i.e., the immigrants), which is culturally different from the resident population, may take longer to adapt, although the strong family ties and enterprise of some immigrant groups may help them to adapt more rapidly, at least in the economic realm. In addition, an important aspect of the adaptation of the new wave of immigrants is the attitude of Americans to the origins of the new residents. The ease of acceptance of immigrants is a critical feature in their adaptation to the new society.

As with previous waves of immigrants, the new immigrants concentrate in a few large cities and in selected states and regions. They will have a profound impact on population change in Los Angeles, Miami, and New York City, for example, repopulating some previously declining neighborhoods and altering the ethnic composition of local schools, communities, and commerce. Although no local level studies are reported in this book, Muller and Espenshade (1985) have described the impact of immigration on southern California; Winnick (1990) has prepared an excellent document on new immigrants in Brooklyn, New York; and Rothman and Espenshade (1992) have compiled a useful, systematic review of studies of immigration's impact on national and local economies.

Some innovations are required to move immigration studies forward. More interdisciplinary approaches would provide new perspectives, and the latest data, along with new methods of research, should be utilized. An older style of immigration research has changed in several ways. First, the older perspective of immigration tended to view individuals as becoming Americanized on their own. During the past decade, researchers have broadened the perspective and increasingly focused on groups and families. Second, earlier work often made the assumption of equal opportunity and free competition in open labor markets. This assumption is now questioned, as evidenced in several chapters in this volume. Newer work emphasizes discrimination and unequal achievement. Third, instead of the common goal of assimilation, as emphasized in earlier work, newer studies portray a variety of options, including emigration from the United States. The image of the "melting pot" cannot accommodate current perspectives, which emphasize the role of family and groups for immigrants and the importance of discrimination and unequal achievement in the labor market and generally question individual assimilation as the only option for the immigrant. So, rather than an individual immigrant "assimilating" while achieving economic success in the United States, the newer perspective emphasizes three themes in the current realities of U.S. immigration: new immigration patterns, new perspectives on the dimensions of immigrant integration, and new trends toward global migration. We summarize these new themes before beginning a fuller discussion of them.

New Immigration Patterns

Several types of immigrants enter the United States, and these types vary in their socioeconomic conditions and in their course of adaptation in the United States. Chapters in this volume describe legal immigrants, illegal immigrants, and refugees. Their different modes of entry can affect their adaptation to the United States. Several chapters analyze these patterns.

Dimensions of Immigrant Integration

The traditional perspective of immigrant adjustment, the so-called "melting pot," viewed the individual immigrant as assimilating into U.S. society by gradually adopting resident cultural values and the English language and eventually intermarrying with the resident population. Eventually, the descendants of the immigrants would be thoroughly blended and would, regardless of their origin, be "homogenized" Americans. Researchers in this volume either directly question the assimilationist perspective or tend not to assume individual assimilation. It is clear that an assimilationist approach is no longer the guiding theory for immigrant research, either as a beacon for interpreting data or even as a theory that requires testing in terms of alternative theories. The chapters in this volume, as a contrast, ask what adjustments immigrants have made and what the conditions are for their social, economic, and political change.

We offer a more detailed discussion of the dimensions of immigrant integration in two later sections. The first section describes two chapters in this volume that deal with Hispanic and Asian immigrants in separate analyses. A second section reviews four chapters that report on important dimensions of immigrant adaptation: wage trends, language acquisition, internal migration, and political change.

Future Trends

International migration now involves many countries, not only the traditional large immigrant-receiving countries of Australia, Canada, and the United States. People are moving, and the movement involves virtually all countries of the world. Huge numbers of people in Asia (which constitutes one-half of the world's population) have emigrated; and the residents of eastern Europe and the former Soviet Union are already emigrating. The potential for greater emigration is high. The changing size of the world's potential migrant population is leading to a diversification in the characteristics of immigrants and is affecting U.S. immigration. Illegal immigration continues in the United States, in spite of employer sanctions and enhanced Border Patrol activities. Legal immigration is large and will slowly increase under the provisions of the recently enacted Immigration Act of 1990. Refugee flows are moderate at the time of this writing, but one can anticipate one or more major refugee movements to the United States during the next decade. Finally, multinational corporations and internationally based research and collaboration have provided demands for changes in the way the United States handles temporary immigrants. The U.S. economy is becoming increasingly enmeshed in the global economy, a change that will necessitate further changes in immigration.

NEW IMMIGRATION PATTERNS

Immigrants are not an undifferentiated group of men and women, nor do they constitute an inchoate ethnic mass. Three broad groups of new immigrants now enter the United States: legal immigrants, illegal immigrants, and refugees (Portes and Rumbaut 1990). These groups have different social and economic characteristics, dissimilar countries of origin, and distinct starting points in their adjustment in the United States. In addition, an increasing number of non-immigrants (temporary international migrants on special "non-immigrant" visas) also enter the United States. Several chapters in this book refer to non-immigrants, although no specific research on them is reported in this volume because they are, by definition, not permanent residents. It is an important topic, however, for more policy research.

Legal immigrants constitute the bulk of U.S. immigration. Of the almost ten million entrants into the United States during the 1980s, about 900,000 were admitted as refugees, slightly over three million entered illegally (over two million were legalized during the decade), and the remaining more than six million were legal immigrants. Net illegal immigration into the United States continues at about 200,000 per year, and little prospect is seen for a significant reduction in that flow. Nevertheless, the main group of U.S. immigrants enters legally under conditions set by immigration legislation and INS guidelines.

The flow of legal immigrants has come increasingly from countries in the developing world. In fact, legal immigration from Asia, Latin America, the Caribbean, and Africa constituted 82 percent of all legal immigration to the United States in 1990 (U.S. Immigration and Naturalization Service 1991b, Table 7).[1] The decline in European-origin immigrants from 1965 to 1990 is impressive. Canada and Europe provided 51 percent of the immigrant flow in 1965 (U.S. Bureau of the Census 1968, Table 127) but only 17 percent in 1990 (U.S. Bureau of the Census 1992, Table 8). An examination of the individual countries of origin reveals that the greatest declines were for immigrants from western and northern Europe. The small number of immigrants from eastern Europe and the former Soviet Union has fluctuated annually, depending upon events in those countries, but has generally increased proportionate to other European immigrants.

Among legal immigrants from developing countries, Asians have shown the most spectacular increase, from 7 percent in 1965 to 46 percent in 1990. The Asian immigrant stream is currently divided among Chinese (17 percent of total immigrants and coming from Hong Kong, Taiwan, China, and Singapore),[2] Filipino (18 percent), South Asians (13 percent from India, Bangladesh, Sri Lanka, and Pakistan), Koreans (10 percent), and various Indo-Chinese ethnic groups (24 percent from Vietnam, Cambodia, Laos, and Thailand).

Latin American immigrants rank second in terms of legal immigrant flows. About 20 percent of 1990 immigrants came from Latin America. The largest group of Latin American immigrants is Mexican (42 percent), and smaller numbers of Latin American immigrants have come from Central America (particularly El Salvador and Guatemala) and South America (especially Colombia) in recent years.

A smaller number of immigrants come from the Caribbean (13 percent of all legal immigrants), although their numbers are significant because of their contribution to the growth of the U.S. black population. Caribbean immigrants in recent years have principally arrived from the Dominican Republic, Jamaica, and Haiti.

Africa provides relatively few immigrants. However, whereas African immigrants constituted only 2,600 immigrants in 1965, their total has increased steadily and is now 20,000, or 3 percent of the legal immigration flow.

As global migration becomes widespread, the characteristics of immigrants have also become more diverse. Much of the immigration flow into the United States (and other countries) is legal immigration, governed by legislative limits and legal qualifications. Illegal immigrants also manage to enter, however, and few industrial nations are immune from the entrance of undocumented migrants. Many of those who do not try the underground route will apply for entrance as refugees. About 135,000 applied for refugee status in the United States in 1990 (U.S. Immigration and Naturalization Service 1991b, 97). Over 550,000 persons sought refugee status in 1990 in European countries (U.S. Department of State 1991, Table 11). An additional 36,000 sought refugee status in Canada; and about 10,000 in Australia. The flow of refugees today is unprecedented, with about 750,000 persons annually seeking refugee status in the industrialized nations (Edmonston and Lee 1990). Although industrial nations maintain a theoretical distinction for the motivation for refugees ("economic refugees" need not apply), most illegal entrants and asylum-seekers stay in their new country, once having entered.

Illegal immigrants are now a persistent problem in all industrial societies. Net illegal immigration into the United States is currently estimated to be in the range of 100,000 to 300,000 per year (Edmonston and Passel in chapter 11 of this volume). Apprehensions of illegal entrants decreased after IRCA, but the decrease occurred principally because many illegal aliens became legal residents. The flow of undocumented migrants into the United States has again increased and, thus, has changed little since the beginning of the decade. Illegal immigrants also slip into European countries, and southern European countries are rapidly installing better immigration controls to comply with the Schengen accord (which will end intra-European Community passport checks). In Asia, many illegal migrants work in Japan, usually as contract workers and on jobs that Japanese workers shun.

The definition of refugees is a matter of international law and national considerations. Although some 15 million refugees were counted worldwide by United Nations agencies in the late 1980s, most of these people were living close to their country of origin and most want to and probably eventually will return to their homes (Edmonston and Lee 1990). The bulk of the world's refugees are accounted for by only a few countries at the moment. Afghanistan provides most of the world's refugees (4.6 million), but this number has been reduced by the cessation of widespread civil war in early

1992. Palestinians contribute the next largest group (2.1 million), and Ethiopia accounts for the third largest group (1.1 million).

The United States accepted about 900,000 refugees during the 1980s. U.S. refugee admission requirements, specified under the Refugee Act of 1980, define a refugee in general accordance with United Nations conventions, viewing refugees as persons who are outside their country of nationality and who are unable or unwilling to return to that country because of persecution or a well-founded fear of persecution because of race, religion, ethnicity, or political opinion or because of conditions that threaten their physical or mental well-being. Future levels of refugee admissions in the United States depend on events in other countries and their associated refugee emigration.

Passel and Edmonston review the major trends for recent U.S. immigration in their chapter, entitled "Immigration and Race: Recent Trends in Immigration to the United States." The immigration chart that we are all familiar with shows two waves: high numbers of immigrants from 1880 to 1920 and again since 1970. Estimates developed by the authors and presented in the chapter show that the decade of the 1980s saw the largest migration to the United States in its history. Counting illegals, asylees, and SAWs (Special Agricultural Workers), more than 9 million immigrants entered the United States in the 1980s, compared to 8.9 million during 1901–1910 (the decade with the next largest immigration). In addition, emigration is much lower now than in previous decades. Thus, the United States experienced net immigration of 8.2 million during 1980–1990, compared to 4.9 million during 1900–1910. The decade from 1970 to 1980 also showed very large net immigration (6.9 million).

The U.S. population has grown considerably since the turn of the century. Has the relative importance of immigration changed? Yes and no. Net immigration was much larger relative to the total population; net immigrants during 1900–1910 represented 10.5 percent of the initial population. This ratio declined to 4.4 percent for the decade 1980 to 1990. On the other hand, fertility decreased significantly between 1900 and 1990. Thus, net immigration contributed 37 percent to population growth during the 1980–1990 decade, compared to 28 percent for the 1900–1910 decade.

Large recent immigration numbers mean that the foreign-born population has been increasing absolutely and proportionately since 1970. Passel and Edmonston (in this volume) estimate that, as of 1990, about 21 million U.S. residents were born outside the country. This represents about 8.5 percent of the population, a marked increase from the low of 5.1 percent in 1970, but significantly below the 13 to 15 percent levels of 1880 to 1910.

Recent immigrants have been predominantly Asian and Hispanic. Both of these groups experienced rapid population increase compared to the black and the white non-Hispanic populations. As a result of recent immigration, the minority share of the U.S. population increased substantially to almost 25 percent in 1990. At that time, the black population represented less than one-half (48 percent) of the U.S. minority population.

Passel and Edmonston also present new estimates of the contribution of twentieth century immigration to U.S. population growth, by decades for Asian, black, Hispanic, and white non-Hispanic groups. This investigation suggests that recent "new" immigration is behaving in a demographically similar manner to the way that immigration shifted from northern and western Europe to southern and eastern Europe from 1850 to 1920. The United States is once again on the eve of large ethnic transformations. In the past, major ethnic changes in the pattern of immigration have given rise to social disturbances, followed by periods of adaptation and integration of the immigrants (and adaptation by the U.S. society). The new phase will also likely involve some disturbances and raise new questions about the identity of the "American."

DIMENSIONS OF IMMIGRANT INTEGRATION: HISPANICS AND ASIANS

The traditional assimilation paradigm was developed by Robert Park (1928) and other Chicago sociologists in the 1920s as an explanation of changes in ethnic identity and behavior of immigrants. Their paradigm described a linear progression from Old World traits to Americanization as the immigrants adapted to life in the United States. They viewed immigrants as improving their language and occupational skills in the years after arrival, then slowly absorbing U.S. cultural values. In subsequent generations, the children of immigrants would increasingly absorb the culture and values of the majority society by intermarrying with other groups and eventually shedding their original ethnic identity.

The assimilationist perspective reinforces the idea of the United States as a melting pot in which a diversity of ethnic origins eventually blends into a single American identity. The notion of a melting pot has been challenged by many critics (Lieberson and Waters 1988) who cite the persistence of ethnic (and racial) identities. Although melting pot critics have advanced alternative perspectives, such as cultural pluralism or ethnic resilience, it is fair to say that most researchers now consider either the traditional assimilationist or alternative single perspectives too simplistic for guiding empirical analysis. Nevertheless, an assimilationist perspective has influenced immigration studies for decades. Oscar Handlin's (1951) influential work, among others, was grounded in the notion of many ethnic groups becoming one group.

More recent research tends not to assume individual assimilation but rather asks questions about the social and economic adjustment of immigrants. Several chapters in this volume occasionally address an assimilationist perspective, but it is no longer the guiding paradigm for immigrant research. Rather, the discussions focus on what adjustments immigrants make, what social and economic changes occur with duration of residence, how successive generations make political and social adjustments, and what the conditions for social, political, and economic change are.

Sociological research has greatly improved our understanding of ethnic identity in recent years. Lieberson and Waters (1988) examined ethnic groups on a range of social and economic dimensions in their census monograph prepared with 1980 data. Their work emphasizes European-origin ethnic groups, however, with less attention to the newer Asian and Hispanic groups. Waters (1990) presents an interesting report of European-origin residents, who are often fourth, fifth, or higher generation descendants of immigrants. Her work is useful for its description of the ways in which U.S. residents think of their ethnicity, given their very mixed ethnic origins. Finally, Alba's (1990) research offers one of the best recent studies analyzing ethnic identity for European-origin Americans. His research greatly improves our understanding of the dynamics of ethnic identity and helps us to think about the changing situation under current immigration. Current research, on the other hand, offers only an untested description of ethnic identity for our newer immigrants from Asia and Latin America.

The chapters in the volume display a preference now for studying group behavior and emphasizing the social and economic structures through which immigrants find a role for themselves in U.S. society. Hence, we find the empirical work offering a strong focus on the assembling of human capital as a key ingredient for the adjustment of immigrant groups in the United States.

Chapters three and four present findings on the adjustment to the United States of the two major recent immigrant groups, Hispanics and Asians. Frank D. Bean, Jorge Chapa, Ruth R. Berg, and Kathryn Sowards discuss the integration of Hispanic immigrants in their chapter, entitled "Educational and Sociodemographic Incorporation among Hispanic Immigrants to the United States." Immigration to the United States increased substantially during the 1970s and 1980s, as did the fraction of immigrants coming from Spanish-speaking countries, especially Mexico. The growing populations of immigrants from such countries and the likelihood of continuing increases in immigration during the 1990s raise anew questions about the prospects for immigrant integration and about whether the pattern and degree of such integration has changed in recent years. Their chapter examines the social characteristics of recent Latino immigrants, focusing on education, fertility, marital status, and patterns of residential location. It seeks to ascertain whether the patterns of variation in these characteristics by duration of residence in the United States and by generational status are more consistent with assimilationist or ethnic structuralist theories concerning immigrant incorporation. The results are discussed in terms of their implications for these theories and for issues pertaining to both immigration and immigrant policy.

Sharon M. Lee and Barry Edmonston analyze data on recent Asian immigrants in their chapter, entitled "The Socioeconomic Status and Integration of Asian Immigrants." Immigration policies that excluded or severely restricted Asian immigration to the United States in the nineteenth and early twentieth centuries often referred to the "unassimilable" character of Asian immigrants. The 1965 amendments to the Immigration and Nationality Act of 1952 opened immigration to Asians once again. Today, Asians are almost a majority of legal immigrants to the United States, representing 44 percent of legal immigrants during the 1980s. The question of how well Asian immigrants are integrating into or adapting to the United States has attracted much attention.

Lee and Edmonston use data from the 1980 Census of Population and the 1986, 1988, and 1989 Current Population Surveys (CPSs) to examine the socioeconomic dimension of Asian immigrant integration. The socioeconomic status of Asian immigrants (classified by country of origin and recency of immigration) is compared with that of native-born Asian and white non-Hispanic U.S. residents. The main sociological theories on immigrant adaptation and progress have focused on the role of human capital characteristics, structural variables, and assimilation factors. Lee and Edmonston examine these factors in terms of their relative importance as determinants of Asian household income. The chapter examines the effects of immigrant status and minority status on Asian immigrants' socioeconomic status and discusses the findings with reference to the larger question of how well Asian immigrants are adjusting to the United States.

SOCIAL, ECONOMIC, AND POLITICAL DIMENSIONS OF IMMIGRANT INTEGRATION

Past work on immigrants, comparing them to the native-born population, has revealed that immigrants have lower average incomes after first arriving, but that their incomes improve over time (Muller and Espenshade 1985). These findings could imply that immigrants may have some initial disadvantages, possibly related to the disruption of resettlement and the shock of arriving in a new society. However, after a certain period, the immigrants become better adapted to U.S. society and become able to take advantage of their skills and training. The specific interpretation of this type of result has important policy implications. If analysis of past data suggests that immigrants adjust on their own, then there is no need to worry about the initial disadvantages of immigrants. One policy conclusion is, therefore, to let time take care of the situation. If, however, impediments exist to the adjustment of immigrants, then it behooves an immigrant policy to acknowledge these difficulties and to consider programs for successful adaptation.

The question of the adjustment of immigrants clearly deserves further attention. In particular, we want to examine the trajectories of immigrants on a variety of dimensions. Among the trajectories that are useful to analyze are geographic distribution, language, education, income, and labor force status. This volume includes chapters that examine a number of trajectories at the same time. Chapters five through eight consider four specific dimensions of primary interest for studies of ethnic integration of recent immigrants: wage returns, language acquisition, migration, and political culture.

Elaine Sorensen and María E. Enchautegui, in their chapter entitled "Immigrant Male Earnings in the 1980s: Divergent Patterns by Race and Ethnicity," analyze an important aspect of the economic mobility of immigrants in their work on wage trends. The average weekly pay, in constant dollars, declined for male workers between 1979 and 1989. This decline occurred both for native-born males and foreign-born males, but with a greater proportionate decline for foreign-born males. In examining the factors behind this increasing disparity, Sorensen and Enchautegui find an interplay of offsetting trends.

In spite of the overall decline of wages for immigrants and natives, recent immigrants in 1989 had virtually identical real wages to recent immigrants in 1979. This relative improvement of recent immigrants in the 1980s represents a reversal of the trends for the two previous decades. Education levels of natives and immigrants mirror the trends in real wages. Average education levels of male immigrants increased in the 1980s, but less than those of native males. Recent immigrants, however, showed even greater improvements than native males.

Sorensen and Enchautegui also find very different earning trends for race and ethnic groups in the 1980s. The general decline in male wages during the 1980s was found for Hispanic immigrants, but not for white, black, or Asian immigrants. White immigrants benefited from increased education and English language skills, whereas the Asian immigrants showed improved earnings mainly because of less recent immigration and increased potential work experience in the United States.

The lack of improvement in earnings among Hispanic immigrants in the 1980s could not be traced directly to some conventional causes, such as experience or language ability. These factors should have led to relative increases in earnings for Hispanic male immigrants. Rather, their work points to the earnings structure of the Hispanic male immigrants and that their extremely low levels of education act as a bar to economic progress.

Gillian Stevens discusses language changes in her chapter, entitled "Immigration, Emigration, Language Acquisition, and the English Language Proficiency of Immigrants in the United States." Stevens notes that political frictions have arisen regarding bilingualism in areas with large numbers of immigrants. Bilingual policies promulgated by federal and state governments, coupled with increasing evidence of non-English speakers and signs, have led to organization of active opposition groups at local and national levels. Proposition 38, entitled "Voting Materials in English Only," for example, obtained over 600,000 signatures in California in 1984. This proposition was then adopted with a 72 percent majority in the election. Referenda in Dade County, Florida, led to a prohibition of public expenditures on bilingual activities. Similar activities have been undertaken in other locales and states, as English-speakers have reacted adversely to the presence of new immigrants. A major concern, as part of this controversy, Stevens argues, is the English language adaptation of immigrants.

In her survey of past research, Stevens concludes that the language adjustment of second and third generation Asian- and Hispanic-origin groups is rapid. Thus, like other immigrant groups before them, these new immigrants should improve their English language skills with time. Cultural reinforcement, however, retards language acquisition. A constant influx of new arrivals, especially in predominantly immigration neighborhoods, keeps the language alive among immigrants and their children.

Lack of English proficiency clearly retards the general educational progress of immigrants. But the use of a home language other than English is not always a detriment. Although educational levels are generally higher for immigrant children who grew up using English at home, Cubans outpace other Hispanics in high school achievement and college entrance, even though sons and daughters of Cuban immigrants are the Hispanic group most likely to use Spanish at home. Finally, Stevens suggests that the high rates of college attendance for some non-English speaking Asian immigrant groups also attest the importance of parental encouragement and educational aspiration, factors that offset problems of a non-English home language.

Kristin E. Neuman and Marta Tienda address the issue of internal migration of immigrants after they enter the United States in "The Settlement and Secondary Migration Patterns of Legalized Immigrants: Insights from Administrative Records." This chapter examines the residential patterns and secondary migration flows of illegal aliens who successfully applied for legal resident status under IRCA. Using data from the Legalization Application Processing System (LAPS) file, this chapter describes the residential distribution at the time of application, the major migratory streams from place of initial U.S. residence to place of residence at application, and determinants of secondary migrant status for several national and regional origin groups.

The results in this chapter show that the settlement patterns of legalization applicants are similar to those of previous immigrants. Furthermore, extensive secondary migration reduces residential concentration slightly for all groups except Asians, Australians, and Canadians. Although gender differences in secondary migration were negligible, there were appreciable differences in rates of internal geographic movement among regional-origin groups, with immigrants originating in Mexico least likely (19 percent) and those originating in Africa or Asia most likely (68 percent) to change residence across state boundaries subsequent to illegal entry to the United States.

California is the single most important gateway for most undocumented aliens, but particularly for those arriving from Mexico and Central America. This state also attracts undocumented aliens who enter in other locations, particularly those originating in Asia. Latin Americans are responsible for substantial migrant streams from California and Texas to Illinois and to the Northeast, while non-Latin Americans make up somewhat smaller streams in other directions. Those from Asia and Africa left New York/New Jersey and Other West States for California and Texas, whereas Europeans and Others left New York/New Jersey and Florida for California and Illinois.

A fairly consistent story emerges from the influence on migration of the circumstances defining the most recent entry: Legal entry on a non-immigrant visa reduced the likelihood of secondary migration among Mexicans, Other Latin Americans, Asians, Europeans, and the residual group. The presence of other relatives in the United States significantly increased the likelihood of movement for the sample as a whole and for illegals from Mexico, El Salvador, and Africa but decreased the likelihood of movement for Europeans and Other Latin Americans. Also, longer residence in the United States increased the likelihood of secondary movement. Finally, immigrants with managerial and professional occupations at first entry were significantly more prone to move within the United States than their counterparts engaged in farming.

Rodolfo O. de la Garza, Angelo Falcon, F. Chris Garcia, and John Garcia consider political changes for immigrants in the chapter entitled "Mexican Immigrants, Mexican Americans, and American Political Culture." They examine the extent to which the Mexican-origin population of the United States holds values that are central to American political culture. The specific values examined are political tolerance, the belief that all residents should learn English, and trust in government. Utilizing new data from the Latino National Political Survey, which was completed in 1990, the chapter analyzes the effect that socioeconomic factors and generational history within the United States have on the degree to which these values are held. The results provide insight into the extent to which ethnic experiences facilitate or impede "Americanization" by comparing the shift in values across foreign-born and native-born generations.

FUTURE TRENDS

The world economy is an increasingly highly stratified labor market, with the United States one of several possible destinations for immigrants. The United States often competes now for skilled and talented labor with other immigrant destinations. International labor flows are growing, and the United States is no longer the one, final destination. Moreover, many immigrants to the United States depart, taking their labor skills to other countries. U.S. immigration involves several types of immigrants: refugees, illegal immigrants, and legal immigrants. Although it is a simplification to classify immigrants in only these three broad types, these immigrant types vary in the country of origin, their social and economic characteristics, and their process of adjustment.

Earlier patterns of international migration have been rapidly reshaped. Migration is now global and no longer unidirectional. Today, few countries are not affected by either immigration or emigration. The large immigrant countries—Australia, Canada, and the United States—may be distinctive in the size of their foreign-born population (with about 10 percent or more foreign-born), but many countries now have sizable immigrant populations. Many European countries have populations with 3 percent or more foreign-born. The high-income oil-exporting nations also employ very high numbers of foreign-born workers. Japan is increasingly home to legal and illegal workers from other Asian countries.

The world is poised for the next wave of emigrants. The world's population of 5.3 billion increases by about 90 to 100 million annually, and many of these people are on the move. Unless the poorer countries can provide jobs and opportunities to absorb the population growth, the export of people will continue to increase. Most of the new emigrants will be Asians because this region is home to half of the world's population. While Australia, Canada, Japan, and the United States keep their eye on Asia for future immigrants and refugees, European countries keep theirs on eastern Europe, the former Soviet Union, and North Africa. From a trickle of only 100,000 moving west to Europe annually in the 1970s and early 1980s, over one million moved to Europe in 1989. Estimates vary considerably, although Russian experts estimated recently that about two million citizens of the former Soviet Union might apply for emigration visas when universal passport applications become available.

An increasingly important new group of "immigrants" are workers who enter the United States on a temporary visas. Non-immigrants are now common in the flow of talented individuals and are expanding with the increase of multinational corporations. Recent revisions of immigration law, incorporated in the Immigration Act of 1990, include tighter restrictions on non-immigrants, workers who enter the United States for temporary work. Non-immigrant visas are widely used by companies for the employment of foreign professionals, including the many multinational corporations that routinely transfer their employees between countries. Yet, while the United States is apparently restricting this type of non-immigrant movement, major corporations have and intend to expand the use of imported managerial and professional staff. With corporations going global, these corporations will increasingly lobby to remove national labor market restrictions.

A final aspect of world migration is emigration. No longer can policymakers assume that immigrants are permanent entrants. A significant proportion of U.S. immigrants eventually depart from the United States (Warren and Kraly 1985). U.S. immigration studies have been almost exclusively concerned with the individual immigrants to the United States and their adjustment to American society. However, several periods of emigration have occurred in U.S. history: the exit of loyalists during the Revolutionary War, the movement of Southern whites (and their black retainers) to the Maritimes during the Civil War, the return migration of European immigrants during the economic downturns of the 1930s, and the departure of young men to avoid the draft during the Vietnam War. Studies have not provided much coverage of the emigration of U.S. citizens or of the substantial return migration of immigrants.

The future population of the United States is being increasingly shaped by world migration trends. At the moment, U.S. population growth is slowing due to two factors: historically low fertility that reduces the rate of natural increase, and immigration levels that have been decreasing relative to overall population size (even though the number of immigrants has increased). The substantial decline in fertility has had the greater impact in recent decades, with the result that the proportion of annual growth dependent upon immigration has risen. Correspondingly, the contribution of immigrants to future population growth has increased. Although the fertility of immigrants (as an overall group) is only slightly higher than the native population, immigrants are generally younger and, given their sizable numbers, will become the parents and grandparents of a rising proportion of future citizens.

Under the current regime of natural increase and emigration, the U.S. population requires about a million immigrants each year in order to offset a potential population decline in the middle of the next century. Given a million immigrants annually, we may anticipate a sustained high proportion of immigrants from Asia and Latin America and the Caribbean; a resulting increase in the proportion of Asians and Hispanics in schools, the labor force, and our society; and an amplification of the impact of these immigrants on policies and programs in our communities.

The final three chapters in this volume focus on future issues for our newest immigrants. In chapter nine, Fix and Zimmermann describe the dimensions of U.S. immigrant policy and, in chapter ten, how de facto immigrant policy works in Massachusetts and Texas. Edmonston and Passel (chapter eleven) present demographic projections for the U.S. population, emphasizing the future racial and ethnic composition of the population.

Michael Fix and Wendy Zimmermann consider the United States' immigrant policy and what a comprehensive immigrant policy might look like in their chapter, entitled "After Arrival: An Overview of Federal Immigrant Policy in the United States." This chapter is an effort to map the nation's express and de facto immigration policies. It discusses federal policy trends that drive immigrant policy, the goals of those policies, and state and local roles in framing immigrant policy. Although admissions of legal and legalized immigrants have increased, federal funding for newcomer programs has decreased, and federal eligibility for assistance programs has been tightened. As a result, the costs of and responsibilities for immigrants have increasingly shifted to state and local governments.

Although not specified in any stated policy, federal immigrant policy seems to be based on five goals: (1) to reinforce immigration policy, (2) to secure individual rights and grant equal protection, (3) to mitigate social service costs, (4) to reimburse state and local governments, and (5) to assist settlement and integration of newcomers. State and local governments play a variety of roles that shape immigrant policy, including implementing federal policy, setting benefit levels for joint federal-state programs, running independent programs and institutions targeted to newcomers, setting benefit levels and eligibility standards for state and local programs, and adapting programs and services to the needs of newcomers.

The chapter by Zimmermann and Fix entitled "Immigrant Policy in the States: A Wavering Welcome" explores more thoroughly the state and local roles in framing and implementing immigrant policy. It presents case studies of immigrant policies in Massachusetts and Texas, two states with widely varying immigrant populations and policies. Massachusetts has a smaller newcomer population than Texas, but refugees make up a larger proportion of the newcomer population. In keeping with the two states' different philosophies, Massachusetts is more generous in its public spending than is Texas and has more programs and institutions targeted to the needs of newcomers. However, the situation in both states may be changing. In Massachusetts, economic difficulties have resulted in increased attempts to restrict services to newcomers, while in Texas, the creation of a new Governor's Office of Immigration and Refugee Affairs may be a sign of more newcomer-targeted policies in the future.

Barry Edmonston and Jeffrey S. Passel present results for a demographic projection of the U.S. population for major racial/ethnic groups in chapter eleven, "The Future Immigrant Population of the United States." They note that the United States is on the eve of substantial shifts in its racial/ethnic composition. These changes will occur as a response to new patterns of immigration that have evolved during the last 30 years. Current immigrants are predominantly Asian and Hispanic, with some black immigrants from Africa and the Caribbean and some white immigrants from Canada, Europe, and Oceania. Present immigrants are different from the overwhelmingly European movements of the nineteenth and early twentieth centuries.

Edmonston and Passel present new information on the racial and ethnic composition of the United States for the next century. The demographic model presents data on the population by generation: a foreign-born first generation, the sons and daughters of immigrants (the second generation), the grandsons and granddaughters of immigrants (the third generation), and the fourth-and-higher generations. This new population projection approach gives estimates of the foreign-born and native-born groups for major racial/ethnic groups.

With annual *net* immigration of 950,000, the total U.S. population of 249 million in 1990 will reach 300 million in 2011 and about 356 million in 2040. Thus, at the level of immigration and emigration assumed in these projections, considerable population growth is in store for the next 50 years.

The racial/ethnic composition will shift markedly during the next 50 years. Assuming the population conditions of the projection, the white non-Hispanic population will increase its numbers from 187 million in 1990 to a peak of 211 million in 2030 and then remain at about that level. This group will become relatively less numerous and drop from 75 percent of the total population to less than 60 percent in 2040. Over the next five decades, the black population will increase from 30 million to 44 million but will remain virtually unchanged as a proportion of the population, increasing from 12.1 percent in 1990 to 12.4 percent in 2040.

Asians and Hispanics will experience substantial growth during the next century. The Asian population will grow from 7 million in 1990 to 35 million in 2040, increasing its proportionate share from 3 percent in 1990 to 10 percent in 2040. Hispanics will increase from 22 million in 1990 to 64 million in 2040, a gain from 9 to 18 percent in the period. The Hispanic population will be a larger numerical group than blacks by about 2010.

Two issues discussed briefly in the Edmonston and Passel chapter are important for the topic of ethnic demography. The first issue is ethnic self-identification. For example, the American Indian population grew by 70 percent from 1970 to 1980 and by 38 percent from 1980 to 1990 (Passel 1992). Yet, most of this population growth was due to changes in the self-designation as American Indian rather than the dynamics of the classic demographic balancing equation (population plus births minus deaths plus net migration). Demographers have succeeded well with the modeling of births, deaths, and migration as they interact to affect population size and structure. The uncertainties of ethnic identity, however, have confounded demographic analysis and have not received the attention that they deserve. Alonso (1987, 125) speculates that the ambiguities of ethnic self-identity make the boundaries of ethnic membership fuzzy and difficult to adapt to standard demographic approaches. It is important, nonetheless, to emphasize the need for population analysis that presents well-defined populations by social groups. This area of research has been pursued by Alba (1990) and Waters (1990) for European-origin persons. Further work is required on Asian and Hispanic persons in order to improve our understanding of ethnic identification for these groups. The second issue briefly mentioned in chapter 11 is the influence of exogamy, the process of members of one racial/ethnic group marrying a member of another group. This is an important consideration because increasing levels of exogamy will produce a future population that includes many members who will not have a single ancestry (i.e., they will have parents of more than one racial/ethnic group). Some limited research has been undertaken on ethnic intermarriage, but demographers have paid little attention to the problem of incorporating exogamy within a population projection framework. This is an important issue for further analysis.

THE CHALLENGE FOR IMMIGRATION POLICY RESEARCH

The demographic effects of recent shifts in the ethnic origins of U.S. immigrants are difficult to predict because of uncertainty about their fertility and mortality patterns and the effects of recent immigration legislation. It seems clear the number and relative proportion of Asians and Hispanics will increase substantially in the next decades, as the relative share for the European-origin population (white non-Hispanics) declines. These declines seem obvious from population projections.

The United States will also face the challenge of avoiding ethnic tensions as new ethnic communities grow rapidly and as native residents worry about economic prospects and social change in their towns and neighborhoods. As the Asian and Hispanic populations grow from immigration—with concentrations in a few states and in the larger metropolitan areas—policies of racial integration focused on black-white relationships will need to be modified to incorporate multiracial/multiethnic issues. Multiracial policies will be especially required as the U.S. population, with its low fertility, finds that future population growth increasingly depends upon immigration from Latin America and Asia.

The chapters in this volume reflect the variety of research going on in the area of immigration policy. The research is necessarily multidisciplinary, involving demographers, economists, political scientists, and sociologists. We hope that this volume serves to expand the basis of research on ethnic demography through an up-to-date, comprehensive survey of the adjustment of America's newest arrivals.

Notes

1. The numbers for legal immigration in 1990 exclude those immigrants residing in the United States under the special provisions of the Immigration Reform and Control

Act of 1986. These immigrants are excluded for the analysis here because they entered the United States several years prior to 1986. Their application for legal resident status, therefore, comes several years after the actual date of their entrance.

2. This percentage for Chinese immigration is a minimum estimate because a significant proportion of immigrants from other countries, such as Vietnam, Malaysia, and Indonesia, are from Chinese ethnic communities and report Chinese ethnicity in U.S. surveys and censuses.

References

Alba, Richard D. 1990. *Ethnic Identity: The Transformation of White America*. New Haven, CT: Yale University Press.

Alonso, William. 1987. "Identity and Population." Pp. 95–125 in William Alonso (editor), *Population in an Interacting World*. Cambridge, MA: Harvard University Press.

Archdeacon, Thomas J. 1983. *Becoming American: An Ethnic History*. New York, NY: The Free Press.

Bean, Frank D., Barry Edmonston, and Jeffrey S. Passel. 1990. *Undocumented Migration to the United States: IRCA and the Experience of the 1980s*. Washington, D.C.: The Urban Institute Press.

Edmonston, Barry, and Sharon M. Lee. 1990. "Factors Affecting Refugee Emigration." Population Studies Center, Discussion Paper Series, Number 3. Washington, D.C.: The Urban Institute.

Fix, Michael. 1991. *The Paper Curtain: Employer Sanctions' Implementation, Impact, and Reform*. Washington, D.C.: The Urban Institute Press.

Fix, Michael, and Jeffrey S. Passel. 1991. "The Door Remains Open: Recent Immigration to the United States and a Preliminary Analysis of The Immigration Act of 1990." Program for Research on Immigration Policy Discussion Paper, Number 14. Washington, D.C.: The Urban Institute.

Fuchs, Lawrence H. 1990. *The American Kaleidoscope: Race, Ethnicity, and the Civic Culture*. Boston, MA: University Press of New England and Wesleyan University Press.

Gordon, Milton M. 1964. *Assimilation in American Life: The Role of Race, Religion, and National Origins*. New York, NY: Oxford University Press.

Handlin, Oscar. 1951. *The Uprooted: The Epic Story of the Great Migrations That Made the American People*. Boston, MA: Little, Brown.

Hirschman, Albert O. 1970. *Exit, Voice, and Loyalty: Responses to Declines in Firms, Organizations, and States*. Cambridge, MA: Harvard University Press.

Lieberson, Stanley, and Mary C. Waters. 1988. *From Many Strands: Ethnic* and *Racial Groups in Contemporary America.* New York, NY: Russell Sage.

Muller, Thomas, and Thomas J. Espenshade. 1985. *The Fourth Wave: California's Newest Immigrants.* Washington, D.C.: The Urban Institute Press.

Park, Robert E. 1928. *Race and Culture.* New York, NY: The Free Press.

Passel, Jeffrey P. 1992. "The Growing American Indian Population: Beyond Demography." Proceedings of the Social Statistics Section of the American Statistical Association: 1992. Washington, D.C.: American Statistical Association.

Portes, Alejandro, and Ruben G. Rumbaut. 1990. *Immigrant America: A Portrait.* Berkeley and Los Angeles, CA: University of California Press.

Rothman, Eric S., and Thomas J. Espenshade. 1992. "Fiscal Impacts of Immigration to the United States." *Population Index* 58(3): 381–415.

U.S. Bureau of the Census. 1968. *Statistical Abstract of the United States, 1968.* Washington, D.C.: U.S. Government Printing Office.

_____. 1992. *Statistical Abstract of the United States, 1992.* Washington, D.C.: U.S. Government Printing Office.

U.S. Department of State, Bureau for Refugee Programs. 1991. *World Refugee Report, September 1991.* Washington, D.C.: Bureau for Refugee Programs, U.S. Department of State.

U.S. Immigration and Naturalization Service. 1991a. *An Immigrant Nation: United States Regulation of Immigration, 1798–1991.* Washington, D.C.: U.S. Government Printing Office.

_____. 1991b. *Statistical Yearbook of the Immigration and Naturalization Service, 1990.* Washington, D.C.: U.S. Government Printing Office.

Warren, Robert, and Ellen Percy Kraly. 1985. "The Elusive Exodus: Emigration from the United States." *Population Trends and Public Policy,* No. 8. Washington, D.C.: Population Reference Bureau.

Waters, Mary C. 1990. *Ethnic Options: Choosing Identities in America.* Berkeley and Los Angeles: University of California Press.

Winnick, Louis. 1990. *New People in Old Neighborhoods: The Role of New Immigrants in Rejuvenating New York's Communities.* New York: Russell Sage.

Chapter Two

IMMIGRATION AND RACE: RECENT TRENDS IN IMMIGRATION TO THE UNITED STATES

Jeffrey S. Passel and Barry Edmonston

A "new wave" of immigrants began to come to the United States following the major revisions in U.S. immigrant admission policy instituted in 1965. Subsequent changes to immigration law have tended to reinforce and expand the new stream of immigrants. Before 1965, U.S. immigration policy restricted annual immigration through a system of country quotas that reflected the ethnic and racial composition of nineteenth century America. The revised rules of 1965 opened the door for immigration from many different countries by eliminating the restrictive (and racist) national quotas. The new law, the Immigration Act of 1965, also raised the annual overall immigration quota to 270,000 while maintaining family reunification as a means for entry outside the quota system. To gain admission to the United States after 1965, a prospective immigrant needed to qualify principally on the basis of selected preference categories. All countries outside the Western Hemisphere were placed on an equal footing, with the result that annual admission ceilings for many countries, notably those in Asia, increased overnight from virtually nil (about 100) to 20,000. In the 1970s, Western Hemisphere countries were brought under the same system.

In recent years, the United States also experienced two additional sources of new residents other than the conventional stream of immigrants. First, several large groups of refugees have arrived in the United States from Cuba, Southeast Asia, and Central America. These refugees are admitted outside the immigration quota and preference system. Second, large-scale illegal immigration to the United States began in the 1960s and increased during the 1970s and 1980s (Passel et al. 1991). Many formerly illegal immigrants acquired legal status under the different legalization programs authorized in 1986 and 1990. For the discussions in this paper, we will make no distinction among the various legal statuses at entry to the country and treat all of the groups as "immigrants" to the United States.

Since the end of World War II, over 25 million immigrants[1] have come to the United States; more than 75 percent of these, or almost 20 million, entered since the immigration law changes of 1965. Moreover, the most recent immigrants have been increasingly from new origin countries, especially Asia, Latin America and the Caribbean, and Africa. Latin America and Asia now account for more than 80 percent of all immigration to the United States. The racial and ethnic characteristics of the new immigrants are distinctive. The age, sex, and educational characteristics, however, are not markedly different from the previous waves of immigrants dominated by Europeans and Canadians.

Immigration to the United States during the past three decades has had a gradual, cumulative impact on the racial and ethnic composition of American society. The effects of the new immigrants on society have become increasingly apparent in recent years. This chapter describes the changes in the racial and ethnic composition of the U.S. population that have taken place in the twentieth century. We use a population projection/estimation methodology to quantify the impact of immigration on the composition of the American population in terms of both the racial/ethnic composition and the generational stock. In chapter 11 of this volume, Edmonston and Passel discuss the future implications of current trends.

HISTORICAL TRENDS

Immigrants have settled in the United States throughout its entire national history. In fact, immigrants from Europe, Mexico, and Asia had come to the present territory of the United States long before national independence. During the past 100 years, the number of immigrants coming to the United States has been quite high compared with other immigrant flows throughout the world. Only Australia and Canada have experienced comparable heavy immigration, albeit relatively smaller numbers of immigrants into much smaller existing populations. Over the course of the twentieth century, immigration flows to the United States have averaged around 500,000 arrivals per year, with a great deal of variation from the peaks of the 1900s and 1980s to the valleys of the 1930s.

Immigration in the Twentieth Century

Figure 2.1 traces the history of immigration to the United States since the inception of official record keeping in 1821 through 1900. This

Figure 2.1 IMMIGRATION TO THE UNITED STATES BY DECADE: 1821–1830
THROUGH 1981–1990

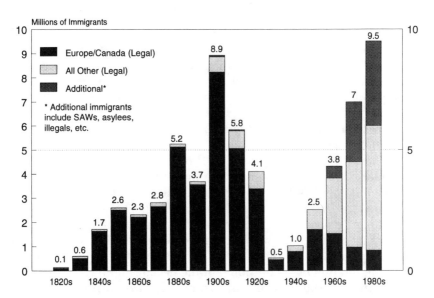

chart[2] shows clearly the immigration boom that occurred during the late decades of the nineteenth century through the period immediately preceding World War I. This period, a time of rapid urbanization and industrialization in the United States, saw especially large immigration from southern and eastern Europe. The peak year for admission of new legal immigrants to the United States was 1907, when almost 1.3 million immigrants entered and added more than 3 percent to the U.S. labor force in that one year alone. In contrast, few immigrants came during World War I, the Depression, and World War II.

Immigration increased steadily in the decades after World War II, since the United States enjoyed a high degree of political freedom and economic prosperity, compared with Europe and many other parts of the world. Available employment in the expanding manufacturing and construction sectors of the U.S. economy gave ample opportunities for a new wave of immigrants. The 1965 changes in immigration law prompted even further increases as the United States began to receive new immigrants from Asia and Latin America. Figure 2.1 also notes the appearance of significant numbers of illegal immigrants in the 1960s and later. Since 1965, both the de jure changes in immigration law and the de facto situation regarding enforcement that affected illegal immigration have dramatically altered the origin countries of immigrants.

Immigration has had considerable impact on population growth in the United States during the twentieth century. To appreciate fully the impact of immigration, however, it is necessary to take into account the effect of emigration as well as immigration. Emigration offsets the population gains stemming from immigration. Moreover, the number of emigrants has changed substantially during the past century. Table 2.1 presents estimates for immigration, emigration, and *net* immigration (immigration minus emigration) during the twentieth century.

Emigration exceeded three million per decade in the first two decades of the twentieth century. Current levels of emigration are now considerably less, both in numerical and percentage terms. There were fewer than two million emigrants over the 1980–1990 decade. As a result, the gains from *net* immigration are now substantially higher than a century ago. In the decade ending in 1910, there were 8.0 million immigrants and 3.1 million emigrants, producing net immigration of 4.9 million. For the decade ending in 1990, there were almost 10.0 million immigrants and 1.8 million emigrants, yielding a net immigration gain of 8.2 million. Furthermore, because of lower emigration rates in the contemporary era, new immigration in the 1970–1980 decade also exceeded the 1900–1910 decade by a great deal, even though gross immigration was roughly the same in the two decades. Thus, compared with a century ago, immigration levels are slightly higher; emigration is considerably lower; and net immigration is substantially greater.

Since the U.S. population has grown considerably since the turn of the century, it is important to consider the volume of immigration compared with population size in assessing the total impact of net immigration. Since 1900, when the U.S. population numbered 76 million, the population has increased more than threefold to 249 million in 1990. Has immigration increased at a comparable rate? The answer is clearly no. As shown in table 2.1, immigration relative to population size is now about one-half of the levels in the early twentieth century. Immigration during the 1900–1910 decade, for example, amounted to 10.5 percent of the 1900 population. The comparable figure for 1980–1990 is 4.4 percent. Relative *net* immigration levels are also lower than a century ago. Net immigration during 1980–1990 is 3.6 percent of the population at the beginning of the decade (1980), compared with 6.5 percent during the 1900–1910 decade. The differences are less for net immigration than for gross

Table 2.1 IMMIGRATION AND POPULATION CHANGE BY DECADE: UNITED STATES: 1900–1990
(populations in thousands)

| Date | Population | Change from Previous Date | Immigration Component During Decade | | | | | | Net Imm. as Percent of Change |
| | | | Amount | | | Percent[a] | | | |
			Net	Immig.	Emig.	Net	Immig.	Emig.	
1990	248,712	22,087	**8,200**	9,972	1,772	**3.6**	4.4	−0.8	**37.1**
1980	226,625	21,058	**6,866**	7,726	860	**3.3**	3.8	−0.4	**32.6**
1970	205,567	23,512	**2,684**	3,738	1,054	**1.5**	2.1	−0.6	**11.4**
1960	182,055	26,899	**2,352**	3,011	660	**1.5**	1.9	−0.4	**8.7**
1950	155,156	18,228	**1,790**	1,849	59	**1.3**	1.4	0.0	**9.8**
1940	136,928	9,343	**−132**	750	882	**−0.1**	0.6	−0.7	**(N)**
1930	127,585	16,838	**2,790**	4,185	1,395	**2.5**	3.8	−1.3	**16.6**
1920	110,747	16,868	**2,530**	5,906	3,376	**2.7**	6.3	−3.6	**15.0**
1910	93,879	17,684	**4,920**	8,024	3,104	**6.5**	10.5	−4.1	**27.8**
1900	76,195	(X)	(X)	(X)	(X)	(X)	(X)	(X)	(X)

Note: Population includes 50 states and the District of Columbia at all dates. Population estimates and net immigration components are derived with POPGEN (Edmonston and Passel 1992) fitted to historical series of census data on the native-born and foreign-born populations, by race. Immigration includes movement between Puerto Rico and the U.S. mainland. See text for further information.
a Expressed as a percentage of the population at the beginning of the decade.
(X) Not applicable.
(N) Negative number—not defined.

immigration alone because of the much higher levels of emigration (both in relative and absolute terms) early in the twentieth century.

Another way to look at immigration and population change is to ask a somewhat different question: "How much of population growth is attributable to immigration?" Table 2.1 also shows net immigration as a percentage of population change during the decade. During 1980–1990, for example, the population grew by 22.1 million. Net immigration for the decade was 8.2 million, or 37 percent of the population change for the 1980s. The trends in table 2.1 reveal that immigration now provides a somewhat greater proportion of population growth than early in the century. The population dynamics are somewhat different, however. Immigration is now at a much lower rate than at the turn of the century, but lower overall fertility rates produce lower levels of natural increase. In the current situation, immigration plays a greater role in affecting overall population growth.

The Foreign-born and Foreign-stock Population

As immigrants enter the country, they affect the composition of the population in several ways. They can change the racial/ethnic makeup of the population if they differ from the resident population. Immigrants always affect the generational composition, since they increase the size of the first generation—i.e., the foreign-born population of the country. The size of the foreign-born population derives principally from past levels of immigration but is also affected by the impact of emigration and mortality. High levels of recent immigration, with little emigration, increase the number of foreign-born persons in the population. As time passes, the effects of mortality begin to diminish various entry cohorts so that the foreign-born numbers decrease if they are not replenished by additional immigrants. Eventually, after about a century, the effect of mortality extinguishes each original cohort of the foreign-born population.

The size of the foreign-born population in the United States has reflected the changing course of immigration over time. Table 2.2 and figure 2.2 display the number of foreign-born persons and their proportion of the total population for the period since 1850. Approximately 2.2 million foreign-born persons resided in the United States in 1850, constituting 9.7 percent of the total population. With the continuing heavy volume of immigration in the late nineteenth century, the foreign-born population grew steadily, reaching a peak of about 14.4 million in 1930. At the same time, the foreign-born popula-

Table 2.2 U.S. POPULATION BY NATIVITY: 1850–1990
(populations in thousands)

| Year | Total Population | Total Foreign Stock | | Foreign-Stock Population | | | | Native-Born of Native Parentage | |
| | | | | Foreign Born | | Native of Foreign or Mixed Parentage | | | |
		Number	Percent	Number	Percent	Number	Percent	Number	Percent
1990	248,712	45,542	18.3	21,188	8.5	24,354	9.8	203,170	81.7
1980	226,625	39,060	17.2	15,054	6.6	24,006	10.6	187,565	82.8
1970	205,567	34,939	17.0	10,462	5.1	24,477	11.9	170,628	83.0
1960	182,055	35,135	19.3	10,351	5.7	24,784	13.6	146,920	80.7
1950	155,156	35,805	23.1	10,633	6.9	25,172	16.2	119,351	76.9
1940	136,928	37,367	27.3	11,568	8.4	25,799	18.8	99,562	72.7
1930	127,585	40,011	31.4	14,428	11.3	25,583	20.1	87,574	68.6
1920	110,747	36,923	33.3	14,106	12.7	22,817	20.6	73,824	66.7
1910	93,879	32,573	34.7	13,688	14.6	18,885	20.1	61,306	65.3
1900	76,195	26,313	34.5	10,443	13.7	15,870	20.8	49,882	65.5
1890	62,622	20,753	33.1	9,250	14.8	11,504	18.4	41,869	66.9
1880	50,156	14,955	29.8	6,680	13.3	8,275	16.5	35,201	70.2
1870	38,558	10,891	28.2	5,567	14.4	5,324	13.8	27,667	71.8
1860	31,443	(X)	(X)	4,139	13.2	(X)	(X)	(X)	(X)
1850	23,192	(X)	(X)	2,245	9.7	(X)	(X)	(X)	(X)

Sources: 1900 to 1990—estimates derived with POPGEN. See text and table 2.1. 1850 to 1890—U.S. Bureau of the Census (1975), Historical Statistics of the United States: Colonial Times to 1970, Part I.
Note: Populations include 50 states and the District of Columbia for 1900–1990; continental U.S. for other years. Foreign-born population includes population born in Puerto Rico. See text.
(X) Not available.

Figure 2.2 FOREIGN-BORN POPULATION OF THE UNITED STATES: 1850–1990

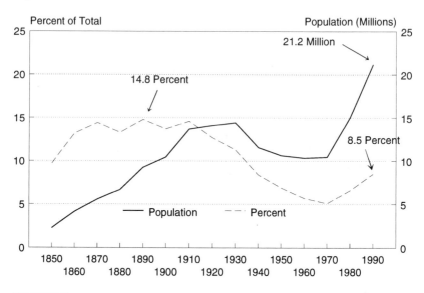

Source: table 2.2.

tion increased as a proportion of the U.S. population. Although the peak proportion of 14.8 percent was reached in 1890, the foreign-born population remained at roughly 13 to 15 percent (or one-seventh) of the population from 1860 to 1920 because the native-born population grew at about the same rate as the foreign-born population during that period.

With the diminution of immigration during World War I, the Depression, and World War II, the foreign-born population decreased in both numbers and proportions as mortality reduced the aging wave of immigrants from the turn of the century. The number of foreign-born residents in the United States declined from 1930 to 1970. By 1970, the foreign-born population had decreased to 10.5 million,[3] or roughly the same number as at the turn of the century. The proportion of foreign-born in the total population began decreasing earlier, after 1910, as the native-born population grew more rapidly. The foreign-born population as a percentage of the total population reached a minimum in 1970, when it accounted for only 5.1 percent, or 1 out of every 20 Americans.

The large increase in immigration that began in the 1960s produced a rapid turnaround in the 40-year decrease of the foreign-born popula-

Figure 2.3 FOREIGN-STOCK POPULATION OF THE UNITED STATES: 1870–1990

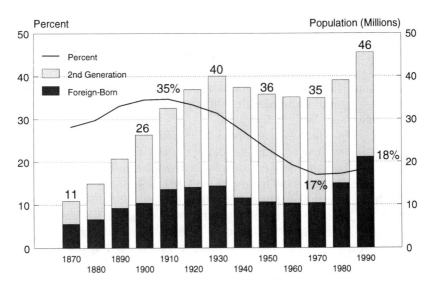

tion. A substantial increase was evident in the 1980 Census, and growth continued through the 1980s. By 1990, the number of foreign-born persons residing in the United States reached the highest levels in the history of the country, more than 20 million. Relative to the rest of the population, however, the foreign-born population is less than two-thirds of the highest levels attained from 1860 to 1920: Just over 8 percent of the population was foreign-born in 1990 versus 13 to 15 percent at the end of the nineteenth century.

The foreign-*stock* population includes the foreign-born population plus residents of foreign parentage. In other words, the foreign stock is the first generation (immigrants) and the second generation (the sons and daughters of one or two immigrant parents). These first two generations are crucial to the understanding of cultural dynamics since they tend to be the segment of the population with the strongest foreign language and cultural experience. Specifically, the immigrant generation (i.e., the foreign-born population) usually speaks a language other than English as a first language and tends to retain fairly close ties with the ancestral country. The second generation (i.e., the children of immigrants) has historically been the crucial one for adaptation to American society.

The dynamics of the foreign-stock population resemble those of the foreign-born, although with a time lag because of reproduction and mortality for the second generation (see figure 2.3). The foreign-stock population peaked at 40 million in 1930 and then declined steadily to 35 million in 1970. As a result of the upturn in immigration that began after World War II, the foreign-stock population began to increase, reaching 46 million in 1990. Proportionately, however, the foreign-stock population was at its highest level—about one-third of the total population—during the period from 1890 to 1930. Currently, the estimated foreign-stock population accounts for about 18 percent of the total population, or only slightly more than half of the highest percentage.

The foreign-stock population has increased in the post–war era principally because of increases in the first, or immigrant, generation. The second generation has hovered between 24 and 25.8 million for the entire 60-year period from 1930 to 1990. With the recent dramatic growth in the first generation (which doubled between 1970 and 1990), the second generation should soon begin to increase also. Thus, the United States is poised for substantial growth in the second generation and foreign-stock population (see chapter 11, this volume).

RACIAL/ETHNIC COMPOSITION OF THE UNITED STATES

The racial and ethnic composition of the United States has changed significantly over the last 30 years and is continuing to change substantially. The principal basis for this change is the shift in origins of immigrants that began in the 1960s. The new immigrants and their descendants are having a dramatic effect on the racial composition of the U.S. population and the racial distribution within the minority population.

Origins of Recent Immigrants

Before the Immigration and Naturalization Act Amendments of 1965 changed the national origin quotas, Europe and Canada were the dominant sources of U.S. immigrants (figure 2.1). As shown in figure 2.4, about two-thirds (66 percent) of immigrants during 1951 to 1960 were from Europe or Canada. The remaining one-third of immigrants were from Asia (6 percent), Mexico (12 percent), and other countries of Latin America (14 percent). As the number of legal immigrants

Figure 2.4 LEGAL IMMIGRATION BY REGION OR COUNTRY: 1951–60 TO
1981–90

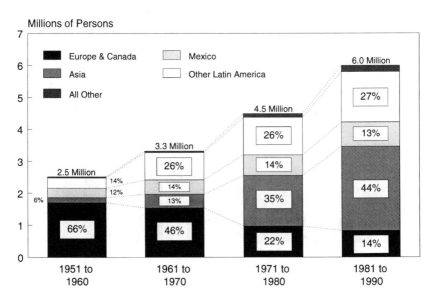

increased during each of the past four decades, from 2.5 million in the
1950s to 6 million in the 1980s, the racial composition (as reflected in
the regions of origin) has also changed.

The proportion of immigrants from Europe and Canada has
decreased steadily both in relative and absolute numbers during
the past four decades. By the 1980s, only about 14 percent of legal
immigrants came from the traditional sources of Europe and Canada.
In relative terms, the biggest gains in immigration have come from
Asia, which sent only 6 percent of legal immigrants in the 1950s,
but 44 percent in the 1980s. About 2.6 million Asians entered legally
in the 1980s, or more than *all* immigration during the 1950s.

Latin American immigration expanded from 26 percent of legal
immigration in the 1950s to 40 percent in the 1960s, where it has
remained since. In the 1980s, Latin America accounted for 2.4 million
legal immigrants. Mexico is the largest single source of legal immigrants, accounting for 12 to 14 percent of the flow during each of
the past four decades. When illegal immigration is included, Latin
America far surpasses Asia as the major source for immigration in
the 1970s and 1980s.

Figure 2.5 U.S. POPULATION BY RACE: 1850–1990

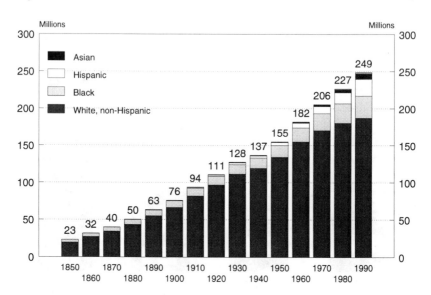

Composition of the U.S. Population

Throughout most of its history, the United States has been essentially a biracial society, comprised of a white majority and a black minority (along with a small American Indian population). This situation is now changing. The United States is becoming a multiracial society. Figure 2.5 and table 2.3 display the population growth of U.S. racial groups[4] for the period from 1850 to 1990. We focus on 1900, the first year for which adequate data on the five "racial" groups have been developed. At the turn of the century the population in areas that now comprise the United States[5] was 87 percent white, 12 percent black, and about 1 percent other racial groups. The 1900 population included about 240,000 American Indians, 240,000 Asians (primarily Chinese, Japanese, and Hawaiians, with a large concentration of all groups in Hawaii), and 660,000 Hispanics (predominantly Mexican-origin population living in the five southwestern states).[6]

All racial groups in the population increased numerically from 1900 to 1960, although the relative shifts were small (see figure 2.5 and table 2.3). By 1960, the white population's share had dropped only slightly from 86.9 percent to 85.1 percent. The proportion of blacks in the population had decreased slightly, from 11.6 percent

Table 2.3 U.S. POPULATION BY RACE/HISPANIC ANCESTRY: 1850–1990
(populations in thousands)

Year	Total	White non-Hispanic	Black	Hispanic	Asian	American Indian
Population						
1990	248,712	187,139	29,986	22,354	7,274	1,959
1980	226,625	180,392	26,482	14,604	3,726	1,420
1970	205,567	170,371	23,005	9,616	1,782	793
1960	182,055	154,969	19,071	6,346	1,146	524
1950	155,156	134,351	15,668	4,039	739	357
1940	136,928	119,425	13,767	2,814	577	345
1930	127,585	111,543	12,736	2,435	527	343
1920	110,747	96,969	11,512	1,632	389	244
1910	93,879	82,049	10,255	999	299	277
1900	76,195	66,225	8,834	656	243	237
1890	62,948	55,101	7,489	(X)	171	248
1880	50,156	43,403	6,581	(X)	145	66
1870	39,818	34,337	5,392	(X)	63	26
1860	31,443	26,923	4,442	(X)	35	44
1850	23,192	19,553	3,639	(X)	(X)	(X)
Percent						
1990	100.0	75.2	12.1	9.0	2.9	0.8
1980	100.0	79.6	11.7	6.4	1.6	0.6
1970	100.0	82.9	11.2	4.7	0.9	0.4
1960	100.0	85.1	10.5	3.5	0.6	0.3
1950	100.0	86.6	10.1	2.6	0.5	0.2
1940	100.0	87.2	10.1	2.1	0.4	0.3
1930	100.0	87.4	10.0	1.9	0.4	0.3
1920	100.0	87.6	10.4	1.5	0.4	0.2
1910	100.0	87.4	10.9	1.1	0.3	0.3
1900	100.0	86.9	11.6	0.9	0.3	0.3
1890	100.0	87.5	11.9	(X)	0.3	0.4
1880	100.0	86.5	13.1	(X)	0.3	0.1
1870	100.0	86.2	13.5	(X)	0.2	0.1
1860	100.0	85.6	14.1	(X)	0.1	0.1
1850	100.0	84.3	15.7	(X)	(X)	(X)

Note: Populations include 50 states and the District of Columbia for 1900–1990; continental U.S. for earlier years. Estimates for 1900–1990 generated by POPGEN fitted to census data by race and nativity. Census data are used for 1850–1890. The five racial/ethnic groups are mutually exclusive and exhaustive. See text for definitions. (X) Not available.

to 10.5 percent. The other three racial/ethnic groups had increased their combined proportion from about 1.5 percent to 4.4 percent.

Since 1960, the shifts in origins of immigrants have led to substantial absolute and relative increases in the Asian and Hispanic popula-

Figure 2.6 MINORITY POPULATION BY RACE: 1850–1990

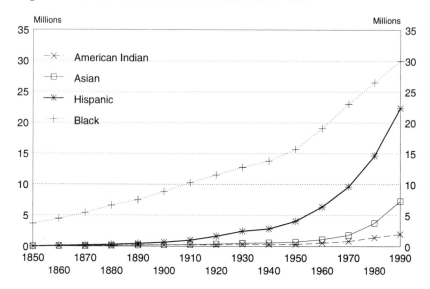

tions. Over the last 30 years, the combined proportion of Hispanics, Asians, and American Indians increased from 4.4 percent in 1960 to 12.7 percent in 1990. These three groups, which accounted for just over 1 million people in 1900, had grown to a total of more than 31 million people by 1990. Differences in size and growth among the various groups can be seen more clearly in figure 2.6, which focuses only on the "minority"[7] races.

The black population has grown steadily from 8.8 million in 1900 to 30 million in 1990. In contrast, the Hispanic population shows much more dramatic growth—from less than 1 million at the turn of the century to 22.4 million in 1990. This 34-fold growth represents a compounded growth rate of 48 percent per decade, or 4 percent per year sustained over 90 years. (The corresponding figures for the remaining white non-Hispanic population are 12 percent per decade, or less than 1.2 percent per year.) The Asian population has shown a similar pattern of rapid growth—from less than 250,000 in 1900 to 7.3 million in 1990, or a 30-fold increase, with an average annual growth rate of 3.8 percent.

As a result of rapid growth of the Asian and Hispanic groups, the composition within the minority population is also changing. The minority population of the United States was almost exclusively black during the nineteenth century, with only a small number of

Figure 2.7 COMPOSITION OF THE MINORITY POPULATION: 1850–1990

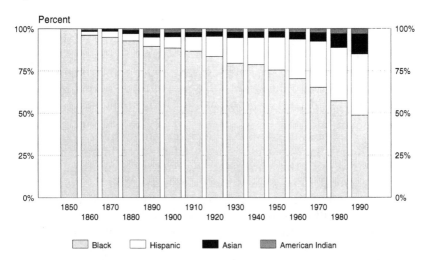

persons of other races. While the black population has increased at a steady pace, the Asian and Hispanic groups have grown at much more rapid rates during the past three decades. Consequently, the proportion of the minority population that is black has been dropping steadily (see figure 2.7). Small gains occurred in the relative size of the Asian, Hispanic, and American Indian groups in the early decades of the twentieth century. The large relative shifts occurred after 1960 with the upturn in legal immigration for Asians and Hispanics and increases in illegal immigration (principally for the Mexican-origin population). The once much smaller Hispanic population, for example, is rapidly gaining on the total numbers in the black population. These trends passed a little-noticed threshold in the 1990 Census. The black population had declined to 48 percent of the total minority population; for the first time, blacks were no longer the "majority" group of the minority population.

IMMIGRATION'S CONTRIBUTION TO POPULATION GROWTH

The preceding sections reviewed the number of immigrants by racial and ethnic groups and discussed the changes in the racial composition of the U.S. population. This section examines explicitly the contribution of immigration to population growth, including how immigration has affected the population changes within each racial group. Immigration affects a population demographically in two ways: directly, through the contribution of new members (immigrants) to the population and, indirectly, through future births to the immigrants and their descendants. To measure the first impact, we need to take into account net immigration (the number of immigrants minus the number of emigrants). To measure the second effect, we must examine the future reproduction of the population after the immigration has occurred.

The impact of immigrants on future reproduction in a population is a function of their age and sex, levels of childbearing, and mortality rates. Determining their impact, thus, requires a population model that disaggregates the population by age, sex, *and generation* and takes into account the four components of population change—immigration, emigration, fertility, and mortality. Edmonston and Passel (in chapter 11 of this volume) describe the model of population change used to determine the impact of immigration on population change in the twentieth century. Edmonston and Passel (1992) present greater detail on methods for projecting a population by generation.

We first used the population "projection" model to fit the time series of U.S. population, fertility, mortality, and immigration by race based principally on data from census sources. Then, to study the impact of immigration on population growth in the twentieth century United States, we use this model to imagine what would have happened *if immigration (legal and illegal) had not occurred.* In the model, we first set immigration to zero for a period and hold all other components fixed. This "experiment"—i.e., the difference between the zero-immigration scenario and the actual case—provides an estimate of the overall effect of the immigrants *plus* the future generations born to the immigrants. Such an estimate is, hence, a measure of the overall direct and indirect effects of immigration on population growth.[8]

Total U.S. Population

From 1900 to 1990, the total population of the United States increased from 76 million to 249 million, an average annual rate of 1.3 percent. Figure 2.8 displays the impact of immigration on the size of the U.S. population for the period from 1900 to 1990. This graph shows the contribution of immigration to population for four key periods of immigration: 1900–1930, 1930–1950, 1950–1970, and 1970–1990.

Figure 2.8 CONTRIBUTION OF IMMIGRATION, TOTAL POPULATION:
1900–1990

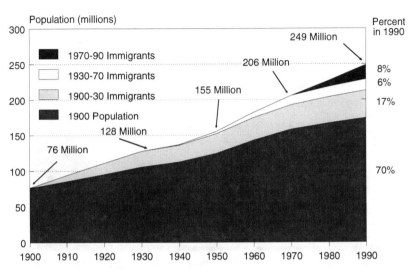

The overall graph represents the growth of the total population from 1900 to 1990. The darker, bottom portion of the graph shows the hypothetical population size under conditions of no immigration since 1900. The different shaded components in the upper portions of the graph show the population growth attributable to different waves of immigrants and *their descendants.*

Figures 2.9 through 2.12 contain the numbers and graphical representations for the different race groups. (Detailed tables containing the supporting numerical data are in appendix 2.A as tables 2.A.1 through 2.A.5. Table 2.4 contains extracts from these detailed tables.) These numbers, derived from our research, represent demographic constructs, not genealogical derivations. For example, 8 percent of the U.S. population of 249 million in 1990, or about 20.3 million people, can be attributed to immigrants who entered the country since 1970 and their offspring (the top band in figure 2.8). However, because immigrants can and do marry natives, the number of people in the U.S. population with such ancestries is actually greater. The 20.3 million figure represents a demographic "what if" calculation— an answer to the question: "If immigration to the United States had stopped between 1970 and 1990, how much less would the U.S. population have been in 1990?"

As shown in figure 2.8, the 1990 U.S. population would have

Figure 2.9 CONTRIBUTION OF IMMIGRATION, ASIAN POPULATION:
1900–1990

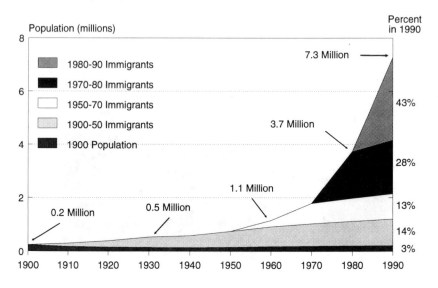

Figure 2.10 CONTRIBUTION OF IMMIGRATION, HISPANIC POPULATION:
1900–1990

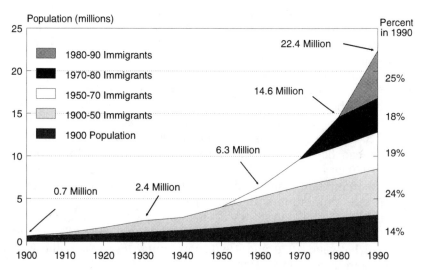

Figure 2.11 CONTRIBUTION OF IMMIGRATION, BLACK POPULATION:
1900–1990

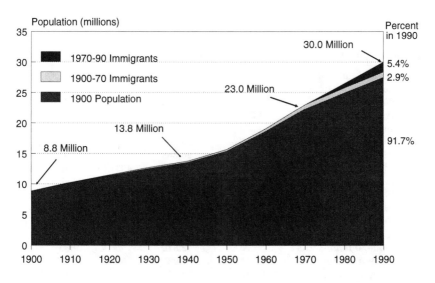

Figure 2.12 CONTRIBUTION OF IMMIGRATION, WHITE NON-HISPANIC
POPULATION: 1900–1990

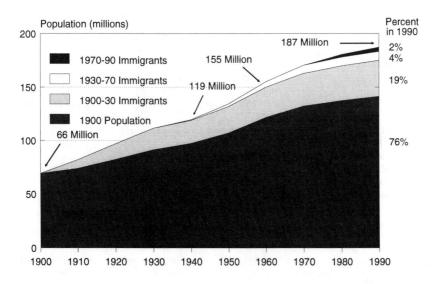

Table 2.4 CONTRIBUTION OF POST-1900 IMMIGRATION AND 1990
POPULATION FOR THE POPULATION OF THE UNITED STATES IN
1990, BY RACE
(populations in thousands)

Contribution from Component	Total	White non-Hispanic	Black	Hispanic	Asian
Estimated Population	**248,712**	187,139	29,986	22,354	7,274
Contribution from:					
1900 Population	**174,145**	141,369	27,493	3,108	216
1st Generation	8,534	8,184	29	301	20
2nd Generation	35,574	34,118	392	956	108
3rd Generation	38,547	36,735	941	869	2
4th + Generations	90,055	60,868	26,151	991	85
Immigation since 1900	**74,567**	45,769	2,493	19,246	7,058
1900–10 Immigrants	17,286	16,398	125	606	157
1910–20 Immigrants	14,487	12,624	196	1,257	409
1920–30 Immigrants	9,305	6,661	167	2,182	295
1930–40 Immigrants	1,439	1,021	22	312	83
1940–50 Immigrants	3,590	2,389	68	1,055	77
1950–60 Immigrants	5,272	2,870	158	1,885	359
1960–70 Immigrants	5,214	1,930	266	2,433	584
1970–80 Immigrants	9,518	2,658	834	4,013	2,014
1980–90 Immigrants	10,756	1,341	774	5,525	3,116

Population Size in 1990 if Immigration Had Been Cut off After:

1900	174,145	141,369	27,493	3,108	216
1910	189,309	155,645	27,618	3,714	373
1920	203,795	168,269	27,814	4,971	782
1930	213,100	174,929	27,980	7,153	1,077
1940	214,539	175,951	28,002	7,465	1,161
1950	218,128	178,340	28,070	8,521	1,238
1960	223,400	181,210	28,228	10,405	1,597
1970	228,614	183,140	28,494	12,839	2,181
1980	238,133	185,798	29,329	16,851	4,195
No Cut-Off (Actual)	248,712	187,139	29,986	22,354	7,274

Percent Distribution in 1990 if Immigration Had Been Cut off After:

1900	100.0	81.2	15.8	1.8	0.1
1910	100.0	82.2	14.6	2.0	0.2
1920	100.0	82.6	13.6	2.4	0.4
1930	100.0	82.1	13.1	3.4	0.5
1940	100.0	82.0	13.1	3.5	0.5
1950	100.0	81.8	12.9	3.9	0.6
1960	100.0	81.1	12.6	4.7	0.7
1970	100.0	80.1	12.5	5.6	1.0
1980	100.0	78.0	12.3	7.1	1.8
No Cut-Off (Actual)	100.0	75.2	12.1	9.0	2.9

Source: Tables 2.A.1 through 2.A.5.

numbered 174 million (or 70 percent of the observed 1990 population) if there had been no immigration since 1900. Immigration during the 1900–1930 period contributed about 39 million people to the 1990 population, or 17 percent of the total population. Immigration during 1930–1950 and 1950–1970 provided a relatively small contribution; combining the periods produces a contribution of 15 million, or only about 6 percent of the total 1990 population. Immigration during the last 20 years, from 1970 to 1990, has, in fact, produced a greater impact on the 1990 population than the previous 40 years. Immigration from 1970 to 1990 has contributed over 19 million persons, or 8 percent of the 1990 U.S. residents. Thus, as of 1990, the 1900–1930 immigrant cohorts have had somewhat more overall impact than all of the post-1930 immigrants. This pattern may change in the future because the more recent immigrant cohorts have higher fertility than the descendants of the 1900–1930 immigrants.

ASIAN AND PACIFIC ISLANDER POPULATION

The Asian and Pacific Islander population (shown in figure 2.9 and table 2.A.2) grew very slowly during the period from 1900 to 1960. Asian immigration has been affected by a succession of immigration laws. Immigration from Japan and China, the principal sources in Asia during the second half of the nineteenth century, began modestly, but even these flows were increasingly restricted from the 1880s to the 1960s. The Chinese Exclusion Act of 1882 had effectively ended immigration from China. Immigration from Japan and the Philippines to Hawaii and the continental United States began in the late 1800s and continued into the early decades of this century. However, Japanese immigration was restricted by the Gentleman's Agreement of 1907. Virtually all Asian immigration was effectively ended by the Immigration Acts of 1917 and 1924. Only Filipinos continued to immigrate—largely because of their special status as residents of a Commonwealth governed by the United States— although legislation in 1934 ended immigration from the Philippines. Then, in 1965, legislation was enacted that abolished the national origins system that had discriminated particularly against Asians (see U.S. Immigration and Naturalization Service 1991 for a summary of all legislation affecting immigrant admissions). The 1965 law also raised the overall numerical ceiling for annual immigration to 270,000, although no more than 20,000 could come from any one country. Many Asians took advantage of the new immigration rules, and Asian immigration began to increase dramatically in the 1960s.

The Asian and Pacific Islander population in the United States numbered 7.3 million in 1990. Of this total, only 1.3 million, or one-sixth of the 1990 population, derive from the 1900 population and immigrants during 1900 to 1950. Stated otherwise, 83 percent of the 1990 Asian population, or six million people, came from immigrants entering since 1950 or their descendants. The contribution of immigration has been increasing, with 0.9 million persons attributable to 1950–1970 immigrants, 2 million from 1970–1980, and 3.1 million from 1980–1990. The current Asian population is noteworthy for its recency in the United States, with 70 percent of the 1990 population consisting of immigrants who entered during the last 20 years or their offspring.

HISPANIC POPULATION

The Hispanic population has also experienced remarkable growth in the twentieth century, increasing from 0.7 million in 1900 to 22.4 million in 1990. Like the Asian population, growth in the Hispanic population has been fueled largely by immigration. If there had been no immigration since 1900, the estimated 1990 Hispanic population would be 3.1 million, or less than one-seventh of the actual 1990 level (figure 2.10 and table 2.4). Some Hispanic immigration took place during 1900–1950, but only a modest portion (4.9 million, or 22 percent) of the 1990 population derives from immigration during that 50-year period (see also figure 2.10). However, immigration during the past 40 years has made major contributions to the 1990 population: 1950–1970 immigrants contributed 4.3 million (19 percent); 1970–1980 immigrants, 4.0 million (18 percent); and 1980–1990 immigrants, 5.5 million (25 percent). Like the Asian population, the Hispanic population is characterized by the recency of immigration, but the concentration in the most recent 20 years is not as great. Almost two-thirds of the 1990 Hispanic population consists of either immigrants who came since 1950 or descendants of those immigrants.

BLACK POPULATION

The pattern of growth for the black population is very distinctive. The black population grew steadily during the period from 1900 to 1990, from 8.8 million to 29.9 million, but the growth was predominantly due to natural increase with very little impact from immigration. If there had been no immigration since 1900, the 1990 black population would have increased to 27.5 million in 1990, or 92 percent of its enumerated count (see figure 2.11 and table 2.4). A modest number of blacks from Africa and the Caribbean have immigrated during the past 20 years but immigrants during the 1900–1970 period and their offspring contributed only 1 million people (3 percent) to the 1990 population, whereas immigration during 1970–1990 contributed 1.6 million (5 percent). Nevertheless, the black population in 1990 is distinctive in that the bulk of the residents are descendants of the population residing in the United States in 1900.

WHITE NON-HISPANIC POPULATION

The white[9] population grew from 66 million in 1900 to 187 million 1990 (figure 2.12). If there had been no immigration during 1900–1990, the population would have grown to only 141 million in 1990 (table 2.4). Thus, three-quarters of the 1990 white population is attributable to the original 1900 population. A majority of the twentieth century immigration of whites occurred in the first three decades of the century. The relative impact of this early immigration wave on the 1990 population is very apparent (figure 2.12). About 36 million, or 19 percent of the 1990 white population was contributed by immigration during 1900–1930. Even though there has been moderate immigration from Europe and Canada in the postwar period (especially in the 1950s), only 11 million, or 6 percent of the 1990 white population can be attributed to post-1930 immigrants and their descendants. For whites, the 1900–1930 wave has had more than *three* times the impact of all post-1930 immigrants.

Alternative Immigration Scenarios

Another way to assess the impact of immigration on population size is to ask the question: "What would the 1990 population be if there had been no immigration since . . .?" Table 2.4 organizes the detailed information from tables 2.A.1 through 2.A.5 in such a way as to address this question and questions concerning the composition of the population under these hypothetical scenarios.

The actual black population was about 30 million in 1990. Even if there had been no black immigration since 1900, the black population would have been 27.5 million, close to its present size. On the other hand, both the Hispanic and Asian populations have been greatly affected by immigration in the twentieth century. Moreover, if there had been no Asian and Hispanic immigration during the past 40 years, these populations would be a noticeably smaller fraction of their 1990 levels. For example, if immigration had stopped in 1950, the 1990 Hispanic population would be about 8.5 million, or only one-third of the actual 1990 population. A similar 1950 cutoff of Asian immigration would have led to an Asian population only one-sixth of actual 1990 levels.

The numerical results from table 2.4 can also be used to consider the hypothetical racial composition of the 1990 population under different conditions of immigration. For example, the white population comprised 75 percent of the 1990 population. If there had been no immigration since 1900 for any racial groups, the 1990 white population would have represented 81 percent of the total population. The actual black population in 1990 is also a smaller proportion of the total population than under hypothetical conditions of no immigration. On the other hand, the Asian and Hispanic populations are a substantially larger proportion of the 1990 population than if there had been no immigration since 1900. These results also confirm that immigration during the past 20 to 30 years has provided the major proportionate increases for the Asian and Hispanic populations.

CONCLUSION

Important changes in U.S. immigration over the past three decades will have a gradual, cumulative impact on the future racial and ethnic composition of American society. In some ways, the effects of the "new" immigrants have been very minor up to this moment. The new immigrants are relatively recent in their acquisition of English language and their adjustment to American society. Many have not yet secured citizenship and begun to vote in elections. All these changes will occur in the future. Also, the relative flow of immigrants to the United States has been small (compared to the size of the U.S. population) and has been concentrated in a few states and major metropolitan areas.

Unprecedented as the current shifts in the ethnic origin of the U.S. population may seem to some observers, has American society ever experienced similar change? During the early decades of this century, some worried about the dramatic increase of "new" immigrants (i.e., those from eastern and southern Europe). How does this earlier ethnic shift in immigration compare to the current one?

Consider an earlier period, from 1850 to 1920, and the shift of immigration from northern and western Europe and Germany to

Figure 2.13 COMPOSITION OF THE FOREIGN-BORN POPULATION: 1850–1920
           AND 1920–90

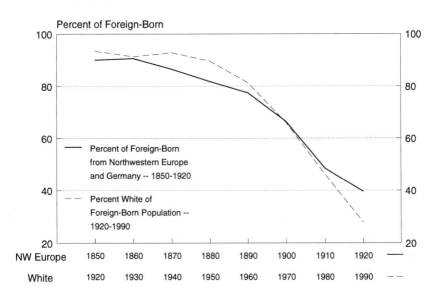

immigration from southern and eastern Europe. During this period,
the composition of the foreign-born population shifted greatly (figure
2.13). The northwestern European component of the foreign-born
population was 90 percent in 1850. This group declined to 40 percent
in 1920, as southern and eastern European immigrants became the
dominant proportion of the foreign-born population.

We can make a similar comparison for the 70-year period from
1920 to 1990. Let us use the white population, the proportion of the
foreign-born population that originated in Europe and Canada, as a
basis for comparison. The proportion of white foreign-born population declined from 90 percent in 1920 to about 30 percent in 1990,
as the Asian and Hispanic proportions of the foreign-born population
increased. This shift is remarkably similar to the shift from northern
and western European immigration to southern and eastern European
immigration that the United States experienced about a century ago.

As a result of the changing composition of the foreign-born population and high levels of immigration, the United States has experienced massive shifts in the ethnic origins of its population. Today's
immigration patterns continue those changes in the racial/ethnic
composition of the population. The impact of past and continuing

immigration on the future population of the United States will depend on three demographic changes that are already taking place.

First, the European-origin population of the United States is large but aging and growing slowly because of low fertility and low immigration. This population is composed largely of descendants of those who arrived before about 1880, the large wave of immigrants during 1880 to 1914, and the last smaller wave in the two decades after World War II. The absolute number of European-born persons in the United States peaked in the 1930s and has declined steadily since then. Over the next decades, the European-born population in the United States will diminish, and European ethnic communities will become relatively less numerous. The source of new immigrant communities will continue to shift to Asia, Latin America, and the Caribbean.

Like previous waves of immigrants, America's newest immigrants are not evenly distributed across the United States. Thus, new immigrant communities tend to be concentrated in only a few places. Although significant numbers of Mexican-origin persons live in the southwestern border states, most recent immigrants choose metropolitan destinations. Immigration is concentrated in Los Angeles, Chicago, New York, Miami, and the dozen or so other largest metropolitan areas. These are the areas where the new immigrants settle and are the places where the new ethnic communities will develop.

Third, the racial/ethnic makeup of the U.S. population is likely to continue to change. However, the demographic consequences of current patterns of immigration are difficult to assess. Even knowing the number of immigrants by country of origin is extremely difficult because of questions concerning the levels of emigration and illegal immigration. In addition, significant questions about the fertility and mortality levels of new immigrant groups remain unanswered.

U.S. population growth is slowing down for two reasons. Substantial fertility declines in the decade from the early 1960s to early 1970s have had the greatest impact. Even though immigration levels have been increasing during recent years—with a higher proportion of annual U.S. population growth deriving from immigration—until recently, immigration has not been sufficient to counterbalance the long-term effects of declines in natural increase. Correspondingly, the rate of natural increase among America's newest immigrants provides a rising proportion of the national population growth, primarily because they are an increasing proportion of the U.S. population, but also because they have slightly higher fertility than the native-born population.

Edmonston and Passel discuss the demographic implications of immigration for the future course of the U.S. population in chapter 11 of this volume. However, a review of past trends and new legislation suggests continued high levels of immigration in the 1990s (Fix and Passel 1991). We anticipate that there will be a sustained high proportion of immigrants arriving from the developing countries of Asia, Latin America, and the Caribbean. New flows may also occur. At this time, the principal major alteration in the current patterns appears to be the potential for new flows from eastern Europe and the states of the former Soviet Union. Such changes are difficult to predict because of uncertainty about the changes that might occur in political and economic conditions and the response of the former Warsaw Pact countries and the U.S. to them. The Middle East is another potential source of new immigrants.

The contribution of immigration to total population growth in the United States, mainly directly through the volume of immigration but also indirectly through slightly higher fertility, will increase the relative proportion of the new immigrant groups in the U.S. population. There is no doubt that the response to the new immigrants will be a major determinant of the country's future, as it has been in the past. The increased absolute and relative size of the new immigrant groups will amplify any anticipated impacts that they will have on American society.

Notes

This chapter is a revised version of a presentation at the conference, "Immigration and Ethnicity: The Integration of America's Newest Immigrants," held at the Urban Institute in Washington, D.C., June 17–18, 1991 and sponsored by the Program for Research on Immigration Policy at the Urban Institute.

1. Unless otherwise noted, all figures for immigration during the twentieth century are from estimates derived by the authors.

2. The numbers in figure 2.1 are derived from data published by the U.S. Immigration and Naturalization Service (1991) and estimates of undocumented immigration (Bean et al. 1991). They differ from the estimates shown in table 2.1, which were derived by fitting demographic components to the series of census counts for the twentieth century with POPGEN, a projection/estimation program (Edmonston and Passel 1992). See also Passel and Edmonston (1992).

3. The foreign-born population in table 2.2 and the asssociated figures 2.2 and 2.3 include persons born in Puerto Rico, even though they are U.S. citizens by birth. In addition, persons whose parents were born in Puerto Rico are included in the foreign-stock population. From a demographic point of view, movement between the United

States and Puerto Rico functions like immigration rather than natural increase—i.e., persons moving from Puerto Rico enter the population at ages other than zero. Thus, we have chosen for POPGEN, our estimation program, to treat this movement as immigration into the first generation (Edmonston and Passel 1992). From socioeconomic and cultural perspectives, the Puerto Rican-born population also has much in common with the immigrant population, even though Puerto Ricans are U.S. citizens by birth.

4. In the context of this paper, the term "race" is used to designate five mutually exclusive groups: blacks, Hispanics, Asians and Pacific Islanders (referred to as "Asians" for brevity), the American Indian and Alaskan Native population (referred to as "American Indians"), and the white population, not of Hispanic origin (referred to as "white non-Hispanic" or simply "white"). Strictly speaking, these groups are not races; for example, according to the U.S. Bureau of the Census, persons of Hispanic origin may be of any race. For brevity and clarity, we use the terms "race" or "racial/ ethnic group."

5. The data refer to the population in the combined area of the 48 conterminous states and the District of Columbia plus Alaska and Hawaii.

6. All figures for the Asian and Hispanic populations before 1980 are estimates derived by the authors, principally from census sources. See Passel and Edmonston 1992.

7. The "majority" population in the context of this paper is the white non-Hispanic population. The remaining population is designated as the "minority" population; it includes blacks, Hispanics, Asians, and American Indians.

8. Gibson (1991) provides somewhat different estimates of the contribution of immigration to population growth. Gibson's methodology involves solving for the rates of natural increase for residents and immigrants during each intercensal period. With estimates of the rates, he then estimates the effect on long-term population growth of immigration during each decennial period from 1790 to 1990. Gibson (1975) describes his methodology in an earlier paper.

9. The term "white" refers to the white non-Hispanic population. See note 4.

APPENDIX 2.A
CONSTRUCTION OF POPULATION ESTIMATES BY RACE AND ESTIMATION OF THE CONTRIBUTION OF IMMIGRATION TO POPULATION GROWTH: 1900–1990

The population estimates and estimated components of change presented in this paper were developed with the estimation/projection program called POPGEN developed by the authors. POPGEN uses a modified cohort-component methodology to develop population estimates by age, sex, and immigrant generation. The program keeps track of four generations: the first generation (i.e., the immigrants); the second generation (i.e., children of immigrants); the third generation (i.e., grandchildren of immigrants); and fourth-or-higher generations (i.e., persons whose most recent immigrant ancestor is at least a great-grandparent). The data presented in the paper follow the designations used in U.S. decennial censuses: An individual's generation is defined by the most recent immigrant ancestor. Thus, an individual with one immigrant parent and one native-born parent is a member of the second generation (see chapter 11, this volume, and Edmonston and Passel 1992 for a more detailed explanation of POPGEN).

POPGEN combines data on fertility, mortality, immigration, and emigration to produce its population estimates (or projections). For this study, POPGEN was applied separately to each of four racial/ethnic groups: Hispanic, Asian, black, and white non-Hispanic. The basic strategy for developing the estimates for each group involved fitting information on each of the four components to the series of population counts from the decennial censuses of 1900 through 1990. The fitting involved an iterative process of progressively fitting the component series to the population targets. Because our interest is primarily in immigration, the targets for each date were the foreign-born population, the second-generation population (i.e., the native-born population of foreign or mixed parentage in census parlance), and the third-and-higher generation population (i.e., the native-born of native parentage). See Passel and Edmonston (1992) for detailed source information on the components.

The result of the fitting process is a detailed set of fertility, mortality, and immigration estimates for each 5-year period in the interval 1900–1990 for each racial/ethnic group by sex. To estimate the contribution of immigration to 1900–1990 population growth, the immigration component for a decade was set to zero. Then, the entire "projection" for 1900–1990 was computed with the zero-immigration component. The difference between the full estimate and this new, diminished estimate was taken to represent the contribution of each decade's worth of immigrants and their descendants to population growth in the United States.

Tables 2.A.2 through 2.A.5 show the estimates of immigration's contribution to population growth by decade for each racial/ethnic group. Table 2.A.1 sums the racial/ethnic groups to give the total for the entire U.S. population.

Table 2.A.1 CONTRIBUTION OF POST-1900 IMMIGRATION AND 1900 POPULATION FOR THE TOTAL POPULATION OF THE UNITED STATES: 1900–1990
(populations in thousands)

Contribution from Component	Census Year									
	1990	1980	1970	1960	1950	1940	1930	1920	1910	1900
Population Size										
Estimated Population	248,712	226,625	205,591	182,024	155,131	136,928	127,573	110,734	93,877	76,195
Contribution from:										
1900 Population	**174,145**	**166,804**	**158,114**	**142,960**	**124,546**	**112,724**	**105,596**	**95,111**	**85,392**	**76,195**
1st Generation	8,534	8,627	8,122	6,954	6,427	6,449	6,650	7,803	9,413	10,443
2nd Generation	35,574	34,713	33,249	30,235	26,944	24,620	22,948	21,114	19,000	15,870
3rd Generation	38,547	39,923	38,286	34,989	31,408	29,007	27,458	25,607	23,294	19,817
4th + Generations	90,055	84,431	79,287	71,551	60,472	53,244	49,126	41,128	34,072	30,066
Immigration since 1900	**74,567**	**59,821**	**47,453**	**39,095**	**30,610**	**24,204**	**21,988**	**15,636**	**8,487**	**(X)**
1900–10 Immigrants	17,286	16,708	15,427	14,180	12,743	10,993	10,272	9,555	8,487	
1910–20 Immigrants	14,487	13,574	12,729	11,917	10,068	8,531	8,184	6,787		
1920–30 Immigrants	9,305	8,841	8,467	7,563	6,332	5,462	4,831			
1930–40 Immigrants	1,439	1,417	1,314	1,193	1,042	800				
1940–50 Immigrants	3,590	3,375	3,084	2,732	2,143					
1950–60 Immigrants	5,272	4,847	4,425	3,537						
1960–70 Immigrants	5,214	4,828	4,196							
1970–80 Immigrants	9,518	8,448								
1980–90 Immigrants	10,756									
Percent of Estimated Population										
Total	100.0	100.0	100.0	100.0	100.0	100.0	100.0	100.0	100.0	100.0
Contribution from:										
1900 Population	**70.0**	**73.6**	**76.9**	**78.5**	**80.3**	**82.3**	**82.8**	**85.9**	**91.0**	**100.0**
1st Generation	3.4	3.8	4.0	3.8	4.1	4.7	5.2	7.0	10.0	13.7
2nd Generation	14.3	15.3	16.2	16.6	17.4	18.0	18.0	19.1	20.2	20.8
3rd Generation	15.5	17.6	18.6	19.2	20.2	21.2	21.5	23.1	24.8	26.0
4th + Generations	36.2	37.3	38.6	39.3	39.0	38.9	38.5	37.1	36.3	39.5
Immigration since 1900	**30.0**	**26.4**	**23.1**	**21.5**	**19.7**	**17.7**	**17.2**	**14.1**	**9.0**	**(X)**
1900–10 Immigrants	7.0	7.4	7.5	7.8	8.2	8.0	8.1	8.6	9.0	
1910–20 Immigrants	5.8	6.0	6.2	6.5	6.5	6.2	6.4	6.1		
1920–30 Immigrants	3.7	3.9	4.1	4.2	4.1	4.0	3.8			

Table 2.A.1 CONTRIBUTION OF POST-1900 IMMIGRATION AND 1900 POPULATION FOR THE TOTAL POPULATION OF THE UNITED STATES: 1900–1990 (continued)
(populations in thousands)

Contribution from Component	Census Year									
	1990	1980	1970	1960	1950	1940	1930	1920	1910	1900
1930–40 Immigrants	0.6	0.6	0.6	0.7	0.7	0.6				
1940–50 Immigrants	1.4	1.5	1.5	1.5	1.4					
1950–60 Immigrants	2.1	2.1	2.2	1.9						
1960–70 Immigrants	2.1	2.1	2.0							
1970–80 Immigrants	3.8	3.7								
1980–90 Immigrants	4.3									
Growth Since 1900										
Amount	172,517	150,429	129,396	105,829	78,936	60,733	51,378	34,539	17,681	(X)
Percent Contribution from:										
1900 Population	**56.8**	**60.2**	**63.3**	**63.1**	**61.3**	**60.1**	**57.2**	**54.8**	**52.0**	**(X)**
1st Generation	−1.1	−1.2	−1.8	−3.3	−5.1	−6.6	−7.4	−7.6	−5.8	(X)
2nd Generation	11.4	12.5	13.4	13.6	14.0	14.4	13.8	15.2	17.7	(X)
3rd Generation	10.9	13.4	14.3	14.3	14.7	15.1	14.9	16.8	19.7	(X)
4th + Generations	34.8	36.1	38.0	39.2	38.5	38.2	37.1	32.0	22.7	(X)
Immigration since 1900	**43.2**	**39.8**	**36.7**	**36.9**	**38.8**	**39.9**	**42.8**	**45.3**	**48.0**	**(X)**
1900–10 Immigrants	10.0	11.1	11.9	13.4	16.1	18.1	20.0	27.7	48.0	
1910–20 Immigrants	8.4	9.0	9.8	11.3	12.8	14.0	15.9	19.7		
1920–30 Immigrants	5.4	5.9	6.5	7.1	8.0	9.0	9.4			
1930–40 Immigrants	0.8	0.9	1.0	1.1	1.3	1.3				
1940–50 Immigrants	2.1	2.2	2.4	2.6	2.7					
1950–60 Immigrants	3.1	3.2	3.4	3.3						
1960–70 Immigrants	3.0	3.2	3.2							
1970–80 Immigrants	5.5	5.6								
1980–90 Immigrants	6.2									

Source: Estimates are the sum of separate estimates for the black population, Hispanic population, Asian and Pacific Islander population, white non-Hispanic population, and the Native American population. Estimates for the first four populations are shown separately in tables 2.A.2 through 2.A.5.
Note: Estimates include 50 states and the District of Columbia for all years.
(X) Not applicable.

Table 2.A.2 CONTRIBUTION OF POST-1900 IMMIGRATION AND 1900 POPULATION FOR THE ASIAN AND PACIFIC ISLANDER POPULATION OF THE UNITED STATES: 1900–1990
(populations in thousands)

Contribution from Component	Census Year									
	1990	1980	1970	1960	1950	1940	1930	1920	1910	1900
Population Size										
Estimated Population	7,274	3,726	1,807	1,115	715	577	516	376	297	243
Contribution from:										
1900 Population	**216**	**206**	**194**	**178**	**153**	**138**	**145**	**157**	**180**	**243**
1st Generation	20	19	18	16	15	22	45	76	113	186
2nd Generation	108	102	96	89	75	32	42	40	28	22
3rd Generation	2	2	2	2	1	1	1	1	0	1
4th + Generations	85	82	78	72	64	56	50	44	41	35
Immigration since 1900	**7,058**	**3,520**	**1,588**	**968**	**586**	**439**	**383**	**232**	**119**	**(X)**
1900–10 Immigrants	157	147	130	113	97	83	89	95	119	
1910–20 Immigrants	409	373	340	304	242	187	182	148		
1920–30 Immigrants	295	275	256	225	180	145	134			
1930–40 Immigrants	83	79	73	64	56	43				
1940–50 Immigrants	77	69	61	52	36					
1950–60 Immigrants	359	325	300	237						
1960–70 Immigrants	584	534	458							
1970–80 Immigrants	2,014	1,752								
1980–90 Immigrants	3,116									
Percent of Estimated Population										
Total	100.0	100.0	100.0	100.0	100.0	100.0	100.0	100.0	100.0	100.0
Contribution from:										
1900 Population	**3.0**	**5.5**	**10.7**	**15.9**	**21.4**	**24.0**	**28.1**	**41.7**	**60.6**	**100.0**
1st Generation	0.3	0.5	1.0	1.5	2.1	3.8	8.7	20.1	37.9	76.4
2nd Generation	1.5	2.7	5.3	8.0	10.5	5.5	8.2	10.6	9.5	8.9
3rd Generation	0.0	0.0	0.1	0.1	0.2	0.2	0.2	0.2	0.0	0.2
4th + Generations	1.2	2.2	4.3	6.5	8.9	9.7	9.7	11.7	13.7	14.5
Immigration since 1900	**97.0**	**94.5**	**87.9**	**86.8**	**82.1**	**76.0**	**74.2**	**61.7**	**40.3**	**(X)**
1900–10 Immigrants	2.2	3.9	7.2	10.1	13.6	14.5	17.3	25.3	40.3	
1910–20 Immigrants	5.6	10.0	18.8	27.3	33.8	32.3	35.2	39.4		
1920–30 Immigrants	4.1	7.4	14.2	20.2	25.2	25.2	26.0			

Table 2.A.2 CONTRIBUTION OF POST-1900 IMMIGRATION AND 1900 POPULATION FOR THE ASIAN AND PACIFIC ISLANDER POPULATION OF THE UNITED STATES: 1900–1990 (populations in thousands) (continued)

Contribution from Component	Census Year									
	1990	1980	1970	1960	1950	1940	1930	1920	1910	1900
1930–40 Immigrants	1.1	2.1	4.0	5.8	7.8	7.4				
1940–50 Immigrants	1.1	1.8	3.4	4.7	5.0					
1950–60 Immigrants	4.9	8.7	16.6	21.3						
1960–70 Immigrants	8.0	14.3	25.3							
1970–80 Immigrants	27.7	47.0								
1980–90 Immigrants	42.8									
Growth Since 1900										
Amount	7,030	3,483	1,563	871	471	334	272	132	54	(X)
Percent Contribution from:										
1900 Population	**-0.4**	**-1.1**	**-3.1**	**-7.5**	**-19.2**	**-31.5**	**-36.1**	**-65.4**	**-118.6**	**(X)**
1st Generation	-2.4	-4.8	-10.7	-19.4	-36.2	-49.1	-51.7	-83.3	-137.0	(X)
2nd Generation	1.2	2.3	4.8	7.7	11.4	3.1	7.6	13.7	12.0	(X)
3rd Generation	0.0	0.0	0.1	0.1	0.2	0.2	0.1	0.0	-0.1	(X)
4th + Generations	0.7	1.4	2.7	4.2	6.0	6.3	5.4	6.6	10.3	(X)
Immigration since 1900	**100.4**	**101.1**	**101.6**	**111.1**	**124.4**	**131.5**	**140.5**	**175.2**	**223.3**	**(X)**
1900–10 Immigrants	2.2	4.2	8.3	13.0	20.6	25.0	32.8	71.8	223.3	
1910–20 Immigrants	5.8	10.7	21.7	34.9	51.2	55.9	66.7	112.0		
1920–30 Immigrants	4.2	7.9	16.4	25.8	38.2	43.6	49.2			
1930–40 Immigrants	1.2	2.3	4.7	7.4	11.8	12.8				
1940–50 Immigrants	1.1	2.0	3.9	6.0	7.5					
1950–60 Immigrants	5.1	9.3	19.2	27.2						
1960–70 Immigrants	8.3	15.3	29.3							
1970–80 Immigrants	28.6	50.3								
1980–90 Immigrants	44.3									

Source: Estimates made using POPGEN program fitted to approximate census counts for total population, first generation, and second generation. The contribution of each immigration component is the difference between the complete estimation and a "projection" for 1900–1990 with that immigration component set to zero. For the 1900 populations, the contribution is estimated by setting all other components to zero in a "projection" for 1900–1990. See text for methods and sources.

Note: Estimates include 50 states and the District of Columbia for all years.

(X) Not applicable.

Table 2.A.3 CONTRIBUTION OF POST-1900 IMMIGRATION AND 1900 POPULATION FOR THE HISPANIC POPULATION OF THE UNITED STATES: 1900–1990
(populations in thousands)

Contribution from Component	Census Year									
	1990	1980	1970	1960	1950	1940	1930	1920	1910	1900
Population Size										
Estimated Population	22,354	14,604	9,616	6,346	4,039	2,814	2,435	1,632	999	656
Contribution from:										
1900 Population	**3,108**	**2,798**	**2,473**	**2,060**	**1,624**	**1,327**	**1,106**	**908**	**786**	**656**
1st Generation	301	270	234	186	144	121	108	114	135	145
2nd Generation	956	861	758	630	496	401	325	259	204	149
3rd Generation	869	781	694	583	460	375	312	243	198	159
4th + Generations	991	893	794	666	529	435	365	295	250	203
Immigration since 1900	**19,246**	**11,806**	**7,143**	**4,286**	**2,415**	**1,487**	**1,330**	**725**	**213**	**(X)**
1900–10 Immigrants	606	538	463	382	307	254	240	237	213	
1910–20 Immigrants	1,257	1,091	941	787	615	488	496	491		
1920–30 Immigrants	2,182	1,872	1,600	1,240	895	693	612			
1930–40 Immigrants	312	269	224	173	135	92				
1940–50 Immigrants	1,055	907	773	658	505					
1950–60 Immigrants	1,885	1,594	1,386	1,089						
1960–70 Immigrants	2,433	2,137	1,808							
1970–80 Immigrants	4,013	3,444								
1980–90 Immigrants	5,525									
Percent of Estimated Population										
Total	100.0	100.0	100.0	100.0	100.0	100.0	100.0	100.0	100.0	100.0
Contribution from:										
1900 Population	**13.9**	**19.2**	**25.7**	**32.5**	**40.2**	**47.2**	**45.4**	**55.6**	**78.6**	**100.0**
1st Generation	1.3	1.8	2.4	2.9	3.6	4.3	4.4	7.0	13.5	22.0
2nd Generation	4.3	5.9	7.9	9.9	12.3	14.2	13.4	15.9	20.5	22.7
3rd Generation	3.9	5.4	7.2	9.2	11.4	13.3	12.8	14.9	19.9	24.3
4th + Generations	4.4	6.1	8.3	10.5	13.1	15.5	15.0	18.1	25.0	30.9
Immigration since 1900	**86.1**	**80.8**	**74.3**	**67.5**	**59.8**	**52.8**	**54.6**	**44.4**	**21.4**	**(X)**
1900–10 Immigrants	2.7	3.7	4.8	6.0	7.6	9.0	9.9	14.5	21.4	
1910–20 Immigrants	5.6	7.5	9.8	12.4	15.2	17.3	20.4	30.1		
1920–30 Immigrants	9.8	12.8	16.6	19.5	22.2	24.6	25.1			

Table 2.A.3 CONTRIBUTION OF POST-1900 IMMIGRATION AND 1900 POPULATION FOR THE HISPANIC POPULATION OF THE UNITED STATES: 1900–1990 (continued)

(populations in thousand) (continued)

Contribution from Component	Census Year									
	1990	1980	1970	1960	1950	1940	1930	1920	1910	1900
1930–40 Immigrants	1.4	1.8	2.3	2.7	3.3	3.3				
1940–50 Immigrants	4.7	6.2	8.0	10.4	12.5					
1950–60 Immigrants	8.4	10.9	14.4	17.2						
1960–70 Immigrants	10.9	14.6	18.8							
1970–80 Immigrants	18.0	23.6								
1980–90 Immigrants	24.7									
Growth Since 1990										
Amount	21,698	13,949	8,961	5,691	3,384	2,158	1,780	977	344	(X)
Percent Contribution from:										
1900 Population	**11.3**	**15.4**	**20.3**	**24.7**	**28.6**	**31.1**	**25.3**	**25.8**	**37.9**	**(X)**
1st Generation	0.7	0.9	1.0	0.7	–0.0	–1.1	–2.0	–3.1	–2.9	(X)
2nd Generation	3.7	5.1	6.8	8.5	10.3	11.7	9.9	11.3	16.1	(X)
3rd Generation	3.3	4.5	6.0	7.4	8.9	10.0	8.6	8.6	11.4	(X)
4th + Generations	3.6	5.0	6.6	8.1	9.7	10.8	9.1	9.4	13.7	(X)
Immigration since 1900	**88.7**	**84.6**	**79.7**	**75.3**	**71.4**	**68.9**	**74.7**	**74.2**	**62.1**	**(X)**
1900–10 Immigrants	2.8	3.9	5.2	6.7	9.1	11.8	13.5	24.3	62.1	
1910–20 Immigrants	5.8	7.8	10.5	13.8	18.2	22.6	27.9	50.3		
1920–30 Immigrants	10.1	13.4	17.9	21.8	26.5	32.1	34.4			
1930–40 Immigrants	1.4	1.9	2.5	3.0	4.0	4.3				
1940–50 Immigrants	4.9	6.5	8.6	11.6	14.9					
1950–60 Immigrants	8.7	11.4	15.5	19.1						
1960–70 Immigrants	11.2	15.3	20.2							
1970–80 Immigrants	18.5	24.7								
1980–90 Immigrants	25.5									

Source: Estimates made using POPGEN program fitted to approximate census counts for total population, first generation, and second generation. The contribution of each immigration component is the difference between the complete estimation and a "projection" for 1900–1990 with that immigration component set to zero. For the 1900 populations, the contribution is estimated by setting all other components to zero in a "projection" for 1900–1990. See text for methods and sources.

Note: Estimates include 50 states and the District of Columbia for all years.

(X) Not applicable.

Table 2.A.4 CONTRIBUTION OF POST-1900 IMMIGRATION AND 1900 POPULATION FOR THE BLACK POPULATION OF THE UNITED STATES: 1900–1990 (populations in thousands)

Contribution from Component	Census Year									
	1990	1980	1970	1960	1950	1940	1930	1920	1910	1900
Population Size										
Estimated Population	29,986	26,482	23,005	19,071	15,668	13,767	12,736	11,512	10,255	8,834
Contribution from:										
1900 Population	**27,493**	**24,953**	**22,300**	**18,655**	**15,404**	**13,566**	**12,562**	**11,410**	**10,217**	**8,834**
1st Generation	29	27	24	20	16	15	16	17	20	20
2nd Generation	392	357	318	265	223	207	205	205	217	202
3rd Generation	941	855	763	638	529	474	448	418	394	344
4th + Generations	26,151	23,732	21,210	17,746	14,646	12,879	11,902	10,777	9,591	8,267
Immigration since 1900	**2,493**	**1,530**	**705**	**415**	**264**	**201**	**173**	**102**	**38**	**(X)**
1900–10 Immigrants	125	113	100	82	67	58	52	46	38	
1910–20 Immigrants	196	175	153	126	101	84	75	61		
1920–30 Immigrants	167	149	131	107	83	69	58			
1930–40 Immigrants	22	20	18	14	12	9				
1940–50 Immigrants	68	61	52	42	30					
1950–60 Immigrants	158	137	117	86						
1960–70 Immigrants	266	240	196							
1970–80 Immigrants	834	716								
1980–90 Immigrants	774									
Percent of Estimated Population										
Total	100.0	100.0	100.0	100.0	100.0	100.0	100.0	100.0	100.0	100.0
Contribution from:										
1900 Population	**91.7**	**94.2**	**96.9**	**97.8**	**98.3**	**98.5**	**98.6**	**99.1**	**99.6**	**100.0**
1st Generation	0.1	0.1	0.1	0.1	0.1	0.1	0.1	0.1	0.2	0.2
2nd Generation	1.3	1.3	1.4	1.4	1.4	1.5	1.6	1.8	2.1	2.3
3rd Generation	3.1	3.2	3.3	3.3	3.4	3.4	3.5	3.6	3.8	3.9
4th + Generations	87.2	89.6	92.2	93.1	93.5	93.5	93.5	93.6	93.5	93.6
Immigration since 1900	**8.3**	**5.8**	**3.1**	**2.2**	**1.7**	**1.5**	**1.4**	**0.9**	**0.4**	**(X)**
1900–10 Immigrants	0.4	0.4	0.4	0.4	0.4	0.4	0.4	0.4	0.4	
1910–20 Immigrants	0.7	0.7	0.7	0.7	0.6	0.6	0.6	0.5		
1920–30 Immigrants	0.6	0.6	0.6	0.6	0.5	0.5	0.5			

Table 2.A.4 CONTRIBUTION OF POST-1900 IMMIGRATION AND 1900 POPULATION FOR THE BLACK POPULATION OF THE UNITED STATES: 1900–1990 (continued)
(populations in thousands) (continued)

Contribution from Component	Census Year									
	1990	1980	1970	1960	1950	1940	1930	1920	1910	1900
1930–40 Immigrants	0.1	0.1	0.1	0.1	0.1	0.1				
1940–50 Immigrants	0.2	0.2	0.2	0.2	0.2					
1950–60 Immigrants	0.5	0.5	0.5	0.5						
1960–70 Immigrants	0.9	0.9	0.9							
1970–80 Immigrants	2.8	2.7								
1980–90 Immigrants	2.6									
Growth Since 1900										
Amount	21,152	17,648	14,171	10,236	6,834	4,933	3,901	2,678	1,420	(X)
Percent Contribution from:										
1900 Population	**88.2**	**91.3**	**95.0**	**95.9**	**96.1**	**95.9**	**95.6**	**96.2**	**97.4**	**(X)**
1st Generation	0.0	0.0	0.0	–0.0	–0.1	–0.1	–0.1	–0.1	–0.0	**(X)**
2nd Generation	0.9	0.9	0.8	0.6	0.3	0.1	0.1	0.1	1.0	**(X)**
3rd Generation	2.8	2.9	3.0	2.9	2.7	2.6	2.7	2.7	3.5	**(X)**
4th + Generations	84.6	87.6	91.3	92.6	93.3	93.5	93.2	93.7	93.2	**(X)**
Immigration since 1900	**11.8**	**8.7**	**5.0**	**4.1**	**3.9**	**4.1**	**4.4**	**3.8**	**2.6**	**(X)**
1900–10 Immigrants	0.6	0.6	0.7	0.8	1.0	1.2	1.3	1.7	2.6	
1910–20 Immigrants	0.9	1.0	1.1	1.2	1.5	1.7	1.9	2.3		
1920–30 Immigrants	0.8	0.8	0.9	1.0	1.2	1.4	1.5			
1930–40 Immigrants	0.1	0.1	0.1	0.1	0.2	0.2				
1940–50 Immigrants	0.3	0.3	0.4	0.4	0.4					
1950–60 Immigrants	0.7	0.8	0.8	0.8						
1960–70 Immigrants	1.3	1.4	1.4							
1970–80 Immigrants	3.9	4.1								
1980–90 Immigrants	3.7									

Source: Estimates made using POPGEN program fitted to approximate census counts for total population, first generation, and second generation. The contribution of each immigration component is the difference between the complete estimation and a "projection" for 1900–1990 with that immigration component set to zero. For the 1900 population, the contribution is estimated by setting all other components to zero in a "projection" for 1900–1990. See text for methods and sources.
Note: Estimates include 50 states and the District of Columbia for all years.
(X) Not applicable.

Table 2.A.5 CONTRIBUTION OF POST-1900 IMMIGRATION AND 1900 POPULATION FOR THE WHITE NON-HISPANIC POPULATION OF THE UNITED STATES: 1900–1990
(populations in thousands)

Contribution from Component	Census Year									
	1990	1980	1970	1960	1950	1940	1930	1920	1910	1900
Population Size										
Estimated Population	187,139	180,392	170,371	154,969	134,351	119,425	111,543	96,969	82,049	66,225
Contribution from:										
1900 Population	**141,369**	**137,428**	**132,354**	**121,543**	**107,007**	**97,348**	**91,440**	**82,392**	**73,932**	**66,225**
1st Generation	8,184	8,311	7,846	6,732	6,253	6,290	6,481	7,597	9,146	10,092
2nd Generation	34,118	33,393	32,076	29,251	26,150	23,980	22,375	20,609	18,550	15,497
3rd Generation	36,735	38,285	36,827	33,767	30,417	28,157	26,697	24,945	22,701	19,313
4th + Generations	60,868	58,303	56,413	52,543	44,876	39,529	36,467	29,767	23,913	21,323
Immigration since 1900	**45,769**	**42,964**	**38,017**	**33,426**	**27,344**	**22,077**	**20,103**	**14,578**	**8,116**	**(X)**
1900–10 Immigrants	16,398	15,909	14,734	13,604	12,272	10,598	9,891	9,177	8,116	
1910–20 Immigrants	12,624	11,935	11,295	10,700	9,111	7,773	7,431	6,087		
1920–30 Immigrants	6,661	6,546	6,480	5,991	5,174	4,554	4,027			
1930–40 Immigrants	1,021	1,049	999	942	840	656				
1940–50 Immigrants	2,389	2,338	2,199	1,979	1,572					
1950–60 Immigrants	2,870	2,790	2,621	2,126						
1960–70 Immigrants	1,930	1,917	1,734							
1970–80 Immigrants	2,658	2,536								
1980–90 Immigrants	1,341									
Percent of Estimated Population										
Total	100.0	100.0	100.0	100.0	100.0	100.0	100.0	100.0	100.0	100.0
Contribution from:										
1900 Population	**75.5**	**76.2**	**77.7**	**78.4**	**79.6**	**81.5**	**82.0**	**85.0**	**90.1**	**100.0**
1st Generation	4.4	4.6	4.6	4.3	4.7	5.3	5.8	7.8	11.1	15.2
2nd Generation	18.2	18.5	18.8	18.9	19.5	20.1	20.1	21.3	22.6	23.4
3rd Generation	19.6	21.2	21.6	21.8	22.6	23.6	23.9	25.7	27.7	29.2
4th + Generations	32.5	32.3	33.1	33.9	33.4	33.1	32.7	30.7	29.1	32.2
Immigration since 1900	**24.5**	**23.8**	**22.3**	**21.6**	**20.4**	**18.5**	**18.0**	**15.0**	**9.9**	**(X)**
1900–10 Immigrants	8.8	8.8	8.6	8.8	9.1	8.9	8.9	9.5	9.9	
1910–20 Immigrants	6.7	6.6	6.6	6.9	6.8	6.5	6.7	6.3		
1920–30 Immigrants	3.6	3.6	3.8	3.9	3.9	3.8	3.6			

continued

Table 2.A.5 CONTRIBUTION OF POST-1900 IMMIGRATION AND 1900 POPULATION FOR THE WHITE NON-HISPANIC POPULATION OF THE UNITED STATES: 1900–1990
(populations in thousands) (continued)

Contribution from Component	Census Year									
	1990	1980	1970	1960	1950	1940	1930	1920	1910	1900
1930–40 Immigrants	0.5	0.6	0.6	0.6	0.6	0.5				
1940–50 Immigrants	1.3	1.3	1.3	1.3	1.2					
1950–60 Immigrants	1.5	1.5	1.5	1.4						
1960–70 Immigrants	1.0	1.1	1.0							
1970–80 Immigrants	1.4	1.4								
1980–90 Immigrants	0.7									
Growth Since 1900										
Amount	120,914	114,167	104,146	88,744	68,127	53,201	45,318	30,745	15,824	(X)
Percent Contribution from:										
1900 Population	**62.1**	**62.4**	**63.5**	**62.3**	**59.9**	**58.5**	**55.6**	**52.6**	**48.7**	**(X)**
1st Generation	-1.6	-1.6	-2.2	-3.8	-5.6	-7.1	-8.0	-8.1	-6.0	(X)
2nd Generation	15.4	15.7	15.9	15.5	15.6	15.9	15.2	16.6	19.3	(X)
3rd Generation	14.4	16.6	16.8	16.3	16.3	16.6	16.3	18.3	21.4	(X)
4th + Generations	32.7	32.4	33.7	35.2	34.6	34.2	33.4	27.5	16.4	(X)
Immigration since 1900	**37.9**	**37.6**	**36.5**	**37.7**	**40.1**	**41.5**	**44.4**	**47.4**	**51.3**	**(X)**
1900–10 Immigrants	13.6	13.9	14.1	15.3	18.0	19.9	21.8	29.8	51.3	
1910–20 Immigrants	10.4	10.5	10.8	12.1	13.4	14.6	16.4	19.8		
1920–30 Immigrants	5.5	5.7	6.2	6.8	7.6	8.6	8.9			
1930–40 Immigrants	0.8	0.9	1.0	1.1	1.2	1.2				
1940–50 Immigrants	2.0	2.0	2.1	2.2	2.3					
1950–60 Immigrants	2.4	2.4	2.5	2.4						
1960–70 Immigrants	1.6	1.7	1.7							
1970–80 Immigrants	2.2	2.2								
1980–90 Immigrants	1.1									

Source: Estimates made using POPGEN program fitted to approximate census counts for total population, first generation, and second generation. The contribution of each immigration component is the difference between the complete estimation and a "projection" for 1900–1990 with that immigration component set to zero. For the 1900 populations, the contribution is estimated by setting all other components to zero in a "projection" for 1900–1990. See text for methods and sources.
Note: Estimates include 50 states and the District of Columbia for all years.
(X) Not applicable.

References

Bean, Frank D., Barry Edmonston, and Jeffrey S. Passel. 1990. *Undocumented Migration to the United States: IRCA and the Experience of the 1980s.* Washington, D.C.: The Urban Institute Press.

Edmonston, Barry, and Jeffrey S. Passel. 1992. "Immigration and Immigrant Generations in Population Projections." *International Journal of Forecasting* 8: 459–476.

Fix, Michael and Jeffrey S. Passel. 1991. "The Door Remains Open: Recent Immigration to the United States and a Preliminary Analysis of the Immigration Act of 1990." Program for Research on Immigration Policy, Policy Discussion Paper PRIP-UI-14. Washington, D.C.: The Urban Institute. January.

Gibson, Campbell. 1975. "The Contribution of Immigration to United States Population Growth: 1790–1970." *International Migration Review* 9 (2, Summer): 157–177.

_____. 1991. "The Contribution of Immigration to the Growth and Ethnic Diversity of the American Population." Paper presented at the biannual meeting of the American Philosophical Society. Philadelphia, Pennsylvania, November 7–8.

Passel, Jeffrey S., and Barry Edmonston. 1992. "Methodology for Estimating the Population of the United States by Race and Generation: 1900–1990." Unpublished memorandum. Washington, D.C. The Urban Institute. May.

Passel, Jeffrey S., Frank D. Bean, and Barry Edmonston. 1991. "Undocumented Migration Since IRCA: An Overall Assessment." In *Undocumented Migration to the United States: IRCA and the Experience of the 1980s*, edited by Frank D. Bean, Barry Edmonston, and Jeffrey S. Passel. Washington, D.C.: The Urban Institute Press.

U.S. Bureau of the Census. 1975. *Historical Statistics of the United States: Colonial Times to 1970, Part I.* Washington, D.C.: U.S. Government Printing Office.

U.S. Immigration and Naturalization Service. 1991. *1990 Statistical Yearbook of the Immigration and Naturalization Service.* Washington, D.C.: U.S. Government Printing Office.

Chapter Three

EDUCATIONAL AND SOCIODEMOGRAPHIC INCORPORATION AMONG HISPANIC IMMIGRANTS TO THE UNITED STATES

Frank D. Bean, Jorge Chapa, Ruth R. Berg,
and Kathryn A. Sowards

The volume of immigration to the United States appears likely to increase during the 1990s, just as it did during the 1980s (Bean and Fix 1992). The vast bulk of this immigration will probably originate in Third World countries, continuing a pattern in which the "new" immigrants of the 1980s and 1990s are relatively less skilled (show a greater gap in educational levels between themselves and natives) than the "old" immigrants of the 1950s and 1960s (Borjas 1990; Chiswick 1990). These trends and the prospect of their continuation raise questions about the degree and pattern of immigrant incorporation into American society. Such questions are particularly salient in the case of Hispanic immigrants because of their generally lower education compared with other immigrant groups and their greater concentration in certain parts of the country (Bean and Tienda 1987; Portes and Rumbaut 1990). While the policy concerns about the rapidity with which immigrants move into the mainstream of society often seem preoccupied with economic issues (Borjas 1990; Borjas and Tienda 1987), questions about social incorporation are of policy and theoretical interest, especially when patterns of economic incorporation depend on social structural factors (Nee 1990; Bean and Tienda 1987; Portes and Bach 1985).

A major element in the current policy debate about incorporation patterns among Hispanic immigrants centers on whether these groups, and especially Mexicans, are following the same incorporation processes as earlier European immigrants or slower and more difficult (and perhaps even non-linear) processes owing either to their own characteristics or to the likelihood that they are facing greater discrimination and barriers to socioeconomic advancement than earlier arrivals. Readings of the available evidence have led some observers to conclude the former, and others, the latter. Linda Chavez (1989, 66–67), for example, argues that "Hispanics are making precisely the kind of progress one would expect from a group so heavily dominated by non–English-speaking immigrants—slow but steady movement into the middle class by successive generations born in the United States." McCarthy and Valdez (1985, 77) reach a similar conclusion: "Mexican immigrants are following the historical pattern of integration into U.S. society, a pattern that is tied to occupational mobility across generations. Intergenerational advances in education play a critical role in that process." Valdivieso and Davis (1988, 5–6), however, argue: "Hispanics have faced discrimination in schools and housing, and in obtaining jobs and promotions. . . Many earlier immigrant groups suffered from similar injustices. However, in part because substantial immigration from Latin America is still occurring, Hispanics continue to experience ethnic discrimination." And Chapa (1991, 13) notes: "The historical experience of most Hispanics contradicts the claim that they are achieving parity in measures of social or economic attainment."

Resolving this debate requires information that sheds light on the social incorporation experiences of Hispanic immigrant groups. Recent data on dimensions of social incorporation, however, are relatively limited. Because many immigrant groups are small and because information on nativity is not ordinarily collected in Current Population Surveys (CPSs), descriptive information about even basic social and demographic characteristics of immigrants is readily available only from decennial census data or from the somewhat sketchy information collected by the Immigration and Naturalization Service on new entrants at the time of their arrival. Data from the 1990 Census, which will allow assessments of immigrant social and demographic characteristics to be updated for many of the new immigrant groups, are not yet available (as of the date of this writing: summer, 1992). Moreover, studies of immigrant incorporation based on 1980 or 1990 Census data, because questions on the nativity of parents were deleted after the 1970 Census, can only focus on short-run incorporation patterns. Thus, studies using 1980 and 1990 Census data can only compare immigrants with natives and examine how immigrants themselves fare the longer they have been in the country.

Studies of the social and demographic characteristics of second- and third- or higher generation Hispanics in comparison with those of natives, which are what would be desirable for inferences to be drawn about the longer-term incorporation patterns of immigrant groups, have generally not been possible since 1970 because the data have not been available (for an exception see the study by Neidert and Farley [1985]). Information allowing such comparisons, however, is now available from two recent CPSs. The purposes of this chapter are thus threefold. First, we seek to present the most recently available descriptive data on the social and demographic characteristics of Hispanic immigrants viewed in comparison with other immigrant groups. Second, we seek to ascertain to what degree Hispanic immigrants who have been in the United States the longest show evidence of greater or lesser incorporation compared with more recent arrivals. Third, we seek to ascertain to what extent third-or-later generation Mexican Americans show evidence of greater or lesser social and demographic incorporation compared with second-generation Mexican Americans as well as the extent to which the latter show evidence of greater or lesser incorporation compared with Mexican immigrants (the first generation).

THEORETICAL BACKGROUND

The policy debate about the degree of social and demographic incorporation of immigrant groups often centers on the issue of how rapidly such groups enter the mainstream of American life. The theoretical paradigm that thus constitutes the point of departure for examining this issue is that of *assimilation*, as represented in the classic work of Thomas and Znaniecki (1927), Park (1950), Handlin (1951), and Child (1943) and in more contemporary writers such as Gordon (1964), Sowell (1981), and Chavez (1989). This perspective sees immigrants as gradually absorbing the cultural values and norms of the majority group, a process sometimes called cultural assimilation. In the most well-developed treatment of the subject, Gordon (1964) postulates several assimilation stages. After cultural assimilation will come structural (educational and occupational), marital, and identificational assimilation. Within the structural category, others draw a useful distinction between secondary and primary structural assimilation. The former refers to "sharing . . . by subordinate group and dominant group members of occupational, educational, political, neighborhood, and public recreational settings" (McLemore 1990, 53). The latter refers to close, personal interactions between dominant and subordinate group members.

The different stages of assimilation may occur at different rates among different groups. Cultural assimilation is viewed not only as a precursor for other kinds of assimilation but as irreversible. While the overall process may proceed through the stage of secondary structural assimilation without going further, once the process reaches primary structural assimilation, it is likely to proceed to completion. In general, immigrant/ethnic and majority groups are seen as becoming more similar in terms of norms, values, behaviors, and characteristics. While considerable debate has arisen over the question of whether this similarity involves the subordinate group becoming more like the dominant group (an "Anglo conformity" model) or the two groups becoming more like each other (a "melting pot" model), in either case, a convergence of behavior and characteristics over time would be predicted.

In the assimilationist paradigm, the social and demographic characteristics of Hispanic immigrants and their descendants and of non-Hispanic whites would be expected to converge over time. Those groups in the Spanish-origin population that have been in the United States the longest (the later generational groups) would show the smallest differences in behavior compared with the majority group. Because this perspective assumes convergence of norms and values as well as access to schooling and jobs between immigrant/ethnic and the majority groups the longer the minority group has been in the country, any differences between the two groups remaining by the third-or-later generation would be assumed to owe to incomplete assimilation. Incomplete assimilation, for example, could result in differences between groups in educational attainment. If structural assimilation were complete, however, the assimilationist perspective would expect secondary behavioral differences between immigrant/ethnic and majority groups to have disappeared by some point and certainly to decline with rising generational status.

The assimilationist model, however, has often been found insufficient to explain fully the incorporation patterns of immigrant groups. Another major (and more recent) stream of thought emphasizes what we would term discrimination and lack of opportunities as explanatory factors. This perspective, reflected in the writings of Greeley (1971), Suttles (1968), Glazer and Moynihan (1970), and Portes and Bach (1985), emphasizes that increasing knowledge of the language of the new country and familiarity with its culture and customs do not necessarily lead to increasing assimilation with respect to behavior. Any lingering discrimination and continuing lack of equal access to socioeconomic opportunities constitute barriers to complete assimilation. Because socioeconomic opportunities for the first generation are evaluated relative to those in the country of origin, it is not until the second and third generations that the realization emerges that the goal of full assimilation may be difficult. Such realities and the evaluation of them have social and cultural consequences, including the reemergence of ethnic consciousness. As Portes and Bach (1985, 25) note: "The rejection experienced by immigrants and their descendants in their attempts to become fully assimilated constitutes a central element in the reconstitution of ethnic culture."

This perspective would expect the immigrant generation to exhibit different characteristics than natives, even after adjusting for other differences between immigrants and natives. With the second generation, language patterns and reference groups are in the process of shifting. Whereas most first-generation Mexican-origin women, for example, have been found to use only Spanish at home (84 percent) (Portes and Rumbaut 1990), by the third generation, the shift to English has been observed to be nearly complete, with 84 percent using only English at home and 12 percent using both English and Spanish (Lopez 1978). These patterns are consistent with the notion that the immigrant generation retains the country of origin as a primary reference group, whereas the third generation makes the transition to the country of destination as the reference group.

Part of the cultural conflict experienced by the second generation derives from the fact that it is socialized by the first generation, the group whose socioeconomic experience in the United States is evaluated most positively. The result is strong efforts by the first generation to inculcate achievement aspirations in the second generation. Reinforcing the second generation's motivation to achieve is its desire to overcome the marginality involved in being caught between the old and the new (Child 1943). The second generation also begins to become more cognizant of the barriers that block access to complete assimilation, as it shifts its reference group to the United States instead of the old country. The experience of discrimination, together with a growing awareness of its relative socioeconomic standing compared to natives, undermines the second generation's motivation to transmit achievement aspirations to its children. Consistent with this view, Neidert and Farley (1985) report a drop in average socioeconomic index scores for third-generation groups. Similarly, levels of educational attainment in the third generation would be expected to fall below those of the second generation.

The discrimination perspective implies that the real and perceived barriers to socioeconomic attainment operate to discourage socioeconomic achievement, to reinforce the distinctiveness of the ethnic group, and to reaffirm and revitalize ethnic patterns and customs. The perspective would predict divergence in the characteristics of the third generation compared with natives. Across generations, then, the perspective would predict a curvilinear relationship between the magnitude of differences by generational status between Hispanic-origin and non-Hispanic white native-born persons, with the first and third generation showing greater differences than the second generation.

DATA AND METHODS

The data for this study were obtained by pooling the individual records from the June 1986 and June 1988 CPSs. The sample universe for each survey included approximately 71,000 households, and in both years, actual interviews were conducted with about 57,000 households. For the two survey years examined, an immigration supplement obtained information on year of immigration, citizenship, and country of birth of both individuals and their parents. The June supplement to the CPS also includes several questions on fertility and birth expectations of females within relevant age ranges. Our sample includes all persons who identified themselves as Hispanic (as indicated by a response to the Hispanic ethnicity question), all persons born abroad, and a quarter sample of non-Hispanic white natives aged 18 to 64. The resulting sample consists of 41,681 persons (5,117 Mexican-origin, 562 Cuban-origin, 1,216 Central/South American-origin, 340 Other Hispanic-origin, 2,624 Asian-origin, 1,143 Canadian/European-origin, 1,070 Other Foreign-born, and 32,609 non-Hispanic white natives). The analyses of the data are based on the weighted cases in order to reflect the actual age, sex, racial/ethnic, and regional composition of persons in the United States.

We define those persons who identified themselves as "Mexican American," "Chicano," or "Mexican(o)" as Mexican-origin and those who classified themselves as "Cuban," "Central/South American," or "Other Hispanic" as Cuban-origin, Central/South American-origin, or Other Hispanic-origin, respectively. We classify non-Hispanic white natives as those who reported themselves as white, of an ethnic origin other than Spanish, and as born in the United States. Since the CPS limits the ethnicity question to Hispanics, we estimate the ethnicity of non-Hispanic groups according to the respondent's reported country of birth, a procedure which limits the specification of ethnic origin for non-Hispanics to first-generation immigrants. Thus, Asian-origin persons are those born in Asian countries (China, India, Iran, Japan, Korea, Laos, Philippines, and Vietnam), Canadian-origin persons are those born in Canada, European-origin persons are those born in Europe (Germany, Greece, Ireland, Italy, Poland, Portugal, United Kingdom, the former U.S.S.R., and the former Yugoslavia); and Other Foreign-born persons are others who reported themselves as foreign-born. First-generation Hispanics were those who are not citizens at the time of the survey or who were naturalized citizens or who reported that both they and their parents were born in a Spanish-speaking country.

In the case of Hispanics only, ethnic groups can be further classified into second- and third-or-later generational groups. The second generation consists of Hispanic-origin persons who were born in the United States or abroad to an American parent and who reported that at least one parent was born in a Spanish-speaking country. The third generation includes men and women who were born in the United States or abroad to American parents and who reported that both parents were born in the United States. Definitions of all the variables are listed in appendix 3.A.

Our empirical investigation involves (1) comparisons of the groups of Hispanic immigrants to other immigrant groups and to non-Hispanic whites in terms of several social and demographic characteristics, (2) comparisons of period-of-entry cohorts within and among the Hispanic immigrant groups, and (3) comparisons of generational differences on selected social and demographic characteristics for the Mexican-origin population, the only group from a single country with a large enough number of cases in the second and third generations for analysis. In interpreting the results of the analyses, it is important to emphasize that the two theoretical perspectives—the assimilationist model and the discrimination model—are not mutually exclusive. The kinds of forces alluded to in both could be operating simultaneously. Given the pattern involved in each of the predictions, however, if the hypothesized forces were operating to generate both patterns, this should be evident in the data, assuming no other factors were operating to affect the patterns.

FINDINGS

Immigrant Group Differences

The first research question we examine concerns the pattern of differences in social and demographic characteristics among different immigrant groups, including Hispanic immigrant groups. The means presented in tables 3.1 and 3.2 reveal patterns of differences between Hispanic immigrant groups and other immigrant groups similar to those noted in previous research. It is overly simplistic, however, to speak of "Hispanic immigrants" as a homogeneous category. The groups often differ as much from each other as they do from other immigrant groups or from non-Hispanic white natives (Bean and Tienda 1987). The differences in regional concentration offer the sharpest example of this: Mexican immigrants concentrate in the census region West; Cubans, in the South; and Other Hispanics, in the Northeast. Stated differently, many Mexican immigrants live in California; many Cuban immigrants, in Miami; and many Dominicans, in New York City. Only Central/South Americans show considerable regional dispersion, and even they are similar to the remaining groups in not residing in the North Central region, a tendency that distinguishes Hispanic from non-Hispanic immigrants.

Interestingly, hardly any variation exists among any of the immigrant groups, whether Hispanic or non-Hispanic, in their tendencies to reside in metropolitan locations, suggesting that the groups find similar degrees of labor market advantage in such locales. This contrast with the findings observed for regional concentration suggests a structure of regional labor market opportunities that is substantially influenced by ethnic origins. That the concentrations for three of the four Hispanic groups are so much greater than they are for Asians or Canadian/European groups suggests a distinctive pattern of incorporation for these groups compared with other immigrants (Portes and Rumbaut 1990). This apparent greater reliance by Hispanic immigrants on enclave employment and network connections that facilitate migration and labor market incorporation (Portes and Bach 1985; Massey et al. 1987) remains a subject for further comparative study, as does the question of whether this concentration impedes, facilitates, or reflects economic and social incorporation.

The various groups do not show evidence of substantial variations in marriage patterns among males. Mexican and Asian male immigrants report a somewhat lower prevalence of divorce, separation, and widowhood than do the other groups, but all of the major groups are characterized by rather similar proportions currently married. In the case of females, however, the Hispanic immigrant groups are less likely to be currently married than Asian or Canadian/European immigrants. Central/South American women in particular show a very low proportion currently married and a high proportion never married, a result that may be connected to their recent immigration

Table 3.1 MEAN VALUES ON SOCIAL AND DEMOGRAPHIC CHARACTERISTICS FOR IMMIGRANT AND NON-HISPANIC WHITE NATIVES, MALES AGED 18–64

	EDU	AGE	NC	NE	S	W	MET	MAR	DSW	NVM	NAT	N
Mexican	7.4	33.2	.077	.016	.257	.650	.910	.684	.047	.027	.256	1021
Cuban	11.2	41.9	.038	.193	.710	.059	.995	.700	.100	.200	.488	281
Central/South American	11.2	35.2	.045	.343	.267	.345	.978	.649	.065	.286	.293	474
Other Hispanic	12.1	39.5	.082	.532	.182	.204	.957	.702	.072	.226	.397	142
Asian	13.7	36.6	.150	.203	.180	.467	.951	.686	.022	.292	.434	1194
Canadian/European	12.9	43.0	.133	.469	.143	.255	.952	.697	.125	.178	.559	737
Other Foreign-born	12.9	35.5	.128	.443	.219	.211	.951	.572	.062	.366	.350	293
Non-Hispanic White Natives	13.1	38.6	.274	.219	.320	.186	.753	.649	.097	.254	1.000	15,855

Source: 1986 and 1988 June CPS.
Key: EDU = education; AGE = age; NC = North Central; NE = North East; S = South; W = West; MET = metropolitan residence; MAR = currently married; DSW = divorced, separated, or widowed; NVM = never married; NAT = naturalized citizen.

Table 3.2 MEAN VALUES ON SOCIAL AND DEMOGRAPHIC CHARACTERISTICS FOR IMMIGRANT GROUPS AND NON-HISPANIC WHITE NATIVES, FEMALES AGED 18–64

	EDU	AGE	NC	NE	S	W	MET	MAR	DSW	NVM	NAT	N
Mexican	7.5	34.9	.074	.013	.249	.665	.931	.672	.143	.185	.239	883
Cuban	11.3	42.6	.036	.186	.718	.059	.994	.689	.164	.147	.516	281
Central/ South American	11.0	37.1	.050	.367	.258	.325	.977	.556	.204	.240	.267	609
Other Hispanic	10.6	38.4	.084	.541	.198	.178	.981	.591	.166	.243	.354	198
Asian	12.8	37.4	.124	.162	.200	.514	.944	.723	.096	.180	.452	1,430
Canadian/ European Other	12.3	44.1	.178	.388	.193	.241	.895	.731	.177	.092	.576	406
Foreign-born	11.9	36.8	.112	.472	.222	.194	.969	.548	.187	.264	.390	777
Non-Hispanic White Natives	12.9	38.8	.278	.221	.322	.179	.754	.648	.160	.192	1.000	16,754

Source: 1986 and 1988 June CPS.
Key: EDU = education; AGE = age; NC = North Central; NE = North East; S = South; W = West; MET = metropolitan residence; MAR = currently married; DSW = divorced, separated, or widowed; NVM = never married; NAT = naturalized citizen.

and to their disproportionate reliance on domestic employment in the United States.

The most interesting differences between the Hispanic immigrant groups and other immigrant groups are in the prevalence of naturalization and education. With the exception of Cuban immigrants, who report quite high levels of naturalization for both males and females, the other Hispanic immigrant groups indicate lower levels of naturalization, and Mexican immigrants report the lowest levels of all. With the exception of the Cubans, who have enjoyed the special benefit of accelerated naturalization procedures (Pedraza-Bailey 1985), the Hispanic immigrant groups also differ in whether males or females show the highest levels of naturalization. In the case of the Hispanic groups, males show higher levels of naturalization, whereas in the case of Asian, Canadian/European, and Cuban immigrants, females are more likely to be naturalized. Age differences do not explain this pattern because in two of the three Hispanic groups, male immigrants are younger, on average, than female immigrants.

Several factors examined thus far suggest the existence of a distinctive pattern of immigration and incorporation in the case of several of the Hispanic immigrant groups, at least when compared with Asian and Canadian/European immigrants. This contention is reinforced when we examine education, on which the sharpest differences between the Hispanic and other immigrant groups emerge. All the Hispanic groups are characterized by fewer years of school completed than the other immigrant groups or non-Hispanic white natives. In most cases, the differences average about one to one-and-a-half fewer years of schooling, irrespective of whether males or females are examined. In the case of Mexican immigrants, the differences are much larger, averaging about five fewer years of schooling compared to non-Hispanic immigrants or natives.

Period of Entry Differences

When we look at educational differences by period of entry for Mexicans and Central/South Americans, the two groups large enough to allow a breakdown, we see that the recent entrants have even lower levels of schooling than the earlier immigrants (tables 3.3 and 3.4). For Mexicans, the difference is as much as two fewer years of schooling completed on average. These differences are all the more significant because schooling generally increases for later birth cohorts (younger persons). Because the recent entry groups predominantly consist of persons in later birth cohorts (i.e., of younger persons), the differences

Table 3.3 MEAN VALUES ON SELECTED SOCIAL AND DEMOGRAPHIC CHARACTERISTICS FOR MEXICAN AND CENTRAL/SOUTH AMERICAN IMMIGRANTS BY PERIOD OF ENTRY, MALES AGED 25–64

Mexican

	EDU	AGE	EAE	NC	NE	S	W	MET	NAT	N
Pre 1960	7.2	50.4	NA	.141	.000	.336	.523	.901	.518	73
1960–64	8.3	43.6	19.1	.129	.032	.197	.642	.981	.600	55
1965–69	7.9	39.4	19.9	.077	.000	.258	.664	.910	.357	70
1970–74	7.1	37.9	23.4	.101	.100	.189	.699	.926	.210	152
1975–79	6.9	34.2	24.3	.092	.026	.308	.574	.888	.256	195
1980–84	6.8	31.2	26.6	.051	.007	.304	.638	.948	.164	127
1985–86	5.5	32.8	31.3	.035	.057	.311	.597	.969	.000	23
1987–88	5.7	33.8	33.3	.000	.000	.154	.846	.475	.000	25

Central/South American

	EDU	AGE	EAE	NC	NE	S	W	MET	NAT	N
Pre 1960	14.1	47.1	NA	.000	.334	.223	.444	.960	.857	17
1960–64	13.0	42.3	17.8	.127	.368	.190	.315	.100	.601	26
1965–69	12.6	42.5	23.1	.042	.540	.121	.297	.984	.553	47
1970–74	11.3	40.1	25.6	.070	.539	.136	.255	.100	.502	61
1975–79	11.5	35.8	26.3	.024	.266	.257	.452	.960	.227	72
1980–84	10.1	34.6	30.1	.041	.228	.354	.376	.980	.061	108
1985–86	10.3	35.2	30.7	.000	.311	.556	.133	.977	.000	29
1987–88	11.1	35.7	35.2	.000	.351	.550	.098	.100	.000	7

Source: 1986 and 1988 June CPS.
Key: EDU = education; AGE = age; NC = North Central; NE = North East; S = South; W = West; MET = metropolitan residence; MAR = currently married; DSW = divorced, separated, or widowed; NVM = never married; NAT = naturalized citizen. Also, EAE = estimated average age at entry.

Table 3.4 MEAN VALUES ON SELECTED SOCIAL AND DEMOGRAPHIC CHARACTERISTICS FOR MEXICAN AND CENTRAL/SOUTH AMERICAN IMMIGRANTS BY PERIOD OF ENTRY, FEMALES AGED 25–64

	EDU	AGE	EAE	NC	NE	S	W	MET	NAT	N
					Mexican					
Pre 1960	7.7	50.4	NA	.105	.009	.410	.476	.923	.582	81
1960–64	8.5	42.6	18.1	.138	.022	.131	.709	.928	.464	59
1965–69	7.6	41.7	22.2	.091	.009	.205	.695	.940	.374	84
1970–74	8.1	38.1	23.6	.085	.009	.229	.677	.935	.193	136
1975–79	6.4	34.8	25.3	.066	.020	.257	.656	.925	.120	175
1980–84	6.4	33.8	29.3	.039	.017	.234	.710	.960	.159	103
1985–86	6.8	35.4	33.9	.000	.019	.430	.551	.971	.041	29
1987–88	6.4	34.6	34.1	.000	.000	.465	.535	.591	.115	10
	EDU	AGE	EAE	NC	NE	S	W	MET	NAT	N
					Central/South American					
Pre 1960	13.1	49.3	NA	.067	.340	.300	.293	.892	.657	26
1960–64	12.6	45.0	20.5	.106	.526	.160	.206	.100	.509	41
1965–69	10.8	44.4	24.9	.061	.463	.243	.233	.984	.475	75
1970–74	10.9	39.8	25.3	.103	.483	.120	.293	.966	.465	78
1975–79	11.0	36.0	26.5	.045	.390	.193	.382	.994	.181	100
1980–84	9.7	35.5	31.0	.021	.194	.327	.458	.982	.066	133
1985–86	10.9	37.3	35.8	.000	.507	.414	.079	.100	.018	25
1987–88	8.0	39.7	39.2	.000	.344	.463	.193	.100	.000	14

Source: 1986 and 1988 June CPS.
Key: EDU = education; AGE = age; NC = North Central; NE = North East; S = South; W = West; MET = metropolitan residence; MAR = currently married; DSW = divorced, separated, or widowed; NVM = never married; NAT = naturalized citizen. Also, EAE = estimated average age at entry.

Table 3.5 AGE STANDARDIZED MEANS ON EDUCATION AND
NATURALIZATION FOR MEXICAN AND CENTRAL/SOUTH
AMERICAN IMMIGRANTS BY PERIOD OF ENTRY, AGED 25–64

	Mexican			
	Males		Females	
	Education	Naturalization	Education	Naturalization
Pre 1960	9.0	.514	9.3	.587
1960–64	9.2	.606	9.1	.462
1965–69	8.2	.370	8.1	.372
1970–74	7.2	.226	8.0	.187
1975–79	6.5	.278	6.0	.111
1980–84	6.0	.190	5.8	.149
1985–86	4.9	0	6.4	0
1987–88	5.3	0	5.8	0

	Central and South American			
	Males		Females	
	Education	Naturalization	Education	Naturalization
Pre 1960	14.5	.866	13.9	.648
1960–64	13.2	.605	13.0	.498
1965–69	12.8	.558	11.2	.463
1970–74	11.4	.504	11.0	.451
1975–79	11.4	.224	10.8	.163
1980–84	10.0	.058	9.3	.048
1985–86	10.2	0	10.8	0
1987–88	11.1	0	8.0	0

Source: 1986 and 1988 June CPS.
Key: EDU = education; AGE = age; NC = North Central; NE = North East; S =
South; W = West; MET = metropolitan residence; MAR = currently married; DSW
= divorced, separated, or widowed; NVM = never married; NAT = naturalized
citizen.

in education between the recent and earlier entry cohorts shown in
tables 3.3 and 3.4 are actually understated. A clearer picture of the
true differences can be seen from the age-standardized values in table
3.5, which, in the case of Mexicans, reveal declines of nearly four
years of schooling from the earlier to the more recent entry groups.
These findings lend support to the contention that at least some
immigrant groups are less skilled than either other immigrant groups
or earlier entrants for the same group (Borjas 1990).

This conclusion holds even when we restrict the analyses shown
in tables 3.3, 3.4, and 3.5 only to persons who immigrated after age
18 (results not shown here), a restriction that can be applied to the

1960–64, 1965–69, 1970–74, and 1975–79 entry cohorts. Anywhere from about 25 to 45 percent of these cohorts came to the United States as children. While their average educational level is higher than that of those coming as adults, this alone is not sufficient to account for the lower levels of education observed in the more recent entry groups.

The data in tables 3.3 and 3.4 for regional and metropolitan location shed some light on the question of whether differences between Mexican and Central/South American immigrants and non-Hispanic white natives become less pronounced the longer the immigrant group has been in the country. In the case of Mexicans, some indication of less regional concentration is evident for the earlier cohorts. With cross-sectional data, we cannot tell whether this reflects a different settlement pattern on their part or dispersion over time. In whatever event, the recent arrivals are more concentrated than the earlier arrivals. Given the lower education of the recent arrivals, this increasing concentration may lead to greater competition for access to jobs and social services among more recent entrants than the competition experienced by earlier entrants. A similar pattern of decreasing regional concentration the longer the time spent in the United States is not evident in the case of Central/South Americans, perhaps because groups from different countries have predominated in the migration flows at different points in time. No pattern of increasing metropolitan concentration is evident for either group.

Another way of examining these data in the case of Mexicans is in terms of what have been called immigrant status groups (Bean, Browning, and Frisbie 1984; Bean and Tienda 1987). Based on Warren and Passel's (1987) inference from analyses of 1980 Census data that about two-thirds of post-1975 Mexican immigrants were undocumented, whereas only about one-third of pre-1975 non-citizen immigrants were illegal, immigrant status groups can be delineated consisting of post-1975 non-citizens, pre-1975 non-citizens, and naturalized citizens. The advantage of this grouping is that it may be interpreted as roughly reflecting degree of attachment to the United States, ranging from the least attachment in the case of the post-1975 group, which probably contains the largest fraction of undocumented immigrants, to the greatest attachment in the case of naturalized citizens. When the data are examined in terms of this classification (table 3.6), we see a strong correspondence, especially between attachment and education. The post-1975 groups have the least education. Together with the findings discussed above, these results

Table 3.6 MEAN VALUES ON SELECTED SOCIAL AND DEMOGRAPHIC CHARACTERISTICS FOR MEXICAN IMMIGRANT STATUS GROUPS, MALES AND FEMALES, AGED 25–64

Generation	EDU	AGE	NC	NE	S	W	MET	NAT	N
					Males				
Post 1975	6.7	32.4	.063	.024	.280	.633	.879	.000	295
Pre 1975	7.1	40.7	.101	.012	.200	.687	.921	.000	222
Naturalized Citizen	7.5	39.8	.106	.004	.309	.582	.944	.100	221
NA	6.7	39.4	.042	.006	.121	.831	.980	.000	33
	EDU	AGE	NC	NE	S	W	MET	NAT	N
					Females				
Post 1975	6.7	34.5	.045	.019	.247	.689	.933	.000	270
Pre 1975	7.5	41.5	.089	.009	.207	.695	.931	.000	223
Naturalized Citizen	8.0	40.9	.102	.015	.339	.544	.936	.100	193
NA	7.7	36.4	.116	.006	.299	.579	.994	.000	33

Source: 1986 and 1988 June CPS

Key: EDU = education; AGE = age; NC = North Central; NE = North East; S = South; W = West; MET = metropolitan residence; MAR = currently married; DSW = divorced, separated, or widowed; NVM = never married; NAT = naturalized citizen. NA = missing data.

support the claim of many observers that including recent immigrants in statistical comparisons between Mexican Americans and natives tends to exaggerate the differences between the groups (Chavez 1989).

Generational Differences

If the education levels of more recent immigrants are declining, this raises concerns about the facility with which immigrants will advance socioeconomically in the future (Borjas 1990). However, the experience of the immigrant generation may hold few implications for the facility with which the children and grandchildren of the immigrants will advance socioeconomically. As Chavez (1989) and others have argued, native-born Mexican Americans may make rapid strides socioeconomically, even if the prospects for the immigrant generation itself might be deteriorating. The key test of whether the native-born groups are assimilating thus inheres in comparisons between the second and third-or-later generation and non-Hispanic white natives. These results are presented in table 3.7, where we find that education steadily increases with generation. Although the third generation on average has not achieved the educational level of non-Hispanic white natives, it surpasses the achievement of the second generation for both males and females.

This result is seemingly consistent with the predictions of assimilationist theory and with the claims by observers like Chavez (1989) that Mexican Americans are undergoing structural assimilation. Certainly these aggregate education statistics, as well as the nearly universal acquisition of English by the third generation, as noted above, lend support to this view. But the aggregate statistics by generation may mask important variations by birth cohort. Given that very little growth has occurred in real wages over the past 20 years (Levy 1987), that immigration has been increasing, and that the size of the Hispanic population has grown tremendously since 1970 (Bean and Tienda 1987, Valdivieso and Davis 1988), discriminatory reactions against Hispanics could easily have increased over this same period. More recent birth cohorts may not have had the same kind of experiences as earlier cohorts.

To investigate this possibility, we examined education by generation patterns separately for different birth cohorts for both males and females. The results are shown in table 3.8. As can be seen, the earlier cohorts are more likely to be characterized by the curvilinear pattern predicted by the discrimination perspective. That is, the years of schooling completed by the third generation falls below that of the

Table 3.7 MEAN VALUES OF SELECTED SOCIAL AND DEMOGRAPHIC CHARACTERISTICS FOR MEXICAN AMERICANS BY GENERATION, MALES AND FEMALES AGED 25–65

Generation	EDU	AGE	NC	NE	Males S	W	MET	NAT
First	7.0	37.2	.085	.014	.258	.643	.914	.279
Second	11.1	41.9	.087	.009	.375	.529	.935	NA
Third	11.5	37.3	.072	.010	.432	.486	.866	NA
NHW Natives	13.1	41.6	.269	.220	.319	.191	.756	NA

Generation	EDU	AGE	NC	NE	Females S	W	MET	NAT
First	7.3	38.4	.076	.014	.260	.650	.935	.251
Second	10.4	43.3	.088	.004	.377	.531	.892	NA
Third	11.1	36.9	.083	.010	.417	.489	.860	NA
NHW Natives	12.9	41.9	.278	.220	.324	.178	.751	NA

Source: 1986 and 1988 June CPS
Key: EDU = education; AGE = age; NC = North Central; NE = North East; S = South; W = West; MET = metropolitan residence; MAR = currently married; DSW = divorced, separated, or widowed; NVM = never married; NAT = naturalized citizen. NHW = Non-Hispanic white.

Table 3.8 MEAN EDUCATION BY BIRTH COHORT AND GENERATION FOR THE
MEXICAN-ORIGIN POPULATION

	Means							
	Males				Females			
Generation	25–29	30–34	35–44	45–64	25–29	30–34	35–44	45–64
First	8.3	6.9	6.6	6.1	8.3	7.8	7.4	6.1
Second	12.3	12.1	11.8	9.6	11.9	12.2	11.6	8.8
Third	12.2	11.9	12.1	9.5	11.7	12.1	11.0	9.5
NHW Natives	13.2	13.5	13.7	12.6	13.2	13.3	13.3	12.3
	Sample Sizes							
	Males				Females			
Generation	25–29	30–34	35–44	45–64	25–29	30–34	35–44	45–64
First	209	164	207	191	159	146	198	216
Second	84	65	111	177	75	70	114	232
Third	172	136	195	178	217	179	224	185
NHW Natives	2,139	2,236	3,696	5,051	2,294	2,285	3,782	5,332

Source: 1986 and 1988 June CPS
NHW = Non-Hispanic white.

second generation. Interestingly, from both a substantive and methodological point of view, this pattern is completely masked unless the data are disaggregated, illustrating the important effects composition can have on aggregate measures of social and economic characteristics.

The lower levels of educational attainment for third-or-later generation Mexican-origin males and females in comparison to the second generation in more recent birth cohorts suggest that something more than assimilationist notions are required to explain the contemporary experience of Mexican Americans with respect to educational attainment. The kinds of forces emphasized by the structural ethnicity approach also need to be considered. Supporting this view are recent data showing that Hispanic perceptions of discrimination increase from the first to higher generations (de la Garza 1991). As reference groups shift across the generations (Alvarez 1984) and as immigrants and their offspring become more aware of the obstacles they face in further socioeconomic advancement, the second generation may not put as much emphasis on the further educational attainment of their children as their parents put on their own education. Whether this or something else is the causal mechanism involved, that the educational gap between third-generation Mexicans and non-Hispanic

Table 3.9 PROPORTION OF MEXICAN-ORIGIN PERSONS WHO COMPLETED
LESS THAN 12 YEARS, 12 YEARS, AND MORE THAN 12 YEARS OF
EDUCATION BY BIRTH COHORT AND GENERATION FOR SELECTED
HISPANIC GROUPS

| | Less than 12 Years | | | | | | | |
| | Males | | | | Females | | | |
Generation	25–29	30–34	35–44	45–64	25–29	30–34	35–44	45–64
First	.687	.816	.816	.865	.697	.694	.762	.842
Second	.223	.252	.261	.552	.279	.268	.321	.604
Third or Later	.221	.282	.251	.593	.294	.242	.437	.604
NHW Natives	.106	.087	.096	.236	.098	.087	.096	.207

| | 12 Years | | | | | | | |
| | Males | | | | Females | | | |
Generation	25–29	30–34	35–44	45–64	25–29	30–34	35–44	45–64
First	.215	.114	.124	.087	.198	.217	.181	.120
Second	.449	.383	.399	.241	.394	.295	.357	.289
Third or Later	.516	.445	.339	.229	.486	.421	.375	.281
NHW Natives	.434	.400	340	.375	.436	.439	.441	.497

| | More than 12 Years | | | | | | | |
| | Males | | | | Females | | | |
Generation	25–29	30–34	35–44	45–64	25–29	30–34	35–44	45–64
First	.097	.069	.060	.047	.106	.089	.058	.038
Second	.328	.365	.340	.207	.326	.436	.322	.106
Third or Later	.263	.272	.410	.178	.220	.337	.188	.115
NHW Natives	.459	.512	.564	.388	.466	.474	.463	.296

Source: 1986 and 1988 June CPS
NHW = Non-Hispanic white.

white natives is not narrowing provides discouraging news concerning the prospects for future assimilation.

This picture receives further support from the data presented in
table 3.9, which shows the proportions of the generational groups
and of non-Hispanic white natives that have completed less than 12,
12, and more than 12 years of schooling. The proportions of second-
and third-generation Mexican American males who have completed
less than 12 years of schooling are similar to one another, and both
are much higher than those for non-Hispanic white natives. The
levels of the second-generation cohorts who had completed more
than 12 years of schooling (i.e., some college) are similar for the three
youngest cohorts born since World War II. In contrast, the levels for
the same cohorts of third-or-later generation Mexican Americans

drop sharply between the 35- to 44-year-olds and the two younger cohorts. The 35 to 44 cohort turned 18 during the 1960s—an era of expanding higher education opportunities for minorities and an era of Vietnam draft deferments. In general, though, the third generation shows lower proportions attending college than the second generation.

Does this stem from increasing difficulties in meeting the high financial cost of college attendance? Or does it result from second-generation parents becoming disappointed with their own progress and thus not encouraging achievement aspirations as strongly in their own children? While the lower college attendance levels of the younger cohorts may reflect decreased opportunities and incentives for college attendance, these factors do not explain the differences between the second and third generations. That the second generation, for which little reason exists to think it enjoys any economic advantage over the third, shows higher rates of college attendance than the third-or-later generation suggests the pattern is not entirely due to economic forces but rather may reflect other factors.

DISCUSSION AND CONCLUSIONS

The data on Mexican immigration from 1960 to 1988 suggest a change in the pattern of migration. Recent Mexican immigrants have lower educational attainment than earlier migrants and recent immigrants seem to be migrating at older ages than previous immigrants. Table 3.3 shows that Mexican immigrants who entered the United States between 1960 and 1964 were, on the average, 19 years old and had finished more than eight years of school. Since 1960, the average age of immigrants who remain in the United States has increased and the average educational level has decreased. Mexican males who immigrated to the United States since 1985 have completed less than six years of school and have an average age of over 30. The same pattern is found among females. The young ages and relatively higher educational levels of the early Mexican immigrants suggest that they might well have been typical economic immigrants. They may have had the aspirations and attitudes classically attributed to this group.

The lower educational levels of recent immigrants indicate that immigration no longer selects for relatively better educated Mexicans. In fact, the opposite is true; recent immigrants have lower than average educational levels. The fact that they are older than the earlier immigrants indicates that they spent more of their adult life in Mexico. The decision to migrate at an older age may reflect the increasingly difficult situation of the Mexican economy. Mexico's recent relatively poor economic health may now be more of a "push" factor for migration than it once was. The decreasing educational level is consistent with the view of Mexican migration to the United States as a social process which now involves a wider range of Mexicans, as Cornelius (1991) has argued.

The same pattern of decreasing education and increasing age can generally be seen among the male and female Central/South American immigrants. The fact that these immigrants come from different countries of origin at different points of time makes it difficult to speculate about possible reasons for this trend. Nonetheless, the older average age and lower educational levels of this group and of the Mexican immigrants suggest that all recent Hispanic immigrants will have a more difficult time becoming incorporated in the United States than earlier immigrants.

One of the key concerns in the immigration debate focuses on the future incorporation or lack of incorporation of the children of immigrants. The sex-, generation-, and cohort-specific educational attainment levels in table 3.8 show that third-generation Hispanics have lower educational levels than the second generation. Among Mexican Americans, both U.S.-born generations have much lower attainment levels than U.S.-born non-Hispanic whites. Both institutional barriers and perceptions of discrimination may explain the apparent ceiling on the educational achievement of Mexican Americans as a whole. When Mexican Americans have been disaggregated into class groups, the results indicate that economic and social incorporation is possible for the proportion of Mexican Americans who do well in terms of educational attainment (Chapa 1992). The large proportion who do not do well in school have lower degrees of social and economic incorporation (Chapa 1990). If the distinction between earlier and recent Hispanic immigrants previously discussed is valid, this suggests that the strength of the "second-generation effect" might be mitigated in the future.

The data presented above have shown that both second- and third-generation Mexican Americans have lower average educational levels than non-Hispanic whites and a much higher proportion of high school dropouts and a lower proportion of college attendees. The level of Hispanic educational attainment is a valid indicator of social incorporation and a key predictor of economic success. The apparent ceiling on the educational attainment of Mexican Americans may be the consequence of unequal access to educational resources. School finances in states with large Hispanic populations have been found to be grossly unequal. The financial and political support for broad-based access to higher education has withered. The proportion of Hispanic high school graduates who had ever enrolled in college was much lower in 1990 than in 1973 (Chapa 1991). Other factors behind the persistence of large numbers of second- and third-generation Mexican Americans with low educational attainment are uneven access to preschool programs, limited means of language-appropriate communication with parents, and low expectations of those who teach Hispanics, which may well become self-fulfilling prophesies.

Whatever the future level of Hispanic immigration, the age structure and fertility levels of current Hispanic residents of the United States indicate a high probability of an increase of the Hispanic population, particularly among younger age groups. Hispanic immigration is likely to be a source of substantial growth in the future. The economic costs of not adequately educating Hispanics will be substantial, and the social consequences of having a large group of Hispanics who are not fully incorporated into U.S. society may be negative and far-reaching.

APPENDIX 3.A
DEFINITIONS OF VARIABLES

Variables	Definitions
Age	— age in years.
Age of entry	— estimated age of entry into the United States.
Education	— completed years of education.
Ethnicity	
Asian-origin	— respondent was born in Asian country (China, India, Iran, Japan, Korea, Laos, Philippines, or Vietnam).
Canadian-origin	— respondent was born in Canada.
Central/South American-origin	— respondent is self-reported as Central or South American and is not a citizen or is a naturalized citizen.
Cuban-origin	— respondent is self-reported as Cuban and is not a citizen or is a naturalized citizen.
European-origin	— respondent was born in European country (Germany, Greece, Ireland, Italy, Poland, Portugal, United Kingdom, former U.S.S.R., or former Yugoslavia).
Mexican-origin	— respondent is self-reported as Mexican American, Chicano, or Mexican(o) and is not a citizen or is a naturalized citizen.
Non-Hispanic White Natives	— respondent is self-reported as white and non-Hispanic.
Other Foreign-born	— respondent is not self-reported as Hispanic and was born in a country other than those listed under Asian, Canadian, or European origin.

Other Hispanic-origin	— respondent is self-reported as Other Hispanic and is not a citizen or is a naturalized citizen.
Generation	
First Generation Hispanic	— respondent is not a citizen or is a naturalized citizen.
First Generation All other	— respondent is born abroad and is not born to U.S. parents.
Second Generation	— respondent is Mexican origin or Central/South American and is born in the United States or abroad to an American parent and has at least one parent who was born in the parent country.
Third-or-Later Generation	— respondent is Mexican origin or Central/South American origin and is born in the United States or abroad to American parents and has parents who were both born in the United States.
Marital Status	
Divorced, Separated or Widowed	— respondent is divorced, separated, or widowed at the time of the survey.
Married	— respondent is married at the time of the survey.
Never Married	— respondent has never been married at the time of the survey.
Metropolitan	— respondent lives in metropolitan area.
Naturalized Citizen	— respondent reported that he/she is a naturalized citizen.
Region	
Northeast	— respondent lives in Maine, New Hampshire, Vermont, Massachusetts, Rhode Island, Connecticut, New York, New Jersey, or Pennsylvania.
North Central	— respondent lives in Ohio, Indiana, Illinois, Michigan, Wisconsin, Minnesota, Iowa, Missouri, North Dakota, South Dakota, Nebraska, or Kansas.
South	— respondent lives in Delaware, Maryland, District of Columbia, Virginia, West Virginia, North Carolina, South Carolina, Georgia, Florida, Kentucky, Tennessee, Alabama, Mississippi,

	Arkansas, Louisiana, Oklahoma, or Texas.
West	— respondent lives in Montana, Idaho, Wyoming, Colorado, New Mexico, Arizona, Utah, Nevada, Washington, Oregon, California, Alaska, or Hawaii.

References

Alvarez, Rodolfo. 1985. "The Psycho-Historical and Socioeconomic Development of the Chicano Community in the United States." In *The Mexican American Experience*, edited by R. de la Garza, F. Bean, C. Bonjean, and R. Alvarez (33–56). Austin: University of Texas Press.

Bean, Frank D., H. L. Browning, and W. P. Frisbie. 1984. "The Sociodemographic Characteristics of Mexican Immigrant Status Groups: Implications for Studying Undocumented Mexicans." *International Migration Review* 18: 672–691.

Bean, Frank D., and M. Fix. 1992. "The Significance of Recent Immigration Policy Reforms in the United States." In *Nations of Immigrants: Australia, the United States and International Migration*, edited by G. Freeman and J. Jupp (41–55). Melbourne: Oxford University Press.

Bean, Frank D., and Marta Tienda. 1987. *The Hispanic Population of the United States*. New York: Russell Sage.

Borjas, George. 1990. *Friends or Strangers: The Impact of Immigrants on the U.S. Economy*. New York: Basic Books.

Borjas, George, and M. Tienda. 1987. "The Economic Consequences of Immigration." *Science* 235: 645–651.

Chapa, Jorge. 1990. "The Myth of Hispanic Progress." *Journal of Hispanic Policy* 4: 3–18.

————. 1991. "Special Focus: Hispanic Demographic and Educational Trends." In *Ninth Annual Status Report on Minorities in Higher Education*, edited by Deborah J. Carter and Reginald Wilson. Washington, D.C.: American Council of Education.

————. 1992. "Longitudinal Trends and Class Differences in the Social-Structural Incorporation of Mexican Americans." Paper presented at the Conference on the Peopling of the Americas: International Union for the Scientific Study of Population. Vera Cruz, Mexico.

Chavez, Linda. 1989. "Tequila Sunrise: The Slow but Steady Progress of Hispanic Immigrants." *Policy Review* (Spring): 64–67.

Child, Irving L. 1943. *Italian or American? The Second Generation in Conflict.* New Haven, Conn.: Yale University Press.

Chiswick, Barry. 1990. "Opening the Golden Door." *The Washington Post,* October 7: D3.

Cornelius, Wayne. 1991. "From Sojourner to Settler: The Changing Profile of Mexican Migration to the United States." Unpublished paper.

de la Garza, Rodolfo O. 1991. Personal communication about data from the Hispanic supplement to the Panel Study of Income Dynamics.

Glazer, Nathan, and Daniel P. Moynihan. 1970. *Beyond the Melting Pot: The Negroes, Puerto Ricans, Jews, Italians and Irish of New York City.* Cambridge, Mass.: The M.I.T. Press.

Gordon, Milton M. 1964. *Assimilation in American Life: The Role of Race, Religion, and National Origins.* New York: Oxford University Press.

Greeley, Andrew. 1971. *Why Can't They Be Like Us? America's White Ethnic Groups.* New York: E. P. Dutton.

Handlin, Oscar. 1941. *Boston's Immigrants: A Study of Acculturation.* Cambridge, Mass.: Harvard University Press.

————. 1951. *The Uprooted: The Epic Story of the Great Migrations that Made the American People.* Boston: Little, Brown.

Levy, Frank. 1987. *Dollars and Dreams: The Changing American Income Distribution.* New York: Russell Sage.

Lopez, David. 1978. "Chicano Language Loyalty in an Urban Setting." *Sociology and Social Research* 62:267–278.

Massey, Douglas S. 1990. "Social Structure, Household Strategies, and the Cumulative Causation of Migration." *Population Index* 56:3–25.

Massey, Douglas S., R. Alarcon, J. Durand, and H. Gonzalez. 1987. *Return to Aztlan: The Social Process of International Migration from Western Mexico.* Berkeley: University of California Press.

McCarthy, Kevin and R. B. Valdez. 1985. *Current and Future Effects of Mexican Immigration in California.* R-3365-CR. Santa Monica, Calif.: The RAND Corporation.

McLemore, S. Dale. 1990. *Racial and Ethnic Relations in America,* 3rd ed. Boston: Allyn and Bacon.

Nee, Victor, and Jimmy Sanders. 1990. "A Theory of Immigrant Incorporation." Cornell University, Ithaca, N.Y.: Sociology Working Paper.

Neidert, Lisa, and R. Farley. 1985. "Assimilation in the United States: An Analysis of Ethnic and Generation Differences in Status and Achievement." *American Sociological Review* 50: 840–850.

Park, R.E. 1950. *Race and Culture.* Glencoe, IL: Free Press.

Pedraza-Bailey, Sylvia. 1985. *Political and Economic Migrants in America.* Austin: University of Texas Press.

Portes, Alejandro, and R. Bach. 1985. *Latin Journey.* Berkeley: University of California Press.

Portes, Alejandro, and R. Rumbaut. 1990. *Immigrant America: A Portrait.* Berkeley: University of California.

Sowell, Thomas. 1981. *Ethnic America: A History.* New York: Basic Books.
Suttles, Gerald D. 1968. *The Social Order of the Slum: Ethnicity and Territory in the Inner City.* Chicago: University of Chicago Press.
Thomas, William I., and Florian Znaniecki. 1927. *The Polish Peasant in Europe and America,* Vol. 2. New York: Alfred A. Knopf, Inc.
Valdivieso, Rafael, and Cary Dains. 1988. "U.S. Hispanics: Challenging Issues for the 1990s." *Population Trends and Public Policy* (December): 1–16.
Warren, Robert, and Jeffrey S. Passel. 1987. "A Count of the Uncountable: Estimates of Undocumented Aliens Counted in the 1980 Census." *Demography* 24: 375–393.

Chapter Four

THE SOCIOECONOMIC STATUS AND INTEGRATION OF ASIAN IMMIGRANTS

Sharon M. Lee and Barry Edmonston

Over the last decade, Asian Americans[1] have overtaken Hispanics as the faster-growing minority population in the United States. For the nation as a whole, the Asian American population increased from 3.7 million in 1980 to 7.3 million in 1990. This doubling comes on top of the 140 percent increase recorded between 1970 and 1980 (U.S. Bureau of the Census 1991).[2]

The role of immigration in the growth of the Asian population is well-known. Following the implementation of the 1965 Amendments to the Immigration and Nationality Act of 1952, immigration has been the main factor in the growth and diversification of the Asian American population. In recent years, immigrants from Asia have comprised close to half of all legal immigrants admitted to the United States. Indeed, among immigrants from developing countries, Asian immigrants have shown the most spectacular increase during the past 25 years, increasing from 7 percent of all immigrants in 1965 to 46 percent in 1990.

Barring changes in current immigration policies, we can expect immigration to continue its impact on the future growth of the Asian American population. This underlines the importance of understanding how Asian immigrants are adapting to U.S. society. The Asian populations will also be changing U.S. society through the diffusion of Asian cultural elements into American culture, and the fertility behavior of Asian immigrants and their descendants will influence the future demography of the United States.[3]

We begin with a review of how immigration and ethnicity can influence group status and integration in general, and more specifically, what these effects may be for Asian Americans, followed by a discussion of theories of group inequality. In the remainder of the chapter, we report and discuss the results of empirical analyses of Asian Americans' socioeconomic status.

IMMIGRANT AND ETHNICITY EFFECTS ON GROUP STATUS

In general, the United States takes pride in its immigrant heritage. After all, except for Native American groups, every American is either an immigrant or the descendant of immigrants. Analyses of how different immigrant communities adjusted, adapted, or assimilated into U.S. culture and society have always formed an important part of sociological research. Research on the progress of immigrants and their U.S.-born descendants and the relationships among different groups of immigrants and with native-born Americans furthered the development of sociological theories of intergroup relations, social stratification, social mobility, and urban ecology, to name but a few areas in sociology that have been profoundly affected by the flow of immigrants to the United States.

Asian immigrants are both old and new players in the American migration story. The first Asian immigrants arrived from China in the 1840s. Until recently, however, Chinese and other Asian immigrants had only a minor role because discriminatory policies had kept Asian immigration at negligible levels. Since the 1970s, Asian immigrants, together with Hispanics, have dominated the immigration scene. As their absolute and relative numbers increase, we can expect greater awareness of the Asian American population and more interest in how Asian Americans form a part of the larger society.

The adjustment of Asian immigrants in the United States can be expected to be influenced by their status as immigrants and as non-Europeans. With few exceptions, immigrants have to deal with obstacles that may delay their economic and social integration into society. Prejudice against foreigners, lack of proficiency in English, and unfamiliarity with American customs and the labor market are just some of the many difficulties that immigrants typically face. Often, the process of integration takes several generations and varies across dimensions. For example, acculturation, or the learning of such aspects of American culture as English language and clothing, is quick and generally achieved by the second generation (U.S.-born children of immigrants), but structural and broader social integration takes much longer. Many groups who are the descendants of more recent arrivals find it hard to be completely accepted by the longer-settled groups.

In general, immigrants tend to have lower earnings than native-born workers, although the gap may not be permanent. Indeed, some researchers report that after about 10 to 12 years, most foreign-born male workers reach parity in earnings with native-born males (Borjas 1985, Carliner 1980, Chiswick 1978). Other research indicates that the disparity in earnings between native-born and some foreign-born males persists (Nee and Sanders 1985). Long (1980) extended this area of research for foreign-born women and reported generally similar experiences for male and female immigrants, although some female immigrants showed higher earnings than native women. An alternative perspective on the socioeconomic disadvantages experienced by females is provided by Woo's (1985) analysis of Asian American women, which examined the double discrimination that minority immigrant women face (see also Boyd 1984 on immigrant women in Canada).

In addition to the disadvantages associated with foreign birth and immigrant status, Asian immigrants can expect their adjustment process to be affected by racial prejudice and discrimination. Racial minority groups include those "whose membership is derived from a shared racial identity, with high visibility in the society and a devalued social status" (Staples and Mirande 1980). The tenacious effect of race in stratifying groups, historically as well as presently, has been extensively documented (Blau and Duncan 1967; Duncan, Featherman, and Duncan 1972; Hirschman and Kraly 1990; Jaynes and Williams 1989; Lieberson 1980; Nee and Sanders 1985; Passell 1991; Siegel 1965). Recent data show that blacks' median family income is just 56 percent of whites', and the poverty rate of blacks has remained at around 30 to 33 percent for the last 20 years, three times that of whites (*The Economist* 1991; O'Hare, Dollard, Mann, and Kent 1991). Similar statistics on Hispanics suggest that while better off compared to blacks, almost one-fifth of Hispanic families are poor and the median income of Hispanic families is about 66 percent that of non-Hispanic families (Barringer 1991a). In contrast, aggregate statistics for Asian Americans depict a better profile, with median family incomes about the same as those of non-Hispanic whites. However, the poverty rate for Asians is almost twice that of non-Hispanic whites, and the poverty rate among some groups, for example, Indo-Chinese refugees, has been well over 33 percent (Lee 1994, O'Hare and Felt 1991). Compared to whites, Asian Americans receive lower income and occupational returns for similar amounts of education (Barringer, Takeuchi, and Xenos 1990) and experience other disadvantages related to their status as a racial minority (U.S. Commission on Civil Rights 1988, U.S. General Accounting Office 1990).

This analysis focuses on the socioeconomic dimension of Asian immigrants' adjustment to the United States. We recognize that immigrants' adaptation to their adopted society varies across many dimensions (Lee 1990b). However, the ability to make a living and provide for oneself and one's family forms the critical base for other dimensions of integration. An immigrant who is able to obtain a full-time job with adequate pay will not be dependent on public assistance, will be better able to provide economic and social resources (in the way of a stable family context) for his/her children's schooling, and will have a better opportunity to own a home. In addition to these benefits, a secure and favorable socioeconomic status is positively related to other dimensions of integration—for example, social and political participation and integration, as discussed by Massey (1981). Therefore, we limit our analysis to the socioeconomic status and integration of Asian immigrants because we see this as perhaps the most important aspect of immigrant adjustment.

THEORIES OF GROUP INEQUALITY AND STATUS

Many theories have been proposed to explain group differentials in socioeconomic status and mobility. Model (1988) provides a useful review of cultural, resource, demographic, and labor market factors that are often employed in explaining group differences. In particular, she reviews the possible effects of these factors on the relative economic success of European and East Asian groups compared with blacks and Hispanics. The various theories of socioeconomic differences can be usefully classified into three main types: assimilationist, human capital, and structural theories.

Assimilationist theories generally assume that immigrants accumulate experiences and skills over time that will facilitate their eventual assimilation (Gordon 1964, Yinger 1985). Education plays a major role in the mobility and assimilation of immigrants and their descendants. Assimilation theories are mainly based on studies of the European immigrants who dominated migration to the United States until the 1960s.

The *human capital* perspective has some similarities with assimilationist theories but draws a more explicit connection between individual characteristics and achievement. This perspective predicts that individuals or groups that have invested in labor market-relevant characteristics—for example, education, vocational training, and work experience—will be more successful (Becker 1964, Berg 1969).

This perspective may be appropriate in situations where jobs, earnings, promotions, and other rewards are obtained through purely market processes that match the most qualified person to the job. In reality, of course, this seldom is the case because of the intrusion of other factors into the labor market. The shortcomings of the human capital perspective have been shown to be particularly significant from research into the economic experiences of minority groups.

The *structural* perspective identifies two general sets of factors that influence immigrant or minority group achievement. One cluster of factors comes from the community or locale in which the group resides. Such community-level factors may act to differentiate the labor market such that immigrant or minority workers tend to be segregated into lower-paid and secondary-sector jobs. In other words, the labor market is not homogeneous, and employers respond accordingly. Minorities or immigrants can expect to be less likely to be employed and more likely to be paid lower wages, if employed, all other things being equal. In addition, minority and immigrant workers may be excluded by organized labor from better-paid jobs, either through formal mechanisms of exclusion (Boswell 1986, Saxton 1971) or informal mechanisms (Bailey and Waldinger 1990). The other structural factor that is external to the minority or immigrant group is the racial composition of the local area and how employers respond. The higher the concentration of some minority groups— for example, blacks—the lower the earnings of minority workers, although research does not demonstrate consistent effects of this structural factor (Brown and Fuguitt 1972, Frisbie and Neidert 1977, Tienda and Lii 1987). The theoretical reasoning behind the effects of minority concentration is unclear. Lower minority wages and higher unemployment may be due to greater competition for jobs or to a defensive response by majority group members to the perceived threat of growing numbers of non-majority people—in short, discrimination.

Some proponents of the structural approach (including Bonacich 1973, Bonacich and Modell 1980, Wilson and Portes 1980) do not necessarily view the segmented labor market as negative. Such segmentation may sometimes provide opportunities for employment and mobility that would otherwise be absent. The concepts of ethnic solidarity, ethnic or cultural resources, and middleman minority are used to discuss positive structural effects for some minority groups— for example, Cubans and Koreans. This interpretation of structural factors derives from group-based characteristics that can either facilitate or hinder socioeconomic progress. Portes and Bach (1985) wrote about "ethnic resilience," or the ability of some groups to gain strength and support from group identification and culture. Thus, groups that encourage schooling, parental sacrifice for children, and informal ethnic networks are expected to do better. On the other hand, the potentially negative effects of an ethnic enclave economy—for example, low wages and limited occupational choices—have also been discussed (Hurh and Kim 1989, Lee 1989, Min 1990, Sanders and Nee 1987).

Both individual and structural variables influence how immigrants and minority group members fare. The relatively high economic achievements of some groups—Cubans, Koreans, Jews, and Chinese—are partly explained by referring to the existence of ethnic enclaves among these groups. The lack of economic mobility among others—for example, blacks—was partly attributed to the absence of established enclave economies (Boyd 1990, Wilson and Martin 1982). While it is far from clear that the ethnic enclave plays such a dominant role in either immigrant or minority group achievement because groups also differ along many other dimensions, the concept of an ethnic economy and its importance to group attainment is generally acknowledged (Light and Bonacich 1988, Wilson and Portes 1980, Zhou and Logan 1989).

In addition to the above factors, recent research has identified ways through which family and household structure may affect minority groups. For example, the higher earnings and generally higher socioeconomic status of minorities such as Cubans and several Asian groups have been shown to be mainly due to more workers per family and a greater dependence on close family ties and intergenerational help (Cummings 1980, Lee 1990a, Perez 1986). Other researchers have looked into the effect of extended household composition on female labor force participation (Tienda and Glass 1985, Lee and Yamanaka 1989), cultural versus economic determinants of household structure among blacks and Hispanics (Angel and Tienda 1982, Tienda and Angel 1982), and the role of household composition on labor force participation among Southeast Asian refugees (Bach and Carroll-Seguin 1986). The growing interest in the role of the family and household can be traced, in part, to the recognition that culture, reflected in family and household organization, can significantly influence a wide range of behavior, including income distribution, economic achievement, and poverty (Duncan, Featherman, and Duncan 1972; McLanahan 1985) and immigrant adaptation (Nee and Wong 1985; Tienda 1980). Even when data cannot directly measure these cultural factors, their potential impact should be acknowledged.

Our study of Asian Americans is particularly significant for theoretical discussions of group achievement. Asian Americans generally have high levels of conventional measures of human capital. Aggregate statistics confirm the outstanding levels of schooling that Asians have. In addition, Asian Americans, both males and females, have high labor force participation rates, and Asian American women continue to work even when they have young children (below six years old) at home. If the human capital perspective is correct, we would expect few differences between Asian and white Americans' socioeconomic status, given roughly similar investments in human capital, experience, and occupational status. On the other hand, disparities between these two groups may lend support to the strength of structuralist arguments—specifically, that minority groups are still disadvantaged, despite heavy investments in human capital. In this way, an examination of the socioeconomic status of Asian Americans provides a unique opportunity for evaluating competing theories of group inequality.

DATA AND METHODS

While research on Asian Americans has increased significantly in recent years, many problems related to availability of data make comparisons with other minority populations—for example, blacks and Hispanics—difficult. The recent growth of this population is impressive, but the Asian American population is still small in absolute numbers. National sample surveys usually do not contain sufficient cases for meaningful analysis, and most surveys do not oversample Asians, although they routinely oversample blacks and Hispanics. U.S. Bureau of the Census data, therefore, often represent the only adequate source of data on Asian Americans. The public use individual data released by the Census Bureau have been invaluable for generating research on Asian Americans because census publications tend to overlook the Asian American population. Published census data on Asian Americans are few compared with the extensive and detailed publications on blacks, whites, and Hispanics. In many census publications, Asians are simply placed in the "Other" racial category. We hope that the statistical neglect by official agencies of this fast-growing population will be redressed in the near future.

The data for our analysis are drawn from two main sources that span the 1980s—the Public Use Microdata 1 Percent Sample (PUMS) files of the 1980 Census of the U.S. Population provide one source of data (U.S. Bureau of the Census 1983) and the 1986, 1988, and 1989 Current Population Surveys (CPSs) provided more recent information. Using several data sets allows us to examine the effects of increased Asian immigration (in volume and diversity) on socioeconomic status.

The PUMS data are suitable for the analysis because of the large number of racial and ethnic minority groups included, thus yielding sufficient cases for the Asian groups. Complete samples of males and females, aged 18 to 64, from the six largest Asian groups, were drawn from the PUMS files.[4] A 20 percent subsample of non-Hispanic whites was also included for comparison. The two data files, one of males and another of females, were then weighed to be proportionately representative of the U.S. population by these groups. All findings in this chapter using the 1980 Census data are based on the weighted files.

The CPS is a monthly survey, conducted by the Bureau of the Census, designed to provide estimates of employment and related characteristics of the U.S. population. About 57,000 households are interviewed monthly. The sample is representative of the civilian, noninstitutionalized population. The 1986 and 1988 CPS files use only three categories for measuring race, classifying respondents into White, Black, and "Other." However, supplements to the monthly survey also collect data on additional topics; for example, the June 1986 and June 1988 surveys added questions on the country of origin of the household members and the country of origin of their parents. We created the Asian sample by using responses to the country of origin questions for the respondent and his/her parents. All respondents who reported that they or one of their parents were born in an Asian country were included in our sample.[5] This approach yields information on foreign-born Asians (those who report being born in an Asian country and whose parents were not U.S. citizens) and second-generation Asians (those who report that they were born in the United States or born abroad to U.S. citizens and who had at least one parent who was born in an Asian country).

Beginning with the 1989 CPS, a separate, additional racial code for Asians and Pacific Islanders was used in the survey. In addition, the 1989 CPS also allowed us to identify three generations of Asian

Americans: the first or foreign-born, the second generation (U.S.-born children of immigrants), and the third-and-higher generations.

For each of the three CPS surveys used in this analysis, a smaller subsample of non-Hispanic whites was drawn for comparison. The non-Hispanic whites were selected from respondents who reported their race as white and indicated that they were not Hispanic. Non-Hispanic whites could be foreign- or native-born.

There are several advantages in using CPS data for studying immigration and ethnicity. If appropriate, we can combine data from the 1986, 1988, and 1989 surveys and have sufficient cases to examine the characteristics of Asian immigrants. In addition, until the 1990 public use microdata are available, the CPS data are the only source for more recent information. However, the use of CPS has some disadvantages. First, for 1986 and 1988, ethnicity is coded only for the white and black populations. As a result, the code for "other" races included Asians, Pacific Islanders, and Native Americans. The number of third-generation Asian Americans is about the same (approximately one million) as the number of Native Americans. If the data do not differentiate between Asians and Native Americans, then analysis of third-and-higher generation people would include a mixture of about one-half Asians (primarily Chinese and Japanese) and one-half Native Americans. Our imputation procedure did not allow us to remove Native Americans from this "other" race category. A second potential problem may come from errors in extracting the Asian samples from the 1986 and 1988 CPSs. The Asian samples were obtained by inferring Asian ethnicity from responses to the country of origin and country of birth questions. It is possible that the procedure may either include some non-Asians or exclude some Asians.[6] Finally, while the 1989 CPS allowed us to identify Asian Americans directly from responses to the ethnicity question, a small number of Pacific Islanders are grouped in the "Asian" category.

In this analysis, we use our male samples only because of the generally greater role of men in defining a household's socioeconomic status and more stable labor force participation history. This does not mean that women's role is not considered important. In future research, we will focus directly on Asian American women and their impact on households' socioeconomic status.

Table 4.1 ASIAN AMERICAN POPULATION BY NATIONAL ORIGIN
(Ethnicity)[a]: 1970, 1980, and 1990 Censuses

Group	1970 Number	1970 Percent[b]	1980 Number	1980 Percent	1990 Number	1990 Percent
Total Asians	1,439,562	100.0	3,443,354	100.0	6,950,339	100.0
Chinese	436,062	30.3	806,040	23.4	1,645,472	23.7
Filipino	343,060	23.8	774,652	22.5	1,406,770	20.2
Japanese	591,290	41.1	700,974	20.2	847,562	12.2
Indian	(NA)[c]	—	361,531	10.5	815,447	11.7
Korean	69,150	4.8	354,593	10.3	798,849	11.5
Vietnamese	(NA)	—	261,729	7.6	614,547	8.8
Other Indo-Chinese	(NA)	—	68,931	2.0	386,507	5.6
All others	(NA)	—	114,904	3.5	435,185	6.3

Sources: Gardner, Robey, and Smith (1985) for the 1970 and 1980 Census figures; U.S. Bureau of the Census (1991) for the 1990 data.
Notes:
a. The data in this table refer to Asian Americans only; where Pacific Islanders were included with Asians (as in the 1990 census), they have been removed from the totals shown.
b. The percentages refer to the percent of the Asian American population.
c. In the 1970 census, some groups that are not counted as Asian Americans (e.g., Indians) were not included or were not tabulated but were published separately. These latter groups are, however, included in the total.

FINDINGS

Ethnicity and National Origin

We begin with descriptive statistics that compare changes in the national origin of Asian Americans over the last decade. The growth of the Asian American population in recent years has been accompanied by shifts in ethnicity and national origin, as shown in table 4.1. Before 1970, Japanese Americans were the largest Asian ethnic group, comprising over 41 percent of the Asian population in the United States, followed by Chinese (30 percent) and Filipinos (24 percent). By 1980, the largest Asian ethnic groups were Chinese and Filipinos, each making up about one-quarter of the total Asian count, while Japanese had declined to 21 percent of the total. In addition, percentages of Koreans, Indians, and Vietnamese had grown significantly (Gardner, Robey, and Smith 1985). These trends have continued through the 1980s, according to the latest data released by the Census Bureau (Vobejda 1991, Barringer 1991b). The three largest Asian ethnic groups are Chinese (24 percent), Filipino (20 percent), and

Indo-Chinese (Vietnamese, Cambodian, Hmong, and Laotian, adding to over 14 percent).

Nativity and Period of Immigration

Changes in the composition and national origins of Asian Americans are mainly due to the effects of differential immigration. Low immigration by Japanese to the United States will continue the relative decline of the Japanese American population within the Asian population, while groups with large recent immigrant flows—for example, Vietnamese, other Indo-Chinese, Chinese, Filipinos, Koreans, and Indians—will all continue to grow. The growth of the Indo-Chinese population through the 1980s is particularly noteworthy. Except for Japanese Americans, the Asian American population is primarily a first-generation population with a fast developing second generation, as shown in table 4.2. The recency of arrival among groups such as the Indo-Chinese is also seen from the bottom two panels of table 4.2, while the Chinese and, to a lesser degree, Filipinos, have been immigrating into the United States over several decades.

Schooling and Quality of Immigrants

A question that frequently arises in discussing immigrant policy and integration is the "quality" of immigrants. By this, we often mean the education and occupation of immigrants and whether their skills are consistent with those needed for economic success and contributions to the U.S. economy. The 1965 amendments to U.S. immigration policy use family reunification as the primary factor in visa allocations. The family reunification principle has intensified discussions of immigrant quality, since family members may not be particularly educated or skilled when compared with immigrants admitted solely on the basis of their education and skills.

The majority of Asian immigrants, like other legal immigrants to the United States, enter as family members. This trend will continue and may even grow as more Asian immigrants become permanent residents or citizens and are able to sponsor more family members. Has the quality of Asian immigrants changed in recent years? We examined data on mean years of schooling as an approximate measure of immigrant quality, comparing native-born Asian Americans with immigrants by period of entry and national origin, as shown in table 4.3.

Table 4.2 ASIAN AMERICAN HOUSEHOLD HEADS BY NATIVITY, PERIOD OF
IMMIGRATION, AND NATIONAL ORIGIN: 1980, 1986, 1988, AND 1989

Year	Sample Size[a]	Percent Distribution for Asian Americans							
		Total	Japanese	Chinese	Filipino	Korean	Indian	Viet-namese	Other Asian
Native-Born[b]									
1980	2,836	100.0	59.1	25.0	10.9	2.5	2.1	0.4	—
1986	121	100.0	45.2	26.0	21.4	4.4	1.9	—	1.1
1988	127	100.0	40.8	22.3	26.1	3.2	3.9	2.1	1.6
1989	154	100.0	46.8	19.6	25.3	1.9	0.6	1.3	4.5
Foreign-Born, Immigrated 10 or More Years Ago[c]									
1980	1,842	100.0	7.6	43.1	25.2	6.9	16.6	0.6	—
1986	220	100.0	8.1	26.9	23.4	15.3	17.5	2.2	6.6
1988	183	100.0	5.2	20.7	29.5	10.0	13.9	13.0	7.7
1989	358	100.0	3.2	20.8	23.2	15.4	12.4	12.2	12.8
Foreign-Born, Immigrated 5 to 10 Years Ago[d]									
1980	1,369	100.0	5.0	29.9	20.4	16.8	26.6	1.3	—
1986	273	100.0	1.7	14.8	15.0	12.9	17.6	26.5	11.5
1988	258	100.0	4.6	22.0	12.5	7.0	14.3	20.5	19.1
1989	182	100.0	3.8	14.4	19.0	12.0	15.0	11.0	24.8
Foreign-Born, Immigrated Within Last 5 Years[e]									
1980	2,470	100.0	7.7	24.3	13.0	14.0	17.2	23.8	—
1986	144	100.0	9.8	19.6	14.9	21.3	10.6	8.0	15.8
1988	109	100.0	10.4	17.8	14.8	15.8	16.5	8.3	16.4
1989	177	100.0	13.3	28.1	9.6	14.1	11.0	7.3	16.6

Sources: 1980 data are from PUMS (U.S. Bureau of the Census 1983); 1986 and 1988
data are from June CPS; and 1989 data are from November CPS.
Notes:
a. The sample size is the number of households in each data set.
b. Because of differences across data sets, the "native-born" in this table refers to
second generation and above for 1980 and 1989, but to the second generation alone
for 1986 and 1988. Data from 1980 refer to the six largest Asian ethnic groups only.
c. In 1986, this is more than 11 years; in 1988, more than 8 years; and for 1989, more
than 9 years.
d. For 1986, this is 5 to 11 years ago; for 1988, 4 to 8 years ago; and for 1989, 5 to 9
years ago.
e. For 1988, the most recent immigrants refer to those who immigrated within the
last 4 years.

Bearing in mind the caution needed in comparing across data sets
(as noted in the table), three general observations can be made. First,
native-born Asian Americans have very high mean years of schooling,
as shown in the first column, first row of table 4.3. Only immigrants

Table 4.3 MEAN YEARS OF SCHOOLING FOR ASIAN AMERICANS BY
NATIVITY, PERIOD OF IMMIGRATION, AND NATIONAL ORIGIN[a]:
1980, 1986, 1988, AND 1989

Year	All Asians	Japanese	Chinese	Filipino	Korean	Indian	Viet-namese	Other Asian
Native-Born[b]								
1980	16.0	15.9	16.7	14.7	15.9	15.9	14.8	—
1986	13.9	13.7	14.8	13.2	13.1	15.9	—	18.0
1988	13.4	13.5	13.7	12.7	13.6	13.9	13.2	14.1
1989	13.8	14.0	15.1	13.3	9.8	11.0	15.1	14.5
Foreign-Born, Immigrated 10 or More Years Ago[c]								
1980	13.4	16.6	15.9	15.5	18.9	19.8	17.2	—
1986	14.8	14.2	14.1	14.5	14.8	16.9	11.6	14.7
1988	14.2	13.6	14.4	14.5	14.0	16.1	13.1	11.3
1989	14.2	14.7	13.6	14.4	13.4	16.4	13.4	14.4
Foreign-Born, Immigrated 5 to 10 Years Ago[d]								
1980	17.1	16.6	16.3	16.7	16.8	18.9	17.4	—
1986	12.4	13.3	12.2	13.7	12.6	14.9	11.3	9.1
1988	13.2	13.8	13.5	15.3	15.4	15.5	12.3	9.9
1989	12.8	15.0	13.1	14.8	15.3	15.5	10.7	8.7
Foreign-Born, Immigrated Within Last 5 Years[e]								
1980	15.5	16.7	14.4	15.9	16.0	17.7	14.0	—
1986	13.1	14.7	13.9	14.6	13.6	15.7	8.9	9.4
1988	13.5	15.2	14.2	14.0	15.4	15.3	9.4	9.6
1989	14.1	15.8	14.7	14.7	13.4	16.2	10.1	12.5

Sources: 1980 data are from PUMS (U.S. Bureau of the Census 1983); 1986 and 1988 data are from June CPS: and 1989 data are from November CPS.
Notes:
a. Mean years of schooling refers to the highest grade of school attended in 1980 and highest grade completed in the CPS samples. For the 1980 PUMS, data are for the six largest Asian ethnic groups only.
b. Because of differences across data sets, the "native-born" in this table refers to second generation and above for 1980 and 1989, but to the second generation alone for 1986 and 1988. Data from 1980 refer to the six largest Asian ethnic groups only.
c. In 1986, this is more than 11 years; in 1988, more than 8 years; and for 1989, more than 9 years.
d. For 1986, this is 5 to 11 years ago; for 1988, 4 to 8 years ago; and for 1989, 5 to 9 years ago.
e. For 1988, the most recent immigrants refer to those who immigrated within the last 4 years.

who immigrated between 1970 and 1975 surpass native-born Asian males' schooling (comparing the first row of the top and third panels). Second, important variations exist among ethnic groups. These variations hold for the native-born as well as the foreign-born. For example, Japanese, Indians, Koreans, and Filipinos have higher mean educational attainment than Chinese and Vietnamese. Third, some evidence indicates a decline in educational attainment over time among some groups of Asian immigrants. Immigrants who came in the 1970s have higher mean years of schooling. For example, those who arrived between 1970 and 1975 had an average of 17 years of schooling (first row of the third panel), whereas immigrants who arrived after 1976 and through the early 1980s have an average of about 12.4 to 13.2 years of schooling (other rows in the third panel of table 4.3). A similar pattern is shown in the bottom panel of the table, although the differentials are smaller.[7] This decline is largely due to the lower schooling of Vietnamese and "other" immigrants (these would include Cambodian, Laotian, Hmong, and other smaller Asian ethnic groups) who began to make up a larger part of Asian immigrant flows in the 1980s. The majority of the most recent arrivals entered the United States under the principle of family reunification or as refugees, whereas most Asian immigrants who arrived in the early 1970s gained entry based on professional qualifications. An important implication of these data is the prospect for economic progress among Asian Americans if more recent Asian immigrants arrive with low educational attainment.

ANALYSIS OF HOUSEHOLD INCOME

Variables

Next, we turn our attention to the relationships among household income, Asian ethnicity, household structure, immigrant status, and selected individual characteristics. A listing of the variables used in this analysis, their definitions, and their availability across the four data sets can be found in appendix 4.A. Most of the variables included in our analysis are conventionally used in similar research and require no additional explanation. However, we briefly describe some of the variables that are particularly important for our research goals.

These include nativity and period of immigration, extended household, English proficiency, and residence in Pacific states.

Nativity and period of immigration are among the more important predictor variables in our model of Asian American socioeconomic status. As discussed earlier, compared with native-born workers, immigrants are often disadvantaged for several reasons: Foreigners often experience prejudice; immigrants may be excluded from certain jobs, and they are unfamiliar with the U.S. labor market; and their schooling may not transfer easily to the United States. Some of these handicaps may be overcome with longer residence in the United States; therefore, it is necessary to separate immigrants by recency of immigration. This variable allows us to examine first, the effects of foreign birth, and second, the effects of duration of residence in the United States. The categories used to measure duration of residence are not exactly similar for the four data sets (as noted in appendix 4.A) but are as similar as possible.

We included the effects of extended household in our model because members of immigrant and some minority groups are more likely to reside in such households (instead of nuclear family households). Extended households may facilitate higher socioeconomic attainment by allowing members to save on housing costs, by pooling resources, and by offering other forms of social support (for example, child care).

A variable that is related to nativity and period of immigration is English proficiency. This factor is particularly significant for examining Asian immigrants' socioeconomic integration because most Asian immigrants come from societies where English is not the indigenous language. Little or no English serves to reduce participation in the labor market. At the same time, we note that for Asian immigrants, the ethnic economy may provide opportunities that do not require English language skills (refer to the earlier section on theories of group inequality). We compared the effects of self-reported English proficiency.

We included a measure of geographical distribution in our analysis. We follow the Bureau of the Census's definition of the Pacific region and include California, Hawaii, Washington, and Oregon (but not Alaska). The Asian American population is concentrated on the West Coast. Over half of all Asian Americans live in California (40 percent) or Hawaii (11 percent), and the West Coast remains the top destination for many Asian immigrants (O'Hare and Felt 1991). This variable is, therefore, an indirect measure of the effects of minority concentration on minority income, given the large representation of Asians in the Pacific states. At the same time, we recognize that wage levels are generally higher in some metropolitan areas of the Pacific states, complicating the interpretation of this factor's influence.

Household income is an important outcome variable because of growing appreciation of the household as the context for socioeconomic behavior and base for social mobility, particularly among immigrants and some minority groups. We attempt to compare four data points in this part of our empirical analysis, but it should be noted that such a comparison is severely constrained by variable measurements and availability. For example, the 1980 Census data include all households identifying themselves as Asian, including foreign- and native-born, regardless of generations in the United States (in other words, the 1980 PUMS sample can be divided into just two groups—the foreign-born first generation and the U.S.-born second and higher generations). The 1986 and 1988 CPS data include only the first- and second-generation Asian-origin persons; third- and higher-generation individuals are not included. The 1989 CPS contains first, second, third, and higher generations. This complicates any evaluation of the effect of generational status. Missing data also make it impossible to include every variable for each of the four data sets. In spite of variable measurement and availability problems, we still believe that a comparison across the four data points can yield important information that would otherwise be absent altogether.

Table 4.4 contains descriptive statistics from all four data sets and compares Asians and whites on the dependent and main predictor variables. Measured in 1980 dollars, mean Asian household incomes are higher than whites for all years except 1989, when we see that whites' mean household income is slightly higher. Among Asian Americans, the general pattern shows much higher household incomes for the native-born (the 1986 CPS sample deviates from this overall pattern). Of all the major groups, foreign-born Asian Americans' household incomes tend to be lowest (again, with the exception of the 1986 CPS sample).

Turning to the predictor variables shown in table 4.4, we note that our samples of white males are slightly older. Compared with whites, Asian Americans have more years of schooling; live in larger households that are more likely to be extended and to contain young children below six years old; are concentrated in the Pacific states; have more people in the labor force per household; and are generally more likely to have a married head of household. We note that because of the high percentage of foreign-born among Asian Ameri-

Table 4.4 DESCRIPTIVE STATISTICS FOR OUTCOME AND PREDICTOR VARIABLES, ASIANS AND WHITES[a]

Variable	1980 PUMS Asians	Whites	1986 CPS Asians	Whites	1988 CPS Asians	Whites	1989 CPS Asians	Whites
Outcome variable								
Mean household income (in 1980 constant dollars)	27,421	25,843	22,635	20,928	22,640	22,205	24,868	24,898
Foreign-born	25,806	—	22,659	—	21,692	—	24,360	—
Second generation	30,656[b]	—	22,458	—	28,859	—	27,892	—
Third generation	N.A.	—	N.A.	—	N.A.	—	24,495	—
Predictor variables								
Mean years of schooling	16.2	14.8	13.4	13.0	13.7	13.2	13.8	13.2
Mean age (18–64)	36.9	38.1	39.6	40.6	39.6	40.5	39.5	40.9
Mean household size	3.8	3.3	3.5	2.8	3.4	2.7	3.3	2.7
Mean number of workers in the household[c]	1.8	1.6	N.A.	N.A.	N.A.	N.A.	1.3	1.2
Percent native-born	33.3	96.8	12.6	96.9	13.5	97.0	27.2	97.2
Percent married	66.2	68.2	73.7	64.8	70.8	62.6	69.0	61.9
Percent in extended households	22.9	11.1	16.2	6.0	17.4	6.0	14.6	5.5
Percent residing in Pacific region	54.8	14.4	46.6	13.9	47.8	12.4	51.4	12.4
Percent native English speaker	27.9	94.9	N.A.	N.A.	N.A.	N.A.	30.7	91.4
Percent with children younger than 6 years	14.7	10.5	31.2	19.7	27.4	19.7	28.0	20.1

continued

Table 4.4 DESCRIPTIVE STATISTICS FOR OUTCOME AND PREDICTOR VARIABLES, ASIANS AND WHITES[a]

Variable	1980 PUMS		1986 CPS		1988 CPS		1989 CPS	
	Asians	Whites	Asians	Whites	Asians	Whites	Asians	Whites
Percent in managerial occupations	12.9	12.9	N.A.	N.A.	N.A.	N.A.	12.8	14.2
Percent in service occupations	12.7	6.9	N.A.	N.A.	N.A.	N.A.	11.0	7.5
Sample size	8,517	104,590	758	3,425	677	3,104	981	3,213

Notes:
a. "Whites" include about 3 percent who are foreign-born.
b. For the 1980 data, the native-born are not separated by generation, so this number refers to all U.S.-born Asian Americans, regardless of generation.
c. For the 1989 CPS, this variable refers to the number of employed people in the family.

cans, only about 30 percent are native English speakers compared to over 90 percent of whites. Finally, Asian Americans are as likely as whites to be in managerial occupations but much more likely to be in service occupations.

Results

In this section, we report the findings from testing an additive model in which all predictor variables are entered into the regression equation. We do not report the results from examining several models with interactive terms because these did not reveal statistically significant interactive terms. In particular, we estimated a model predicting household income separately for whites and Asians. Then, we tested for statistically significant different regression coefficients for each explanatory variable between the two groups. Given the absence of statistically significant differences, we decided to exposit a simpler model. The presented model has fewer conceptual ambiguities and estimates only main effects for the included explanatory variables.[8] The regression coefficients in table 4.5 are to be interpreted in the standard way—each coefficient shows the difference (either positive or negative) that the particular term makes to the constant term, after controlling for all other variables in the equation.

ETHNICITY

We begin with the effects of ethnicity on Asian Americans' household income. Compared to non-Hispanic whites, only Japanese Americans show consistently higher returns to household income from their ethnicity (statistically significant in 1980 and 1989). Some Asian groups that had a similar positive effect in 1980 (for example, Indians) were no longer advantaged by 1989. While most of the effects of Asian ethnicity are not significant, we note that first, the negative effect for Chinese ethnicity was observed throughout the 1980s and was significant in 1980 and 1988 and continues (although not significant) throughout the 1980s, and second, at some point during the 1980s, Koreans and Vietnamese experienced significantly lower returns to their household incomes, holding all other variables in the equation constant.

EDUCATION

The effects of this important human capital individual characteristic are strong and consistent and are in the expected direction. Higher

Table 4.5 REGRESSION ANALYSIS OF HOUSEHOLD INCOME
(in 1980 constant dollars)

Variable	1980 Coefficient	1980 Standard Error	1986 Coefficient	1986 Standard Error	1988 Coefficient	1988 Standard Error	1989 Coefficient	1989 Standard Error
Constant	2,604*	247	13,475*	1,498	9,270*	1,591	14,279*	1,848
Ethnicity								
White	0	—	0	—	0	—	0	—
Japanese	951**	310	1,737	2,710	2,405	2,722	4,386*	1,814
Chinese	-1,316**	317	-1,911	2,182	-4,441*	2,199	-2,112	1,749
Filipino	401	403	-3,089	2,223	-2,535	2,204	120	1,768
Korean	-72	529	-2,533	2,343	-3,308	2,665	-4,202*	2,159
Indian	1,703**	403	-1,202	2,454	-2,780	2,394	-929	2,200
Vietnamese	-167	613	53	2,676	-7,232**	2,536	1,945	2,474
Education								
<12 years	0	—	0	—	0	—	0	—
12 years	5,148**	114	3,666**	823	4,551**	865	4,203**	880
13–15 years	6,730**	133	6,150**	945	8,185**	969	7,142**	997
16+ years	10,840**	143	12,312**	880	20,383**	906	14,045**	1,039
Marital Status								
Married	0	—	0	—	0	—	0	—
Widowed	-5,194**	449	-9,959**	1,702	-13,464**	1,633	-7,614**	1,744
Divorced	-1,183**	160	-6,959**	835	-10,438**	841	-5,499**	917
Single	667**	117	-7,338**	841	-10,276**	861	-4,761**	934
Nativity and Immigration								
Native	0	—	0	—	0	—	0	—
<5 years	-5,921**	343	-2,571**	2,157	-7,874**	2,465	-6,701**	1,879
5–10 years	-2,208**	397	22	2,017	-4,406*	2,139	-4,348*	1,871
10+ years	642**	247	4,138**	1,618	1,534	1,597	3,279**	1,345

Children								
<6 years	-2,180**	140	-250	747	-1,011	775	-1,112	710
Extended Household	2,677**	125	1,881	1,068	4,023**	1,056	986	1,065
No. Workers	7,512**	46	N.A.	—	N.A.	—	4,563**	343
Age	199**	4	89**	27	180**	28	193**	27
English Proficiency								
Native	0	—	N.A.	—	N.A.	—	0	—
Well +	-572**	188	N.A.	—	N.A.	—	-1,489	1,153
Poor	-3,584**	419	N.A.	—	N.A.	—	-2,433	1,869
None	-5,254**	912	N.A.	—	N.A.	—	-5,585	3,971
Pacific	1,701**	1,12	1,688*	830	2,156*	955	1,487*	730
Occupation								
Managers	0	—	N.A.	—	N.A.	—	0	—
Professionals	-67	159	N.A.	—	N.A.	—	-2,095*	1,017
Technical	-2,885**	245	N.A.	—	N.A.	—	-8,798**	1,578
Sales	-1,336**	167	N.A.	—	N.A.	—	-5,399**	1,071
Clerical	-3,293**	180	N.A.	—	N.A.	—	-12,511**	1,232
Crafts	-2,774**	133	N.A.	—	N.A.	—	-11,003**	1,038
Service	-5,918**	177	N.A.	—	N.A.	—	-12,986**	1,204
Operators	-3,621**	135	N.A.	—	N.A.	—	-12,104**	1,059
Farm	-6,553**	219	N.A.	—	N.A.	—	-16,865**	1,740
R^2	0.290		0.106		0.254		0.348	
F-ratio	1,494**		23.56**		60.78**		65.29**	
Sample Size	113,107		4,182		3,780		4,193	

Notes:
*Statistically significant, $p < .05$.
**Statistically significant, $p < .01$.

educational attainment by the head of household consistently translates into higher returns to household incomes.

MARITAL STATUS

Compared to the reference category of "married," all other categories (except for "single" in 1980) show negative effects. The negative effects from being widowed or divorced or single are all statistically significant for the 1986, 1988, and 1989 CPS data.

NATIVITY AND IMMIGRATION PERIOD

Nativity and period of immigration is a variable of particular interest because of this research's focus on immigrant adaptation. Compared to the native-born, we expect immigrant households to be poorer, and for this negative effect to be larger among the most recent immigrants. This pattern appears to be confirmed for all immigrants except those who arrived ten or more years ago. Relatively recent immigrants—that is, those who arrived in the United States within the last ten years—all experience a significant negative effect on their household incomes. However, all four data points reveal that longer-term immigrants—that is, those who have been in the United States ten or more years—have statistically significant higher returns to household income (the coefficient for the 1988 CPS is not significant but is in the same direction). It appears that not all foreign-born households are always poorer than native-born households; however, it appears that the households of the most recently arrived are consistently the poorest. The disruptive effects of immigration are most intense on arrival and disappear slowly over time. Judging from these results, it may take at least ten years before immigrant households leave behind the disadvantages associated with foreign birth and immigrant status.

PRESENCE OF YOUNG CHILDREN

The presence of young children (below six years old) in a household can decrease household income by creating additional expenses and discouraging women's work outside the home. As expected, its effect is negative, but it is statistically significant only with the 1980 data.

EXTENDED HOUSEHOLD

An extended household contains others besides members of a nuclear family. Such households are expected to have higher incomes because of the presence of other adults to help with child care or because more people are available for labor force participation. The results are in the expected direction, and the positive effects of extended households are statistically significant in the 1980 and 1988 data.

NUMBER OF WORKERS

This variable was available only for the 1980 and 1989 data, and its effect on household income is as expected and is also statistically significant. Households with more workers have higher incomes, although we should note that this does not necessarily mean that such households are always economically advantaged over those with fewer workers. Many workers in a household, each earning a low income, may add up to a substantial household income, but the individual earnings of such workers are substantially lower than that of a single-worker household with a comparable household income. Multiple-worker households may, therefore, contain adults with less ability to obtain jobs that pay well.

AGE

Age of household head is generally used as a proxy measure of experience in the labor force; more experience commands higher incomes. The effects of age are all positive and significant across the four data points.

ENGLISH PROFICIENCY

This important variable relates directly to immigrant integration and adjustment. Proficiency in English is probably one of the most crucial factors in facilitating immigrants' socioeconomic success and related adaptation. For Asian immigrants whose native languages are not English or who have never been exposed to an English-language environment, lack of facility in English can be a major obstacle. We have data from 1980 and 1989 to evaluate the effects of this variable and note that while the coefficients are all in the expected direction, they are significant with the 1980 data but not with the 1989 data. As expected, the negative effects of non-native English language are much larger among those without any English or who speak it poorly, although it is interesting that even those who believe that they speak English very well or well still suffer a disadvantage compared to native English speakers.

RESIDENCE IN PACIFIC STATES

We include this variable because of the geographical concentration of so many Asian Americans in these states. Residence in the Pacific states adds to household income, and the effects of this factor are all statistically significant. Thus, the concentration of Asian Americans in this part of the United States is related to their observed higher household incomes.

OCCUPATIONAL GROUP

We use the occupational classification system that evolved from the 1980 Standard Occupational Classification system. This classification of occupations into nine broad categories has been used by the decennial census beginning in 1980 and the CPS since January, 1983. The nine occupational groups are: (1) executives, administration, and managers; (2) professionals; (3) technical and related support; (4) sales; (5) clerical and administrative support; (6) service; (7) crafts and precision production; (8) operators, fabricators, and laborers; and (9) farming, forestry, and fishing. The excluded category is executive, administrative, and managerial occupations, and we are able to compare 1980 and 1989 data. All occupational groups have lower returns compared to the reference category of managerial and administrative occupations. In addition, all the coefficients are significant except for professional occupations in 1980. According to these data, the household income gap between managerial/administrative occupations and all other occupations increased rather substantially during the 1980s.

Summary

Summarizing the results from the regression analysis of household income, we can conclude (with caution, given the data and measurement problems already described) that Asian immigrant households are generally poorer than households headed by native-born whites, after controlling for the explanatory variables included in table 4.5. The socioeconomic disadvantages of immigrant households are particularly large for recent arrivals. Immigrant households without many workers or without an extended family structure will be even poorer. Immigrants who are not native English speakers (and most Asian immigrants fall into this group) experience lower incomes, even if they speak English well or very well. Finally, comparisons from 1980 to 1989 suggest that except for Japanese households, many

Asian American households appear to have lower household incomes than non-Hispanic white households, after holding constant all other variables in the equation.

Figure 4.1 summarizes in graphical form the findings from the regression analysis. This graph shows the observed difference in household income in a solid bar at the top of the graph, comparing the observed household income for each Asian American ethnic group to the observed household income for the white population. The graph also shows the composition effects for the ten variables included in the regression analysis, reported in table 4.5. The composition effect for a specific variable is calculated by multiplying two items: (1) the difference in the observed composition of the ethnic group, compared with the white population, and (2) the estimated regression coefficient. For example, the composition effect for the age variable for Indians (the third shaded line for composition effects) is calculated by multiplying the observed difference in mean age for Indians, compared with the white population, times the estimated regression coefficient for age. In this instance, Indians tend to be younger and hence, given a positive regression coefficient of 193 for the effect of age on household income, a moderate negative composition effect of age on household income is shown for Indians.

Overall, the Indian and Japanese groups have considerably higher observed household incomes, compared with white households. Chinese and Filipino households exceed white household incomes by a smaller extent, and Korean and Vietnamese households have lower observed household incomes than the white population. Three groups of composition variables can be distinguished.

The first group, education and occupation, reflects the human capital qualities of the head of the household. On these measures, the Indian, Chinese, Japanese, and Korean groups have positive effects derived from the education and occupation of the household head. Filipino households derive a positive effect from education, but a small negative effect from occupation. Only the Vietnamese have a negative effect from both education and occupation.

A second group of variables reflects the impact of household structure: age of household head, extended household, marital status of household head, number of workers, and the presence of young children. Our analysis reveals that this set of variables has a generally modest impact on difference in observed household income. Most Asian American households derive a mixed positive and negative set of effects due to their household structure. A few notable exceptions are shown. Filipino households have a relatively high number

Figure 4.1 DECOMPOSITION OF HOUSEHOLD INCOME FOR ASIAN AMERICAN ETHNIC GROUPS, 1989

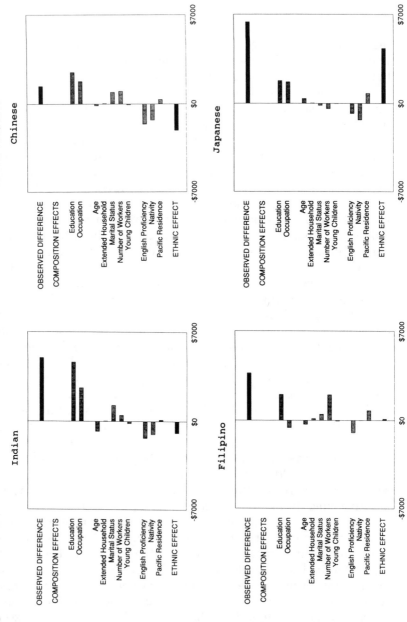

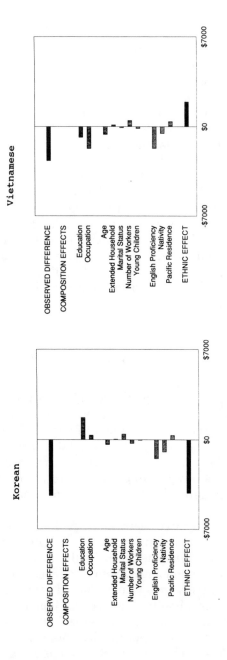

of workers per household and, as a result, receive a moderate composition effect (positive $2,000).

Finally, a third set of variables indicates immigration-related effects: proficiency in English, nativity and recency of immigration, and residence in the Pacific region. All Asian American groups experience a negative impact on their household income related to English proficiency and their immigrant origins. Residence in the Pacific region, however, partially offsets this negative impact with the slightly higher household incomes.

Overall, the regression analysis summarized in figure 4.1 suggests sizable effects on household income for some Asian American groups from human capital characteristics (Indian, Chinese, Filipino, Japanese, and Korean), mixed and counterbalancing effects from family structure characteristics, and negative impacts from immigration-related variables. These compositional variables do not account for the entire difference of Asian Americans' household income compared with white households. Our analysis also reveals that each Asian American group experiences specific (and generally negative) household income differences not accounted for by the variables in this regression analysis.

DISCUSSION AND CONCLUSION

The research reported here is part of a body of research addressing the integration of America's newest immigrants. Within this framework, we approach the issue of Asian immigrants' integration by examining the effects of immigrant status, Asian race and ethnicity, and individual and household characteristics on socioeconomic status. We see socioeconomic integration as fundamental to other dimensions of immigrant adjustment, including social and political integration.

We briefly summarize five main findings. First, the growth and increased diversity of the Asian American population, first observed in the 1970s, continued unabated through the 1980s. Immigration is the main reason for these changes. Some evidence suggests that the increased ethnic diversity may also include diversity of individual characteristics such as schooling and socioeconomic status. Second, our analysis of household income shows that households headed by Asian immigrants tend to be poorer than households headed by native-born Americans. The poorest households are those with the most recently arrived Asians. At least ten years are apparently needed before immigrant households leave behind the socioeconomic disadvantage associated with immigrant status. Third, the role of extended households and multiple workers in raising household income is particularly important among immigrants. Fourth, lack of proficiency in English exacts a heavy price on the earnings of Asian American households. While not as large as the negative impact of poor English, even those Asian Americans with good English facility are at a disadvantage compared to native speakers. Fifth, of all the Asian ethnic groups we examined, only the Japanese continued to maintain a consistent edge over whites in household income during the last decade. While the effects of Asian ethnicity on socioeconomic status are generally not statistically significant, nevertheless, the findings are suggestive of an ethnicity-based disadvantage that is possibly related to persistent discrimination against Asian Americans.

On the whole, our results are consistent with previous research on the effects of various predictor factors on Asian Americans' status. Those individual characteristics that increase Asian Americans' household incomes include their high levels of education, their greater likelihood to be married, and their higher participation in professional occupations. Individual characteristics that negatively affect socioeconomic status include immigrant status and recency of immigration, younger age, employment in service occupations, and lack of native English (and almost all Asian immigrants fall into this category). Among the structural factors that we examined, Asian ethnicity is generally a negative factor, whereas residence in extended households that are more likely to have more workers and in the Pacific states raised household incomes. Our results provide support for theories of attainment that stress the role of individual characteristics. At the same time, an apparent individual characteristic such as Asian ethnicity may function more as a structural factor in maintaining a lower socioeconomic status for Asian Americans than would be expected based on their other individual and structural characteristics.

Our ability to examine four different data sets throughout the 1980s led to the identification of certain trends that suggest significant changes in the aggregate socioeconomic status of Asian Americans. The decline in average years of schooling among Asian Americans and the dominance of immigrant households in this population contribute to what appears to be a retreat in socioeconomic well-being, as measured by household incomes.

We note, however, that the findings reported here require better data for confirmation. Additionally, for several reasons, the results should be interpreted with much caution. Given the role played by immigration in the Asian American population, this population is characterized by a high degree of flux, which vastly complicates research efforts to identify the factors that are most important in influencing its integration into American society. We remind the reader of the many caveats regarding the data used in this analysis (see earlier sections on data, results from the analysis of household income, and note 8).

This research points to several questions or issues that can be usefully explored to further understanding on the larger issue of integrating Asian immigrants into U.S. society. Given the different profile of Japanese Americans from other Asian ethnic groups (in terms of nativity and other dimensions), future analyses of Asian Americans must specify ethnicity as a basic variable or risk distorting analysis by grouping sociologically different groups together. A more accurate analysis of Asian Americans can be obtained by classifying Asian Americans by nativity and generational status. This would also highlight the role of immigration in studying the Asian population, a factor that is central to research on Asian Americans.

How will changes in Asian immigrants' characteristics potentially affect this population's prospects for integration into U.S. society? The observed social stratification within the Asian American population is closely tied to immigrant status and duration of residence in the United States. More recent arrivals tend to be less well-educated and experience greater socioeconomic disadvantages. This relationship between immigrant status and period of immigration and socioeconomic well-being holds important implications for both immigration policy and immigrant integration. If current immigration policy remains unchanged, then we expect that this pattern of declining socioeconomic status among Asian Americans will continue, mainly because the Asian American population will be even more immigrant-based and will be continually replenished by new arrivals. Thus, socioeconomic and other forms of integration of Asian Americans will be very slow, simply because of the effects of immigrant status and other immigrant-related factors in this process, as reported in this paper.

Finally, we ask what this research means for the acceptance of Asian Americans as Americans. The integration of a particular immigrant group into U.S. society depends upon the relationship between immigrant and host. The history of the treatment of Asians in the United States suggests that the dominant white society had, in the past, either remained ignorant of the presence of Asians or had explicitly rejected their right to be in the United States through formal and informal actions. Now that Asian Americans are a growing population and have the formal right to immigrate to the United States and become U.S. citizens, it is timely to ask whether the identity of "American" has broadened to include people of Asian ancestries. The answers are many and range from optimistic "America as the world's first universal nation" to pessimistic accountings of all the ways in which Asian Americans are reminded of their "otherness" by Americans of European descent. In the end, therefore, when researchers attempt to examine the question of immigrant integration through empirical analyses, we cannot forget the role of public opinion, politicians, and other social institutions in affecting the immigrant's journey to integration and acceptance.

Notes

1. Asian Americans include native-born Americans of Asian ancestries and foreign-born Asians who may or may not be U.S. citizens.

2. The percentage increases refer to the combined Asian American and Pacific Islander population. However, the Pacific Islanders are a small part of this combined group: in 1990, Pacific Islanders were 4.4 percent of the combined Asian/Pacific Islander population.

3. Bouvier and Agresta (1987) report on fertility variations among Asian ethnic groups—for example, Vietnamese fertility is higher than the national average, whereas Chinese, Japanese, and Indian fertility levels are lower than the national average. More recent immigrants also tend to start with higher fertility but are expected to converge to the national average over time.

4. Our selection of Asian groups was based on the need to have sufficient sample sizes for analysis. We also restricted our samples to people between ages 18 and 64 because of our interest in earnings. The age brackets will bias certain characteristics—for example, the mean age of our samples.

5. We used "hot-deck" imputation procedures to impute the country of birth for respondents or parents with missing data on the country of birth question. We created a hot deck of prior valid responses classified by age, sex, and ethnicity and then imputed missing data by a random selection from the prior responses. The hot deck was continuously updated whenever a valid response was selected. We used hot deck imputation for about 6 percent of the respondents and about 15 percent of the parents for the 1986 and 1988 CPS. Examination of bivariate distributions before and after the imputation revealed a satisfactory use of the procedure.

6. To examine the potential bias in the selection of Asians for the 1986 and 1988 samples, we applied the same hot deck procedures to the 1989 CPS, where respondents' self-identification as Asian was known. We found a modest proportion (2 percent) of persons born in an Asian country who indicated that they were not Asian. Most of

these individuals reported their race as "white," suggesting that they were born to "white" parents who were temporarily residing in an Asian country. On the other hand, a similarly modest proportion (3 percent) of foreign-born persons, who self-identified as Asian, were born in regions other than Asia. Some gave their country of birth as an African country (for example, Indians born in Uganda) or Canada or Europe. Overall, our imputation procedure gives a slight underestimate of Asian immigrants and includes a modest amount of misidentification of Asian ancestry.

7. The data in table 4.3 suggest that changes in the national origins, conditions of entry into the United States, and recency of arrival of Asian immigrants in the 1980s have produced a decline in the average schooling of Asian immigrants. It may well be the case that such a decline may not be observed when only aggregate levels of schooling for all foreign-born Asians are examined (see Sorensen and Enchautegui in this volume).

8. It should also be noted that we did not test for interaction terms for each Asian ethnic group. The small sample sizes for each ethnic group limited separate analyses for statistical tests between groups. The results reported assume, therefore, that income returns to education are similar for each Asian ethnic group. This assumption needs to be tested with additional analysis using larger samples.

APPENDIX 4.A
DESCRIPTION OF VARIABLES USED IN
ANALYSIS OF HOUSEHOLD INCOME

(Available Variables Marked With an X)

Variable Name and Categories	Variable Description	Availability 1980	1986	1988	1989
Ethnicity					
Non-Hispanic Whites (excluded category) Japanese Chinese Filipino Korean Asian Indian Vietnamese Other	A series of dummy variables coded 1 if the respondent is of that ethnicity, and otherwise 0.	X	X	X	X
Education					
Less than High School (excluded category) High School Post High School College and More	A series of dummy variables measuring highest grade of schooling attained.	X	X	X	X
Marital Status					
Married (excluded category) Widowed Divorced Single	A series of dummy variables	X	X	X	X
Nativity and Period of Immigration					
Native-born (excluded category) Immigration less than 5 years ago (1980, 1986, and 1989; for 1988, less than 4 years ago) Immigration between 5 and 10 years ago (1980;	A series of dummy variables. As noted, the categories are not exactly the same across the samples because of the way the data were originally collected. We use the closest approximation.	X	X	X	X

Variable Name and Categories	Variable Description	Availability			
		1980	1986	1988	1989
for 1986, between 5 and 11 years ago; for 1988, between 4 and 8 years ago; for 1989, between 5 and 9 years ago)					
Immigration more than 10 years ago (1980; for 1986, more than 11 years ago; for 1988, more than 8 years ago; for 1989, more than 9 years ago)					
Presence of Children Under 6 years	A dichotomous variable.	X	X	X	X
Extended Household	A dichotomous variable. An extended household contains others besides members of the nuclear family.	X	X	X	X
Number of Workers in Household		X	NA	NA	X
	Measured as a continuous variable.				
Age	Actual age.	X	X	X	X
English Proficiency Native English Speaker (excluded category) Speak Well or Very Well Speak Poorly No English	A series of dummy variables based on self-report.	X	NA	NA	X
Pacific States Residence	Dichotomous variable.	X	X	X	X
Occupational Group Managerial and administrative (excluded category) Professional Technical Sales Clerical Crafts Service Operators Farm	A series of dummy variables. Occupations were grouped into nine main categories.	X	NA	NA	X

References

Angel, Ronald, and Marta Tienda. 1982. "Determinants of Extended Household Structure: Cultural Pattern or Economic Need?" *American Journal of Sociology* 87: 1360–83.
Bach, Robert L., and Rita Carroll-Seguin. 1986. "Labor Force Participation and Sponsorship among Southeast Asian Refugees." *International Migration Review* 20: 381–404.
Bailey, Thomas, and Roger Waldinger. 1990. "The Continuing Significance of Race: Racial Discrimination and Racial Conflict in Construction." Paper presented at the American Sociological Association Annual Meeting. Washington, D.C., August 11–15.
Barringer, Felicity. 1991a. "Despite Some Hispanic Gains, Report Finds They Still Lag." *The New York Times*, 11 April.
————. 1991b. "Immigration Brings New Diversity to Asian Population in the U.S." *The New York Times*, 12 June.
Barringer, Herbert R., David T. Takeuchi, and Peter Xenos. 1990. "Education, Occupational Prestige, and Income of Asian Americans." *Sociology of Education* 63: 27–43.
Becker, Gary S. 1964. *Human Capital*. New York: Columbia University Press.
Berg, Ivar. 1969. *Education and Jobs*. New York: Praeger.
Blau, Peter, and O. D. Duncan. 1967. *The American Occupational Structure*. New York: John Wiley and Sons, Inc.
Bonacich, Edna. 1973. "A Theory of Middleman Minorities." *American Sociological Review* 38: 583–94.
Bonacich, Edna, and John Modell. 1980. *The Economic Basis of Ethnic Solidarity: Small Business in the Japanese American Community*. Berkeley: University of California Press.
Borjas, George J. 1985. "Assimilation, Changes in Cohort Quality, and the Earnings of Immigrants." *Journal of Labor Economics* 3: 463–489.
Boswell, Terry E. 1986. "A Split Labor Market Analysis of Discrimination against Chinese Immigrants, 1850–1882." *American Sociological Review* 51: 352–71.
Bouvier, Leon F., and Anthony J. Agresta. 1987. "The Future Asian Population of the United States." *Pacific Bridges: The New Immigration from Asia and the Pacific Islands*, edited by James T. Fawcett and Benjamin V. Carino (285–301). New York: Center for Migration Studies.
Boyd, Monica. 1984. "At a Disadvantage: The Occupational Attainments of Foreign-born Women in Canada." *International Migration Review* 18: 1091–1119.
Boyd, Robert L. 1990. "Black and Asian Self-Employment in Large Metropolitan Areas: A Comparative Analysis." *Social Problems* 37: 258–74.
Brown, David L., and Glenn V. Fuguitt. 1972. "Percent Non-white and Racial Disparity in Nonmetropolitan Cities in the South." *Social Science Quarterly* 53: 573–82.

Carliner, Geoffrey. 1980. "Wages, Earnings and Hours of First, Second, and Third Generation American Males." *Economic Inquiry* 18: 87–102.

Chiswick, Barry R. 1978. "The Effect of Americanization on the Earnings of Foreign-born Men." *Journal of Political Economy* 86: 897–921.

Cummings, Scott, ed. 1980. *Self-help in Urban America: Patterns of Minority Business Enterprise.* Port Washington, N.Y.: Kennikat.

Duncan, Otis Dudley, David L. Featherman, and Beverly Duncan. 1972. *Socioeconomic Background and Achievement.* New York: Seminar.

The Economist. 1991. "America's Blacks: A World Apart." 30 March, 17–21.

Frisbie, W. Parker, and Lisa Neidert. 1977. "Inequality and the Relative Size of Minority Populations: A Comparative Analysis." *American Journal of Sociology* 82: 1007–1030.

Gardner, Robert, Brian Robey, and Peter C. Smith. 1985. "Asian Americans: Growth, Change, and Diversity." *Population Bulletin* 40 (4). Washington, D.C.: Population Reference Bureau.

Gordon, Milton M. 1964. *Assimilation in American Life.* New York: Oxford University Press.

Hirschman, Charles, and Ellen P. Kraly. 1990. "Racial and Ethnic Inequality in the United States, 1940 and 1950: The Impact of Geographic Location and Human Capital." *International Migration Review* 24: 4–33.

Hurh, Won M., and Kwang C. Kim. 1989. "The 'Success' Image of Asian Americans: Its Validity and Its Practical and Theoretical Implications." *Ethnic and Racial Studies* 12: 512–538.

Jaynes, Gerald, and Robin M. Williams, eds. 1989. *A Common Destiny.* Washington, D.C.: National Academy of Science.

Lee, Sharon M. 1989. "Asian Immigration and American Race Relations: From Exclusion to Acceptance?" *Ethnic and Racial Studies* 12: 368–390.

————. 1990a. "Minority Group Household Structure and Economic Well-Being." Paper presented at the American Sociological Association Annual Meeting. Washington, D.C., August 11–15.

————. 1990b. "Integrating America's Newest Immigrants: Some Lessons from the Past." Paper presented at the Social Science History Association Annual Meeting. Minneapolis, October 18–21.

————. 1994. "Poverty and the U.S. Asian Population." *Social Science Quarterly* (forthcoming, September).

Lee, Sharon M., and Keiko Yamanaka. 1989. "Household Structure, Minority Group Labor Force Participation, and Income Attainment." Paper presented at the American Sociological Association Annual Meeting. San Francisco, August 9–13.

Lieberson, Stanley. 1980. *A Piece of the Pie: Black and White Immigrants since 1880.* Berkeley: University of California Press.

Light, Ivan, and Edna Bonacich. 1988. *Immigrant Entrepreneurs: Koreans in Los Angeles, 1965–1982.* Berkeley: University of California Press.

Long, James E. 1980. "The Effect of Americanization on Earnings: Some Evidence for Women." *Journal of Political Economy* 88: 620–29.

McLanahan, Sara. 1985. "Family Structure and the Reproduction of Poverty." *American Journal of Sociology* 90: 873–901.

Massey, Douglas S. 1981. "Dimensions of the New Immigration to the United States and the Prospects for Assimilation." *Annual Review of Sociology* 7: 57–85.

Min, Pyong Gap. 1990. "Immigrant Entrepreneurship and Wives' Overwork: Koreans in New York City." Paper presented at the American Sociological Association Annual Meeting. Washington, D.C., August 11–15.

Model, Suzanne. 1988. "The Economic Progress of European and East Asian Americans." *Annual Review of Sociology* 14: 363–380.

Nee, Victor, and J. Sanders. 1985. "The Road to Parity: Determinants of the Socioeconomic Achievements of Asian Americans." *Ethnic and Racial Studies* 8: 75–93.

Nee, Victor, and Herbert Y. Wong. 1985. "Asian American Socioeconomic Achievement: The Strength of the Family Bond." *Sociological Perspectives* 28: 281–306.

O'Hare, William P., and Judy C. Felt. 1991. *Asian Americans: America's Fastest Growing Minority Group.* Population Trends and Public Policy Occasional Papers, No. 19. Washington, D.C.: Population Reference Bureau.

O'Hare, William P., Kelvin M. Pollard, Taynia L. Mann, and Mary M. Kent. 1991. "African Americans in the 1990s." *Population Bulletin* 46 (1). Washington, D.C.: Population Reference Bureau.

Passel, Jeffrey. 1991. "Demography of the United States." Unpublished charts. Washington, D.C.: The Urban Institute.

Passell, Peter. 1991. "Chronic Poverty, Black and White." *New York Times,* 6 March.

Perez, Lisandro. 1986. "Immigrant Economic Adjustment and Family Organization: the Cuban Success Story Re-examined." *International Migration Review* 20: 4–20.

Portes, Alejandro, and Robert L. Bach. 1985. *Latin Journey: Cuban and Mexican Immigrants in the United States.* Berkeley: University of California Press.

Sanders, J. M., and Victor G. Nee. 1987. "Limits of Ethnic Solidarity in the Enclave Economy." *American Sociological Review* 52: 745–773.

Saxton, Alexander. 1971. *The Indispensable Enemy: Labor and the Anti-Chinese Movement in California.* Berkeley: University of California Press.

Siegel, Paul M. 1965. "On the Cost of Being a Negro." *Sociological Inquiry* 35: 41–57.

Staples, Robert, and Alfredo Mirande. 1980. "Racial and Cultural Variations among American Families: A Decennial Review of the Literature on Minority Families." *Journal of Marriage and the Family* 42: 887–903.

Tienda, Marta. 1980. "Familism and Structural Assimilation of Mexican Immigrants in the United States." *International Migration Review* 14: 383–408.

Tienda, Marta, and Ronald Angel. 1982. "Headship and Extended Household Composition among Blacks, Hispanics, and Whites." *Social Forces* 61: 508–531.

Tienda, Marta, and Jennifer N. Glass. 1985. "Household Structure and Labor Force Participation of Black, Hispanic, and White Mothers." *Demography* 22: 381–394.

Tienda, Marta, and Ding-Tzann Lii. 1987. "Minority Concentration and Earnings Inequality: Blacks, Hispanics, and Asians Compared." *American Journal of Sociology* 93: 141–165.

U.S. Bureau of the Census. 1983. *Census of Population and Housing, 1980: Public Use Microdata Samples, Technical Documentation.* Washington, D.C.: U.S. Government Printing Office.

————. 1991. "Census Bureau Completes Distribution of 1990 Redistricting Tabulations of States." Release: March 11, 1991, CB91-100.

U.S. Commission on Civil Rights. 1988. *The Economic Status of Americans of Asian Descent: An Exploratory Investigation.* Washington, D.C.: U.S. Commission on Civil Rights, Clearinghouse Publication 95.

U.S. General Accounting Office. 1990. *Asian Americans. A Status Report.* Washington, D.C.: U.S. General Accounting Office.

Vobejda, Barbara. 1991. "Asians, Hispanics Giving Nation More Diversity." *The Washington Post,* 12 June.

Wilson, Kenneth L., and W. Allen Martin. 1982. "Ethnic Enclaves: A Comparison of the Cuban and Black Economies in Miami." *American Journal of Sociology* 88: 135–160.

Wilson, Kenneth L., and Alejandro Portes. 1980. "Immigrant Enclaves: An Analysis of the Labor Market Experiences of Cubans in Miami." *American Journal of Sociology* 86: 295–319.

Woo, Deborah. 1985. "The Socioeconomic Status of Asian American Women in the Labor Force: An Alternative View." *Sociological Perspective* 28: 307–338.

Yinger, J. Milton. 1985. "Assimilation in the United States: the Mexican Perspective." In *Mexican Americans in Comparative Perspective,* edited by W. Connor. Washington, D.C.: The Urban Institute.

Zhou, Min and John R. Logan. 1989. "Returns on Human Capital in Ethnic Enclaves: New York City's Chinatown." *American Sociological Review* 54: 809–820.

Chapter Five

IMMIGRANT MALE EARNINGS IN THE 1980s: DIVERGENT PATTERNS BY RACE AND ETHNICITY

Elaine Sorensen and María E. Enchautegui

During the 1980s, the U.S. economy experienced the deepest recession since the Great Depression, followed by the longest peacetime recovery since World War II. These dramatic swings in the business cycle coincided with significant changes in the distribution of earnings. Virtually all research analyzing the events of the 1980s has found that real earnings declined (or stagnated) and that income inequality increased for male workers (Levy 1988, Burtless 1990, Ryscavage and Henle 1990). Recent studies have analyzed the reasons for these trends (Harrison and Bluestone 1988, Blackburn and Bloom 1987, Kosters 1991). Much of this literature points to the general deterioration of wages for low-skilled workers caused by shifts in labor demand (Blackburn, Bloom, and Freeman 1990, Juhn, Murphy, and Pierce 1991). Black men have received particular attention since the earnings disparity between white and black men grew during the 1980s (Bound and Freeman 1992, O'Neill 1990, Juhn et al. 1991).

This chapter considers the male immigrant population within the context of the broader debate on earnings trends in the 1980s. Immigrants are particularly vulnerable to the changes taking place in the economy because many of them are high school dropouts. In 1989, almost one-third of the immigrant male work force had not completed high school, whereas only 13 percent of the native male work force was without a high school diploma. Despite their high school dropout rates, immigrant males have increased their presence in the work force; their share of the work force rose from 6 to 9 percent between 1979 and 1989.

Several explanations can be advanced for the decline in earnings for the population as a whole and for immigrants in particular. These explanations traditionally fall into three categories: changes in individual characteristics, changes in labor demand, and changes in institutional factors. Two other elements are relevant when analyzing immigrants—immigration policies and the overall supply of immigrants to the labor market. In this chapter, we focus on trends in individual characteristics. Although changes in demand conditions, institutional factors, and the broader effects of immigration are not specifically addressed in this chapter, their consequences are revealed through examination of changes in the structure of earnings.

Our analysis examines how the trends in skill composition and duration of residence in the United States have affected the earnings status of immigrants. These two elements, skill and U.S. residence, have been the subject of many scholarly discussions within the immigration literature (Greenwood and McDowell 1986, Borjas 1990, LaLonde and Topel 1991). Some researchers have characterized recent migrant cohorts as less skilled than prior migrants, concluding that the "quality" of immigrants has declined over time (Borjas 1991). The most recent data in these analyses are from 1980, which are now more than a decade out of date. We assess whether this trend has continued during the 1980s. By analyzing more recent information, we fill a gap in the immigration literature, which up to now has focused on earlier time periods.

Asian, Hispanic, black, and white male immigrants are analyzed separately to document the ethnic and racial diversity in the patterns of economic progress of immigrants during the 1980s. This kind of analysis provides a better identification of the causes of stagnation or progress for the immigrant population. We demonstrate that diversity means more than diversification in the country of origin of the immigrant population. Diversity carries over to the U.S. labor market in the form of different paths of economic progress for different immigrant groups.

This chapter is organized as follows. Following this introduction, a literature review focuses on the economic status of immigrants. The third section describes the data collection process. The fourth section presents the data analysis, which is divided into two parts. The first part gives a descriptive analysis of wages, skills, and duration of residence of the immigrants by ethnic and racial group. The second part estimates earnings equations for different immigrant groups using data from 1979 and 1989. These results are used to determine which factors contributed to wage growth and decline in the 1980s. The last section summarizes our findings and discusses the policy implications of this research.

THE LITERATURE

Studies on the economic status of immigrants are numerous. A primary concern in this literature has been the economic progress of immigrants relative to natives. Most of this research is based on decennial censuses, since they offer large enough sample sizes for analyzing the foreign-born population. Consequently, today, most of our knowledge of the economic status of immigrants ends in 1980.

Recognizing the diversity of the immigration flow, most of the studies conduct separate analyses for the major immigrant groups (LaLonde and Topel 1991, Reimers 1985, Carliner 1980, Borjas 1985, Kossoudji 1988). There is overall agreement that the rate of economic progress of the major immigrant groups differs; for example, Asians are more economically mobile than Hispanics (LaLonde and Topel 1991, Kossoudji 1988, Chiswick 1986). Among Hispanics, Cubans show the highest rate of upward economic mobility (Borjas 1982, Reimers 1985). After controlling for personal characteristics, little difference is discerned between the earnings of European immigrants and natives (LaLonde and Topel 1991, Carliner 1980, Chiswick 1978). In contrast, the earnings of black immigrants differ from those of black natives according to year of arrival: Recent arrivals have lower earnings than earlier arrivals, and these, in turn, have lower earnings than black natives (Woodbury 1989).

A variable that mediates in these results is English language proficiency. Labor market experience acquired in the United States is more productive for immigrants from English-speaking countries (Chiswick 1978). McManus, Gould, and Welch (1983) find that virtually all of the earnings differential usually associated with national origins disappears after accounting for English language proficiency. Kossoudji (1988) finds that the cost of English language deficiency is higher among Hispanics than Asians. Earnings of non-English-speaking black immigrants never catch up with the earnings of black natives (Woodbury 1989).

More than ten years have passed since Chiswick (1978) reported that the earnings of immigrants are initially lower but rise more rapidly than the earnings of natives, resulting in an overtaking point that occurs after about 15 years of residence in the United States. Since then, various papers have indicated that Chiswick's assimilation effects were overstated. Borjas (1985) argues that cross-sectional results such as Chiswick's mix within-cohort and across-cohort earnings changes and hence the dynamic interpretation of earnings growth from cross-section data is invalid. Borjas constructed panel data with the 1970 and 1980 Censuses and illustrated that Chiswick's assimilation effects were overstated. More recently, LaLonde and Topel (1991) report sizable assimilation effects after constructing cross-section and within-cohort earnings differentials for immigrants, results that dispute Borjas's conclusions. These authors conclude that most of the earnings differential between immigrants and the base group disappears after ten years in the United States and that this is true in panel as well as in cross-section data.

The trends in "quality" of the immigrant population have also captured a great deal of attention in the immigration literature, since quality is related to the economic progress of immigrants as well as the design of immigration policy. Chiswick (1986) evaluates quality of immigrants by measuring the earnings differential between the immigrant group relative to natives for specific migration cohorts at two points in time. Under this analysis, an increase in the earnings differential is interpreted as a decline in quality. The earnings differentials of Mexicans, Cubans, and white immigrants relative to comparable natives of the same ethnicity increased between 1970 and 1980, whereas the earnings differentials of Japanese, Chinese, and Filipinos decreased. Chiswick attributes the increase in quality of Asians to the higher proportion of them entering under occupational preference visas during the 1970s.

In his critique of Chiswick, Borjas (1985, 1990) claims that the assimilation effects on cross-section data are large because earlier immigrants were of a better quality than recent immigrants. Borjas's decomposition of the total cross-section growth into within- and across-cohort components points to a decline in quality. Borjas finds that in comparison to 1970, the earnings of recent arrivals in 1980 were 12 percent lower among Mexicans, 61 percent lower among Cubans, and 30 percent lower among blacks.

LaLonde and Topel (1991) suggest that although the relative earnings and education of immigrants point to a deterioration in the quality of immigrants, the trends within immigrant groups show no decline in quality. The decline in overall quality can be explained by the increased representation of countries with low levels of education. They argue that the decline in the price of low-skilled labor during the 1970s tends to overstate the decline in quality of recent immigrant cohorts.

The issues of economic assimilation and the quality of immigrants are still under debate. The data that we use here for 1979 and 1989 are intended to shed light on these questions by evaluating the skill composition and earnings trends of immigrants during the 1980s. Group-specific analyses provide further evidence on the differential rates of economic assimilation of immigrants and whether these were altered during the 1980s.

DATA

This study uses the Current Population Surveys (CPSs) conducted in November 1979 and 1989. The CPS is particularly well-suited for this project because it is a large nationally representative sample that collects a wide array of labor market and demographic attributes about individuals. These two months of the CPS are used because they include special immigration supplements involving questions about nativity, language skills, and country of origin. The supplement files only contain earnings information for one-quarter of the sample, but the other households in the immigration supplement were asked about the earnings of individual members over the next three months. We merged the earnings data from these later months onto the immigration supplement file to create a larger database.[1]

About 4 percent of the CPS samples did not answer the questions regarding nativity and year of entry to the United States, so we imputed these variables for cases that were missing this information. This was done by first searching within the household for the information from a family member. If no suitable information was available from a family member, the values were assigned from a record of the same sex, age group, and race/ethnicity from the same state and CMSA (Consolidated Metropolitan Statistical Area).[2]

These data have weaknesses as well as strengths for this research project. One limitation of those two particular months of the CPS is that they only ask respondents about their usual weekly earnings and usual weekly hours worked; they do not ask respondents about their annual income or number of weeks worked last year. Hence, we are unable to examine changes in annual income or weeks worked. Due to this limitation, our research focuses on hourly pay (i.e., weekly pay divided by weekly hours). The advantage of the CPS supplements is that as the only large-scale survey conducted in the 1980s that contains information on immigrants, using it allows us to supplement previous research based on the 1980 decennial census. Our analysis is limited to men between the ages of 18 and 64 who are civilian wage and salary workers with positive earnings and hours worked.

DESCRIPTIVE ANALYSIS

Labor Force Composition

Table 5.1 presents the composition of the U.S. male wage and salary work force in 1979 and 1989. During the 1980s, immigrants increased

Table 5.1 COMPOSITION OF THE MALE WORK FORCE: 1979 AND 1989

	1979	1989
Native-born	94.2%	91.4%
Foreign-born	5.8	8.6
Race and Ethnic Composition of Native-born		
White[a]	81.6%	76.7%
Black[b]	8.7	9.3
Hispanic	3.2	4.2
Other Race[c]	0.8	1.2
Race and Ethnic Composition of Foreign-born		
White	2.7%	2.1%
Hispanic	2.0	4.1
Asian[d]	0.7	1.6
Black	0.4	0.6
Other[e]	0.1	0.2

Source: Authors' analysis of the Current Population Survey, 1979 and 1989.
a. White refers to non-Hispanic whites.
b. Black refers to non-Hispanic blacks.
c. Other Race refers to those who did not identify themselves as white, black, or Hispanic.
d. Asian refers to those who identified themselves as Other Race and were born in a country in the Far East.
e. Other includes those who identified themselves as Other Race and were not born in the Far East.

their share of the male work force from 5.8 to 8.6 percent, representing almost a 50 percent increase in their share of the male work force in ten years. The racial and ethnic composition of the male work force also changed during this period. Hispanic immigrants, for example, doubled their presence in the work force, from 2 to 4.1 percent. The share of Hispanic natives increased from 3.2 to 4.2 percent. Hence, Hispanics now represent 8.3 percent of the male work force. Blacks represent 10 percent of the male work force, up from 9 percent in 1979. The Asian immigrant male work force also doubled during the 1980s but still accounts for less than 2 percent of the male work force. White natives now represent 76.7 percent of the male work force, down from 81.6 percent in 1979.

The most dramatic change took place in the composition of the foreign-born work force, shown in table 5.2. In a ten-year period, the proportion of white immigrants declined precipitously from 45.6 percent of the foreign-born work force in 1979 to 24.5 percent in 1989. Hispanics became the largest group in 1989, accounting for

Table 5.2 RACE AND ETHNIC COMPOSITION OF THE MALE IMMIGRANT
WORK FORCE

	1979	1989
Total	100%	100%
White	45.6	24.5
Hispanic	33.8	48.2
Asian	12.7	18.5
Black	7.1	6.4
Other	0.8	2.5
0–5 years in U.S.	100%	100%
White	24.9	23.2
Hispanic	35.3	48.0
Asian	22.0	22.1
Black	16.5	4.0
Other	1.2	2.7

Source: Authors' analysis of the Current Population Survey, 1979 and 1989.

48.2 percent of all male immigrant workers. Asians also increased their share, from 12.7 to 18.5 percent, but their share of the foreign-born work force is still relatively small in 1989.

Table 5.2 also shows a similar but less dramatic shift among immigrant workers with zero to five years in the United States. Whites' share of the recent immigrant work force fell from 25 to 23 percent between 1979 and 1989. Blacks lost ground as well, representing 4 percent of the recent foreign-born work force in 1989, down from 16.5 percent in 1979. Hispanics showed the greatest increase; their share rose from 35 to 48 percent.

Hourly Wages

Table 5.3 presents the real hourly pay of immigrants and natives for 1979 and 1989.[3] Overall male earnings declined during the 1980s in part because of the increased representation of the foreign-born in the U.S. work force. Between 1979 and 1989, male hourly pay dropped an average 5.3 percent. When immigrants are excluded, the overall decline in real wages was only 4.7 percent. During the same period, the hourly wage of immigrant males declined 8 percent. The larger wage loss of immigrant men caused a deterioration in their relative status. In 1989, immigrants earned 12 percent less than natives compared to 9 percent less in 1979.

Male immigrants who entered the United States during the last five years experienced a 0.2 percent decline in real pay, representing

Table 5.3 REAL HOURLY PAY OF MEN: 1979 AND 1989 (in 1989 dollars)

	Geometric Means[a]		
	1979	1989	Percent Change
Males	$11.20	$10.61	−5.3%
Natives	11.26	10.73	−4.7
Foreign-born	10.23	9.41	−8.0
0–5 years in U.S.	7.77	7.75	−0.2
6+ years in U.S.	11.15	9.84	−12.5
Natives by Race and Ethnicity			
White	11.58	11.18	−3.5
Black	9.12	8.38	−8.1
Hispanic	9.76	8.92	−8.6
Other Race	10.53	10.05	−4.6
Foreign-born by Race and Ethnicity			
White	12.42	12.98	+4.5
0–5 yrs in U.S.	10.18	10.93	+7.4
6+ yrs in U.S.	12.79	13.48	+5.4
Hispanic	8.19	7.61	−7.0
0–5 yrs in U.S.	6.50	5.89	−9.4
6+ yrs in U.S.	8.84	8.07	−8.7
Asian	10.32	10.87	+5.3
0–5 yrs in U.S.	8.29	10.12	+22.1
6+ yrs in U.S.	12.04	11.11	−7.7
Black	8.36	9.29	+11.1

Source: Authors' analysis of the Current Population Survey, 1979 and 1989.
a. The geometric mean is the antilog of the mean of the natural log of earnings.

a much smaller decline in pay than that experienced by natives or earlier cohorts of immigrants. Thus, the relative wages of recent immigrants (compared with natives and earlier immigrants) improved in the 1980s, in contrast to earlier decades (Borjas 1991). The earnings disparity between recent immigrants and natives, for example, declined between 1979 and 1989, from 31 to 28 percent. This suggests that the "quality" of recent immigrants increased slightly.

Table 5.3 also shows a divergent pattern in earnings trends according to race/ethnicity. During this period, the four racial and ethnic groups of native males examined in this study—white, black, Hispanic, and Other Race—experienced a deterioration in real pay. White native earnings declined 4 percent during the 1980s, while black natives experienced an 8 percent decline in real pay. The 9 percent decline in wages of Hispanic natives was the largest among native male workers. This large drop in Hispanic male earnings represents an interruption to the economic progress that this group had enjoyed in previous decades (DeFreitas 1991).

At the same time, however, white, Asian, and black foreign-born men experienced increases in real wages ranging from 4.5 to 11.1 percent. Somehow these groups managed to improve their economic situation during a period of general decline in real earnings. This suggests that the composition of these groups shifted toward a more skilled population or that these groups were less affected by changes in labor market conditions taking place during the 1980s.

Hispanics were the only foreign-born group that experienced a deterioration in real wages between 1979 and 1989; their real hourly pay dropped 7 percent. This figure is even larger for Hispanic immigrants once duration of residence in the United States is taken into account. The real hourly pay of Hispanic immigrants with at most five years of residence in the U.S. declined 9.4 percent; earlier Hispanic immigrants experienced an 8.7 percent drop in real pay.

Asian immigrant earnings also differ by duration of residence in the United States. In 1989, recent Asian immigrants had wages that were 22 percent higher than the comparable cohort in 1979, while earnings of earlier Asian immigrant cohorts declined by 8 percent. This suggests that the skills of Asians migrating during the late 1980s were considerably higher than those of Asians migrating during the late 1970s.

The wage pattern observed among white foreign-born men, recent as well as early arrivals, is different from all other groups in the table. Their wages increased in both migration cohort categories. White immigrants during the 1980s seem to have become an increasingly select group.

THE ROLE OF CHANGING RACE AND ETHNICITY

To determine how much of the overall 8 percent decline in real pay of immigrants in the 1980s was due to a shift in their race and ethnic composition, we employed a decomposition method used by Borjas (1991). The decomposition method divides the decline in real pay of immigrants into two parts: shifts in the racial and ethnic composition of the immigrant work force and declines in pay within each racial and ethnic group. This decomposition can be written as follows:

$$W_{89} - W_{79} = \Sigma_j \, p_{j89} \, w_{j89} - \Sigma_j \, p_{j79} \, w_{j79} \tag{1}$$

$$= \Sigma_j \, (p_{j89} - p_{j79}) \, w_{j89} + \Sigma_j \, (w_{j89} - w_{j79}) \, p_{j79}$$

Table 5.4 EDUCATION LEVELS OF MALE WORKERS

			Education Level in Percent				
		Mean # of Years	Less Than 9 Years	9–11 Years	12 Years	13–15 Years	16+ Years
Natives	1979	12.7	7.7	12.8	39.7	18.9	20.9
	1989	13.2	3.7	9.5	40.1	21.6	25.1
Immigrants	1979	11.4	28.4	8.5	25.8	14.0	23.3
	1989	11.8	23.5	8.5	27.0	16.2	24.9
Immigrants	1979	10.5	38.4	6.3	22.1	13.3	19.9
0–5 yrs in U.S.	1989	11.9	20.1	13.0	28.5	11.7	26.6
Immigrants by Race and Ethnicity							
White	1979	12.5	17.6	7.6	32.6	14.9	27.3
	1989	13.5	9.8	4.4	28.5	18.7	38.6
Hispanic	1979	8.9	50.7	10.7	19.4	10.3	8.9
	1989	9.7	39.7	13.0	24.9	14.3	8.1
Asian	1979	14.1	7.4	6.2	19.2	20.5	46.8
	1989	14.2	7.4	3.4	24.4	17.8	47.0

Source: Authors' analysis of the Current Population Survey, 1979 and 1989.

where: W is the average (logarithmic) wage of foreign-born male workers; the subscripts 89 and 79 refer to the relevant year; p is the proportion of immigrants in a particular race or ethnic group; and w reflects the average (logarithmic) wage for that immigrant group.

The two parts of the decomposition are presented in the second row. The first summation reflects changes in the racial composition of the work force; the second reflects changes in wages within racial/ethnic groups.

Our results show that all of the decline in real pay of immigrant males during the 1980s can be attributed to a shift in their racial and ethnic composition. Wage changes within racial and ethnic groups did not contribute to the overall decline in pay for immigrant males. As explained earlier, the racial composition of the foreign-born work force shifted in the 1980s from whites to Hispanics and Asians. Since white immigrants earn more, on average, than Hispanics or Asians, the average earnings of immigrants fell as the immigrant work force shifted its racial and ethnic composition.

Education

To understand why the earnings of immigrant males changed in the 1980s, we first examined changes in their education. Table 5.4 shows that the mean education of all foreign-born male workers increased slightly—from 11.4 to 11.8 years—during the 1980s. The largest improvement took place among those with eight years of education or less, who represented 28 percent of the work force in 1979 and 24 percent in 1989. Foreign-born males also made gains at the higher end of the educational spectrum. In 1989, a quarter of all foreign-born male workers had a college degree, up from 23 percent in 1979.

Recent immigrants increased their average education 1.4 years during the 1980s. The percentage with less than nine years of education was halved within ten years, dropping from 38 to 20 percent. The gains in college education were also remarkable, going from 20 to 27 percent. The gains in educational attainment of recent migration cohorts occurred across all racial/ethnic groups. For example, the average education of recent Hispanic immigrants increased 2.3 years, from 7.2 to 9.5 years of education. Recent Asians increased their education 1.5 years, from 13.4 to 14.9 years.

Table 5.4 also shows that the educational attainment of immigrant male workers increased across all racial and ethnic groups. It increased most among white immigrant males, from 12.5 to 13.5 years, on average, between 1979 and 1989. Asians are the most educated among all foreign-born male workers, averaging over 14 years of education. In 1989, 47 percent of all Asians had a college degree, but their average level of education increased only 0.1 years during the 1980s, the smallest increase of any immigrant group.

The education levels of Hispanic immigrant male workers are considerably lower than that of other immigrant workers, but they did increase during the 1980s from an average of 8.9 to 9.7 years. Hispanic education increased in the 1980s because of a reduction in the percentage of Hispanics with eight years of education or less. This percentage declined from 51 to 40 percent during the 1980s. On the other hand, Hispanic immigrant males are the only ethnic group that experienced a decline in percentage of college graduates, from 8.9 to 8.1 percent.

Some researchers have argued that absolute educational level is meaningless in evaluating immigrant performance. For these researchers the relevant indicator is how immigrants are doing relative to natives. To inquire on this issue, table 5.5 reports the educational characteristics of native male workers in 1979 and 1989. In the past decade natives experienced a larger gain in educational attainment than immigrants. Mean educational level of natives increased 0.5 years while mean education level of immigrants increased 0.4 years. As a result the education of all immigrants rela-

Table 5.5 ENGLISH LANGUAGE FLUENCY OF FOREIGN-BORN MALE WORKERS

		Speaks No or Little English	Speaks English Well	Speaks English Very Well	Speaks Only English
Foreign-born	1979	26.9%	19.3%	25.8%	27.9%
	1989	28.8	24.5	25.6	21.1
0–5 yrs in U.S.	1979	48.1	16.4	13.8	21.6
	1989	45.0	22.4	17.4	15.2
By Race and Ethnicity					
White	1979	13.5	17.0	26.5	42.9
	1989	7.5	16.9	30.9	44.7
Hispanic	1979	50.7	21.9	22.5	4.9
	1989	47.1	27.5	20.6	4.8
Asian	1979	27.0	26.9	36.7	9.4
	1989	18.8	33.2	35.7	12.3

Source: Authors' analysis of the Current Population Survey, 1979 and 1989.

tive to natives declined during the past decade. However, because recent male immigrants experienced large gains in education, the educational level of recent immigrants relative to natives increased during the 1980s. In 1979, the educational disparity between recent immigrant male workers and natives was 2.2 years. In 1989, this gap had narrowed to 1.3 years.

The major difference in educational attainment between natives and immigrants is that immigrants are more likely to drop out before entering high school. These high school dropouts account for almost a fourth of foreign-born workers. Immigrant and native male workers have the same percentage of college graduates, around 25 percent of both groups.

English Language Proficiency

Another indicator of skill for male immigrants is English language fluency. Table 5.5 presents information related to the English abilities of the immigrant population. In 1989 foreign-born male workers were less likely to speak only English than they were in 1979. This proportion went from 28 percent in 1979 to 21 percent in 1989. In addition, the proportion speaking little or no English increased in the 1980s. These changes can be attributed to shifts in the country of origin of immigrants away from English-speaking countries.

A slightly different pattern is apparent in the English language abilities of recent immigrants. As with all immigrants, the proportion of recent immigrants speaking only English declined in the 1980s, but in contrast to all immigrants the proportion of recent immigrants speaking little or no English also declined. On the other hand, the proportion of recent immigrants who speak English well or very well increased.

Improvements in English language skills varied by race and ethnicity. White immigrants showed the greatest improvement in their English language abilities over the 1980s. The percentage of white immigrant male workers who spoke only English or spoke English very well increased from 68 to 76 percent. At the same time, the percentage who spoke no English fell from 13.5 percent to 7.5 percent. Asian immigrants also showed modest improvement in their English language skills. Their greatest improvement was the result of a large decline in the percentage of Asians who spoke no English, from 27 to 19 percent.

Hispanic immigrants are the most constrained by English language abilities, and improvements in the ten year period under analysis were negligible. In 1979, over half of all Hispanic immigrants spoke little or no English. This figure declined to 47 percent in 1989. The percentage who spoke only English or spoke English very well also declined, however, from 27 to 25 percent.

Duration of U.S. Residence

Table 5.6 presents the distribution of U.S. residential duration for immigrant male workers. It shows that recent migrants represent a lower percentage of the total immigrant work force in 1989 than in 1979 for all immigrant groups, except whites. For example, in 1979, 41 percent of the Asian immigrant work force had arrived during the last five years. By 1989, this figure dropped to 23 percent. The relative recency of the Asian flow is also seen in the low percentage of earlier immigrants in 1979. In 1979, only 11 percent of the Asian immigrant work force had been in the United States more than 15 years. By 1989, this group more than doubled in size, to 27 percent of the Asian immigrant work force. Hispanic immigrant workers show a similar but less dramatic trend in their duration of U.S. residence. In 1979, one-fourth of Hispanic immigrant workers had migrated to the United States during the past five years. By 1989, this figure had declined to 19 percent.

Declines in the proportion of recent immigrants occurred among

Table 5.6 DURATION OF U.S. RESIDENCE OF FOREIGN-BORN MALE WORKERS

		Years Since Arrival				
		0–5 Years	6–10 Years	11–15 Years	16–20 Years	21+ Years
Foreign-born	1979	23.8%	20.1%	14.9%	11.0%	30.2%
	1989	19.1	23.7	17.3	13.8	26.2
By Race and Ethnicity						
White	1979	13.0	12.9	12.6	12.0	49.4
	1989	18.0	10.5	9.8	13.0	48.8
Hispanic	1979	24.9	26.4	17.1	13.3	18.2
	1989	19.0	28.4	18.8	13.3	20.6
Asian	1979	41.3	27.6	19.6	3.9	7.6
	1989	22.8	25.7	24.3	14.5	12.7

Source: Authors' analysis of the Current Population Survey, 1979 and 1989.

Asians and Hispanics because the relatively small inflows of these groups prior to the 1970s were followed by rather large inflows during the 1970s. Although Asian and Hispanic migration to the United States during the 1980s was larger than it was in the 1970s, the increase was not as dramatic as it was in the 1970s. Whites are the only immigrant group that experienced an increase in the percentage of the immigrant work force migrating to the United States during the last five years, from 13 to 18 percent. Despite this change, white immigrants have the longest presence in the United States, as reflected in the large percentage who have resided in the United States over 20 years.

MULTIVARIATE ANALYSIS OF EARNINGS

We showed above that the decline in real earnings among immigrant men could be explained by a shift in the racial and ethnic composition of immigrants. This explanation, however, does not account for the divergent trends in real pay among different racial and ethnic groups. Although immigrant men in each of the racial/ethnic categories increased their education during the 1980s, Hispanic immigrant men experienced a decline in real pay, while white, black, and Asian immigrant men experienced an increase in real pay.

Analytic Approach

To determine why earnings trends differed by race and ethnicity, we estimated separate earnings equations for white, Asian, and Hispanic foreign-born men using pooled data from 1979 and 1989.[4] The samples were restricted to wage and salary workers between the ages of 18 and 64. The following equation illustrates our efforts:

$$\ln w_{it} = a_0 + a_1 X_{it} + a_2 D89_t + a_3 D89_t^* X_{it} + u_{it} \qquad (2)$$

where: i is the subscript for men who belong to a particular racial/ethnic subgroup; t is the subscript that indicates the data is either from 1979 or 1989; ln w is the logarithm of real hourly wages; X is a vector of explanatory variables; D89 is equal to 1 if the data are from 1989 and zero otherwise; the a's are the regression coefficients; and u is the disturbance term assumed to be normally distributed.

The dependent variable in the regressions is the logarithm of real hourly pay. The vector of explanatory variables includes the following: (1) the level of education completed; (2) potential work experience (i.e., age minus education minus 5); (3) potential experience squared; (4) a dummy variable that equals one if the immigrant lived in the south; (5) a dummy variable that equals one if the immigrant could not speak English or could not speak English well; and (6) four dummy variables indicating the length of residence in the United States. A dummy variable is added to the model that equals one if the data are from 1989 and zero if they are from 1979. A full set of interaction terms between this dummy variable and the other explanatory variables is also included.

This model allows us to control for personal attributes of the individuals while simultaneously permitting any structural change in the earnings equation. The estimated coefficients for the personal attributes measure the impact of these attributes on real earnings in 1979. The interaction terms measure the change in these estimated coefficients in 1989. In other words, they indicate whether the impact of these attributes on real pay changed during the 1980s. These results are presented in table 5.7.

Education

Table 5.7 shows that the rate of return to educational investments varies by race and ethnicity. In 1979, Asian immigrant males had the highest return to education—at 5.5 percent. Each additional year

Table 5.7 REAL EARNINGS REGRESSION RESULTS FOR IMMIGRANT MEN IN
1979 AND 1989
(T-statistics in parentheses)

	White		Hispanic		Asian	
Constant	1.628*	(15.26)	1.785*	(15.83)	1.476*	(6.86)
Education	.039*	(6.74)	.029*	(5.40)	.055*	(5.14)
Potential Exp.	.035*	(6.53)	.025*	(4.36)	.026*	(2.98)
Potential Exp. Sq.	−.0005*	(−4.98)	−.0004*	(−3.77)	−.0004*	(−2.02)
South	−.040	(−.69)	−.059	(−1.40)	−.094	(−1.10)
Poor or No English	−.190*	(−2.92)	−.081*	(−1.76)	−.189*	(−2.35)
0–5 yrs in U.S.	−.067	(−.98)	−.286*	(−4.26)	−.203*	(−1.70)
6–10 yrs in U.S.	.025	(.39)	−.194*	(−3.14)	−.086	(−.72)
11–15 yrs in U.S.	−.051	(−.84)	−.104*	(−1.67)	.047	(.38)
16–20 yrs in U.S.	.047	(.78)	−.064	(−.97)	.154	(.84)
Imputed	.008	(.09)	.059	(.48)	−.087	(−.58)
1989 Data	−.095	(−.59)	−.232	(−1.62)	−.179	(−.65)
89 × Education	.015*	(1.72)	.012*	(1.73)	.018	(1.27)
89 × Pot Exp	−.010	(−1.14)	−.005	(.76)	.009	(.75)
89 × Pot Exp Sq	.0002	(1.17)	−.00003	(−.23)	−.0002	(−.88)
89 × South	−.077	(−.94)	−.040	(−.75)	−.140	(−1.27)
89 × Poor English	−.085	(−.80)	−.139*	(−2.46)	.060	(.56)
89 × U.S. 0–5	−.012	(.13)	.037	(.43)	−.070	(−.46)
89 × U.S. 6–10	−.048	(−.49)	.008	(.10)	−.157	(−1.04)
89 × U.S. 11–15	.018	(.18)	−.013	(−.17)	−.326*	(−2.11)
89 × U.S. 16–20	.006	(.06)	.042	(.50)	−.292	(−1.41)
89 × Imputed	−.162	(−1.35)	−.068	(−.49)	−.109	(−.57)
R^2	.18		.30		.31	
N	1269		1306		658	

Source: Authors' analysis of the Current Population Survey, 1979 and 1989.
*Significant at the 10 percent level (two-tailed tests).

of education increased the hourly pay of Asian immigrant males by
5.5 percent. For white immigrant males, the rate of return to education
was 3.9 percent. Hispanic immigrants had the lowest rate of return,
2.9 percent for each additional year of schooling.

We also find that the returns to education increased for immigrant
men between 1979 and 1989, a result that others have already noted
for the labor market in general (Kosters 1991, O'Neill 1990). The
increased returns to education was a major change in the labor market
in the 1980s and contributed to the rise in earnings inequality, since
it exacerbated the earnings differential between better-educated and
less-educated workers. This trend extended to immigrant men. The
estimated coefficients for education increased significantly for white
and Hispanic immigrant men and increased by a similar magnitude

for Asian immigrant men, although this increase was not significantly different from its 1979 value.

English Language Fluency

During the 1980s, the penalty for speaking English poorly or not at all increased for all immigrants. In 1979, Hispanic male immigrants with poor English abilities earned 8 percent less than other Hispanic immigrants after controlling for education, potential work experience, and duration of residence in the United States. Asian and white immigrants were penalized more than Hispanic immigrants for poor English abilities. Asians and whites with poor English made 19 percent less than their counterparts with good English abilities. By 1989, the penalty for poor English increased among Hispanics, to the extent that the earnings of Hispanic immigrants with poor English were 22 percent below the earnings of otherwise comparable Hispanic immigrants. The penalty for poor English did not increase significantly for Asians or whites.

Duration of U.S. Residence

Table 5.7 shows that recent migrant cohorts tended to earn less than earlier immigrants in 1979, but these differences were only significant among Asians and Hispanics. In 1979, Asian immigrants who came to the United States between 1975 and 1979 earned 20 percent less than Asian immigrants who had come to the United States prior to 1960. Similarly, the most recent cohort—those residing in the United States from 0 to 5 years—in 1979 earned 29 percent less than Hispanic immigrants who had been in the United States at least 20 years. We find no significant difference in pay by U.S. residence among white immigrant men in 1979. These results provide further evidence that the rate of economic progress of immigrants differs by race and ethnicity.

Table 5.7 also shows that the cross-section assimilation profiles have been relatively stable during the last ten years. We find that none of the U.S. tenure coefficients in the white or Hispanic equations changed significantly between 1979 and 1989. One interpretation of these results is that the "quality" of white and Hispanic migration during the 1980s did not change significantly.

The only exception to this pattern is for Asians, whose cross-section assimilation profile changed in the 1980s. This change was significant for those who came to the United States 11 to 15 years earlier. In 1979, Asian immigrants who had resided in the United States 11 to 15 years (i.e. they came in the late 1960s) earned about the same as those who had been in the United States at least 20 years. Ten years later, however, Asian immigrants who entered the United States during the late 1970s and resided in the United States for 11 to 15 years earned 28 percent less than Asian immigrants who entered the United States more than 20 years earlier. This difference could be viewed as evidence that Asians who migrated to the United States during the late 1970s were of lower "quality" than those who migrated in the 1960s, but these findings could also reflect other factors, such as the large size of this immigrant cohort. One million Asians entered the United States during the late 1970s, compared to about 430,000 during all of the 1960s. The large size of this particular Asian immigrant cohort may result in more difficulty increasing their earnings through assimilation.

Decomposition of the Earnings Trends

To examine the reasons why wages changed in the 1980s, we divided the total change in wages into two components: (1) the part due to changes in the characteristics of the individuals and (2) the part due to changes in the earnings structure. This method is similar to that employed by Oaxaca (1973) and Blinder (1973), who examined male/female and black/white wage gaps. We estimated separate wage equations for each racial/ethnic group in 1979 and 1989. We decomposed these results in the following manner:

$$\overline{\ln w}_{89j} - \overline{\ln w}_{79j} = (\overline{X}_{89j} - \overline{X}_{79j}) \hat{A}_{89j} + \overline{X}_{79j} (\hat{A}_{89j} - \hat{A}_{79j}) \quad (3)$$

where: j is one of the racial/ethnic groups; $\overline{\ln w}$ is the mean value of the logarithmic wage for group j in year t; $\overline{X}$ is a vector of mean values for the characteristics of group j at time t; and the A's are the estimated coefficients.

The first term measures the change in characteristics; the last term measures the change in the earnings structure. Note that the changes in the regression coefficients are weighted by the mean characteristics in 1979. An alternative procedure would use the mean characteristics from 1989 as the weights. We get similar results with this alternative. However, the first approach is more appropriate since we are interested in the question: What would have happened to earnings in 1989 if the characteristics of men remained as they were in 1979?[5]

Table 5.8 RESULTS FROM THE REGRESSION DECOMPOSITION FOR
IMMIGRANT MEN

| | Total Change in Log Pay, 1979–1989* | Due to: | |
		Changes in Characteristics	Changes in Coefficients
Whites	4.9	5.3	−1.4
Asians	4.4	8.5	−4.1
Hispanics	−7.0	3.4	−10.4

Source: Authors' analysis of the Current Population Survey, 1979 and 1989.
*Figures in this column are slightly different from those reported in table 5.3. The figures in table 5.3 are the percentage change in the weighted value of hourly pay, which equals $e^b − 1$ where $b = \ln w_{89} − \ln w_{79}$. In this table, wages are not weighted, and we are simply reporting b.

According to this decomposition method, we find that the real hourly pay for white and Asian immigrant men increased by 4.9 and 4.4 percent, respectively, during the 1980s because of changes in their personal characteristics. Table 5.8 shows that if the characteristics of white and Asian immigrant men had not changed, their real pay would have declined during the 1980s. The largest change in personal characteristics among white immigrant men was in their education level, which increased from 12.5 to 13.5 years. In addition, the English language skills of white immigrant males improved, contributing to their higher earnings. Among Asian immigrant men, their potential work experience increased an average 1.4 years between 1979 and 1989, from 16.2 years to 17.6 years. In addition, the proportion of Asian immigrants who entered the United States during the last five years declined dramatically, from 40 percent in 1979 to 24 percent in 1989.

In contrast, Hispanic immigrant men experienced a decline in real pay during the 1980s because of changes in their earnings structure. In other words, changes in the estimated coefficients for Hispanic immigrant men reduced their wages more than the estimated coefficients for white or Asian immigrant men reduced theirs. Table 5.8 shows that Hispanic immigrant men would have experienced a 10.4 percent decline in real pay during the 1980s if their personal attributes had not changed, but white and Asian immigrant men would have only experienced a 1.4 and 4.1 percent decline in real pay, respectively.

The question remains: Why did the real earnings of Hispanic immigrant men decline in the 1980s more than white and Asian immigrant men once changes in individual characteristics were controlled?

Recent research shows that the real earnings of less-skilled male workers declined in the 1980s, both in absolute terms and in relation to more skilled workers (Blackburn et al. 1990, Juhn et al. 1991). We suspect that this large decline in the relative earnings of low-skilled workers has taken its toll on Hispanic immigrants, over half of whom did not possess a high school diploma in 1989. Further research is necessary, however, to confirm this hypothesis. The sizable immigration flow during the 1980s and the legalization of over two million illegals are also potential explanations which merit further research.

SUMMARY AND POLICY IMPLICATIONS

Between 1979 and 1989, the real hourly pay of immigrant males dropped 8 percent. In comparison, native males lost 5 percent of their real hourly pay. The larger wage drop for immigrants caused the immigrant/native pay disparity to increase from 9 to 12 percent. In contrast, the real hourly pay of recent immigrants declined only 0.2 percent over the ten-year period. Thus, the wage disparity between recent immigrants and natives declined during the 1980s, from 31 to 28 percent. This represents a reversal from the previous two decades, during which time the pay disparity between recent immigrants and natives increased (Borjas 1991).

We also find that the education of male immigrants increased slightly during the 1980s but increased more dramatically among recent male immigrants. Native male workers increased their education by slightly more than immigrant males. Thus, the relative education of immigrants declined somewhat during the 1980s. In contrast, the educational position of recent immigrants relative to natives improved.

Borjas (1985, 1990) and others have argued that the "quality" of immigrants to the United States declined after 1965, when immigration policy eliminated the national-origin quota system and emphasized family reunification. This assertion was based, in part, on the declining relative earnings and education of recent immigrants when compared to natives. We find that these trends reversed in the 1980s.

We also examined the earnings trends of immigrants from different racial and ethnic groups. We found that increased diversity in country of origin of immigrants translated into a diversity of achievement in the U.S. labor market. The general decline in hourly wages of foreign-born immigrants extended only to Hispanic immigrants, who experienced a 7 percent loss in real hourly pay. White, Asian, and black immigrants all experienced an increase in real wages during the 1980s. Native workers also experienced a decline in real earnings, which extended to all racial and ethnic groups examined.

The multivariate analysis of earnings reveals that the factors most responsible for the increase in real wages for white foreign-born men were education and English language skills, both of which improved during the 1980s. A sharp drop in recency of migration and an increase in potential work experience can explain most of the wage improvements for Asians.

The results of the earnings equation for Hispanic immigrants demonstrates that we cannot attribute the decline in real earnings in the 1980s to changes in education, English language fluency, or recency of migration. If characteristics analyzed here were the only factors that changed in the 1980s, the earnings of Hispanic men would have been higher in 1989 than in 1979. Instead, changes in their earnings structure led to the decline in earnings for Hispanic immigrants.

The very low educational level of Hispanic immigrants limits their economic progress. In the 1980s, when returns to education increased, their low educational levels became an even greater liability. Reforming immigration policy to reduce illegal immigration and increase visa allocation to high-skilled immigrants are two methods of improving the educational level of immigrants, but they do not adequately address the difficult question of increasing the educational attainment of foreign-born Hispanic men. Hispanic immigrants who come to the United States as adults may see their migration as an activity expected to generate immediate income to support their families or to send remittances back home. To postpone income-generating activities for formal schooling may not be a viable alternative. The educational prospects of Hispanics who enter the United States as children are also gloomy. High school drop-out rates are very high among Hispanic students. Future immigrant policies need to address these critical issues.

Notes

1. We found earnings information for over 90 percent of individuals over the next three months, an extremely high matching rate. We thank Anne Bergsman, a computer specialist at the Urban Institute, for constructing these data files.

2. We want to thank Jeff Passel and Jim Youngberg, both at the Urban Institute, for designing and executing this imputation process.

3. We used the CPI-U-X series to correct for inflation. This is the price index that incorporates a rental equivalence measure for homeowner costs. It has been the official consumer price index since 1983. The 1979 figure is reported in an unpublished table available from the U.S. Bureau of Labor Statistics. The salaries reflect 1989 prices.

4. We omitted black and other immigrant men from this analysis because our sample sizes were too small.

5. Sociologists usually apply weights from the same year, either 1979 or 1989, rather than apply one weight from each year as we have done. Using weights from the same year results in three components to the wage decomposition: that due to changes in characteristics, that due to changes in coefficients, and an interaction term. The approach used here eliminates the interaction term.

References

Blackburn, McKinley L., and David E. Bloom. 1987. "Earnings and Income Inequality in the United States." *Population and Development Review* 13(4): 575–609.

Blackburn, McKinley L., David E. Bloom, and Richard B. Freeman. 1990. "The Declining Economic Position of Less Skilled American Men." In *A Future of Lousy Jobs? The Changing Structure of U.S. Wages.* edited by Gary Burtless. Washington, D.C.: Brookings Institution.

Blinder, Alan S. 1973. "Wage Discrimination: Reduced Form and Structural Variables." *Journal of Human Resources* 8 (Fall): 436–455.

Borjas, George J. 1985. "Assimilation, Changes in Cohort Quality, and the Earnings of Immigrants." *Journal of Labor Economics*, 3(4), Chicago, IL: University of Chicago Press.

————. 1990. *Friends or Strangers: The Impact of Immigrants on the U.S. Economy.* New York: Basic Books.

————. 1991. "Immigrants in the U.S. Labor Market: 1940–80." *American Economic Review Paper and Proceedings* 81(2): 287–291.

Bound, John, and Richard Freeman. 1992. "What Went Wrong? The 1980's Erosion of the Economic Well-being of Black Men." *Quarterly Journal of Economics*, February.

Burtless, Gary, ed. 1990. *A Future of Lousy Jobs? The Changing Structure of U.S. Wages.* Washington, D.C.: Brookings Institution.

Carliner, G. 1976. "Returns to Education for Blacks, Anglos, and Five Spanish Groups." *Journal of Human Resources*, 11(2): 172–184.

————. 1980. "Wages, Earnings and Hours of First, Second, and Third Generation American Males." *Economic Inquiry* 18: 87–102.

Chiswick, B. R. 1978. "The Effect of Americanization on the Earnings of Foreign-born Men." *Journal of Political Economy* 86(34): 807–921.

————. 1986. "Is the New Immigration Less Skilled than the Old?" *Journal of Labor Economics* 4(2): 168–192.

DeFreitas, Gregory. 1991. *Inequality at Work: Hispanics in the U.S. Labor Force.* New York: Oxford University Press.

Greenwood, Michael J., and John M. McDowell. 1986. "The Factor Market Consequences of U.S. Immigration." *Journal of Economic Literature* 24(4): 1738–1773.

Harrison, Bennett, and Barry Bluestone. 1988. *The Great U-Turn.* New York: Basic Books.

Juhn, Chinhui, Kevin M. Murphy, and Brooks Pierce. 1991. "Accounting for the Slowdown in Black-White Wage Convergence." In *Workers and Their Wages*, edited by Marvin H. Kosters. Washington, D.C.: American Enterprise Institute.

Kossoudji, S. A. 1988. "English Language Ability and the Labor Market Opportunities of Hispanic and East Asian Immigrant Men," *Journal of Labor Economics.* 6(2): 205–28.

————. 1989. "Immigrant Worker Assimilation: Is it a Labor Market Phenomenon?" *Journal of Human Resources*, 24(3): 495–527.

Kosters, Marvin H., ed. 1991. *Workers and Their Wages: Changing Patterns in the United States.* Washington, D.C.: American Enterprise Institute.

LaLonde, R. J., and R. H. Topel. 1990. "The Assimilation of Immigrants in the U.S. Labor Market." Paper presented to Ford/NBER Immigration Conference. January, Chicago.

————. 1991. "Immigrants in the American Labor Market: Quality, Assimilation, and Distributional Effects." *American Economic Review Papers and Proceedings.* 81(2): 297–302, May.

Levy, Frank. 1988. *Dollars and Dreams: The Changing American Income Distribution.* New York: W.W. Norton & Company.

Oaxaca, Ronald. 1973. "Male-Female Wage Differentials in Urban Labor Markets." *International Economic Review* 14(3): 693–709, October.

O'Neill, June. 1990. "The Role of Human Capital in Earnings Differences Between Black and White Men." *Journal of Economic Perspectives* 4(4): 25–45.

Reimers, C. 1985. "A Comparative Analysis of the Wages of Hispanics, Blacks and Non-Hispanic Whites." In *Hispanics in the U.S. Economy*, edited by G. Borjas and M. Tienda. Orlando: Academic Press Inc.

Ryscavage, Paul and Peter Henle. 1990. "Earnings Inequality Accelerates in the 1980s." *Monthly Labor Review* (December).

Woodbury S. A. 1989. "Earnings of Black Male Immigrants: Implications for Racial Discrimination." Paper presented at Middlebury College Conference on New Approaches to the Analysis of Discrimination, April.

Chapter Six

IMMIGRATION, EMIGRATION, LANGUAGE ACQUISITION, AND THE ENGLISH LANGUAGE PROFICIENCY OF IMMIGRANTS IN THE UNITED STATES

Gillian Stevens

Although the United States is dominated by the English language, it has never had an official language or an official language policy at the federal level. Perhaps as a result, while the strictness of the U.S. immigration policies in the twentieth century has waxed and waned in terms of restricting the entry of persons with various characteristics, potential immigrants have never been explicitly excluded on the basis of language characteristics (Leibowitz 1984). Nevertheless, American presidents, various judicial bodies, and the general public alike have assumed throughout most of America's history that proficiency in the English language is desirable for immigrants and perhaps necessary for access to American political and economic life (Baron 1990). The accompanying exhortations to immigrants to discard their native language and to learn to speak English, although more or less vociferous at various times, have never really stopped.

In this chapter, I describe the linguistic characteristics of adult immigrants in the United States. The focus is on how well immigrants speak English, a particularly important aspect of overall competency in English. I first review the major processes—differential immigration, emigration, and English language acquisition—that produce the linguistic characteristics of immigrants currently resident in the United States. I then use data from the November 1989 and November 1979 Current Population Surveys (CPSs) to outline the impact of these processes on the levels of proficiency in speaking English among immigrants resident in the United States in 1989.

HOW WELL IMMIGRANTS SPEAK ENGLISH

How well immigrants in the United States speak English is the product of three sets of processes. The first set includes processes of selective immigration. How likely are immigrants to arrive in the United States already proficient in English? The second set of processes concerns emigration. Are immigrants who lack proficiency in English at time of arrival or who do not learn English while in the United States more likely to leave the country than other immigrants? The third set of processes concerns the extent of language acquisition or "linguistic adaptation" occurring among immigrants living in the United States. To what extent do immigrants learn or increase their level of proficiency in English while living in the United States?

Immigration and Language Characteristics

With the exception of very young children, immigrants arrive in the United States with an extant linguistic repertoire. Whether or not that linguistic repertoire includes facility in English is an important consideration in the necessity, the rapidity, and the ease with which immigrants adjust to an English-language-dominated environment. The linguistic attributes of immigrants arriving in the United States can be viewed as the product of language-specific selection processes operating at two levels of aggregation. First, all other things being equal, potential immigrants born and raised in countries in which English is a dominant or official language have a large advantage over potential immigrants born and raised in non-English-language countries. Presumably, immigration to the United States, an English-language-dominated society, is thus a less formidable undertaking.

Within each country, self-selection occurs at the individual level. Within specific countries, potential immigrants vary in their knowledge of English, in their willingness and ability to learn English, and in their anticipation of problems associated with immigrating to an English-language-dominated society (Fawcett et al. 1990). Potential immigrants who have prior knowledge of English or who anticipate few difficulties in the learning of English may be more likely to move to the United States.

Although the linguistic characteristics of immigrants at time of arrival in the United States are an important consideration in immigrants' eventual levels of proficiency in English, data on the linguistic characteristics of immigrants at time of arrival are generally unavailable. No major recent U.S. survey contains information on immigrants' linguistic repertoires at time of arrival in the United States. Moreover, no major recent national survey[1] or census[2] contains retrospective information on immigrants' language characteristics at time of arrival in the United States.

One remedy for this lack of information on immigrants' linguistic characteristics is to infer levels of proficiency in English from country of birth. If English is the dominant language of an immigrant's country of birth, then it is very likely that the immigrant is a "native" speaker of English. Countries in which English is the dominant language include Anguilla, Australia, Canada, and the United Kingdom. Although some of these countries (e.g., Canada) have sizable non-English-language populations, it is probably reasonable to infer that the majority of the populations living in these countries learn English in childhood as a first language. For most immigrants from these countries, linguistic assimilation or adaptation in the United States is not much of an issue.

In countries in which English is not a dominant language, English may be an official language and thus used in important social institutions such as the government or the educational system. Countries in which English is an official (but not dominant) language include several very large countries, such as India. Although in many cases, English is only one of several official languages, it is probably reasonable to assume that a large portion of the country's population learns English as a first language or as a second language in that country's educational system. As a result, immigrants from countries in which English is an official language probably arrive in the United States with some knowledge of the English language.

In the remainder of the world's countries, potential migrants to the United States are much less likely to learn English as a first or second language or to use English in major social institutions. As a result, immigrants from these countries are less apt to be proficient in English on arrival in the United States. This large and heterogeneous group of countries can be further classified by whether or not Spanish is a dominant language.

Table 6.1 shows the percentages of immigrants admitted legally to the United States during the 1970s and the 1980s and the estimated percentages residing in the United States in November 1979 and November 1989 cross-classified by the linguistic characteristics of the immigrant's country of birth.[3] Countries were classified by whether English is the dominant language, English is an official but non-dominant language, Spanish is a dominant language, or some other languages were dominant.

For several reasons, the percentages in table 6.1 are only rough estimates. The first two columns, for example, include only legally admitted immigrants; the other two columns refer only to adults. In addition, the percentages of immigrants from countries in which

Table 6.1 PERCENTAGES OF ADMITTED AND RESIDENT IMMIGRANTS BY THE OFFICIAL LANGUAGE(S) OF THEIR COUNTRIES OF ORIGIN

Official or Dominant Language in Country of Birth	Immigrants Admitted Between		Adult Immigrants Resident in U.S. in:	
	1970–1979	1980–1989	1979	1989
English: dominant	6.2[1]	5.2[2]	14.7[3]	11.6[4]
English: official	19.0[5]	21.5[6]	9.0[7]	12.3[8]
English: total[9]	25.2	26.7	23.7	23.9
Spanish	32.2[10]	32.3[11]	24.9[12]	33.1[13]
Other[9]	42.6	41.0	47.6	42.9
Country of birth unknown	—	—	3.8	1.8
Total	100.0	100.0	99.9	100.0
Source:	INS Yearbook, 1979	INS Yearbook, 1989	CPS, November 1979	CPS, November 1989

1. Includes Australia, Canada, Ireland, and the United Kingdom.
2. Includes Antigua-Barbuda, Australia, Canada, Ireland, New Zealand, St. Kitts and Nevis, and the United Kingdom.
3. Includes Anguilla, Australia, the British Isles, Bermuda, Canada, England, Ireland, New Zealand, North Ireland, St. Kitts and Nevis, Scotland, and Wales.
4. Includes Anguilla, Australia, Bermuda, British West Indies, Canada, England, Ireland, New Zealand, North Ireland, Scotland, St. Kitts and Nevis, and Wales.
5. Includes Barbados, Guyana, Hong Kong, India, Jamaica, Philippines, Trinidad and Tobago.
6. Includes the Bahamas, Bangladesh, Barbados, Belize, Dominica, Fiji, Ghana, Grenada, Guyana, Hong Kong, India, Jamaica, Kenya, Liberia, Malaysia, Nigeria, Pakistan, the Philippines, St. Lucia, St. Vincent and the Grenadines, Sierra Leone, South Africa, Tanzania, Trinidad and Tobago, and Uganda.
7. Includes the Bahamas, Bangladesh, Barbados, Belize, Ghana, Guyana, Hong Kong, India, Jamaica, Kenya, Liberia, Malaysia, Nigeria, Pakistan, the Philippines, St. Lucia, St. Vincent and the Grenadines, Singapore, Suriname, Trinidad and Tobago, and Uganda.
8. Includes the Bahamas, Bangladesh, Barbados, Belize, Ghana, Guyana, Hong Kong, India, Jamaica, Kenya, Liberia, Malaysia, Nigeria, Pakistan, the Philippines, St. Lucia, St. Vincent and the Grenadines, Singapore, South Africa, Trinidad and Tobago, and Uganda.
9. Obtained by addition.
10. Includes Argentina, Chile, Colombia, Costa Rica, Cuba, the Dominican Republic, Ecuador, El Salvador, Guatemala, Honduras, Mexico, Nicaragua, Panama, Peru, Spain, Uruguay, and Venezuela.
11. Includes Argentina, Bolivia, Chile, Colombia, Costa Rica, Cuba, the Dominican Republic, Ecuador, El Salvador, Guatemala, Honduras, Mexico, Nicaragua, Panama, Peru, Spain, Uruguay, and Venezuela.
12. Includes Argentina, Bolivia, Central America, Chile, Colombia, Costa Rica, Cuba, Ecuador, El Salvador, Guatemala, Honduras, Mexico, Nicaragua, Panama, Paraguay, Peru, Spain, Uruguay, and Venezuela.
13. Includes Argentina, Bolivia, Central America, Chile, Colombia, Costa Rica, Cuba, the Dominican Republic, Ecuador, El Salvador, Guatemala, Honduras, Latin America, Mexico, Nicaragua, Panama, Paraguay, Peru, Spain, Uruguay, and Venezuela.

English is a dominant or official language are probably underestimated (and the percentages of immigrants from non-English-language countries correspondingly overestimated). The data based on immigrant admittance statistics did not contain enough detail to code all immigrants' countries of origin by linguistic characteristics; the data obtained from the 1979 and 1989 CPSs contained even less detail on immigrants' countries of origin.[4]

In spite of these shortcomings with the data, it is obvious that sizable percentages of the immigrants legally admitted to the United States during the 1970s and 1980s probably had some exposure to English before migrating. About a quarter of the immigrants legally admitted during the 1970s and 1980s were from English-language countries. For purposes of comparison, about a quarter of the world's population (outside of the United States) lives in countries in which English is a dominant or official language, a comparison that does not suggest a high level of selectivity. However, only about 2 percent of the world's population (excluding the United States) lives in a country in which English is the dominant language, yet over 10 percent of the resident immigrant population in the United States was born in an English-language-dominated country.

The data presented in table 6.2, which are from the 1989 November CPS, support the conjecture that the linguistic characteristics of immigrants' counties of origin are closely related to the immigrants' levels of English language proficiency at time of arrival. The table entries show the percentages of immigrants entering the United States between 1987 and 1989 and between 1985 and 1986 classified by the official or dominant language of their country of birth. Almost all of the immigrants from countries in which English is a dominant language report themselves as speaking English "very well." Immigrants from countries in which English is an official but not dominant language are apt to report themselves as speaking "very well" or "well"; only about 10 percent report speaking English "not well" or "not well at all." Immigrants from non-English-language countries report the lowest levels of proficiency in speaking English: three-quarters of immigrants from Spanish-language countries and almost half of immigrants from non-English, non-Spanish-language countries report speaking English "not well" or "not well at all."

The data in table 6.2 suggest that immigration to the United States is selective for individuals from non-English-language countries who have high levels of English language proficiency. While many of the immigrants who report high levels of proficiency in English are from countries in which English is a dominant or official language (col-

Table 6.2 THE PERCENTAGES OF RECENT IMMIGRANTS WHO REPORT
SPEAKING ENGLISH "VERY WELL," "WELL," "NOT WELL," OR "NOT
WELL AT ALL" BY OFFICIAL OR DOMINANT LANGUAGE OF THEIR
COUNTRY OF BIRTH, 1989 CPS

| | | Official or Dominant Language of Immigrants' Country of Birth[1] | | | |
	Total	English Dominant	English Official	Spanish Dominant	Other
Immigrants Entering the U.S. 1987–89					
Not well at all	21.7	.0	.0	41.6	14.4
Not well	30.1	.0	9.0	40.0	32.9
Well	18.5	3.3	19.8	13.0	25.9
Very well[2]	29.7	96.7	71.2	5.4	26.8
Total	100.0	100.0	100.0	100.0	100.0
Immigrants Entering the U.S. 1985–86					
Not well at all	17.9	—	2.1	29.4	9.3
Not well	33.0	—	9.3	44.1	30.1
Well	19.9	—	17.5	15.4	29.7
Very well[2]	29.2	—	71.0	11.1	31.0
Total	99.9	100.0[3]	99.9	100.0	100.1

1. See notes to table 6.1.
2. Includes immigrants who stated that they spoke only English at home and therefore did not answer the question on English proficiency.
3. Based on fewer than 50 cases.

umns 2 and 3), many immigrants from non-English-language countries also report high levels of proficiency. Between 18 and 26 percent
of recent immigrants from Spanish-language countries report speaking English well or very well (column 4), and over half of the recent
immigrants from non-English, non-Spanish-language countries
report speaking English well or very well (column 5).

Overall, although only about 25 percent of recent immigrants are
from countries in which English is a dominant or official language
(table 6.1), almost half of the immigrants entering the United States
in the late 1980s report speaking English "well" or "very well" (table
6.2). To put this "almost half" into perspective, only about a fifth of
the world's population outside the United States speaks English as
a first or second language (Decsy 1987).

Tables 6.1 and 6.2 thus suggest two major conclusions: (1) the
linguistic characteristics of immigrants' countries of origin are related
to immigrants' levels of English language proficiency at the time of
or soon after arrival in the United States, and (2) immigration to

the United States appears to be selective with respect to language characteristics. The selection processes appear to be operating at aggregate and individual levels. Using the percentages of the world's population living in countries in which English or some other language is a dominant or official language as a rough guide, immigrants to the United States are more likely to come from countries in which English is a dominant language. In addition, many immigrants from non-English-language countries appear to be proficient in English.

Emigration and Language Characteristics

Parallel to the selection processes that influence who immigrates to the United States are selection processes influencing who emigrates from the United States. A sizable percentage of immigrants eventually leave the country and return to their country of origin or move elsewhere. If immigrants who lacked prior facility in English and did not learn English in the American context emigrate, then the levels of English language proficiency among immigrants who stay will appear to increase over time. Immigrants with less knowledge of English at the time of arrival in the United States may be more likely to leave because of the difficulties of living in an English-language-dominated environment. In addition, non-English-speaking immigrants who anticipate leaving the United States may not invest the time and effort needed to learn a new language.

On the other hand, emigration may not be selective of immigrants lacking prior facility in English. New immigrants who lack facility in the English language have, by virtue of entering the United States, declared their willingness to live in an English-language-dominated society. Presumably this includes a commitment to learning the dominant language of their new country. Potential immigrants who were unwilling to make such a commitment may not have left their country of origin or they may have chosen another destination. This strong commitment on the part of non-English-speaking immigrants entering the United States may lower the probability that they leave the United States. Since immigrants who spoke English prior to their arrival in the United States did not have to consider the difficulties of learning a new language when evaluating the costs of immigrating, their decision to immigrate to the United States may have entailed less commitment to their new country and thus a lower likelihood of staying.

Without longitudinal data, it is difficult to assess whether the probability of an immigrant leaving the United States is related to his or her linguistic characteristics at time of entry or to the extent to which he or she learned English after arrival in the United States. However, if the linguistic characteristics of immigrants' countries of birth are related to immigrants' levels of English proficiency at time of arrival and if immigrants with less proficiency have more difficulty adapting to the American environment, then immigrants from countries in which English was the dominant or official language should be more likely to remain in the United States, and immigrants from countries in which other languages are dominant or official should be more likely to leave. On the other hand, if immigrants with less English proficiency are more committed to adapting to the American environment, then immigrants from non-English-speaking countries may be more likely to remain in the United States than immigrants from countries in which English is a dominant or official language.

The data in table 6.3 are from the November 1979 and November 1989 CPSs. The cell entries are the percentages of immigrants residing in the United States in 1979 and in 1989 cross-classified by time period of entry into the United States and by the linguistic characteristics of the immigrants' countries of birth. For example, the numeric entries in the first row, which refer to all immigrants living in the United States in 1989 who entered the United States between 1985 and 1989, show that 4.4 percent of the immigrants in this entry cohort were born in countries in which English was a dominant language, 15.1 percent were born in countries in which English was an official language, 44 percent were born in countries in which Spanish was a dominant language, and 36.6 percent were born in other countries. The entries in the second row show that 3.2 percent and 15.9 percent of the immigrants resident in the United States in 1989 who entered the country during 1980–1984 were born in countries in which English was a dominant language and an official language, respectively; 49.8 percent were born in countries in which Spanish was a dominant language; and 31.2 percent were born in other countries. In the remaining rows, the entries show the percentages of immigrants living in the United States in 1979 and 1989 who were born in countries in which English is the dominant or an official language or Spanish or some other language is the dominant language.

The data in table 6.3 are based on two surveys and are thus subject to sampling error, and the coding of the linguistic characteristics of immigrants' countries of birth suffers from lack of detail. While conclusions from these data are therefore tentative, the data do suggest two insights.

First, there does not appear to be differential emigration by linguis-

Table 6.3 OFFICIAL OR DOMINANT LANGUAGE OF U.S. IMMIGRANTS' COUNTRY OF BIRTH BY TIME OF IMMIGRATION FOR IMMIGRANTS LIVING IN THE U.S. IN 1979 AND FOR IMMIGRANTS LIVING IN THE U.S. IN 1989

	Official or Dominant Language of Immigrants' Country of Birth							
	English is Dominant		English is Official		Spanish is Dominant		Other Language	
	Immigrants Living in U.S. in:		Immigrants Living in U.S. in:		Immigrants Living in U.S. in:		Immigrants Living in U.S. in:	
Time Period of Immigration to U.S.	1979[1]	1989[2]	1979	1989	1979	1989	1979	1989
1985–1989	—	4.4	—	15.1	—	44.0	—	36.6
1980–1984	—	3.2	—	15.9	—	49.8	—	31.2
1975–1979	7.8	2.8	18.6	14.8	32.3	44.3	41.3	38.1
1970–1974	5.8	5.1	17.3	17.9	40.7	40.9	36.2	36.1
1965–1969	12.0	11.2	11.5	12.4	39.4	42.8	37.0	33.6
1960–1964	16.3	16.2	5.0	5.5	36.3	38.8	42.4	39.5
1950–1959	18.0	} 23.3	4.0	} 3.6	20.1	} 17.8	57.9	} 55.3
before 1950	24.9		2.3		10.6		62.2	

1. Source: 1979 November CPS.
2. Source: 1989 November CPS.

tic characteristics between 1979 and 1989 for immigrants entering the United States before the mid-1970s. For example, in 1979, 16.3 percent of the cohort of immigrants who entered the United States in 1960–1964 were born in countries dominated by English (table 6.3, column 1); ten years later, in 1989, almost exactly the same percentage (16.2 percent) of this same cohort of immigrants were born in countries dominated by English (table 6.3, column 2). This conclusion concerning the apparent lack of differential emigration by linguistic characteristics for earlier cohorts may reflect the fact that immigrants are more likely to leave the United States within the first handful of years after entry into the country than later. (Furthermore, if rates of emigration drop quickly after the time of arrival in the country, then the possibility of being able to discern differential emigration also drops correspondingly.) It may also reflect a true drop in differential emigration according to length of time lived in the United States.

The second conclusion from table 6.3 is that differential emigration or retention may be operating for the most recent entry cohort of immigrants, the one entering 1975–1979, that we can analyze with the 1979 and 1989 CPS data. Table 6.3 shows that in 1979, 7.8 percent of the 1975–1979 cohort members were from countries in which English was a dominant language; ten years later, only 2.8 percent of the members of this entry cohort were from countries in which English was a dominant language. The percentage of immigrants from countries in which English is an official (but not dominant) language also drops between 1979 and 1989 (from 18.6 percent to 14.8 percent). Because of the way in which the comparisons across 1979 and 1989 are made, the only plausible[5] way the percentages of immigrants in this entry cohort who are from English-language countries could decrease between 1979 and 1989 is through higher rates of emigration of the immigrants from these countries relative to immigrants from other countries. For this cohort, it appears that the apparently high emigration of immigrants from the English-language countries corresponds to an apparently high retention of the subset of immigrants from Spanish-language countries (table 6.3, columns 5 and 6).

Unfortunately, the data presented here do not leave any clues about the nature of the selection processes responsible for the apparent differential emigration during the first decade or so after arrival in the United States. Not only do the data refer to the linguistic characteristics of the immigrants' countries of birth rather than the immigrants' own linguistic capabilities, the data do not allow any discussion of characteristics such as language learning aptitude or motivation. The wide band of time between the 1979 and the 1989 CPSs also does not allow any description of differential emigration during the first few years after arrival, when the possibility of differential emigration is probably most marked.

In addition, the nature of the data does not allow the disentangling of the apparent differential probabilities of retention versus emigration among immigrants in the 1975–1979 entry cohort. For example, the apparently higher probability of emigration of immigrants from English-language countries may be a product of their lesser commitment or lesser investment in language learning than other immigrants. The apparently higher retention during the 1980s of the immigrants from Spanish-language countries who entered the United States during the late 1970s may be a byproduct of the 1986 immigration legislation (Immigration Reform and Control Act of 1986), which allowed many illegal immigrants to apply for amnesty. The apparently higher retention of immigrants from Spanish-language countries may reflect the special status of Spanish in the United States: It is the second most commonly spoken language in the United States. The apparently higher retention of immigrants from Spanish-language countries versus immigrants from other non-English-language counties could also reflect the availability of Spanish-language communities in the United States in which to live, an option not readily available for immigrants who speak other non-English languages. The retention could, of course, be a product of factors unrelated to language, such as the close proximity of Spanish-language countries to the United States and the relatively low cost of traveling between the United States and the immigrants' home countries.

Linguistic Adaptation after Arrival in the United States

The third major process related to the linguistic attributes of immigrants is the acquisition of English as a second (or higher-order) language, or what is sometimes called "anglicization," after arrival in the United States. Immigrants who know no English or who lack a high level of proficiency in English at time of entry in the United States can acquire English as a second or higher-order language.

Several major theoretical perspectives concern second-language learning and suggest reasons for the cessation of learning in a second language (McLaughlin 1987). Second-language learning, for example, is sometimes considered to be akin to first-language learning in the sense that the acquisition of any order language is seen as the acquisition of a complex cognitive skill. Highly educated people, who presumably have more-developed cognitive skills, may have an advantage in second-language learning. Second-language learning is also sometimes considered to differ from first-language learning. Krashen (1981) differentiates, for example, between "language acquisition," which occurs through the communication of information to and by the learner and is typical of the process through which individuals become proficient in a first language, and "language learning," which involves the presence of a monitor, which reviews and possibly alters utterances before production and is typical of the process through which individuals become proficient in a second language. An allied theoretical perspective that differentiates between first- and second-language acquisition rests on the notion of the "interlanguage" which describes the interim and interlocking grammars constructed by second-language learners as they acquire competence in the new language. A fourth and very general perspective emphasizes the role of social and psychological factors by postulating that "second language acquisition is just one aspect of acculturation and the degree to which a learner acculturates to the target-language group will control the degree to which he acquires the second language" (Schumann 1978).

Linguistic Adaptation and Length of Residence in the United States

All the theoretical perspectives on second-language learning acknowledge the role of time. Over time and with increased exposure to second-language input, individuals' levels of proficiency in a second language tend to increase. Language monitoring becomes more facile and automaticity is achieved; interlanguages more closely approximate the target language; and acculturation occurs in nonlinguistic dimensions.

Table 6.4 shows the distributions across immigrants' self-reported speaking proficiency in English in 1989 by the time period of immigration. Because immigrants from English-language-dominated countries are very likely to be proficient in English at or soon after time of arrival in the United States (table 6.2), they are not included in table 6.4. The data presented in table 6.4 show that English language proficiency increases across the immigrants' entry cohorts and thus presumably increases with time lived in the United States. Among the newest immigrants, those entering the country since 1987, over half report speaking English "not well at all" or "not well," whereas only 1 in 25 of the immigrants entering the country before 1960 report speaking English "not well at all" and only 1 in 9 report speaking English "not well" in 1989.

Table 6.4 PERCENTAGES OF IMMIGRANTS FROM COUNTRIES DOMINATED BY
NON-ENGLISH LANGUAGES BY LEVEL OF SELF-REPORTED
PROFICIENCY IN ENGLISH IN 1989 BY TIME OF IMMIGRATION,
CPS 1989

Time Period of Immigration to U.S.	Level of English Proficiency (and numeric code)					
	Not Well at All (1)	Not Well (2)	Well (3)	Very Well (4)	Total	Average
1987–1989	21.7	30.1	18.5	29.7	100.0	2.43
1985–1986	18.1	32.7	20.3	28.8	99.9	2.60
1982–1984	12.8	29.2	24.4	33.7	100.1	2.79
1980–1981	11.2	30.2	27.6	31.0	100.0	2.78
1975–1979	7.4	22.7	23.6	46.3	100.0	3.09
1970–1974	6.9	16.0	20.2	56.9	100.0	3.27
1965–1969	6.2	14.9	15.0	63.8	99.9	3.36
1960–1964	4.3	11.8	14.4	69.4	99.9	3.49
Before 1960	3.4	8.5	11.9	76.3	100.1	3.61

The last column in table 6.4 shows the average level of speaking proficiency in English calculated by assuming that the levels of reported proficiency can be coded "1" (lowest level of proficiency) through "4" (highest level of proficiency). When English language proficiency is quantified in this way, the average level of proficiency steadily increases over time. This general finding—and the interpretation that this relationship reflects English language acquisition occurring in the United States—is a common one (Jasso and Rosenzweig 1990, Veltman 1983).

The strong relationship between English language proficiency and length of time in the United States as portrayed in table 6.4 may, however, be partly attributable to two other factors. The findings in table 6.4 may reflect differential emigration or retention of individuals with superior language learning aptitudes at time of arrival, or changes across entering cohorts in other characteristics that are relevant to English language proficiency or to learning a second language. It seems unlikely, however, that differential emigration with respect to either entering facility in English and to differential learning of English after entry into the United States accounts for more than a small part of the relationship. The relationship between time and proficiency in English is so strong that the differential retention or emigration on the basis of language characteristics or characteristics relevant to second-language learning would have to be extremely efficient to account fully for it. The differential retention on the basis of language characteristics would also have to persist over the first several decades after arrival of the cohort. Yet the results from table 6.3 suggest that differential retention or emigration on the basis of linguistic and related characteristics is probably most marked within the decade or so after arrival in the States.

If the strong relationship between English language proficiency and length of time lived in the United States is mostly attributable to linguistic adaptation or "anglicization" occurring after arrival, it is surprising that the process of becoming proficient in spoken English stretches over such a long period of time. Linguistic research suggests that exposure to second-language input on the order of 1,000 hours or so should allow adults to attain near native proficiency in a second language (Burke 1974). At two hours a day of English-language input, 2-1/2 years would suffice. At only one hour a day, five years would suffice. Yet the data in table 6.4 suggests that the increases in English language proficiency continue throughout the second decade and into at least the third decade of residence in the United States.

The continuation of increases in immigrants' levels of English language proficiency over such a long period of time could be attributable to immigrants' changing the definition of speaking English "well" or "very well" as they become more facile in English. As their knowledge of English syntax and vocabulary becomes more accurate and more extensive, they may become more discerning about or more critical of their proficiency. This hypothesis fits well with theories of second-language learning that are predicated on iterative and self-conscious processes through which learners acquire near-native proficiency in a second language. On the other hand, if the attainment of proficiency in a second language is indeed limited by degree of acculturation in other social spheres, then the rate of learning English, which is intrinsically associated with American culture, is not driven by the rate at which individuals can learn a second language but by the rate of social acculturation.

LINGUISTIC ADAPTATION AND OTHER SOCIAL AND
DEMOGRAPHIC CHARACTERISTICS

Linguistic theories all expound the role of time or "exposure" to second-language input. Length of residence in the United States is probably the best single measure of amount of exposure to English-language input, but for many immigrants, it is only a crude measure. The regression analyses summarized in tables 6.5 and 6.6 contain several demographic and social variables that measure several differ-

Table 6.5 COEFFICIENTS (AND STANDARD ERRORS) IN REGRESSION MODELS PREDICTING HOW WELL IMMIGRANTS FROM NON-ENGLISH-LANGUAGE COUNTRIES[1] REPORT SPEAKING ENGLISH: CPS, 1989

Independent Variables	I	II	III	IV
Years in U.S.	.040	.044	.044	.055
	(.005)	(.004)	(.004)	(.004)
Years in U.S. squared[2]	−.316	−.420	−.446	−.635
	(.140)	(.121)	(.116)	(.118)
Came to U.S. as a child?	.621	.496	.555	.550
	(.027)	(.024)	(.023)	(.023)
Years of education		.110	.090	.090
		(.002)	(.002)	(.002)
English official in country of birth?[3] (EOCB)			.455	.817
			(.028)	(.049)
Spanish dominant in country of birth?[4] (SDCB)			−.377	−.298
			(.021)	(.036)
Years in US × EOCB[5]				−.029
				(.003)
Years in US × SDCB[6]				−.005*
				(.002)
Constant	2.455	1.212	1.517	1.408
	(.030)	(.036)	(.037)	(.042)
R^2	.168	.379	.443	.449

All coefficients are significant at the .05 level unless marked with an asterisk.
1. Does not include immigrants from countries dominated by English.
2. Coefficients and standard errors multiplied by 1,000.
3. "Yes" coded as '1.' Omitted category is "other." See notes to table 6.1 for list of countries in which English is an official language.
4. "Yes" coded as '1.' Omitted category is "other." See notes to table 6.1 for list of countries in which Spanish is the dominant language.
5. The interaction between the variables years in the United States and whether English is an official language in the immigrant's country of birth.
6. The interaction between the variables years in the United States and whether Spanish is a dominant language in the immigrant's country of birth.

ent aspects of "exposure" to the English language and that, therefore, may influence changes in immigrants' levels of English language proficiency.

The coefficients (and standard errors) presented in table 6.5 are from four regression models in which the dependent variable is English language proficiency coded as an interval level variable ranging from 1 (speaks English not well at all) to 4 (speaks English very

Table 6.6 COEFFICIENTS (AND STANDARD ERRORS) IN REGRESSION MODELS PREDICTING HOW WELL RECENT IMMIGRANTS FROM NON-ENGLISH LANGUAGE COUNTRIES[1] REPORT SPEAKING ENGLISH: CPS, 1989

Independent Variables	I	II	III	IV
Years in U.S.	.078	.064	.037	.041
	(.005)	(.004)	(.004)	(.005)
Years in U.S. squared[2]	−1.251	−.863	−.195*	−.214
	(.153)	(.135)	(.130)	(.141)
Came to U.S. as a child?	.492	.436	.485	.483
	(.031)	(.027)	(.026)	(.026)
Years of education		.102	.083	.084
		(.002)	(.002)	(.002)
English official in country of birth?[3] (EOCB)			.472	.804
			(.027)	(.047)
Spanish dominant in country of birth?[4] (SDCB)			−.447	−.566
			(.030)	(.056)
Years in U.S. × EOCB[5]				−.027
				(.003)
Years in U.S. × SDCB[6]				.034
				(.009)
Constant	2.347	1.242	1.636	1.573
	(.029)	(.037)	(.042)	(.045)
R^2	.224	.401	.466	.475

All coefficients are significant at the .05 level unless marked with an asterisk.
1. Includes only immigrants who entered the country during the 1980s. Does not include immigrants from countries dominated by English.
2. Coefficients and standard errors multiplied by 1,000.
3. "Yes" coded as '1.' Omitted category is "other." See notes to table 6.1 for list of countries in which English is an official language.
4. "Yes" coded as '1.' Omitted category is "other." See notes to table 6.1 for list of countries in which Spanish is the dominant language.
5. The interaction between the variables years in the United States and whether English is an official language in the immigrant's country of birth.
6. The interaction between the variables years in the United States and whether Spanish is a dominant language in the immigrant's country of birth.

well). Because recent immigrants from countries in which English is a dominant language consistently report very high levels of proficiency in English, the models are based on immigrants from countries in which English was not a dominant language.

The first model in table 6.5 summarizes the strong linear relationship between English language proficiency and years lived in the United States. The model also includes a squared term for years lived in the United States and a dichotomous variable indicating whether the respondent immigrated to the United States as a child aged 15 years or less. The results for this model suggest that improvements in English language proficiency taper off across time and that immigration during childhood, rather than in adulthood, substantially increases an immigrant's level of speaking proficiency in English as an adult. Because length of time in the United States has been taken into account, this substantial increase in English language proficiency—0.6 on a scale with a range of 3—may reflect at least some schooling in the United States and thus the effect of participation in a very intensive English-language environment.

The implied importance of schooling in the United States points to a more general effect of education. Model II of table 6.5 includes a measure of educational attainment. Years of completed education has a strong effect on an immigrant's English language proficiency. This effect has been interpreted from a human capital perspective: The costs associated with a continued reliance on a non-English language and thus the impetus for investment in English language proficiency rise with educational attainment (Chiswick and Miller 1992).

Additionally, educational attainment among immigrants may indicate formal instruction in the English language before arriving in the United States. English is taught as a second language in many countries in the equivalent of secondary and postsecondary institutions (Cooper 1982). For immigrants, high educational attainment may thus indicate a jump-start on the acquisition of English before arrival in the United States. On the other hand, higher educational attainment may reflect postsecondary schooling undertaken as a young adult while in the United States. Attendance at and, in particular, the completion of a course of study in an American institution may both require English language skills, and it may add to already extant English skills.

Finally, at the lower end of the educational distribution, linguistic theories imply that individuals with less education are disadvantaged in the acquisition of a complex cognitive skill such as proficiency in a second language. Among lesser-educated individuals who immigrated as adults, lack of literacy in their first language is definitely an impediment to second-language learning. Among lesser-educated individuals who immigrated as children, there is some research, albeit contested, suggesting that children lacking age-appropriate skills in their first language have added difficulties when trying to learn a second language. For these immigrants, their low educational attainment may be, in part, a product of their low levels of English language proficiency.

The last two models in table 6.5 include variables indicating whether the immigrant is from a country in which English is an official language or from a country in which Spanish is a dominant language (the omitted variable is whether or not the immigrant is from a country in which neither Spanish nor English is a dominant or an official language). The inclusion of these variables is an attempt to control for the immigrant's linguistic characteristics at time of immigration. In both Model III and Model IV, the coefficients suggest that immigrants from countries where English is the official language, immigrants who probably knew some English before immigrating, have higher levels of English language proficiency than other immigrants. Furthermore, in Model IV, the interaction term—between having been born in an official English-language country and number of years lived in the United States—has a negative coefficient. Thus, English proficiency among immigrants from countries in which English is an official language does not increase as rapidly with time as for other immigrants, presumably because they arrive in the United States with higher levels of knowledge in English.

The coefficient for the variable indicating whether the immigrant was born in a Spanish-language-dominant country is negative, indicating that immigrants from Spanish-language countries tend to be less proficient in English than immigrants from other non-English-language countries. Yet the interaction term between birth in a Spanish-language-dominant country and years in the United States is insignificant, suggesting that the impact of time in the United States on increases in English language proficiency is the same for immigrants born in Spanish-language- and other non-English-language countries.

Although the regression models presented in table 6.5 are based on cross-sectional data, the results strongly imply that the English language proficiency of immigrants increases with time lived in the United States, although the rate of improvement slows down the longer the immigrants reside in the country. These results could be affected by differences between entering cohorts of immigrants that are relevant to English language proficiency (and are not captured by the variables describing the linguistic characteristics of the immigrant's country of birth) or by a differential emigration of immigrants according to their linguistic attributes, a selection process that earlier analysis suggested may be operating.

Table 6.6 presents regression models based on data only for the immigrants entering the United States in the 1980s in an effort to lessen the possible impact of selective emigration. The results are very similar to those found in table 6.5, with two notable differences.

First, the effect of the squared term for years in the United States is less in the more complex models, suggesting that the larger effect found earlier for the complete sample of immigrants reflected the cessation of English language learning for some immigrants in the earlier entry cohorts. There are several extensively investigated examples of second-language learners whose language learning "fossilized" after a period of time, presumably because of a lack of motivation to progress beyond the level of English language proficiency sufficient for their needs (Schumann 1986).

Second, the coefficient for the interaction between years in the United States and being from a Spanish-language country is significant and positive, suggesting that Hispanic immigrants become proficient in English at a more rapid pace than immigrants from other non-English-language countries. Since immigrants from Spanish-language countries appear to arrive in the United States less proficient in English than other non-English-speaking immigrants, there may be more room for improvement in English. Selective emigration may also influence the coefficient. Many of the immigrants from Spanish-language countries are from Mexico. Repeated movement back and forth across the U.S.-Mexico border is common. Mexican immigrants who have stayed in the country more than a few years may be highly self-selected on accommodation to American culture.

SUMMARY AND DISCUSSION

At any point in time, levels of English language proficiency among immigrants living in the United States are the result of three processes: the selection processes, which encourage or induce potential immigrants with certain linguistic characteristics to immigrate to the United States; the counter-selection processes, which encourage or induce some immigrants in the United States to leave; and the processes through which non-English-language immigrants residing in the United States increase their proficiency in English.

Of these three proccesses, the last has been the most intensively studied by sociologists and economists (Chiswick and Miller 1992, Jasso and Rosenzweig 1990, Stevens 1992, Veltman 1983). However, none of the research has considered, except perhaps in passing, the fact that the three processes are entangled. Without data on the English language abilities of immigrants at time of entry into the United States, it is impossible to establish a benchmark from which to assess progress in English language skills in the American environment. Without data on emigrants, it is impossible to assess the extent to which immigrants' linguistic characteristics are associated with the probability of remaining in or leaving the country. Finally, without longitudinal data, processes of linguistic adaptation occurring within the American context can only be inferred. Yet there is evidence that all three of these processes are operating.

First, some self-selection appears among potential immigrants to the United States on the basis of competency in or knowledge of English. About a tenth of immigrants living in the United States are from countries in which English is a dominant language—a percentage that is much higher than the corresponding percentage of the world's population living in countries dominated by English. Although only about 20% of the world's population speaks English as a first or second language, almost half of the immigrants entering the United States in late 1980s reported speaking English "very well" or "well."

Second, comparisons between the 1979 and 1989 CPSs suggest that differential emigration by linguistic characteristics occurs during the first decade or so after immigrants enter the United States. Immigrants from Spanish-language countries who entered the country during the late 1970s, for example, appear to have been very likely to remain in the United States during the 1980s, while immigrants from English-language countries (who presumably knew some English at time of arrival) appear to have been more likely to emigrate.

Finally, a regression analysis suggested three major factors predicting English language proficiency among immigrants resident in the United States: age at immigration, years lived in the United States, and educational attainment. Although the models are based on cross-sectional data, the results strongly imply that immigrants increase their level of proficiency in English the longer they live in the United States. In addition, the results imply that immigrants who entered the country as children are more proficient in English as adults than immigrants who entered the country after childhood. The accompanying strong effect of educational attainment on English language proficiency could reflect a general academic preparation for the learning of a second language, schooling in English, or formal language training in English in either the United States or in the immigrant's country of birth.

Although all three processes—selective immigration, selective emigration, and the acquisition of English as a second language— affect the distribution of the English language skills of immigrants living in the United States, two appear to be particularly important. In spite of the lack of explicit U.S. legislation concerning the entry of potential immigrants according to their proficiency in English, the majority of new immigrants entering the United States speak English. With time and education, the others learn English. Although there have been several recent attempts to declare English the official language of the United States, the nature of the selection processes underlying who immigrates to the United States and of the extent of the language learning that occurs after they arrive are already much more compelling declarations of the fact that English is, de facto, the nation's official language.

Notes

I am grateful to Sandra Gauvreau and Lisa Kelly-Wilson for research assistance, to Bonny Graham for editorial assistance, and to Barry Edmonston and Harvey Choldin for detailed comments.

1. The Survey of Income and Education, fielded in 1976, and the English Language Proficiency Survey (U.S. Bureau of the Census 1987) do, however, contain information on non-English languages spoken in childhood.

2. The 1970 Census contains data on "childhood home" language, but the responses refer to whether a non-English language was spoken in the respondent's childhood home, not to whether the respondent actually spoke the non-English language in childhood (see Veltman 1983 for a critical discussion of the question).

3. The linguistic characteristics of countries were classified using Decsy's (1987) classification of the world's language populations and Hawkins's (1987) description of official policies concerning the English language.

4. When compared against 1980 U.S. Census data, the CPS-based percentages of immigrants born in countries in which English was either an official or a dominant language seem low.

5. Differential mortality can also produce changes over time in the relative sizes of two components of a population, but it seems implausible that differential mortality by linguistic characteristics could produce noticeable differences in only a ten-year time span.

References

Baron, Dennis. 1990. *The English-Only Question.* New Haven: Yale University Press.

Chiswick, Barry R., and Paul W. Miller. 1992. "Language in the Labor Market" In *Immigration, Language, and Ethnicity: Canada and the United States,* edited by Barry R. Chiswick, 229-296. Washington, D.C.: AEI Press.

Cooper, Robert L., ed. 1982. *Language Spread: Studies in Diffusion and Social Change.* Bloomington, IN: Indiana University Press.

Decsy, Gyula. 1987. *Statistical Report on the Languages of the World as of 1985.* Bloomington, IN: Eurolingua.

Fawcett, James T., Benjamin V. Cariño, Insook Han Park, and Robert W. Gardner. 1990. "Selectivity and Diversity: The Effects of U.S. Immigration Policy on Immigrant Characteristics." Paper presented at the Annual Meetings of the Population Association of America, Toronto, Canada, May 1990.

Hawkins, John A. 1987. "English." In *The Major Languages of Western Europe,* edited by Bernard Comrie, 67–99. New York: Routledge.

Jasso, Guillermina, and Mark R. Rosenzweig. 1990. *The New Chosen People: Immigrants to the United States.* New York: Russell Sage.

Krashen, S. D. 1981. *Second Language Acquisition and Second Language Learning.* Oxford: Pergamon Press.

Leibowitz, Arnold H. 1984. "The Official Character of Language in the United States: Literacy Requirements for Immigration, Citizenship, and Entrance into American Life." *Aztlan* 15: 25–70.

McLaughlin, Barry. 1987. *Theories of Second-Language Learning.* London: Edward Arnold.

Schumann, J. H. 1975. "Second Language Acquisition: The Pidginization Hypothesis." Ph.D. diss., Harvard University, Cambridge, MA.

————. 1986. "Research on the Acculturation Model for Second Language Acquisition." *Journal of Multilingual and Multicultural Development* 7:379–392.

Stevens, Gillian. 1992. "The Social and Demographic Contexts of Language Use in the U.S." *American Sociological Review* 57:171–185.

U.S. Department of Commerce, Bureau of the Census. 1979. *Current Population Survey, November 1979.* [MRDF.] Washington, D.C.

————. 1987. *English Language Proficiency Study (ELPS) 1982 Microdata File.* [Technical Documentation.] Washington, D.C.

————. 1991. *Current Population Survey, November 1989.* [MRDF]. Washington, D.C.

U.S. Immigration and Naturalization Service. 1980. *Statistical Yearbook of the Immigration and Naturalization Service 1979.* Washington, D.C.: U.S. Government Printing Office.

_____. 1990. *Statistical Yearbook of the Immigration and Naturalization Service 1989.* Washington, D.C.: U.S. Government Printing Office.

Veltman, Calvin. 1983. *Language Shift in the United States.* New York: Mouton.

Chapter Seven

THE SETTLEMENT AND SECONDARY MIGRATION PATTERNS OF LEGALIZED IMMIGRANTS: INSIGHTS FROM ADMINISTRATIVE RECORDS

Kristin E. Neuman and Marta Tienda

International immigration as an economic and social problem commanded considerable attention within the research and policy communities during the late 1970s and early to mid-1980s, with considerable emphasis on the problem of illegal immigration. This interest peaked with passage and implementation of the Immigration Reform and Control Act of 1986 (IRCA), the most significant revision of immigration policy since the 1965 Amendments to the Immigration and Nationality Act of 1952. Precipitated in large measure by a desire to reduce U.S.-bound illegal immigration, IRCA included provisions for: (1) stemming the supply of undocumented workers through tightened control of the border; (2) penalizing employers who knowingly and willingly hire undocumented workers, as a measure to curb the demand for unauthorized workers; and (3) an amnesty program through which undocumented aliens residing in the United States could legalize their status as immigrants.

The amnesty program, which began in May 1987, stipulated that undocumented aliens who had resided continuously in the United States prior to January 1, 1982, could apply for temporary residence as Legally Authorized Workers (LAWs). Less stringent requirements were extended to agricultural workers, who were eligible for Special Agricultural Worker (SAW) status if they furnished evidence of employment in agricultural jobs for at least 90 days during 1986.[1] Both categories of undocumented immigrants were required to apply for permanent residence within 12 to 18 months following receipt of their temporary residence status. As a result of the amnesty provisions of IRCA, more than 1.7 million illegal aliens were granted temporary resident status as LAWs, and more than 1.3 million were granted temporary resident status as SAWs.[2]

Although the overall impact of the amnesty program will not be known for some time, the nature and magnitude of these impacts will differ across states and labor markets, with the most pronounced consequences in those areas where the legalized aliens reside. Therefore, a first step toward assessing the impact of the legalization program involves documenting the settlement patterns of diverse groups who legalized their status under the amnesty provision. Accordingly, this chapter examines the residential distribution and secondary migration of newly legalized aliens who began the process of status adjustment under the LAW program.[3] Three aspects of geographic distribution examined include: (1) residential location at first entry and at date of application for amnesty; (2) interstate/inter-region migrant streams; and (3) determinants of secondary migration.

BACKGROUND

Many researchers have identified uneven consequences of immigration. The impact is greatest in areas with high concentrations of immigrants (Bartel 1989; Greenwood 1983; Jones 1982, 1984; Passel 1986; Passel and Woodrow 1984). Historically, most immigrants have been concentrated in a handful of states, and that pattern continues. Not surprisingly, the five states that host the majority of legal immigrants—California, Texas, New York, Illinois, and Florida—also attract the most undocumented migrants. The spatial distribution of LAWs has direct implications for the states and cities most affected by IRCA legalization. The residential distribution of immigrants at any point in time is a function of their initial distribution upon entry to the United States and secondary migration within the United States. Given the historical residential preferences of the foreign-born, three questions arise concerning the geographic distribution of the LAW population. First, how similar is their initial residential profile to that of the legal immigrant population? Second, how pervasive is secondary migration among undocumented aliens? Third, does secondary migration lead to increased or decreased geographic concentration? The practical importance of these questions derives from the social impacts of the amnesty program, which derive, in turn, from volume and settlement patterns of amnestied immigrants and their participation in the labor force and various social institutions. Their theoretical importance is to shed light on the meaning of legal status as a circumstance that shapes opportunity and behavior.

Despite widespread agreement that the impact of immigration is residentially bound, relatively few studies have examined the geographic distribution of legal immigrants, and hardly any have looked

at secondary migration of undocumented U.S. immigrants.[4] Exceptions include Reichert and Massey (1979), Bartel (1989), and Jones
(1982, 1984). In an article examining differences between legal and
illegal migrants from a rural town in Mexico, Reichert and Massey
(1979, 620) found that those with legal status in the United States
were much more likely to move than those who were undocumented,
and they suggested a "strong proclivity of illegals to remain seden-
tary." Using microdata from the 1980 Census, Bartel observed higher
rates of internal migration among the foreign-born compared to the
native-born population, but she also found differences among regional-origin groups. Asian immigrants were more likely to engage in
secondary migration than either Europeans or Latinos. In addition,
she found that secondary migration resulted in greater spatial concentration of the foreign-born, although this varied somewhat by origin
groups. Jones, on the other hand, presented evidence supporting a
"dispersion thesis," at least among undocumented Mexican immigrants. However, he acknowledged only weak evidence of dispersion.
Because Jones used data on undocumented Mexicans only, and Bartel's study was based on the foreign-born population, regardless of
citizenship or legal status, it is not clear that their conclusions apply
to the LAW population. Furthermore, even within the LAW population there will likely be differences in migration patterns by place
of birth. These differences are substantively significant, not only
because individual characteristics differ by place of birth (Keely 1974,
Massey 1981, Passel 1986), but also because assimilation processes
differ markedly by country of origin and time of arrival.

One reason immigrants might be more likely to move than natives
is that they may have shallower social ties in their initial U.S. destination. This suggests a duration dependence between length of U.S.
residence and the propensity to move, with earlier arrivals exhibiting
higher propensities to move than later arrivals. Another reason may
involve selection effects (DaVanzo 1978, DaVanzo and Morrison
1981). Migrants who are not successful in improving their situation
by moving are likely to return to their original place of residence.
Those who are successful may be predisposed to move again in hopes
of improving their circumstances even further. However, given the
role of social networks in shaping international streams in the first
place, the influence of economic factors on secondary migration is
weakened.

The well-established positive association between education and
internal migration (Greenwood 1975, Long 1982) reflects both a
greater willingness on the part of the better-educated to take risks

and their enhanced ability to evaluate the costs and benefits of a move (Findley 1982, DaVanzo 1978). Bartel (1989) found that better-educated immigrants have higher rates of migration and that their geographic movement reduces spatial concentration, despite the absence of a tendency toward dispersion among the foreign-born population as a whole.

Age has been found to be negatively related to migration, with persons in their 20s most likely to move and the probability of movement decreasing with additional years of age (DaVanzo 1978, Findley 1982, Greenwood 1975, Long 1982).[5] Findley claimed that the young have fewer responsibilities and more time to realize the potentially greater earnings stemming from a move. Sandefur and Scott (1981), however, found neither age nor education to be significantly related to internal migration. Because their study was restricted to a ten-year birth cohort of white males, it may not be possible to generalize their findings, but their results underscore the need to examine commonly accepted and intuitively sensible relationships among internal migration and various individual characteristics.

In addition to their direct effects on migration decision-making, age and education have been shown to condition the influence of other variables. For example, DeVanzo (1978, 7) argued that the relationship between unemployment and internal migration "is uneven because workers more prone to unemployment—those in blue-collar occupations, with low skill and educational levels, or of advanced age—tend to be more immobile than others." Greenwood (1975) suggested that the unemployed are more likely to move than the employed but that this relationship may differ by subgroup, a finding supported by the work of Wilson and Tienda (1989). Massey (1981) argued that low rates of mobility for undocumented Mexican migrants largely reflect their lower socioeconomic status compared with other Western Hemisphere immigrants. Also, illegal aliens from Mexico are more likely to be in unskilled occupations compared with immigrants from other regions (Borjas and Tienda 1987). Both characteristics—Mexican origin and incumbency in low-status occupations—are associated with low mobility rates. Whether illegal Mexican immigrants exhibit lower rates of secondary migration is an empirical question we consider below.

DATA AND METHODS

We analyze data from records of illegal aliens who applied for "amnesty" under the Legally Authorized Workers (LAWs) provision of the Immigration Reform and Control Act of 1986 (IRCA), as recorded by an administrative file known as the Legalization Application Processing System (LAPS). As of May 16, 1990, 1,762,143 aliens had applied for amnesty under the LAW program, with an approval rate of 94.5 percent.[6] Approved applicants were granted temporary resident status for a period of 18 months, but were required before the expiration date to petition for permanent residence (regular "green card") and to demonstrate basic English language skills and knowledge of U.S. civics.[7]

One strength of the LAPS database is its size. Our analyses are based on a 15 percent sample of all LAW applicants. We restricted the sample of 259,484 applicants to those age 18 or older who were actually granted temporary resident status by the date the program formally terminated (May 4, 1988), resulting in a final sample of 220,791 applicants granted temporary LAW status. Of these, 70 percent were from Mexico, but the large sample permits further disaggregation by region of origin. For example, although African-born applicants constitute less than 2 percent of LAW applicants, this represents over 3,500 observations. Another important attribute of the LAPS database is that it is nationally representative. Because collecting nationally representative information on illegal aliens has proven virtually impossible, most prior research had been restricted to incidental samples, such as those based on aliens residing in particular locations, working in specific industries, or living temporarily in detention centers. This has precluded micro-level analyses of specific behavioral outcomes, like migratory behavior, that are even approximately nationally representative.[8] Because applicants under IRCA were required to prove continuous residence in the United States since at least January 1, 1982, short-term and seasonal, or "sojourner," migrants have been largely selected out. This means that our results may be generalized to those "settled" illegal immigrants who had been in this country for at least five years as of 1987, who applied for amnesty, and who were successful in satisfying admission requirements. We do not know the proportion of undocumented aliens who either did not qualify for and/or did not apply for amnesty.[9]

Because the residential change data in the LAPS data are retrospective, internal migration patterns of LAWs pertain to those of **illegal aliens**. However, in speculating about the social consequences of spatial distribution patterns of persons granted temporary residence status, we acknowledge that lawful status could shape future impacts. We use the terms **illegal** or **undocumented aliens** in reference to our applicant sample because the patterns examined refer to behavior that occurred prior to regularizing their status.

The LAPS file provides basic demographic information about applicants: their occupation, their place of residence and their place of birth, the date and place of their most recent entry, and some information about their family members living in the United States.[10] Data on place of residence were collected for current and previous residences in the United States. Instructions on the I-687 application form required the applicant to list all previous residences in the United States that lasted six months or more. Only five residences (including current) were keyed.

Data quality varies considerably according to specific variables. Data on applicant's sex, for example, are quite reliable and very rarely missing. Many other items, however, have large quantities of missing data (such as occupation) or were inconsistent with other information in the database. These problems result in large part because the data were collected for administrative purposes and were often collected by private organizations that differed greatly in their experience collecting data and in their familiarity with immigration. Finally, among immigrants with low levels of formal schooling, such as Mexicans and Salvadorans, accuracy of responses certainly affected the reliability of retrospective items. We restricted our analyses to items deemed reliable after extensive editing and cleaning of the LAPS file.

Our dependent variable is whether the applicant is a mover, defined as having made a change of residence across state boundaries subsequent to most recent entry. **Place of origin** is defined as the state of most recent entry and assumes that illegal immigrants live, for at least a short period of time, in the state through which they enter.[11] **Destination** is the state of residence where the immigrant applied for amnesty.

For the descriptive analyses, the sample is divided into seven region-of-birth groups. Mexicans and Salvadorans are treated separately because of their relatively large numbers; other Latin Americans make up a third group. The fourth, fifth, and sixth groups are Asians, Africans, and Europeans, respectively; the residual group, "Other," contains applicants from remaining countries, mainly the non-Spanish-speaking Caribbean, Oceania, and Canada. Details of countries included in each region are reported in appendix 7.A.

In deriving an internal geographic classification for the study of residential mobility, we keep the states hosting the largest immigrant populations separate and collapse those with small shares of immigrants into subregions. Because California, Texas, Illinois, and Florida are each home to a relatively large share of LAWs, they are analyzed separately. New York and New Jersey are combined into one category, and the remaining states are grouped into five regional categories: Other West, Other South, Other Midwest, Other Northeast, and Other (see appendix 7.A for further detail).

RESIDENTIAL AND SECONDARY MIGRATION PATTERNS OF LEGALIZED ALIENS: TABULAR RESULTS

We begin our empirical analysis by comparing the residential profile of the legalized aliens with that of the foreign-born population in the June 1988 Current Population Survey (CPS).[12] A comparison of the country-of-origin distributions in table 7.1 reveals substantial differences. Most salient is the share of Mexicans. In the CPS, Mexicans and Salvadorans account for 23.3 percentage points of all foreign-born. However, these two origin groups account for 70 percent of the LAPS sample. This is consistent with previous work on the character of the illegal population.

The CPS (not shown) and LAPS samples are similar in percentage born in Africa, but other origin places are more highly represented among the foreign-born than among amnestied aliens. For example, Other Latin Americans comprise almost one in ten of legalized aliens compared to 14 percent of all legal immigrants. Asians and Europeans constitute only 4.8 percent and 2 percent of the LAW population, respectively, but roughly one-quarter of legal immigrants. In sum, the population legalizing under IRCA differs appreciably from legal immigrants in terms of national origins.

Settlement patterns of legalized immigrants tend to follow those of previous, and presumably legal, immigrants from similar regional origins. Networks of immigrants from a country provide information and assistance to prospective immigrants from their communities, leading to residential concentration and emergence of "sister" or "daughter" communities in the host society (Massey and Garcia España 1987). Spatial concentration of immigrants is evident for the foreign-born population generally, but it is especially pronounced for recently legalized aliens, who probably have the greatest need for sponsored entry and settlement assistance from earlier arrivals.

Over 90 percent of the LAWs live in the states that traditionally have hosted the lion's share of the foreign-born population, and although the national sample of all foreign-born individuals indicates

Table 7.1 RESIDENTIAL DISTRIBUTION OF IRCA APPLICANTS AND CPS FOREIGN-BORN POPULATION AGED 18+ BY REGION/COUNTRY OF ORIGIN

Residence	CPS			Total	LAPS						
	Foreign Born	Mexico El Salv.	Other		Mexico	El Salvador	Other Latin America	Asia	Africa	Europe	Other
California	26.9	59.6	22.6	58.2	65.1	68.4	41.9	41.3	11.3	14.7	14.0
Texas	6.8	20.7	4.0	14.7	17.9	13.7	5.3	5.6	9.0	1.8	1.7
New York/New Jersey	16.7	2.7	23.3	8.6	1.1	7.6	29.3	27.3	37.2	32.0	49.5
Illinois	4.9	4.9	4.9	6.9	7.7	0.9	3.6	6.3	3.1	31.8	2.4
Florida	7.9	1.4	11.6	2.3	0.5	0.8	9.7	2.4	1.9	6.1	17.9
Other West	6.2	7.4	5.7	4.6	5.9	1.2	1.2	2.8	2.2	2.8	2.1
Other South	10.0	1.8	8.8	2.4	0.9	6.2	3.1	8.0	24.4	2.3	3.3
Other Midwest	10.9	1.0	7.6	0.9	0.8	0.2	0.4	3.2	3.7	2.5	1.2
Other Northeast	8.7	0.3	10.2	1.1	0.1	1.0	3.1	2.8	7.2	5.6	6.9
Other	0.8	0.1	1.3	0.3	0.0	0.0	2.4	0.4	0.0	0.3	0.9
[% of N]	[100]	[23.3]	[76.7]	[100]	[69.3]	[9.0]	[9.6]	[4.8]	[1.7]	[2.0]	[3.6]
[N]	[12,602]a	[1,962]a	[6,454]a	[220,791]	[153,002]	[19,837]	[21,147]	[10,687]	[3,678]	[4,467]	[7,968]

Source: Legalization Application Processing System (LAPS) and pooled April 1983, June 1986, and June 1988 Current Population Survey.
a. The discrepancy between the total foreign-born CPS sample and the sum of the Mexican/Salvadoran and Other subsamples is due to missing information on the place of birth variable for one-third of the sample. This resulted because of cost-saving measures implemented by the Bureau of Labor Statistics. Observations missing place of birth are random relative to those for which valid codes are available.

less concentration, the six top states house over 60 percent of legal immigrants. In both samples, Mexicans and Salvadorans are more likely to live in California than in all other states combined. The index of dissimilarity (ID) for the Mexican/Salvadoran distributions for the two samples is only 7.9, indicating a close correspondence of residential distribution between the undocumented and legal.[13] Other Latin Americans in the LAPS sample are disproportionately concentrated in California, as are Asians, and both groups also have large concentrations in New York/New Jersey. Africans and Europeans are most concentrated in New York/New Jersey; however, the second most popular place of residence for Europeans is Illinois, while for Africans, it is the Other South states.

That such a high proportion of Mexicans and Salvadorans live in California and Texas is no surprise, since residential contiguity of these border states results in a disproportionate share of the illegal "entries without inspection (EWI)," usually by foot or by car. Other groups, such as Africans and Europeans, tend to enter on legal nonimmigrant visas and become illegal because they overstay their allotted time. This mode of entry may allow them wider locational options than EWIs, whose clandestine entry is illegal from the start.

These residential patterns at the time of application for amnesty result from two mechanisms: destination choices at most recent entry and secondary migration. Separate tabulations, not shown here, of secondary migration status by place of birth, provide strong evidence that place of birth is associated with the likelihood of a residential change subsequent to successful entry to the United States (Neuman 1991). Just over one-quarter of amnestied immigrants changed residence at least once between the time of most recent entry and application for amnesty, but the likelihood of secondary moves varied appreciably by place of birth. Mexicans were least likely to move subsequent to their initial entry; Asians and Africans were most likely to do so. Specifically, 19 percent of the Mexicans were secondary movers, compared with more than two-thirds of illegal immigrants from Asia and Africa. Salvadorans are similar to Mexicans with respect to migratory behavior, with just over a quarter moving across state boundaries subsequent to their arrival. After initial entry, 45 percent of Other Latin Americans changed their state of residence. Africans and Europeans are more similar to Asians, with 67.6 percent and 63.6 percent, respectively, classified as movers.

One reason for this association may be the distance of the move. Those who move to the United States from countries farther away, such as Africans, may see the distance involved in secondary migration within the United States as slight by comparison. Another reason may have to do with network migration. Those who arrive already connected to social networks in the destination community, as frequently occurs for Mexicans, may have greater amounts of location-specific capital, in the form of ties to jobs, housing, etc. For them, a subsequent move within the United States might be relatively costly compared to those who come in the absence of such networks.

Locational Choices

Does secondary migration lead to more similar residential patterns between movers and nonmovers, or does it increase the differences between them? Table 7.2 provides three insights into the impact of interstate movement on residential distribution of undocumented migrants at time of application for legalization.

The first insight is that states of entry differed by place of birth. California and Texas were the most common gateways for Mexicans and Salvadorans. Other Latin Americans used Florida in addition to California and Texas. For all non-Latin American groups, New York/New Jersey was important, as was Florida. Second, aliens who entered through the gateways historically used by others from the same place of origin were less likely to move prior to the time of application for legalization. Third, with the possible exceptions of immigrants from Asia and from "Other" countries, movers were less residentially concentrated than nonmovers from the same place of birth. That is, movers were more highly represented (although still fairly small in absolute numbers) in states not among the six high immigrant states.

A comparison of entry and current residence distributions of movers and nonmovers reveals that secondary migration of illegal aliens may lead to greater residential dispersion, although large shares of the mover population remain in the top six immigrant states. If secondary migration leads to greater residential dispersion throughout the country, the social impacts of illegal immigration ultimately will be less acute in the high immigrant states. The extent of dispersion or concentration stemming from secondary migration is easily summarized by the index of dissimilarity. If secondary migration results in dispersion, then the index for place of residence (ID_R) will be higher than that for place of entry (ID_E).

Among Mexicans, nonmovers were more than twice as likely as movers to have entered through California: Three-fourths of nonmovers from Mexico entered through California, compared to just over

Table 7.2 PLACE OF ENTRY AND PLACE OF RESIDENCE, BY PLACE OF BIRTH AND MOVER STATUS: LEGALIZED ALIENS AGED 18+

State/Region of Residence	Total		Mexico		El Salvador		Other Latin Am.	
	Mover	Nonmover	Mover	Nonmover	Mover	Nonmover	Mover	Nonmover
At entry								
California	27.7	72.4	36.5	75.5	36.7	81.8	29.3	65.4
Texas	32.7	19.0	51.0	21.6	49.6	17.3	20.5	7.5
New York/New Jersey	13.4	3.9	0.1	0.1	0.6	0.2	7.1	10.2
Illinois	0.9	0.5	0.2	0.3	0.0	0.0	0.2	0.1
Florida	8.1	1.6	0.1	0.0	3.8	0.3	29.8	11.7
Other West	8.0	2.0	11.7	2.5	7.8	0.3	4.1	0.4
Other South	1.7	0.1	0.1	0.0	1.4	0.1	3.2	0.5
Other Midwest	0.9	0.0	0.1	0.0	0.0	0.0	0.2	0.0
Other Northeast	1.2	0.1	0.1	0.0	0.1	0.0	0.4	0.1
Other	5.5	0.3	0.0	0.0	0.0	0.0	5.2	4.0
At application (1987–88)								
California	20.8		20.3		30.0		13.4	
Texas	3.3		2.2		3.6		2.8	
New York/New Jersey	20.8		5.3		28.5		52.0	
Illinois	23.7		39.4		3.4		7.9	
Florida	4.0		2.6		2.1		7.4	
Other West	11.6		20.6		3.8		2.1	
Other South	8.6		4.7		23.9		6.2	
Other Midwest	3.3		4.2		0.9		0.8	
Other Northeast	3.6		0.4		3.8		6.8	
Other	0.2		0.1		0.1		0.6	
[N]	[60,220]	[159,569]	[28,974]	[123,450]	[5,040]	[14,658]	[9,451]	[11,502]
[% of area total]	[27.4]	[72.6]	[19.0]	[81.0]	[25.6]	[74.4]	[45.1]	[54.9]
Index of dissimilarity between movers and nonmovers								
Place of entry distributions	44.8		39.1		45.1		39.3	
Current residence distribution	67.4		74.5		65.6		65.5	

continued

Table 7.2 PLACE OF ENTRY AND PLACE OF RESIDENCE, BY PLACE OF BIRTH AND MOVER STATUS: LEGALIZED ALIENS AGED 18+ (continued)

State/Region of Residence	Asia		Africa		Europe		Other	
	Mover	Nonmover	Mover	Nonmover	Mover	Nonmover	Mover	Nonmover
At entry								
California	14.9	55.6	4.2	12.9	3.6	18.4	3.7	12.2
Texas	2.3	2.8	4.8	4.5	2.8	1.7	3.2	0.8
New York/New Jersey	32.9	29.3	66.0	69.7	77.4	57.0	26.7	57.8
Illinois	4.2	7.4	3.1	2.1	1.6	12.0	0.7	0.5
Florida	3.2	1.5	1.3	1.7	2.0	6.8	36.8	26.0
Other West	5.5	1.0	2.5	0.3	2.4	0.9	3.0	0.6
Other South	2.6	0.3	7.2	4.6	2.1	0.2	3.7	0.2
Other Midwest	1.4	0.6	3.6	0.7	4.0	0.4	5.1	0.2
Other Northeast	2.5	0.6	7.1	3.4	3.7	2.0	4.6	0.7
Other	30.6	0.9	0.3	0.0	0.6	0.5	12.7	0.9
At application (1987–88)								
California	35.1		10.6		12.5		15.7	
Texas	6.8		11.1		1.9		2.6	
New York/New Jersey	26.2		21.4		17.7		41.6	
Illinois	5.8		3.6		43.2		4.2	
Florida	2.8		2.1		5.7		10.2	
Other West	3.5		3.1		3.8		3.5	
Other South	11.4		34.0		3.5		6.3	
Other Midwest	4.4		5.1		3.7		2.2	
Other Northeast	3.7		9.0		7.7		12.9	
Other	0.2		0.0		0.2		0.8	
[N]	[7,383]	[3,249]	[2,479]	[1,190]	[2,832]	[1,624]	[4,061]	[3,891]
[% of area total]	[69.4]	[30.6]	[67.6]	[32.4]	[63.6]	[36.4]	[51.1]	[48.9]
Index of dissimilarity between movers and nonmovers								
Place of entry distributions	44.5		12.9		30.2		39.8	
Current residence distributions	25.9		50.7		46.6		32.2	

Source: Legalization Application Processing System (LAPS).

one-third of movers. Just over half of Mexican movers entered through Texas, compared to little more than one-fifth of nonmovers. Mexican movers were less residentially concentrated at time of application than at time of entry compared to nonmovers.[14]

The entry patterns of Salvadorans and Other Latin Americans were similar to those of Mexicans. Nonmovers from El Salvador and Other Latin American countries (other than Mexico) were more than twice as likely as movers to have entered through California, and movers were more than two and a half times more likely than nonmovers to have entered through Texas. Movers from Other Latin American countries were more than two and a half times more likely than nonmovers to have entered through Florida. At time of application, residential patterns of Salvadorans were similar to Mexicans, except that Salvadorans preferred Southern to Western states. Like Mexican movers, Salvadoran movers were less residentially concentrated than nonmovers by time of application. Secondary movement resulted in greater residential dispersion of Other Latin Americans, and at time of application, over half of the movers lived in New York and New Jersey.

Migratory behavior of Asians differs from that of Latin Americans. Although New York/New Jersey and California were still the most popular gateways, undocumented immigrants from Asia were less likely than Mexicans to enter through California. Among nonmovers, 56 percent were more likely to have entered through California, compared to less than one-sixth of movers. Nearly a third of Asian movers entered through places in the residual Other category, compared to less than one of every hundred nonmovers. Movers and nonmovers were almost equally likely, at 32.9 and 29.3 percent, respectively, to have entered through New York/New Jersey. Secondary migration among Asians contrasted to secondary migration among undocumented immigrants from Latin America because it resulted in greater residential concentration, a conclusion supported by the lower ID_R compared to the ID_E. This concentration is driven by the preference of Asians for California as a destination state.

Among Africans, a third distinctive residential pattern is evident. For almost all states of entry, differences between movers and nonmovers are fairly small. Over two-thirds of all undocumented African aliens entered through New York/New Jersey. The distribution of movers at time of application indicates that only one in five African movers remained there, with over one-third moving to Southern states. Thus, secondary migration of Africans leads to decreased residential concentration. In fact, for this group the ID_R exceeds the ID_E

by 37.8, a difference greater than for any other group, including Mexicans.

Like Africans, most Europeans who overstayed visas and became undocumented aliens entered through New York/New Jersey. Illinois was the gateway for 12 percent of European origin nonmovers, but only 1.6 percent of movers. By time of application, less than one-fifth of movers remained in New York/New Jersey, while 43.2 percent of all European movers lived in Illinois. Thus, secondary migration decreased residential concentration of illegal aliens from Europe in all locations except Illinois, where it increased concentration substantially.

Applicants from Canada, Australia, and elsewhere generally entered through New York/New Jersey, although nonmovers were more than twice as likely to have entered there as movers. Florida was the second most common port of entry for this group, the gateway for 37 percent of movers and 26 percent of nonmovers. By time of application, the proportion of movers living in New York/New Jersey had increased substantially, although not as much as the proportion of nonmovers, whereas the proportion of movers in Florida had dropped to a level even lower than that of nonmovers. Thus secondary migration resulted in a slight increase in their residential concentration.

In summary, secondary migration reduces the overall residential concentration of the undocumented population slightly, but the distributional consequences of secondary migration vary by place of birth. While secondary migration decreases residential concentration for Mexicans, Salvadorans, Other Latin Americans, Africans, and Europeans, it increases concentration for Asians and migrants from Canada, Australia, and "Other" countries. These patterns appear to be fairly consistent with those of Jones (1982, 1984) and Bartel (1989), which showed increasing overall dispersion resulting from secondary migration, albeit with subgroup differences. From a national standpoint, however, the patterns of concentration and dispersion amount to residential "re-shuffling" among the six immigrant-dominant states, rather than to a change in the overall pattern of dominant states.

Demographic consequences of the residential relocation of undocumented aliens, whose ports of entry are often at variance with places traditionally inhabited by members of like ethnicity, are summarized in table 7.3. These tabulations show the number of LAWs who entered through each state or regional aggregate, the number who currently

Table 7.3 NET POPULATION CHANGE BY STATE AND REGION OF ORIGIN: LEGALIZED ALIENS AGED 18+

	California	Texas	New York/ New Jersey	Illinois	Florida	Other West	Other South	Other Midwest	Other Northeast	Other
Total Population										
Origin N	132,165	49,977	14,310	1,388	7,486	8,048	1,147	592	852	3,824
Destination N	128,027	32,279	18,794	15,091	5,007	10,194	5,355	2,046	2,315	681
Absolute Difference	−4,138	−17,698	4,484	13,703	−2,479	2,146	4,208	1,454	1,463	−3,143
Percent Gain/Loss	−3.1	−35.4	+31.3	+987.2	−33.1	+26.7	+366.9	+245.6	+171.7	−82.2
Mexican and El Salvadoran										
Origin N	117,677	46,472	166	422	303	6,893	127	24	37	1
Destination N	112,651	30,013	3,068	11,937	936	9,287	2,594	1,277	301	40
Absolute Difference	−5,026	−16,459	2,902	11,515	633	2,394	2,467	1,253	264	39
Percent Gain/Loss	−4.3	−35.4	+1,748.2	+2,728.7	+208.9	+34.7	+1,942.5	+5,220.8	+713.5	+3,900.0
Other Latin American										
Origin N	10,294	2,806	1,849	27	4,170	429	365	16	44	953
Destination N	8,797	1,124	6,092	760	2,015	245	646	81	650	513
Absolute Difference	−1,497	−1,682	4,243	733	−2,155	−184	281	65	606	−440
Percent Difference	−14.5	−59.9	229.5	2,714.8	−51.7	−42.9	77.0	406.3	1,377.3	−46.2
Asian and African										
Origin N	3,165	431	5,846	653	339	500	437	216	419	2,295
Destination N	4,808	923	4,249	757	328	374	1,749	479	559	45
Absolute Difference	1,643	492	−1,597	104	−11	−126	1,312	263	140	−2,250
Percent Difference	+51.9	+114.2	−27.3	+15.9	−3.2	−25.2	+300.2	+121.8	+33.4	−98.0
European and Other										
Origin N	1,025	267	6,449	286	2,674	226	218	336	352	575
Destination N	1,767	218	5,367	1,607	1,698	288	366	209	805	83
Absolute Difference	742	−49	−1,082	1,321	−976	62	148	−127	453	−492
Percent Difference	72.4	−18.4	−16.8	+461.9	−36.5	+27.4	+67.9	−37.8	+128.7	−85.6

Source: Legalization Application Processing System (LAPS).

live in each state, the net gain or loss and the percent net gain or loss.[15]

California is the primary gateway for undocumented aliens and retains a large share of those who entered there. Texas and Florida experienced a **net loss** of about one-third of their undocumented entrants who eventually applied for LAW status, while New York/ New Jersey **increased** their undocumented population by one-third. Other West, Other South, Other Midwest, and Other Northeast states also experienced net gains in undocumented aliens. The most startling figures, however, are for Illinois. This state witnessed a tremendous **net gain** of undocumented aliens, winding up with an undocumented population more than tenfold the number who entered there originally. In part this gain reflects the low absolute numbers using Chicago as their port of entry, even though it may be their ultimate destination.

The huge increase in the number of undocumented aliens in Illinois comprised mainly Mexicans, Salvadorans, and Other Latin Americans. The European presence in Illinois increased fourfold, while the number of Africans and Asians in Illinois increased only slightly. The growth of the illegal alien population in New York/New Jersey resulted largely from inflows of Mexicans, Salvadorans, and Other Latin Americans, but this population gain was offset by an exodus of non-Latin American groups. Although Texas and Florida lost similar proportions of their undocumented aliens, the composition of their populations differed, with Texas more than doubling its Asian and African population and Florida tripling its Mexican and Salvadoran population. California's small net loss of illegal aliens resulted from the exodus of Mexicans, Salvadorans, and Other Latin Americans, although California did take in other groups of illegal aliens.

General trends based on the net gains and losses of population, however, may oversimplify the size and direction of secondary migrant streams because small net changes mask large flows (in or out) that partially cancel each other out. Further insight into the patterns of geographic movement is afforded by decomposing net gains and losses into the secondary migration streams that undergird them. Since these patterns differ by place of birth, mobility tables were computed for each place-of-birth group as well as the sample as a whole. In the interest of economy, we report only the pooled results.

Table 7.4 presents outflows and inflows for the entire sample. Entries along the diagonal, in boldface type, represent those who did not move from their state of entry. The most striking result is the

Table 7.4 GEOGRAPHIC MOBILITY OF LEGALIZED ALIENS: TOTAL POPULATION AGED 18+

Origin	Destination										
	California	Texas	New York/ New Jersey	Illinois	Florida	Other West	Other South	Other Midwest	Other Northeast	Other	Total
Outflow Percents											
California	87.4	0.6	3.3	4.7	0.4	2.1	0.8	0.3	0.3	0.0	100.0
Texas	11.2	60.6	3.9	10.9	1.8	6.0	3.6	1.8	0.3	0.0	100.0
New York/New Jersey	10.0	3.5	52.6	9.9	4.5	1.5	8.9	2.6	6.3	0.1	100.0
Illinois	12.1	3.7	8.9	60.7	1.8	1.7	4.0	5.4	1.5	0.1	100.0
Florida	9.1	2.6	36.3	3.8	34.9	0.8	5.7	0.9	5.9	0.2	100.0
Other West	33.7	1.9	4.3	6.9	0.6	49.8	1.3	0.8	0.6	0.1	100.0
Other South	18.7	6.1	22.3	6.7	5.0	2.1	31.9	2.4	4.5	0.3	100.0
Other Midwest	17.4	7.3	19.1	12.2	15.5	3.9	7.9	14.4	2.2	0.2	100.0
Other Northeast	14.4	6.0	31.8	3.3	6.3	2.1	10.4	1.6	23.6	0.4	100.0
Other	38.8	2.4	28.1	3.4	1.5	3.5	3.7	1.3	2.3	15.1	100.0
Total	58.2	14.7	8.6	6.9	2.3	4.6	2.4	0.9	1.1	0.3	100.0
Inflow Percents											
California	90.2	2.6	23.5	41.8	10.6	26.7	19.8	20.4	16.3	5.9	60.1
Texas	4.4	93.8	10.4	36.0	17.8	29.2	33.4	42.8	7.2	2.8	22.7
New York/New Jersey	1.1	1.6	40.1	9.4	12.9	2.0	23.9	18.2	39.2	1.9	6.5
Illinois	0.1	0.2	0.7	5.6	0.5	0.2	1.0	3.7	0.9	0.1	0.6
Florida	0.5	0.6	14.5	1.9	52.2	0.6	7.9	3.2	19.0	2.1	3.4
Other West	2.1	0.5	1.9	3.7	1.0	39.3	1.9	3.2	2.2	1.5	3.7
Other South	0.2	0.2	1.4	0.5	1.1	0.2	6.8	1.3	2.2	0.4	0.5
Other Midwest	0.1	0.1	0.6	0.2	1.8	0.2	0.9	4.2	0.6	0.1	0.3
Other Northeast	0.1	0.2	1.4	0.5	1.1	0.2	1.7	0.7	8.7	0.4	0.4
Other	1.2	0.3	5.7	0.9	1.1	1.3	2.6	2.5	3.8	84.7	1.7
Total	100.0	100.0	100.0	100.0	100.0	100.0	100.0	100.0	100.0	100.0	100.0

Source: Legalization Application Processing System (LAPS).

large proportion of entrants who remained in their state of entry, especially in California, Texas, New York/New Jersey, Illinois, and Other West states. These states retained more than half of all undocumented aliens who entered there, with California keeping a full 87 percent of those who originally entered there.

The outflows present information about the sending states of those who move. Neither California, Texas, New York/New Jersey, Illinois, nor Other Midwest states sent more than one-fifth of their undocumented aliens to any single destination. Florida, Other South states, Other Northeast states, and Other sent between one-quarter to one-third of the illegals who eventually applied for amnesty to New York/New Jersey.

The inflows indicate destination choices and origin of their undocumented populations. In these tabulations, the boldface diagonal tells the proportion of each state's LAW population that entered there, as opposed to moving there from another state. Underscoring results from tables 7.1 and 7.2, California and Texas stand out as major ports of entry for undocumented aliens, 80 percent of whom originated from Mexico. Despite the appeal of these two states as destination choices, less than 10 percent of the undocumented aliens residing in Texas and California at the time of application were secondary migrants. This contrasts with Illinois and Other Midwest states, where 19 of every 20 illegals who applied for amnesty were secondary migrants who entered elsewhere, whether legally or clandestinely. Two-fifths of secondary migrants to Illinois originated in California. A population loss that is proportionally small for California constitutes a relatively large gain for Illinois. New York/New Jersey and Other West and Other Midwest states each received between one-fifth and one-fourth of their undocumented population from California. Illinois and Other West, Other South, and Other Midwest states each received between 29 percent and 43 percent of their illegal aliens from Texas, and Other South and Other Northeast states received 24 percent and 39 percent, respectively, from New York/New Jersey.

MULTIVARIATE ANALYSIS

If social networks account for the strong holding power of the gateway states and high tendency of illegal immigrants to concentrate in a handful of states, what explains their propensity to move? Obviously, high risks are involved. Geographic movement, especially over land and from areas known to harbor large numbers of illegals, increases the possibility of detection. Are movers positively selected vis-à-vis nonmovers, or do social networks also account for the spatial redistribution of undocumented aliens? Answers to this question require a micro-level analysis of migration decision making. We now turn, therefore, to the applicants themselves to observe how their demographic and social characteristics differ by place of birth and to model the migration decision as a function of some of these traits.

COUNTRY PROFILES

We begin by examining the demographic and social characteristics of the major regional and nationality groups as a prelude to modeling. Table 7.5 presents characteristics associated with migration behavior for each of the country and regional groupings.

Although legal immigration to the United States has been dominated by women since 1930, owing largely to marriages with U.S. citizens and legal residents, men were numerically dominant among illegal aliens (Houston, et al. 1984).[16] However, the gender composition of undocumented migrant streams varies according to region of origin. Illegals from Asia and Africa are least likely to be women, with less than 40 percent female. Just 40 percent of undocumented immigrants from Mexico were women, compared to approximately half of those from other Spanish-speaking countries. Those from Other regions, which include Canada and Australia, constitute the only group with more women than men.

The portrait of Mexicans sketched by these data is one of relatively young immigrants who entered illegally approximately eight years before the amnesty program. Mexicans reported more immediate family members in the United States than did other groups. The somewhat lower labor force participation rate of illegal Mexican migrants mostly reflects a younger age composition and lower activity rates among women. Almost a third of the Mexicans who qualified for LAW status were employed as operators or laborers, and nearly one-fifth were in service jobs at the time of legalization. Salvadorans, also a relatively young population, were more likely than Mexicans to have children in the United States but less likely to have a spouse present. As a group, they reported fewer years of illegal residence than any other group. More than a third were service workers, and more than a quarter were operators or fabricators. Other Latin Americans averaged 8.2 years in the United States before their legalization

Table 7.5 SELECTED SOCIAL AND DEMOGRAPHIC CHARACTERISTICS OF LEGALIZED ALIENS AGED 18 + BY COUNTRY OF ORIGIN: MEANS OR PERCENTS
(Standard Errors)

	Total	Mexico	El Salvador	Other Latin America	Asia	Africa	Europe	Other
% Female	44.3	43.3	48.5	47.4	38.7	39.9	45.0	54.5
Mean age	33.1	31.9	33.3	35.4	38.2	33.7	41.0	38.0
	(10.2)	(10.0)	(10.0)	(10.5)	(11.0)	(7.1)	(12.0)	(11.9)
% with spouse in U.S.	15.5	15.9	12.7	13.6	16.6	16.5	15.6	17.1
% with children in U.S.	27.0	27.1	29.3	26.8	20.5	23.2	19.8	34.0
Mean number of other relatives in U.S.	1.8	2.0	1.7	1.1	0.8	0.6	0.4	1.2
	(2.2)	(2.3)	(1.9)	(1.6)	(1.3)	(1.2)	(0.8)	(1.7)
% with legal entry	18.4	7.8	6.1	32.7	82.2	79.6	84.0	64.6
Years since most recent entry	8.2	8.1	7.7	8.2	8.7	8.7	8.0	9.0
	(3.5)	(3.7)	(2.2)	(2.8)	(2.9)	(3.0)	(3.5)	(3.5)
Labor force participation rate	89.2	88.0	92.2	90.9	92.9	94.2	92.7	92.4

Current Occupation

Farming, forestry, fishing	4.5	6.1	1.6	1.0	0.5	0.2	0.9	1.2
Managerial, professional	5.1	2.7	3.6	6.6	27.2	18.2	14.9	10.3
Technical, sales, administrative support	8.7	6.5	8.3	11.7	22.1	23.8	10.9	17.6
Service	24.7	22.1	35.9	30.0	23.1	30.8	25.9	32.6
Precision production, crafts	12.5	12.8	13.2	13.9	5.8	4.8	17.3	10.4
Operators, fabricators, laborers	29.0	32.8	26.6	24.1	7.9	14.3	18.7	15.5
At home	4.4	5.3	2.4	2.8	2.0	1.0	2.1	1.3
Student/child	1.4	1.5	1.1	1.3	1.5	1.1	1.3	1.8
Unemployed, retired	4.5	4.8	2.8	3.4	6.1	2.0	4.0	4.7
Not reported	5.2	5.5	4.4	5.1	3.7	3.8	4.0	4.6
[N]	220,791	153,002	19,837	21,147	10,687	3,678	4,467	7,968

Source: Legalization Application Processing System (LAPS).

process began. Like Mexicans and Salvadorans, they worked predominantly in service jobs and as operators or laborers.

Asians were more likely to be male, were somewhat older, and were more likely to have a spouse in the United States than were illegal aliens from Spanish-speaking countries, but lower shares of Asians had children here. More than four-fifths were visa overstayers, and they averaged nearly nine years of residence prior to being granted LAW status. Their occupational profile is clearly bimodal, with over one-quarter engaged in managerial or professional jobs and just under one-quarter in service jobs. Almost as many were employed in technical, sales, and administrative support jobs. Undocumented immigrants from Africa were predominantly male visa-overstayers with just under nine years of U.S. residence. They had the highest labor force participation rate, and they were concentrated in service, technical, sales, and administrative support jobs. Like Africans, European illegal aliens were visa-overstayers who averaged eight years of U.S. residence by 1987. Although services, as for most groups, were their modal occupation, Europeans were less occupationally concentrated than other groups.

REGRESSION ANALYSIS

Group differences evident in these profiles have direct implications for the likelihood of secondary migration. In addition to a pooled model that generates main effects on secondary migration probabilities for each of the major nationality and regional groupings, we estimate separate models for each regional group as a function of sex, age, marital status, presence of family members in the United States, occupation at first entry, place of entry, mode of entry, and years of residence.

If the gender patterns of the secondary migration among undocumented immigrants are similar to those of most other migrants, being female should decrease the likelihood of a move. Some prior research suggests that migration probabilities decrease with age, but other research shows that age may simply be a proxy for career and family life-cycle stage. Absent data to portray life-cycle states, we expect some age effects, but their direction, magnitude, and possible interaction with birthplace is an empirical question. The marital status variable, a dummy indicating whether the respondent is married or not, should have a negative effect on secondary migration because married persons generally experience constraints and responsibilities that make residential moves more difficult. For similar reasons, the presence of immediate family members in this country should deter secondary migration. The presence of other relatives, on the other hand, could facilitate secondary migration, particularly if they live in different locations and represent a potential resource for prospective movers.

Employment status also influences migration propensities. Workers engaged in farming are least likely to move because their jobs are often tied to particular pieces of land, whereas incumbents of professional occupations should exhibit high probabilities of moving, given that labor markets for such jobs operate at the national, rather than the local, level. Finally, the unemployed should exhibit a high propensity to move in search of better job opportunities (Wilson and Tienda 1989).

Variables in the LAPS file related to entry refer to the most recent entry and include **place** and **manner** of entry as well as **time** since entry. The place of entry will affect secondary migration probabilities, as prospective movers assess the desirability of that location relative to alternative destinations. Entry through preferred destinations by a specific group will, other things equal, deter secondary migration. Manner of entry could influence the likelihood of secondary migration, although its direction is an empirical question. On the one hand, legal entry on a nonimmigrant visa provides a period during which aliens may learn about opportunities and move around freely without fear of apprehension. On the other hand, legal entry on a visa provides access to the preferred residential location, making subsequent movement less necessary. Other things equal, length of U.S. residence, measured as time since most recent entry, should increase the likelihood of secondary migration as a function of greater exposure (longer risk) and longer time to acquire information about how to change residence without detection, but longer residence in a given location increases the probability of establishing roots, or transiting from "sojourner" to "resident" status (Massey et al. 1987). Hence the expected effect of this variable is indeterminant.[17]

Table 7.6 displays the results of regressing migrant status on a vector of individual social and demographic characteristics known to influence migratory behavior. In general, the results conform to expectations but with some surprises. The gender coefficient is negative for every group and is statistically significant for all groups except Africans and Europeans. This result implies a 3 percent lower migration probability for undocumented women compared to their

Table 7.6 LOGIT COEFFICIENTS PREDICTING INTERNAL MIGRATION: LEGALIZED ALIENS AGED 18 + (Standard Errors)

	Total	Mexico	El Salvador	Other Latin America	Asia	Africa	Europe	Other
Female	-0.145** (0.015)	-0.061** (0.022)	-0.343** (0.039)	-0.309** (0.032)	-0.154** (0.052)	-0.030 (0.078)	-0.019 (0.071)	-0.202** (0.053)
Age[a]								
25–34 years	0.015 (0.021)	-0.050* (0.027)	0.174** (0.056)	0.126* (0.052)	0.098 (0.098)	0.167 (0.160)	0.051 (0.155)	0.276** (0.096)
35–44 years	0.031 (0.024)	-0.010 (0.032)	0.163** (0.064)	0.159** (0.055)	-0.108 (0.102)	0.144 (0.169)	0.226 (0.156)	0.192* (0.099)
45–54 years	0.005 (0.030)	-0.050 (0.044)	0.237** (0.086)	0.184** (0.067)	-0.334** (0.115)	-0.122 (0.224)	0.215 (0.165)	0.284 (0.111)
55–64 years	-0.041 (0.042)	-0.080 (0.068)	0.354** (0.129)	0.057 (0.090)	-0.370** (0.142)	-0.456 (0.369)	-0.088 (0.174)	0.380** (0.134)
65 + years	-0.303** (0.064)	-0.421** (0.121)	-0.164 (0.215)	-0.176 (0.132)	-0.275 (0.171)	-0.360 (0.646)	0.044 (0.230)	0.026 (0.179)
Married	0.057** (0.015)	0.070** (0.022)	0.007 (0.039)	-0.104** (0.033)	0.165** (0.054)	-0.054 (0.083)	0.181* (0.074)	0.140** (0.056)
# Immediate family in U.S.	0.005 (0.005)	0.006 (0.006)	0.015 (0.015)	-0.004 (0.013)	0.026 (0.022)	-0.001 (0.033)	0.053 (0.037)	-0.031 (0.020)
# Relatives in U.S.	0.031** (0.004)	0.034** (0.004)	0.054** (0.010)	-0.035** (0.010)	-0.021 (0.018)	0.135** (0.034)	-0.076* (0.044)	-0.019 (0.016)
Legal entry	-0.301** (0.022)	-0.368** (0.039)	0.111 (0.090)	-0.478** (0.044)	-0.343** (0.063)	0.092 (0.097)	-0.245* (0.100)	-0.282** (0.056)

Time since most recent entry	0.015** (0.011)	0.017** (0.001)	0.010* (0.005)	0.015** (0.003)	0.021** (0.006)	0.11* (0.006)	0.006 (0.003)	-0.008* (0.004)
***First Occupation*[b]**								
Managerial, professional	0.166** (0.058)	-0.129 (0.175)	-0.198 (0.254)	-0.127 (0.143)	0.255** (0.102)	0.730** (0.186)	-0.026 (0.207)	0.441** (0.170)
Technical, sales, admin. support	0.141** (0.041)	0.090 (0.093)	-0.067 (0.158)	0.002 (0.083)	0.133 (0.090)	0.404** (0.126)	-0.351* (0.181)	0.407** (0.108)
Service	0.304** (0.024)	0.265** (0.038)	0.531** (0.054)	0.194** (0.050)	0.354** (0.077)	0.485** (0.102)	0.073 (0.112)	0.201** (0.079)
Precision produc., crafts	-0.116** (0.036)	-0.278** (0.055)	0.121 (0.087)	0.105 (0.072)	-0.645** (0.154)	0.308 (0.284)	0.014 (0.146)	0.211 (0.143)
Operators, fabricators, laborers	0.221** (0.024)	0.204** (0.032)	0.207** (0.061)	0.270** (0.052)	-0.051 (0.117)	0.319* (0.146)	0.060 (0.140)	0.172 (0.103)
At home	0.311 (0.194)	e	-0.128 (0.492)	0.150 (0.368)	0.603 (0.972)	-11.780 (142.926)	0.229 (1.192)	-0.658 (1.135)
Student	0.306* (0.126)	e	0.639* (0.316)	-0.394 (0.339)	0.067 (0.379)	-0.298 (0.427)	-0.823 (0.834)	0.757* (0.376)
Unemployed, retired	0.487** (0.092)	e	0.794** (0.258)	0.350* (0.194)	0.061 (0.259)	-0.194 (0.500)	0.379 (0.517)	-0.343 (0.282)
Combined out of labor force	—	-0.155** (0.034)	—	—	—	—	—	—
Not reported	0.389** (0.065)	0.400** (0.092)	0.310* (0.169)	0.508** (0.137)	-0.170 (0.227)	1.441** (0.444)	-0.291 (0.300)	0.230 (0.216)
***Place of entry*[c]**								
Texas	1.679** (0.017)	1.636** (0.021)	1.860** (0.039)	1.827** (0.047)	0.982** (0.139)	1.329** (0.211)	2.185** (0.251)	2.569** (0.220)

continued

Table 7.6 LOGIT COEFFICIENTS PREDICTING INTERNAL MIGRATION: LEGALIZED ALIENS AGED 18 + (Standard Errors) (continued)

	Total	Mexico	El Salvador	Other Latin America	Asia	Africa	Europe	Other
Illinois	0.507** (0.069)	f	11.903 (102.121)	1.713** (0.400)	0.865** (0.096)	1.458** (0.269)	−0.416* (0.203)	1.649** (0.320)
New York/ New Jersey	1.112** (0.030)	f	1.830** (0.273)	0.764** (0.062)	1.470** (0.056)	1.086** (0.137)	1.999** (0.125)	0.568 (0.106)
Florida	1.985** (0.033)	f	3.202** (0.177)	2.077** (0.049)	2.067** (0.162)	0.941** (0.317)	0.454* (0.203)	1.643** (0.105)
Other West	2.490** (0.034)	2.367** (0.039)	3.988** (0.156)	3.206** (0.165)	3.091** (0.189)	3.292** (0.536)	2.643** (0.312)	2.732** (0.246)
Other South	3.080** (0.096)	f	3.873** (0.364)	2.992** (0.147)	3.352** (0.314)	1.510** (0.204)	3.845** (0.531)	4.547** (0.429)
Other Midwest	3.553** (0.166)	f	11.746 (102.129)	3.849** (1.035)	2.244** (0.263)	3.048** (0.395)	3.832** (0.407)	4.469** (0.373)
Other Northeast	2.608** (0.105)	f	2.231* (0.917)	2.887** (0.421)	2.707** (0.242)	1.886** (0.219)	2.285** (0.233)	3.051** (0.223)
Other	2.640** (0.052)	f	−7.852 (144.524)	1.090** (0.070)	5.028** (0.192)	11.767 (94.716)	1.843** (0.447)	4.009** (0.200)
Combined other entry	—	1.767** (0.118)	—	—	—	—	—	—
Place of birth[d]								
Mexico	−1.956** (0.043)		—	—	—	—	—	—

El Salvador	−1.471** (0.045)	—	—	—	—	—	—
Other Latin America	−0.812** (0.041)	—	—	—	—	—	—
Asia	0.223** (0.042)	—	—	—	—	—	—
Africa	−0.041 (0.050)	—	—	—	—	—	—
Other place of birth	−1.063** (0.043)	—	—	—	—	—	—
Constant	−0.459** (0.046)	−2.373** (0.030)	−2.166** (0.069)	−1.038** (0.058)	−0.439** (0.114)	−0.949** (0.208)	−1.158** (0.190)	−1.226** (0.136)
Log likelihood	−51,357	−32,769	−9,171.3	−12,438	−4,992.4	−2,177	−2,557.1	−4,541.1
Percent movers	31.7%	18.9%	25.4%	44.7%	69.1%	67.4%	63.4%	51.0%
[N][g]	[144,290]	[76,501]	[19,837]	[21,147]	[10,687]	[3,678]	[4,467]	[7,968]

Source: Legalization Application Processing System (LAPS).

[a] Omitted category is 18–24 years.
[b] Omitted category is farming, forestry, and fishing.
[c] Omitted category is California.
[d] Omitted category is Europe.
[e] Because not enough cases of Mexicans occurred in these categories, they were combined into one dummy variable called 'Combined out of labor force.'
[f] Because not enough cases of Mexicans occurred in these categories, they were combined into one dummy variable called 'Combined other entry.'
[g] Ns for the pooled and Mexican models are based on a 50 percent sample of Mexicans for computational efficiency.
*Significant at p .05 level.
**Significant at p .01 level.

statistically equivalent male counterparts. For Mexicans, the gender differential is less than 1 percent, compared to 6 and 8 percent, respectively, for Salvadoran and Other Latin Americans.[18]

The age coefficients reveal a complex pattern of migration over the lives of undocumented immigrants from diverse origins. For the sample as a whole, the lower migration probability at later ages emerged, but only among persons over 65. Mexican illegals aged 25 to 34 years or over 65 were less likely to move following a successful border crossing than their counterparts ages 18 to 24. Yet Latin American migrants ages 25 to 54 were more likely than their origin counterparts ages 18 to 24 to undertake an interstate move. Among Salvadorans, the likelihood of moving increased with age up to 64. For undocumented migrants from Africa and Europe, age was an inconsequential correlate of secondary migration, but among those from Asia, the lowest migration probabilities corresponded to persons ages 45 to 64.

Family status variables appear to have mixed effects on migration propensities. Marriage increased the likelihood of migration for undocumented migrants as a whole, particularly for Mexicans, Asians, Europeans, and Others. For Other Latin Americans, its effect on secondary migration is negative, and for Salvadorans and Africans, marriage makes no difference. Surprisingly, the presence of immediate relatives in the United States did not alter migration propensities for any group. However, the presence of other relatives **increased** migration probabilities for the sample as a whole and especially for aliens from Mexico, El Salvador, and Africa. For Other Latin Americans and Europeans, access to other relatives **decreased** secondary migration. Given the proximity of Mexico and El Salvador to the United States, with the possibility of clandestine entry by land, and the relatively longer existence of these migratory streams vis-à-vis those from Asia, the presence of other relatives in diverse parts of this country probably serves to locate undocumented migrants away from the border. Not only does this decrease the likelihood of detection, but it may also enhance probabilities of finding work and housing. The lack of consistent and significant effects of family variables may be due partly to the absence of information about the location of family members. If the family members live in the same location where the applicant initially enters, they probably decrease the probability of secondary migration for the applicant. This may well explain the negative effects for Europeans and Other Latin Americans. In general, our results are consistent with the social network conception of international and secondary migration.

A fairly consistent story emerges from the influence on migration of the circumstances defining the most recent entry. A legal entry on a nonimmigrant visa reduces the likelihood of secondary migration, at least among those groups for whom the effect is significant, including the pooled sample, Mexicans, Other Latin Americans, Asians, Europeans, and Others. This provides some support for the argument that a visa permits aliens to head directly for their desired location, thereby making subsequent movement less likely. Length of U.S. residence significantly increases the probability of secondary migration for every group except Europeans. This may be a simple exposure effect, but in the absence of information about the timing of moves, we cannot assess this effect further.

Coefficients for the labor force variables reveal diverse effects of first U.S. occupation on the likelihood of subsequent geographic movement. Having been in a managerial or professional occupation increases the likelihood of secondary migration compared to farming jobs, at least for the pooled sample as well as for Asians, Africans, and Others. This is consistent with the idea that these occupational labor markets operate at a national level and that occupation serves as a proxy for education differences. Those who initially worked as operators and laborers were significantly more likely to be movers than their counterparts who first worked in agriculture, at least among Mexicans, Salvadorans, Other Latin Americans, and Africans. Immigrants in service work were significantly more likely to be secondary migrants than were agricultural workers, with the exception of Europeans. Finally, for the pooled sample, Salvadorans, and Other Latin Americans, those who were jobless after initial entry exhibited higher probabilities of migration—10 percent, 15 percent, and 9 percent, respectively.

For the pooled model, the coefficients for the place-of-entry variables are uniformly significant and positive, indicating that those who did not enter through California were consistently more likely to move than those who entered there. The single negative place coefficient corresponds to Europeans who enter through Illinois; they were 10 percent **less** likely to move than their statistical counterparts who entered through California. These findings lend strong reinforcement to the tabular results indicating that California has a strong hold on illegal aliens who enter there, while Illinois, although the state of entry for few, is a desired final destination of many.

In summary, the significance and direction of effects of the age and family variables included in the logit models vary considerably by place of birth. This may reflect differences between groups, but it also results from the crudeness of the measures. For example, information on the place of residence of immediate family members may be needed to understand how their presence influences secondary migration. Although coefficients indicating first U.S. occupation also differed by place of birth, this variation partly reflects the distinct recruitment processes and options that operate for groups with very different labor histories and levels of education. The variables related to circumstances of most recent entry into the United States were most consistent with expectations: They confirm our thesis that place of entry is an important determinant of secondary migration, as are the manner of entry and the duration of time since entry.

CONCLUSION

Our analyses reveal that the settlement patterns of illegal aliens who applied for and were granted temporary resident status are quite similar to those of previous immigrants from the same places of origin. As with past immigrants, recent illegal immigrants were heavily concentrated in a handful of states. Secondary migration by illegals is pervasive. Even taking into account only moves across state lines, which constitute only a small share of all residential exchanges, over one-quarter of the sample made at least one interstate move in the time between most recent entry and application for legalization. These moves were made while the immigrants were undocumented.

The rate of secondary migration, however, varies substantially by place of birth: Asians and Africans were most likely to move; Mexicans were least likely to do so. Migration rates were not very sensitive to gender. Place of most recent entry shapes migration prospects: Those who entered through states that are traditional entry points for fellow ethnics were less likely to be secondary migrants. Logit analyses of the determinants of secondary migration confirm that place of entry is a consistently significant determinant of secondary migration, as are manner of entry and time since entry. First U.S. occupation is often related to secondary movement, but effects vary by place of birth, age, and family variables.

Movers from Mexico, El Salvador, Other Latin America, Africa, and Europe become less residentially concentrated than their fellow ethnics who stay in their state of entry, but movers from Asian and Other countries become more concentrated than nonmovers. Although the distributional consequences of secondary migration, as well as the magnitude of those consequences, vary by place of birth, in general, secondary migration seems to lead to some increase in the dispersion of the illegal population as a whole. However, this dispersion is small and does little to alter the persisting concentration of immigrants in the top six immigrant states. California receives the largest share of illegal immigrants and retains most of those who enter there. Other states that have considerable holding power include Texas, New York/New Jersey, Illinois, and Other West states. Illinois is also notable for its enormous net gain of illegal aliens through secondary migration; its illegal population increased by more than ten times the number who originally entered there. Other Midwest states also greatly increased their undocumented populations as a result of secondary migration. Consequently, more than 90 percent of the illegals who applied for amnesty in Illinois and Other Midwest states were secondary migrants. Although these population increases in Illinois and Other Midwest states may be small in absolute number compared to the number of illegal aliens in California, they are important relative to their number of entries.

These patterns of residential settlement and secondary migration are important because of the social and economic impacts on state and local communities that derive from the spatial concentration of illegal migrants. The research of Massey and his colleagues (Massey and Schnabel 1983b; Massey et al. 1987; Massey, Donato, and Liang 1990) suggests that legal status is a powerful determinant of the use of social services, and legalization of more than 1.7 million illegal aliens under IRCA (not counting the 1.3 million SAWs) will almost certainly result in increased demand for welfare and social services, just as North (1983) predicted. This increased demand, at a time when many states are experiencing severe fiscal difficulties, constitutes a potentially substantial burden that, like the immigrants themselves, will be concentrated in a handful of states. Only longitudinal analyses can reveal whether and how the behavior of legalized aliens will change after the amnesty process is complete, and how state and local economies will be affected by their presence.

Notes

This research was supported by a grant from ASPE of the Department of Health and Human Services to the Institute for Research on Poverty of the University of Chicago.

We acknowledge the assistance of Deenie Kinder, project officer from 1987 to 1990; without her relentless support this research would not have been completed. George Yates of the University of Chicago also was instrumental in helping us launch the empirical work presented here.

This research was completed while the first author was an NIH demography trainee and the second author was a fellow at the Center for Advanced Study in the Behavioral Sciences, Stanford, California. Support for this fellowship was provided by the John D. and Katharine T. MacArthur Foundation. We also acknowledge institutional support from the Population Research Center of the University of Chicago.

1. Two kinds of SAW status were available, depending on the number of days worked in agriculture yearly for up to three prior years.

2. Other provisions of IRCA are summarized in various published and unpublished research documents. In the interest of brevity, we focus only on the short-term provisions and requirements of the amnesty program.

3. SAWs are excluded from this analysis because requirements for legalization under the SAW program do not include continuous residence in the United States. A brief discussion of the social and demographic characteristics of this group of amnestied immigrants is provided in Tienda et al. 1991.

4. Some research has examined the secondary migration of refugees. However, this research has focused on formal resettlement programs for refugees controlled by the federal government.

5. A temporary upswing in the probability of moving is often found around retirement age.

6. Although the application period ended as of May 4, 1988, court decisions still pending may increase the number of successful status adjustments. However, these represent a tiny fraction of applications approved for temporary resident status.

7. In addition to the special requirements under IRCA, the applicant must satisfy the health and criminal standards required of all immigrants to the United States.

8. A partial exception are the studies of the illegal population based on residual methods, such as Warren and Passel (1987).

9. Woodrow and Passel (1990), using Current Population Survey data from June 1986 and June 1988, estimate the non-legalizing undocumented population to be over a million. This figure includes aliens who were not eligible for legalization.

10. The appendix describes the variables used in our analysis.

11. An alternative definition of origin, using the applicant's earliest reported residence that was keyed, proved unreliable because the sample mean for duration since most recent entry was greater than mean for duration since earliest residence. Missing values accounted for this discrepancy. The earliest reported residence variable also is systematically biased against applicants with a greater number of residences in the United States, since only the five most recent residences listed on the application form were keyed, even if earlier residences were listed by the applicant.

In the majority of cases, most recent entry refers to 1982 or before. In a small percentage of cases, temporary visits after 1982 for personal reasons were forgiven. Our use of most recent entry to analyze secondary migration assumes that immigrants generally re-enter through the same state, even if at different border points.

12. This comparison is somewhat biased because the CPS includes an unknown number of undocumented aliens. However, the comparison is a meaningful point of departure.

13. This comparison is slightly biased insofar as the CPS sample includes undocumented migrants.

14. This conclusion is supported by the fact that the ID_R is larger than the ID_E by 35

points, indicating that movers and nonmovers were even less similar in their residential patterns after secondary migration than before.

15. Based on similarity of results and in order to reduce the volume of statistics presented, Mexicans and Salvadorans have been pooled, as have Asians and Africans, and Europeans and Others.

16. Women constituted less than 20 percent of the SAW undocumented immigrants.

17. Adding to the ambiguity of this variable is the fact that the application requested the date of most recent entry, which for individuals with a history of circular migration, may not adequately reflect total years of U.S. residence. The problem is more serious for Mexican immigrants, many of whom have shuffled back and forth across the border for years.

18. These probabilities were computed from the logits using the well-known transformation, $b_i p'(1 - p')$ where p' is the percent movers, and b_i is the logit coefficient in question.

APPENDIX 7.A
VARIABLES USED IN ANALYSIS

VARIABLE	OPERATIONAL DEFINITION
AGE	Age at time of application; computed by subtracting the year of birth from the year of application for legalization. Recoded for logit equations as dummy variables designating 25–34; 35–44; 45–54; 55–64; and 65+ age groups.
FEMALE	Equal 1 if female, 0 if male.
MARRIED	Equal 1 if married at time of application, otherwise 0.
SPOUSE IN U.S.	Equal 1 if respondent is married and reports spouse as living in U.S., otherwise 0. (Since family members were not listed in any consistent order, we made the assumption that in cases in which the applicant had been married more than once, the first spousal relationship listed was the current spouse.)
CHILDREN IN U.S.	Equal 1 if respondent reports children who live in the U.S., otherwise 0.
IMMEDIATE FAMILY IN U.S.	Computed as the number of children of the respondent in U.S., plus 1 if spouse in U.S.
OTHER RELATIVES IN U.S.	Number of other close relatives living in U.S. reported by respondent, includes mostly siblings and parents.
PLACE OF BIRTH	Country of birth, recoded into categories (see below).

STATE OF CURRENT RESIDENCE	State of residence, recoded into categories (see below).
STATE OF ENTRY	State through which respondent entered on most recent entry into U.S., recoded into categories (see below).
LEGAL ENTRY	1 if respondent's most recent entry was made on a temporary nonimmigrant visa, otherwise 0.
DURATION SINCE ENTRY	Duration of stay since most recent entry into U.S., computed by subtracting the year of most recent entry from the year of application.
MOVER	Equal 1 if state of current residence is the same as the state of entry, otherwise 0.
OCCUPATION	Occupation at time of application, recoded into categories of occupations as used in the INS Administrative Manual (see below).
IN LABOR FORCE	Equal 1 if in labor force (includes unemployed and retired), otherwise 0.
FIRST JOB IN U.S.	Earliest U.S. occupation keyed from application, recoded into categories (see below).

VARIABLE RECODES

Recoded categories for place of birth

MEXICO

EL SALVADOR

OTHER LATIN AMERICA includes Argentina, Bolivia, Brazil, Chile, Colombia, Costa Rica, Cuba, the Dominican Republic, Ecuador, Guatemala, Honduras, Nicaragua, Panama, Paraguay, Peru, Uruguay, Venezuela.

ASIA includes Afghanistan, Bahrain, Bangladesh, Brunei, Burma, Cambodia, China, Cyprus, Guam, Hong Kong, India, Indonesia, Iran, Iraq, Israel, Jordan, Korea, Kuwait, Laos, Lebanon, Macau, Malaysia, Nepal, North Korea, Oman, Pakistan, Palestine, Philippines, Qatar, Saudi Arabia, Singapore, South Korea, Sri Lanka,

Taiwan, Thailand, Togo, Turks and Caicos Islands, United Arab Emirates, Viet Nam, Yemen.

AFRICA includes Algeria, Angola, Benin, Botswana, Gabon, Burundi, the Cameroons, Cape Verdes, Congo, Djibouti, Egypt, Equitorial Guinea, Ethiopia, Ghana, Guinea Bissau, Ivory Coast, Kenya, Lesotho, Liberia, Libya, Madagascar, Malawi, Mali, Mauritania, Morocco, Mozambique, Namibia, Nigeria, Senegal, Somalia, South Africa, the Sudan, Tanzania, Tunisia, Uganda, Zaire, Zambia, Zimbabwe.

EUROPE includes Albania, Austria, Belgium, Bulgaria, Czechoslovakia, Denmark, East Germany, England, Finland, France, Gibraltar, Greece, Hungary, Iceland, Ireland, Italy, Liechtenstein, Lithuania, Malta, Monaco, the Netherlands, Norway, Poland, Portugal, Romania, Russia, Spain, Sweden, Switzerland, Union of Soviet Socialist Republics, the United Kingdom, West Germany, Yugoslavia.

OTHER includes American Samoa, Antigua, Antilles, Aruba, Australia, Bahamas, Barbados, Belize, Bermuda, British Virgin Islands, Canada, Cayman Island, Cuba, Fiji, Grenada, Guadeloupe, Guinea, Guyana, Haiti, Jamaica, Martinique, Montserrat, Nauru, New Guinea, New Zealand, St. Kitts, St. Lucia, St. Vincent, Surinam, Tonga, Trinidad, Tuvalu, Western Samoa.

Recoded categories for state of residence and state of entry

California

Texas

New York/New Jersey

Florida

Illinois

Other West includes Arizona, Colorado, Idaho, Montana, Nevada, New Mexico, Oregon, Utah, Washington, Wyoming.

Other South includes Alabama, Arkansas, Delaware, Washington, D.C., Georgia, Kentucky, Louisiana, Maryland, Mississippi, North Carolina, Oklahoma, South Carolina, Tennessee, Virginia, West Virginia.

Other Midwest includes Indiana, Iowa, Kansas, Michigan, Minnesota, Missouri, Nebraska, North Dakota, Ohio, South Dakota, Wisconsin.

Other Northeast includes Connecticut, Maine, Massachusetts, New Hampshire, Pennsylvania, Rhode Island, Vermont.

Other includes Hawaii, Alaska, Guam, Puerto Rico, Virgin Islands.

Recoded categories for current occupation and first U.S. occupation

Managerial and professional specialty occupations
  Architect
  Writer, Artist, Entertainer, Athlete
  Educational or vocational counselor
  Physician
  Managerial/Professional specialty
  Other health diagnosing occupations
  Other health accessing occupations
  Lawyer, judge
  Librarian, archivist
  Math/computer scientist, statistician
  Natural scientist
  Nurse
  Social scientist
  Social, recreational or religious worker
  Teacher, except post-secondary
  Teacher, post-secondary

Technical, sales, and administrative support occupations
  Tech, sales, administrative support
  Sales
  Health technologist or technician
  Technological and technical, except health

Service occupations

Precision production, craft, and repair occupations

Operators, fabricators, and laborers

At home

Student, child

Unemployed, retired

References

Bartel, Ann P. 1989. "Where do the New U.S. Immigrants Live?" *Journal of Labor Economics* 7(4): 371–391.

Bean, Frank D., Barry Edmonston, and Jeffrey S. Passel. 1990. *Undocumented Migration to the United States: IRCA and the Experience of the 1980s.* Washington, D.C.: Urban Institute Press.

Bean, Frank D., and Allan G. King. 1982. *Estimates of the Number of Illegal Migrants to the United States.* Research Report. Austin, TX: Governor's Task Force on Illegal Aliens.

Bean, Frank D., Edward E. Telles, and B. Lindsay Lowell. 1987. "Undocumented Migration to the United States: Perceptions and Evidence." *Population and Development Review* 13(4): 671–690.

Bean, Frank D., and Marta Tienda. 1987. *The Hispanic Population of the United States.* New York: Russel Sage Foundation.

Bean, Frank, George Velez, and Charles B. Keely. 1989. *Opening and Closing the Doors: Evaluating Immigration Reform and Control.* Lanham, Md.: University Press of America.

Borjas, George J. 1990. *Friends or Strangers: The Impact of Immigrants on the U.S. Economy.* New York: Basic Books, Inc.

Browning, Harley L., and Nestor Rodriguez. 1985. "The Migration of Mexican Indocumentados as a Settlement Process: Implications for Work." In *Hispanics in the U.S. Economy,* edited by George J. Borjas and Marta Tienda, 277–297. Orlando, Fla.: Academic Press, Inc.

DaVanzo, Julie. 1978. *U.S. Internal Migration: Who Moves and Why?* Rand paper series, P-6133; Santa Monica, Calif.: Rand Corporation.

DaVanzo, Julie S., and Peter A. Morrison. 1981. "Return and Other Sequences of Migration in the United States." *Demography* 18(1): 85–101.

Findley, Sally E. 1982. "Internal Migration: Determinants." In *International Encyclopaedia of Population,* edited by J. A. Ross, 344–351. New York: Free Press.

Forbes, Susan S. 1985. "Residency Patterns and Secondary Migration of Refugees." *Migration News* 34(1): 3–18.

Greenwood, Michael J. 1975. "Research on Internal Migration in the United States: A Survey." *Journal of Economic Literature* 13: 397–433.

————. 1983. "Regional Economic Aspects of Immigrant Location Patterns in the United States." In *U.S. Immigration and Refugee Policy,* edited by Mary M. Kritz, 233–247. Lexington, Mass.: Lexington Books.

Houstoun, Marion F., Roger G. Kramer, and Joan Mackin Barrett. 1984. "Female Predominance in Immigration to the United States Since 1930: A First Look." *International Migration Review* 18: 908–963.

Jones, Richard C. 1982. "Undocumented Migration from Mexico: Some Geographical Questions." *Annals,* Association of American Geographers 72(1).

————. 1984. "Macro-Patterns of Undocumented Migration Between Mexico and the U.S." In *Patterns of Undocumented Migration: Mexico and the United States*, edited by Richard M. Jones. Totowa, N.J.: Rowman and Allanheld.

Jones, Richard C., Richard J. Harris, and Avelardo Valdez. 1984. "Occupational and Spatial Mobility of Undocumented Migrants from Dolores Hidalgo, Guanajuato." In *Patterns of Undocumented Migration: Mexico and the United States*, edited by Richard M. Jones. Totowa, N.J.: Rowman and Allanheld.

Keely, Charles B. 1974. "Immigration Composition and Population Policy." *Science*, 185: 587–593.

―――――. 1977. "Counting the Uncountable: Estimates of Undocumented Aliens in the United States." *Population and Development Review* 3.

Lesko Associates. 1975. *Final Report: Basic Data and Guidance Required to Implement a Major Illegal Alien Study During Fiscal Year 1976*. Washington, D.C.: U.S. Immigration and Naturalization Service.

Long, Larry H. 1982. "Internal Migration: United States." In *International Encyclopaedia of Population*, edited by J. A. Ross, 353–360. New York: Free Press.

―――――. 1988. *Migration and Residential Mobility in the United States*. New York: Russel Sage Foundation.

Massey, Douglas S. 1981. "Dimensions of the New Immigration to the United States and the Prospects for Assimilation." *Annual Review of Sociology* 7: 57–85.

―――――. 1990. "The Social and Economic Origins of Immigration." *The Annals of the American Academy of Political and Social Science* 510: 60–72.

Massey, Douglas, Rafael Alarcon, Jorge Durand, and Humberto Gonzalez. 1987. *Return to Aztlan*. Berkeley: University of California Press.

Massey, Douglas S., Katharine M. Donato, and Zai Liang. 1990. "Effects of the Immigration Reform and Control Act of 1986: Preliminary Data from Mexico." In *Undocumented Migration to the United States: IRCA and the Experience of the 1980s*, edited by Frank D. Bean, Barry Edmonston, and Jeffrey S. Passel. Washington, D.C.: National Academy Press.

Massey, Douglas S., and Felipe Garcia España. 1987. "The Social Process of International Migration." *Science* 237: 733–738.

Massey, Douglas S., and Kathleen M. Schnabel. 1983a. "Recent Trends in Hispanic Immigration to the United States." *International Migration Review* 17(2): 212–244.

―――――. 1983b. "Background and Characteristics of Undocumented Hispanic Migrants to the United States." *Migration Today* 11(1): 6–13.

Neuman, Kristin E. 1991. "The Settlement and Secondary Migration Patterns of Amnesty Immigrants." M.A. Thesis, Department of Sociology, University of Chicago.

North, David S. 1983. "Impact of Legal, Illegal, and Refugee Migrations on U.S. Social Service Programs." In *U.S. Immigration and Refugee Policy*, edited by Mary M. Kritz, 269–285. Lexington, Mass.: Lexington Books.

Passel, Jeffrey. 1986. "Undocumented Immigration." *The Annals of the American Academy of Political and Social Science* 487: 181–200.

Passel, Jeffrey, and Karen A. Woodrow. 1984. "Geographic Distribution of Undocumented Immigrants: Estimates of Undocumented Aliens Counted in the 1980 Census by State." *International Migration Review* 18(3): 642–671.

Portes, Alejandro, and Robert Bach. 1985. *Latin Journey: Cuban and Mexican Immigrants in the United States*. Berkeley: University of California Press.

Portes, Alejandro, and Ruben G. Rumbaut. 1990. *Immigrant America: A Portrait*. Berkeley: University of California Press.

Reichert, Josh, and Douglas S. Massey. 1979. "Patterns of U.S. Migration from a Mexican Sending Community: A Comparison of Legal and Illegal Migrants." *International Migration Review* 13(4): 599–623.

Sandefur, Gary D., and Wilbur J. Scott. 1981. "A Dynamic Analysis of Migration: An Assessment of the Effects of Age, Family and Career Variables." *Demography* 18(3): 355–368.

Tienda, Marta, George Borjas, Hector Cordero-Guzman, Kristin Neuman, and Manuela Romero. 1991. "The Demography of Legalization." *Population Research Center Discussion Paper Series*, OSC (PRC 91-4), Ogburn-Stouffer Center, University of Chicago, Chicago, Ill.

Warren, Robert, and Jeffrey S. Passel. 1987. "A Count of the Uncountable: Estimates of Undocumented Aliens Counted in the 1980 United States Census." *Demography* 24(3): 375–393.

White, Michael J., Frank D. Bean, and Thomas J. Espenshade. 1990. "The U.S. 1986 Immigration Reform and Control Act and Undocumented Migration to the United States." *Population Research and Policy Review* 9: 93–116.

Wilson, Franklin D., and Marta Tienda. 1989. "Employment Returns to Migration." *Urban Geography* 10: 540–561.

Wong, Linda J. 1990. "The Effects of IRCA/SLIAG on Public Education: The California Experience." In *In Defense of the Alien Volume XII*, edited by Lydio F. Tomasi. New York: Center for Migration Studies.

Woodrow, Karen A., and Jeffrey Passel. 1990. "Post-IRCA Undocumented Immigration to the United States: An Assessment Based on the June 1988 CPS." In *Undocumented Migration to the United States: IRCA and the Experience of the 1980s*, edited by Frank D. Bean, Barry Edmonston, and Jeffrey S. Passel, 33–75. Washington, D.C.: National Academy Press.

Chapter Eight

MEXICAN IMMIGRANTS, MEXICAN AMERICANS, AND AMERICAN POLITICAL CULTURE

Rodolfo O. de la Garza, Angelo Falcon, F. Chris Garcia, and John Garcia

This chapter examines the extent to which the Mexican-origin population of the United States holds values that are central to American political culture. The analysis focuses on two principal questions. First, what is the difference between the foreign-born and native-born regarding core American political values? Among the native-born, what differences are there among second, third, and fourth generations? Second, how significant are the differences associated with nativity and generation on these political values relative to the effects of individual attainments and attributes? Answering these questions will inform the current debate regarding the role that the Mexican-origin population (and perhaps Latinos in general) will play in the American polity. The analysis should inform us about how sustained contact with U.S. society affects the support of the Mexican-origin population for core national political values.

THE AMERICAN CREED

As a nation of immigrants, the United States rests on a heterogeneous cultural foundation. No single cultural pattern has ever defined who is an American, and continuous immigration ensures that, culturally speaking, American identity continuously evolves (Fuchs 1991). A shared history and culture, thus, do not serve as the foundation of identity in the United States as they do in France, Germany, Japan, and elsewhere. Lacking that bond, American identity has been molded around an explicit, if imperfectly realized, commitment to liberal democratic principles that have been labeled a "civic culture" (Almond and Verba 1963), a "civil religion," (Fuchs 1991, 31) and the American "creed" (Huntington 1981). In principle, then, whatever one's language, religion, or national origin, if one commits to the creed, one is or may become an American.

The nation takes its creed of liberal, democratic principles seriously. It consistently has barred from immigrating foreigners who have a history of supporting political movements or philosophies defined as incompatible with the creed. More significantly, even native-born citizens may be guilty of becoming "un-American" if they embrace such ideologies; and historically, those who did so risked the dire consequences of being investigated by organizations such as the House Committee on Un-American Activities. This orthodoxy is, to be certain, no longer as rabidly enforced as it was during the Cold War. However, that the 1988 presidential election was dominated by symbols such as support for the Pledge of Allegiance and the call for the return to "real" American values suggests that allegiance to the creed remains essential to the meaning of being American.

One potential exception to the absence of a defining cultural trait is language. Several recent developments illustrate this possibility. From 1981 through 1989, amendments to make English the official language were introduced annually into Congress. In 1988, for only the second time in history, Congress scheduled hearings on an English language amendment to the Constitution. Meanwhile, 14 states passed some form of official English policy in the 1980s (de la Garza and Trujillo 1991).

Thus, while to be French (or German or Japanese) is a permanent state indicating membership in a historically defined cultural community, to be American indicates membership in a self-consciously created political community whose cultural identity continuously evolves. Membership is conditional and fluid because it requires continuous adherence to a particular set of political values. Foreigners forfeit their right to membership—i.e., to immigrate—if they are deemed to hold values incompatible with the American creed, or if they are considered to be "incapable" of absorbing those values. Immigrants become Americans (i.e., naturalize, through publicly pledging allegiance to the creed)—after taking English and civics classes designed to socialize them into the creed. The native-born enjoy membership in the polity as a birthright, and the only requirement for maintaining it is that they not explicitly reject these core national values. However, since the native-born may not share but not explicitly reject these values, some scholars wonder whether formal membership in the polity—i.e., citizenship—should be a birthright (Schuck and Smith 1985).

Despite its rhetorical commitments, the United States has a history of racial and ethnic discrimination that exposes its failure to comply with the tenets of its own creed. Although Mexican-origin persons have continuously sought to become full-fledged members of the polity, this has been denied to most of them (Acuña 1988). Questions about support for American values have been directed against both native-born and immigrant Mexican Americans alike, even though the former have asserted their American identity and explicitly distanced themselves from immigrants, both to avoid discrimination and accelerate incorporation (de la Garza 1985, 95). As continuing voter discrimination litigation across the Southwest illustrates, some of these discriminatory and exclusionary practices continue, and terminating them requires prolonged legal struggles.

The rationale for denying the Mexican-origin populations full access to U.S. society is the racist argument that they are incapable of internalizing American values. Many historical examples illustrate how widely shared this view has been (Romano-V 1973). A 1990 poll on ethnic images conducted by the National Opinion Research Center reveals its continuing prevalence. The survey's results indicate that the "belief that Americans are approaching a color- and creed-blind society is easily disabused." It compares images of Jews, blacks, Asians, Hispanics and Southern whites with the general population regarding six core characteristics. Compared to the general population, Latinos and blacks ranked last or next to last on all of these (Smith 1990).

The survey indicates that Latinos are perceived to be the least patriotic of the six groups (Smith 1990). Similar sentiments have been voiced by organizations such as U.S. English, and by public opinion leaders and elected officials who have suggested that national security is threatened by irredentism at the hand of Mexican-origin secessionists (Fuchs 1991, 255). Thus, Mexican American leaders who have attempted to develop linkages to the Mexican government akin to those common to other American ethnics and their "homelands" have had their loyalties questioned (de la Garza 1980).

This study tests the accuracy of these perceptions by examining the extent to which the Mexican-origin population of the nation supports key elements of the American creed. Specifically, it analyzes support for speaking English, political tolerance, and trust in government. The first is included because the view that English should be considered an essential cultural trait is gaining support (de la Garza and Trujillo 1991). The second is part of the consensual definition of the creed (Fuchs 1991). Trust in government is included for several reasons. It is an indicator of governmental legitimacy and is essential to the maintenance of a democratic polity. Americans have traditionally voiced trust levels far greater than those of citizens in other democratic polities (Almond and Verba 1963), and lack of such trust may portend institutional decay and instability.

DATA AND METHODS

This study is based on data from the Latino National Political Survey (LNPS). A total of 40 primary sampling units (PSUs) were designated for the sample, including 28 self-representing sites. The other 12 sites were randomly selected from a pool stratified by state, metropolitan/nonmetropolitan status, and concentration of Hispanic-origin populations in the PSUs. To be included in the pool, Mexican-, Puerto Rican-, and Cuban-origin populations together had to be at least 5 percent of their state's population.

The sample includes respondents from across the social spectrum. One-fourth come from high-income areas with from 5 to 20 percent Latino density. Another quarter are from middle-income areas in which Latino households constitute 20 to 49 percent of the households. Half are from majority Latino neighborhoods that tend to be working class or poverty areas. It is important to note that the survey includes respondents who reside in regions such as the Southeast and Northeast that are outside traditional Mexican settlement. Over 97 percent of all interviews were completed between August 1989 and February 1990.

The 1,546 Mexican-origin respondents analyzed here are representative of 91 percent of the Mexican-origin population in the nation. That portion of the Mexican population not represented includes those who live in states in which Latinos (Mexicans, Puerto Ricans, and Cubans) make up less than 5 percent of the total population. A respondent is defined as being of Mexican origin if the respondent, one parent, or two grandparents are solely of Mexican origin. The sample is almost equally divided between foreign- and native-born. The latter includes four generations: second generation (those with foreign-born parents), second generation Type II (one native-born parent), third generation (two native-born parents), and fourth generation (two native-born parents and at least one native-born grandparent).[1]

The analysis tests competing interpretations of immigrant political incorporation. The generally accepted assimilationist model posits that it takes approximately three generations for immigrants to become "Americans" (Fuchs 1991, 29; Gordon 1964). This approach assumes that neither long-term obstacles to incorporation nor recurring socializing experiences that result in alienation, i.e., anti-incorporative attitudes, exist. In this model, designated the "three-generation model," socioeconomic incorporation and political incorporation evolve more or less simultaneously.

An alternative model—the "emergent ethnicity model"—suggests that ethnic identities emerge in response to shared experiences such as group-based discrimination (Yancey, Eriksen, and Julani 1976). In the case of U.S. indigenous minorities and of immigrants and their children, their experiences with mainstream society may promote alienation from, rather than attachment to, the polity. This response need not be immutable; in some cases, ethnicity may be converted into a resource used to attain incorporation. In such a context, ethnicity, which often develops in reaction to socioeconomic exclusion, becomes the instrument for realizing inclusion and eroding alienation (Smith 1981; Portes and Bach 1985, ch. 8).

This model also implies that attachment to and experiences with the polity may be inversely correlated. The native-born may be less attached to the American creed than immigrants even if they have higher socioeconomic status. Although they may be prospering relative to the foreign-born, the native-born may consider the creed hypocritical and reject it if they feel unable to advance relative to Anglos (non-Hispanic whites) because of discrimination. Immigrants, on the other hand, may naively embrace the creed because of its bountiful promise (Portes and Bach 1985).

Our analysis begins by relating the sociodemographic characteristics of the sample to both hypotheses. Then we use multiple regression techniques to identify the sources of attitudes toward three dimensions of the American creed—speaking English, political tolerance, and trust in government. The foreign-born are further analyzed to determine the effects of U.S. versus home country experiences on support for core American values.

SOCIODEMOGRAPHIC COMPARISONS

Both the three-generation and emergent ethnicity models predict the foreign-born to have lower socioeconomic attainments than the native-born. The former would also predict systematic gains from the first to the fourth (native-born) generations. The premise of the emergent ethnicity model, however, is that the native-born will not experience socioeconomic mobility across generations.

Overall, over half the respondents were between 18 and 35 years old, a plurality lived in households of five or more, and over 77 percent were Catholic. Less than 44 percent had finished high school, close to 62 percent had household incomes of less than $30,000, and approximately 39 percent owned their own homes. Few were not employed; those who were employed tended to hold low-status positions, with less than 8 percent holding managerial or professional positions (see table 8.1).

The foreign and native-born differed on most of these dimensions. The foreign-born were younger, had substantially larger households, and were more likely to be Catholic. They also had lower household incomes, lower home ownership rates, and significantly lower educational attainment. Overall, they were more likely to be out of the labor force, but this was true only for women (not shown). The foreign-born also tended to hold low-status jobs.

Among the native-born, it is noteworthy that virtually no measure manifests a monotonic increase or decrease across generations. A comparison between the foreign-born and fourth generation natives, however, reveals substantial socioeconomic gains across the generations. For example, the percentage holding managerial and professional jobs increases from 4.7 to 11.6; the percentage of household incomes above $30,000 increases from 27.3 to 35.2; and the percentage of high school and college graduates increases from 24.7 to 49.4 and 5.4 to 9.6, respectively.

A comparison between the nation at large (U.S. Bureau of the Census 1990) and fourth generation LNPS respondents also reveals large gaps. In March 1990, over 24 percent of all households had incomes over $50,000, but less than 11 percent of fourth generation Mexican American households earned over $50,000; 1.7 percent of non-Hispanics had less than five years of school, compared with 16.3 percent of fourth generation Mexican Americans; and 22.2 percent of non-Hispanics and 3.5 percent of fourth generation Mexican Americans had at least a college degree.

These comparisons illustrate two points. First, the native-born Mexican Americans have more education, higher incomes, and better jobs than their foreign-born counterparts. Second, the native-born do not significantly improve their socioeconomic position across generations. Thus, fourth generation Mexican Americans still do sub-

Table 8.1 SOCIOECONOMIC CHARACTERISTICS OF MEXICAN-ORIGIN RESPONDENTS TO THE LATINO NATIONAL POLITICAL SURVEY (LNPS), 1989–1990

Characteristic	Total Sample	Foreign-born	Native-born Generation (*)				
			Total	Second	Second II	Third	Fourth
Number in Sample (N)	1,546	784	762	182	103	113	356
Percentage	100.0	50.7	49.3	11.8	6.7	7.3	23.0
Gender (%):	100.0	100.0	100.0	100.0	100.0	100.0	100.0
Female	47.8	39.7	55.3	55.5	44.7	49.6	60.1
Male	52.2	60.3	44.7	44.5	55.3	50.4	39.9
(N)	(1,546)	(781)	(754)	(182)	(103)	(113)	(356)
Age (%)	100.0	100.0	100.0	100.0	100.0	100.0	100.0
18–35 years	56.6	60.4	52.1	38.9	49.0	53.3	59.3
36–55 years	29.1	30.3	27.7	19.2	36.3	36.0	27.1
Over 55 years	14.3	9.4	20.2	42.0	10.7	10.7	13.6
(N)	(1,544)	(780)	(743)	(182)	(93)	(113)	(355)
Household Size (%)	100.0	100.0	100.0	100.0	100.0	100.0	100.0
1	4.4	3.4	5.4	7.8	5.3	7.9	3.5
2	13.7	9.5	18.1	22.8	16.8	13.4	17.6
3	17.8	14.7	21.2	23.3	19.3	20.2	20.9
4	22.4	19.9	24.7	15.9	19.6	25.9	30.2
5 or more	41.7	52.5	30.5	30.2	39.0	32.5	27.8
(N)	(1,546)	(781)	(744)	(182)	(93)	(113)	(356)
Household Income (%)	100.0	100.0	100.0	100.0	100.0	100.0	100.0
Under $13,000	26.0	30.9	25.6	31.2	17.5	15.7	28.1
$13,000–19,999	16.8	19.2	17.3	14.6	21.4	17.4	17.5
$20,000–29,999	19.2	22.6	18.5	18.6	12.2	20.9	19.2
$30,000–39,999	14.3	12.4	18.4	18.0	21.0	20.2	17.3
$40,000–49,999	8.0	7.8	9.3	7.0	15.3	14.6	7.2
$50,000 or more	8.4	7.1	11.0	10.5	12.7	11.2	10.7
(N)	(1,434)	(710)	(705)	(167)	(88)	(111)	(339)

continued

Table 8.1 SOCIOECONOMIC CHARACTERISTICS OF MEXICAN-ORIGIN RESPONDENTS TO THE LATINO NATIONAL POLITICAL SURVEY (LNPS), 1989–1990 (continued)

Characteristic	Total Sample	Foreign-born	Native-born Generation (*)				
			Total	Second	Second II	Third	Fourth
Own Home	39.2	30.6	48.1	58.6	48.6	55.1	40.3
(N)	(1,546)	(781)	(744)	(182)	(93)	(113)	(356)
Religion (%)	100.0	100.0	100.0	100.0	100.0	100.0	100.0
Protestant	11.3	8.4	15.2	12.4	20.1	13.3	15.9
Catholic	77.4	81.6	73.4	81.5	66.1	81.6	68.6
Other	10.7	10.0	11.4	6.1	13.9	5.1	15.5
(N)	(1,543)	(781)	(741)	(182)	(93)	(111)	(355)
Education (%)	100.0	100.0	100.0	100.0	100.0	100.0	100.0
0–8 years	39.6	61.2	17.6	29.3	21.5	15.2	11.4
9–12 years, No Degree	16.8	8.7	25.3	22.2	24.4	17.8	29.6
High School Degree	36.0	24.7	47.8	39.2	45.3	58.5	49.4
Post-High School	7.4	5.4	9.3	9.3	8.9	8.5	9.6
(N)	(1,542)	(799)	(743)	(182)	(93)	(113)	(355)
Occupation (%)	100.0	100.0	100.0	100.0	100.0	100.0	100.0
Managerial/professional	7.4	4.7	10.2	7.0	12.7	8.7	11.6
Technical, sales, and administrative support	14.5	7.4	21.8	16.0	19.8	24.7	24.2
Service	7.9	15.3	13.4	9.3	16.3	19.5	12.6
Farming, forestry, fishing	14.3	13.5	2.1	1.3	1.4	5.0	1.7
Precision production, craft, repair	10.3	21.1	8.5	10.3	10.4	6.8	7.7
Operator, laborer (non-transportation)	11.2	15.2	6.7	9.4	5.1	1.8	7.4
Operator, laborer (transportation)	9.9	11.4	8.3	3.8	8.7	13.7	8.6
Not in labor force (**)	24.6	20.5	29.1	42.3	25.7	19.6	26.2
(N)	(1,474)	(749)	(707)	(167)	(91)	(110)	(339)

*See text for definition of generations.

**Unemployed and not looking for work, in school, retired, homemaker, disabled, or public assist...

stantially worse on these three measures than Anglos. Overall, then, these results do not support the three-generation model but satisfy the conditions of the emergent ethnicity model.

SUPPORT FOR THE AMERICAN CREED

Both models predict immigrants in general to have lower support for the American creed than the native-born population. The lack of evidence that Mexicans (in Mexico), and particularly the poor, have been socialized into democratic norms supports this hypothesis (Levy and Szekely 1983; Fromm and Maccoby 1970; Segovia 1975; Almond and Verba 1963). The established positive correlation between socioeconomic characteristics (particularly education) and political tolerance (Sullivan et al. 1982; Bobo and Licari 1989), combined with the socioeconomic characteristics of the sample, suggest further empirical support.

The model predictions differ regarding the native-born. The three-generation model predicts complete socioeconomic and political incorporation in the third generation. As has been indicated, however, third and fourth generation Mexican Americans lag substantially behind Anglos in socioeconomic status. Therefore, this model should not be expected to explain Mexican American support for the American creed. The emergent ethnicity model, however, stipulates limited socioeconomic mobility and predicts limited or declining support for the polity's core values among the third and fourth generations.

Our hypotheses, then, are:

1) The native-born will be more supportive of the creed than are immigrants; and,

2) support for the creed decreases from the second to the fourth generation.

English Language

An examination of English competence is the first test of our hypotheses. In part, this analysis anticipates the argument that attitudes toward core values and lack of socioeconomic status gains are linked to low English competence. As table 8.2 illustrates, 56 percent of the total sample say they are English-dominant or bilingual, and about 55 percent report that they speak more English than Spanish, or an equal amount of each language in their homes. Less than 10 percent of the total sample describes itself as monolingual Spanish, but this is more than twice the proportion identifying itself as monolingual English.

The foreign-born differ from all native-born generations regarding English competence (table 8.2). Over 75 percent of the foreign-born evaluate themselves as Spanish-dominant, less than 15 percent as bilingual, very few as English-dominant. The great majority describe Spanish as the language spoken in their home. At least 80 percent of each native-born generation describes itself as bilingual or English-dominant. The Spanish dominants decline from about 25 percent in the second generation to between 3 and 7 percent in the third and fourth.

The respondents were asked whether they agreed with the statement that "all citizens and residents of the United States should learn English." In our judgment, this question taps attitudes toward language and culture more clearly than a question about making English the nation's official language. Responses to the latter may be confounded by attitudes toward free speech, civil liberties, and individual rights.

The two models predict different responses to this question. The three-generation model should yield increasing acceptance from the foreign-born through the fourth generation. According to the emergent ethnicity model, however, native-born generations may assert an increased attachment to their "mother tongue" and articulate ambivalence toward learning English, especially if they equate it with giving up their ancestral language. Among the Spanish-speaking, such proclamations may be more rhetorical than real (Fishman 1985).

What is most significant is the extent to which the native-born and foreign-born both support learning English. Nonetheless, the differences between the foreign-born and native-born, though slight, are surprising. Overall, 93.8 percent of the foreign-born strongly agree or agree, compared to 90.8 percent of the native-born (table 8.3). The native-born vary slightly in their responses; 12 percent of the fourth generation and 8 percent of the second generation, compared to 6 percent of the third generation, disagree that everyone should learn English. Again, there is no monotonic pattern across generations.

These results do not support either model completely. Neither

Table 8.2 LANGUAGE COMPETENCE AND HOME LANGUAGE OF MEXICANS IN THE UNITED STATES, 1989–1990

Measure	Total Sample	Foreign-born	Native-born Generation(*)				
			Total	Second	Second II	Third	Fourth
Self-evaluation of Language Competence							
Total (%)	100.0	100.0	100.0	100.0	100.0	100.0	100.0
Only English	4.2	0.2	8.2	0.6	2.4	14.2	11.7
Better English	32.5	6.5	59.2	46.4	69.6	63.8	61.6
Bilingual	19.2	14.3	24.5	35.3	17.8	19.4	22.4
Better Spanish	34.2	60.3	7.5	16.2	9.7	2.1	4.2
Only Spanish	9.8	18.8	0.6	1.5	0.5	0.5	0.1
Language Spoken at Home							
Total (%)	100.0	100.0	100.0	100.0	100.0	100.0	100.0
Only English	16.3	2.9	29.6	12.3	21.9	42.4	36.3
More English	19.3	6.1	33.0	28.9	41.1	29.8	34.0
Both	19.0	12.6	25.8	34.7	21.7	25.0	22.5
More Spanish	17.6	26.2	8.7	17.1	13.4	1.2	5.6
Only Spanish	27.8	52.3	3.0	7.0	1.8	1.6	1.5
(N)	(1,545)	(781)	(744)	(182)	(93)	(113)	(356)

Source: Latino National Political Survey (LNPS), 1989–1990.
*See text for definition of generations.

Table 8.3 MEASURES OF AGREEMENT WITH THE "AMERICAN CREED" FOR MEXICANS IN THE UNITED STATES, 1989–1990

Measure	Total Sample	Foreign-born	Native-born Generation (*)				
			Total	Second	Second II	Third	Fourth
"Citizens/residents of the United States should learn English."							
Total (%)	100.0	100.0	100.0	100.0	100.0	100.0	100.0
Strongly agree	26.8	23.7	30.1	34.8	27.5	22.5	30.7
Agree	65.5	70.1	60.6	57.6	65.9	72.0	57.2
Disagree	6.5	5.2	7.8	7.1	6.7	4.3	9.6
Strongly disagree	1.2	1.0	1.5	0.5	0.0	1.3	2.5
(N)	(1,499)	(766)	(733)	(180)	(92)	(111)	(350)
Most Disliked Group							
Total (%)	100.0	100.0	100.0	100.0	100.0	100.0	100.0
Communists	20.5	22.7	18.1	21.2	19.0	12.2	18.0
Nazis	13.4	10.5	16.4	12.6	14.9	13.7	19.5
KKK	34.5	26.9	42.5	44.9	39.2	50.3	39.9
Homosexuals	23.2	32.8	13.2	11.3	16.8	8.5	14.5
Black Muslims	1.4	1.3	1.5	3.0	0.0	2.2	0.9
U.S. English	2.4	2.5	2.4	1.0	3.6	3.0	2.6
Atheists	4.6	3.3	6.0	6.0	6.6	10.0	4.6
(N)	(1,487)	(763)	(724)	(181)	(93)	(101)	(349)
Political Tolerance Scale							
Total (%)	100.0	100.0	100.0	100.0	100.0	100.0	100.0
High	0.7	0.7	0.7	0.3	1.9	2.6	0.1
6	0.4	0.4	0.3	0.1	0.0	0.0	0.6
5	4.7	3.5	5.9	4.2	5.7	5.1	7.1
4	8.0	8.2	7.9	11.5	4.5	13.0	5.3

3	40.8	46.5	34.9	35.9	39.2	34.0	33.6
2	12.5	9.5	15.5	15.7	16.1	14.0	15.7
Low	32.9	31.2	34.7	32.1	32.6	31.4	37.6
(N)	(1,450)	(736)	(714)	(175)	(91)	(106)	(342)

Trust in Government Scale

Total (%)	100.0	100.0	100.0	100.0	100.0	100.0	100.0
High	1.2	1.3	1.1	0.8	0.5	3.0	0.9
4	21.4	27.1	15.4	12.5	24.6	12.0	15.8
3	45.9	37.4	54.9	57.1	58.4	59.3	51.5
2	28.8	31.2	26.2	26.3	16.5	22.6	29.6
Low	2.7	3.0	2.3	3.3	0.0	3.1	2.2
(N)	(1,447)	(742)	(705)	(173)	(83)	(107)	(342)

Source: Latino National Political Survey (LNPS) 1989-1990
*See text for definition of generations.

model predicts well the extent to which all respondents support learning English. Both would have expected more disagreement between the foreign-born and native-born. Although this high level of agreement is in keeping with the three-generation model, that model cannot account for why more than 10 percent of the fourth generation disagree that everyone should learn English. That result lends some support to the emergent ethnicity model, especially given that the fourth generation is somewhat less supportive of learning English than is the second.

To evaluate the overall utility of the two models, the responses to "learn English" were analyzed using a series of logistic regressions. The dependent variable, "learn English," was dichotomized into "agree" and "disagree" categories. In the analysis using the entire sample, the independent variables included socioeconomic status indicators (education and household income), indicators of acculturation (foreign-born and native-born generations), racial identification, and total language competence (a combination of home language and self-evaluation of language competence), and age. The socioeconomic variables, income and education, have no systematic effects. Age is the only variable that exhibits statistically significant positive monotonic support for learning English.

Racial identification has two categories constructed from responses to "Do you consider yourself white, black or something else?" Those who identified with terms such as Mexican, Hispanic, or brown were labeled as Latino. Those selecting either white or black were grouped as non-Latino identifiers. Cognizant that U.S. society has been organized around a white-black dichotomy with white as the preferred category, Mexican American leaders have historically campaigned to have the Mexican-origin population identified as white to avoid discrimination (San Miguel 1987). Here, therefore, we consider self-identifying in terms of Latino referents to reflect either nonsocialization into society, as might be the case for recent immigrants, or rejection of society's dominant racial stratification, as might be true for those with a strong ethnic identity. Overall, 48.6 percent of the total sample identified with Latino referents. Among the foreign-born, 52.9 percent did so. Among the native-born generations, the percentages choosing Latino identifiers were 42.1, 36.1, 64.1, and 42 percent, respectively.

Racial identification here does not refer to ethnic identity. A person may identify racially as Latino and have no ethnic identification—that is, he may simply consider himself an American. On the other hand, a person may consider herself white and identify ethnically as a Chicana (Garcia et al. 1991; de la Garza et al. 1991). The regression yields no clear pattern (table 8.4, column 1), perhaps because over 90 percent of respondents strongly agree or agree that everyone in the nation should learn English.

Overall, the indicators of acculturation are not significantly related to attitudes toward learning English. No systematic, statistically significant relationship is found between language competence and attitudes toward learning English. Nonetheless, in contradiction to the emergent ethnicity model, those who know even a little English are more likely than Spanish monolinguals to disagree that everyone should learn English, and English monolinguals are 279 times more likely than Spanish monolinguals to hold this view. In keeping with the emergent ethnicity model, on the other hand, all the native-born generations are less likely than the foreign-born to disagree that everyone should learn English. However, the differences are statistically significant only for the fourth generation, with members of this group being 25 percent more likely than the foreign-born to disagree. Racial identification is not significantly related to attitudes toward learning English.

The model was slightly altered to analyze further the foreign-born. The modified model included all the original variables except the immigrant generation scale and added years of school in Mexico and a ratio of years in the United States divided by age at immigration. We label this variable "mestizo." While the overall model was significant (.0077, df = 23), few variables were. The mestizo variable produced a statistically significant negative coefficient. That is, like the native-born, the longer the immigrants were in the United States, the less likely they were to agree that everyone should learn English. Those with a knowledge of English, from very little to complete (i.e., monolinguals), were more likely than Spanish monolinguals to agree.

Education has a mixed effect on this attitude. Educational achievement is positively associated with support for learning English, and in one case—high school graduates compared to those with less than eight years of school—the relationship is statistically significant. However, years of education in Mexico has a contradictory relationship to views on learning English. Compared to those with no Mexican education, those with one to nine years of Mexican education are significantly more likely to agree that everyone should learn English; however, those with ten or more years of Mexican education are significantly less likely to do so. As was the case with the total sample, respondents over 36 were significantly more likely than those 35 and under to agree. Again, what is most noteworthy is that 93.8

Table 8.4 REGRESSION COEFFICIENTS FOR ELEMENTS OF THE "AMERICAN CREED" FOR MEXICANS IN THE UNITED STATES, 1989–1990

Independent Variable of Measure	Attitude toward Learning English (#) (Logistic)	Political Tolerance Scale (Linear)	Trust in Government Scale (Linear)
Independent Variables			
Age:			
18–35 years (o)	—	—	—
36–55 years	0.55*	−0.0193	−0.0263
Over 55 years	1.34**	0.2245*	0.0155
Education:			
0–8 years (o)	—	—	—
9–12 years, No Diploma	0.89	−0.0334	0.0106
High School Diploma	0.63	0.1149	0.0889
College Degree	0.27	0.3962*	0.0609
Generation (+):			
Foreign-born (o)	—	—	—
Second	−0.69	−0.1533	−0.0253
Second II	−0.20	−0.1619	0.1943
Third	−0.60	0.0042	0.0029
Fourth	−1.25**	−0.2726	−0.0106
Racial Identification:			
Non-Latino (o)	—	—	—
Latino	0.09	0.1721*	−0.0861
Language Total (+):			
Only English	3.79*	0.5004*	−0.1156
2	0.71	0.5965*	−0.0643
3	0.44	0.3913*	−0.0041
4	0.43	0.4621*	0.0666

Bilingual	0.31	0.2463	0.1092
6	0.59	0.6595**	0.0346
7	1.09*	0.3181*	0.0630
More Spanish	0.46	0.4614*	0.0894
Only Spanish (o)	—	—	—
Household Income:			
Under $13,000 (o)	—	—	—
$13,000–19,999	0.20	0.1540	0.0572
$20,000–29,999	-0.15	0.0501	-0.1027
$30,000–39,999	0.26	-0.0474	-0.0327
$40,000–49,999	0.81	0.3259*	0.0510
$50,000 or more	-0.14	0.2520	-0.0565
Measures of Fit			
Sample Size (N)	1485	1465	1466
R-squared	—	0.05	0.02
Chi-squared	46.4	—	—
Degrees of Freedom	23	—	—
Significance	0.0027	—	—

(+) See text for definition of generations.
(o) Omitted category.
*P<0.05
**P<0.01
(#) Base Category is "Disagree."

percent of the foreign-born strongly agreed or agreed that everyone should learn English.

Political Tolerance

The next test of the hypotheses focuses on political tolerance. Political tolerance was operationalized as a scale derived from the responses to the following questions (Sullivan, Pierson, and Marcus 1982):

> There are many controversial groups in the United States. From the groups that I name and the ones you think of, select the one group you dislike the most.
> Tell us how strongly you agree or disagree with the following statements: Members of (selected group)
> 1) should not be allowed to hold elective office in the United States;
> 2) should be allowed to teach in public schools;
> 3) should be allowed to hold public rallies in our city.

The scale includes answers to items 2 and 3; the responses to item 1 did not cohere with the other two and thus are excluded from this analysis.

As table 8.3 illustrates, the foreign-born and native-born differ regarding their most disliked groups. The Ku Klux Klan (KKK) ranks first for each native-born generation, with communists and Nazis ranked a distant second and third overall. The foreign-born rank homosexuals first, with the KKK second. This pattern suggests that foreign-born and native-born have significantly different socialization experiences.

Overall, neither the foreign-born nor the native-born articulate high tolerance (table 8.3). Combining the three top categories reveals that 4.6 percent of the foreign-born, compared to 4.6, 7.6, 7.7, and 7.8 percent of each native-born generation, have "high" tolerance. These differences, though slight, do suggest that the native-born and foreign-born have distinct socialization experiences.

Table 8.4 (second column) presents the results of regressing political tolerance on the same model applied to "learn English." The results yielded two noteworthy patterns. First, the acculturation indicators (native-born generations, language, and racial identification) have different effects. Overall, while the relationship is statistically significant for only the fourth generation, each native-born generation is likely to express lower political tolerance than the foreign-born. Second, except for the pure bilinguals (i.e., those in the middle of the scale), those who know English, whether they are monolingual or know only a little, are significantly more likely to express higher tolerance than are Spanish monolinguals. Finally, racially identifying with Latino referents is associated with higher tolerance.

Surprisingly, only relatively high socioeconomic status has any impact on tolerance. Relative to those with zero to eight years of school, only college graduates are significantly more likely to voice higher tolerance. Similarly, relative to those earning less than $13,000, all but one of the higher income categories are positively linked to tolerance, but only the highest group shows a statistically significant relationship (see table 8.4).

As before, the model was slightly altered to focus only on the foreign-born. The regression produced results similar to those in table 8.4. Those with a post-high school education are significantly more likely than those with less than eight years of school to voice higher political tolerance. Relative to Spanish monolingualism, Spanish dominance has a positive, statistically significant relationship to tolerance, but English monolingualism has a negative, statistically nonsignificant relationship. Those with household incomes over $40,000 are more likely to be tolerant than those with incomes less than $13,000. Those who identified with Latino referents are also significantly more likely than others to voice higher political tolerance.

There is one anomalous result. The mestizo index (years in the United States/age of immigration) does not have a statistically significant effect on political tolerance (tables not shown). This result supports the previous finding that there were no significant differences between the foreign-born and native-born. Those who attended school in Mexico are likely to be less tolerant than those who had no Mexican schooling, but the relationship is not statistically significant. This pattern may suggest that those who were born in Mexico but educated in the United States internalized the American "commitment" to political tolerance. On the other hand, the fact that the mestizo index is statistically unrelated to political tolerance and that total education, including U.S. schooling, has little overall effect on tolerance seems to negate this possibility. The anomaly, then, is why Mexican education is associated with lower political tolerance.

These results support the emergent ethnicity model more than the three-generation model. Explicitly supporting the emergent ethnicity model is the finding that native-born generations are negatively associated with political tolerance, even though this relationship is statistically significant for only one generation. Also, as the emergent ethnicity model predicts, persons who identify racially as Latinos are more tolerant than nonidentifiers. Finally, English competence has a positive systematic, statistically significant relationship to political tolerance. While this finding supports the three-generation model, it also supports the emergent ethnicity model, since learning English is linked to developing ethnic awareness (Portes and Bach 1985).

Trust in Government

The final test of the two models focuses on trust in government. Despite declines in recent years, Americans have long expressed high levels of governmental trust (Abramson 1983: 193–194). The three-generation model would predict increased trust from immigrant to native-born generations, especially among immigrants from polities such as Mexico, which does not have a history of democratic and responsive government. The emergent ethnicity model hypothesizes an initial increase between the foreign-born and the native-born followed by a decrease in governmental trust in the third and fourth generations.

Trust in government was operationalized as a scale incorporating responses to the following items:

How much of the time do you think you can trust government officials to do what is right?
1) just about always,
2) most of the time,
3) some of the time, or
4) almost never.
Would you say that the government is run by a few people looking out for their own interests or run for the benefit of all?

The responses do not consistently support either model. Most notably, and contrary to both models, the foreign-born express higher trust in government (the sum of categories 4 and "high" 5) than do any of the native-born generations (table 8.3). However, in keeping with the emergent ethnicity model, trust in government does not increase from the second through the fourth generations.

To determine any independent effect that sociodemographics and acculturation might have on these patterns, trust in government was regressed on the same set of socioeconomic status and acculturation variables used previously. Overall, the results support neither model (table 8.4, third column). Those who identify racially with Latino referents express lower but not significantly different trust levels than non-Latino identifiers. English competence does not have a statistically significant relationship to trust in government, but English dominance is associated with lower trust, as the emergent ethnicity model predicts.

The regression among the foreign-born lends modest support to the emergent ethnicity model. The mestizo index does not have a statistically significant impact on trust in government—i.e., immigrants who have spent most of their lives in the United States are not more likely to trust government than those more recently arrived. Also, differences in English competence levels are essentially unrelated to how trusting individuals are of government.

DISCUSSION

This chapter examines the extent to which the Mexican-origin population of the United States supports key elements of the American creed. It focuses particularly on the differences between the foreign-born and native-born and on the extent to which these differences are a function of sociodemographic factors rather than indicators of acculturation. We also relate our results to two competing theories of immigrant incorporation to evaluate their utility.

The results of this analysis challenge the assumptions of those who question the extent to which the Mexican-origin populations support the American creed. To the extent that knowing English is defined as essential to American political identity, these populations are committed to Americanizing. They overwhelmingly agree that everyone in the nation should learn English. It is noteworthy that the fourth generation, which is the most English-dominant, is somewhat more likely to disagree with this sentiment than the other Mexican-origin populations.

These populations also act on their judgment regarding the importance of English. While the majority of the foreign-born, not surprisingly, continue to be Spanish-dominant, a majority also report knowing at least some English, and over 45 percent report using at least some English at home. Moreover, virtually all the native-born are at least bilingual, and almost none are Spanish-monolingual.

The findings regarding trust in government reinforce this pattern. Perhaps what is most significant is that both the foreign-born and native-born have significantly higher trust scores than Anglos (de la

Garza, Falcon, Garcia, and Garcia 1991). Educational attainment and income have no statistically significant relationship to trust.

While the results of the analysis are not robust—i.e., the acculturation indicators do not have a statistically significant relationship to trust in government—the patterns they reveal contradict the three-generation model and provide some support for the emergent ethnicity model. English dominance is associated with lower trust. American generational history has a similar though less pronounced effect. None of the four native-born generations have significantly higher trust than the foreign-born. Nevertheless, comparing national results to these data indicates that both foreign-born and native-born Mexicans have significantly higher trust scores than Anglos.

The patterns regarding political tolerance are less clear. Increases in English competence are positively associated with increased political tolerance. However, all the native-born generations voice lower tolerance than the foreign-born, and the fourth generation does so to the greatest degree.

In combination, these results indicate that acculturation has not had a uniform impact on support for American core political values. Attitudinally and behaviorally, the foreign-born and native-born Mexican populations strongly support learning English. This support, however, has a mixed effect on support for core values. Similarly, albeit less uniformly, increased exposure to American society, as indicated by deeper generational roots in American society, tends to be inversely associated with support for core values.

The emergent ethnicity model better explains these results than does the three-generation model. In the latter, economic mobility and political incorporation proceed regularly so that by the third and subsequent generations, the descendants of immigrants are fully incorporated into the polity. The emergent ethnicity model, on the other hand, predicts that the descendants of immigrants will become disaffected minorities if they become frustrated at their lack of socio-economic mobility. This pattern more closely fits the pattern produced by this analysis.

This study focuses exclusively on the Mexican-origin population. It shows that the foreign-born do not in any sense reject core elements of the American creed but rather manifest a strong willingness to embrace the nation's core values. Ironically, those more incorporated into mainstream society, the native-born Mexican Americans, are less supportive of core American values than are the foreign-born. Clearly, then, these results indicate that Mexican heritage in no way impedes support for the American creed.

Notes

The authors express their appreciation to Jerome Hernandez of the University of Texas at Austin for his assistance in preparing this paper.

1. These definitions differ slightly from those used by Edmonston and Passel elsewhere in this volume, but they are similar in that they indicate the distance of the immigrant ancestor in a linear manner.

References

Abramson, Paul. 1983. *Political Attitudes in America: Formation and Change*. San Francisco: W. H. Freeman & Co.

Almond, Gabriel, and Sidney Verba. 1963. *The Civic Culture*. New York: Little, Brown.

Acuña, Rodolfo. 1988. *Occupied America: A History of Chicanos*. New York: Harper and Row.

Bobo, Lawrence, and Frederick C. Licari. 1989. "Education and Political Tolerance: Testing the Effects of Cognitive Sophistication and Target Group Affect." *Public Opinion Quarterly* 53: 285–308.

de la Garza, Rodolfo O. 1980. "Chicanos and U.S. Foreign Policy: The Future of Chicano-Mexican Relations." *Western Political Quarterly* 33 (4, December): 571–582.

————. 1985. "Mexican Americans, Mexican Immigrants and Immigration Reform." In *Clamor at the Gates: The New American Immigration*, edited by Nathan Glazer. San Francisco: Institute for Contemporary Studies.

de la Garza, Rodolfo, and Armando Trujillo. 1991. "Latinos and the Official English Debate in the United States: Language is not the Issue." In *Language and the State: The Law and Politics of Identity*, edited by David Schneiderman. Cowansville (Quebec), Canada: Les Editions Yvon Blais Inc.

de la Garza, Rodolfo, Angelo Falcon, F. Chris Garcia, and John Garcia. 1991. "Will The Real Americans Please Stand Up: A Comparison of Political Values Among Mexicans, Cubans, Puerto Ricans and Anglos in the United States." Paper presented at the American Political Science Association Annual Meeting.

Fishman, Joshua. 1985. *The Rise and Fall of the Ethnic Revival: Perspectives on Language and Ethnicity*. New York: Mouton Publishers.

Fromm, Erich, and Michael Maccoby. 1970. *Social Character in a Mexican Village*. Stanford: Stanford University Press.

Fuchs, L. H. 1991. *The American Kaleidoscope: Race, Ethnicity and the Civic Culture*. Hanover: University Press of New England.

Garcia, John, Rodolfo O. de la Garza, Angelo Falcon, and F. Chris Garcia.

1991. "Ethnicity and National Origin Status: Patterns of Identities among Latinos in the U.S." Paper presented at the Annual Meeting of the American Political Science Association.

Gordon, Milton M. 1964. *Assimilation in American Life: The Role of Race, Religion, and National Origins.* New York: Oxford University Press.

Huntington, Samuel P. 1981. *American Politics: The Politics of Disharmony.* Cambridge: Belknap Press of Harvard University Press.

Levy, Daniel, and Gabriel Szekely. 1983. *Mexico: Paradoxes of Stability and Change.* Boulder: Westview Press.

Portes, Alejandro, and Robert Bach. 1985. *Latin Journey: Cuban and Mexican Immigrants in the United States.* Berkeley: University of California Press.

Romano-V, Octavio. 1973. "The Anthropology and Sociology of the Mexican American." In *Voices: Readings from El Grito, 1967–1973.* Berkeley: Quinto Sol.

San Miguel, Guadalupe Jr. 1987. *Let All of Them Take Heed: Mexican Americans and the Campaign for Educational Equality in Texas, 1910–1981.* Austin: Center for Mexican American Studies, University of Texas.

Segovia, Rafael. 1975. *La politizacion del nin mexicano.* Mexico, D.F.: El Colegio de Mexico.

Schuck, Peter H., and Rogers M. Smith. 1985. *Citizenship Without Consent: Illegal Aliens in the American Polity.* New Haven: Yale University Press.

Smith, Anthony. 1981. *The Ethnic Revival in the Modern World.* Cambridge, England: Cambridge University Press.

Smith, Tom. 1990. "Ethnic Survey," GSS Topical Report No. 19. Chicago: National Opinion Research Center, University of Chicago.

Sullivan, J. L., J. Pierson, and G. E. Marcus. 1982. *Political Tolerance and American Democracy.* Chicago: University of Chicago Press.

U.S. Bureau of the Census. 1990. *The Hispanic Population in the United States.* Current Population Reports, Series P-20, #449, March.

Yancey, W., E. Ericksen, and R. Julani. 1976. "Emergent Ethnicity: A Review and Reformulation." *American Sociological Review* 41: 391–403.

Chapter Nine

AFTER ARRIVAL: AN OVERVIEW OF FEDERAL IMMIGRANT POLICY IN THE UNITED STATES

Michael Fix and Wendy Zimmermann

Two strategic options are available to government as it seeks to ensure that immigration serves the social and economic needs of the country. The one that is most often discussed and that is at the heart of most reform proposals today[1] is controlling who comes and in what numbers, or classical *immigration* policy. Another far less discussed strategy is the investment that federal, state, and local governments choose to make in the human capital and other needs of immigrants. The rules guiding these investments and the resources dedicated to them can be viewed as the nation's *immigrant* policies.

While the United States has an inclusive, open immigration policy, the federal government has a largely laissez-faire, hands-off immigrant policy. The nation's immigrant policies—those policies designed to promote the social and economic integration of newcomers—are skeletal and largely inchoate. As a consequence, public responsibility for incorporating newcomers has fallen, mostly by default, to state and local governments. The result, not surprisingly, is that they vary widely from place to place. At the same time, the limited federal expenditures devoted to immigrant-related programs in the best of fiscal times are now being sharply reduced, despite steadily rising admissions.

The lack of a deliberate integration or settlement policy like those in place in Canada, Israel, or Australia (Rosenthal 1992) is not a simple oversight on the part of Congress but a logical correlate of the way in which most immigrants admitted for family unification or work-related reasons have been viewed historically.[2] Policymakers have viewed legal immigrants coming for family or work reasons as being either responsible for their own well-being or the responsibility of their family, their employer, or a sponsoring nonprofit agency. Most immigrants are, then, presumed to be self-sufficient or at least not the responsibility of government. Hence, it is assumed that they impose few or no costs on the public and that the role government needs to play in their integration is minimal. Moreover, policies have been structured in such a way that to the extent that immigrants do impose costs on state and local governments, those costs are shared only to the extent that social expenditures are generally shared. For the most part, no heightened sense of federal obligation obtains to respond to the community impacts of legal immigration as there has been, say, to the opening or closing of military bases.

While the notion of immigrant self-reliance may make it politically and fiscally possible to admit the comparatively high number of immigrants authorized by federal immigration law, the assumption raises a number of issues. In the first place, this premise may not hold, given the structural changes that have occurred in the economy over the course of the past two decades—specifically, the sharply rising returns to education and skills that have taken place. Its validity may also be questioned given the limited skills and language capacity brought by many immigrants. The assumption may no longer make sense given increasing levels of admissions, federal fiscal retrenchment, and the continuing devolution of responsibilities to state and local governments.

While the federal government may not have adopted a deliberate immigrant policy, governments at all levels have on the books a host of rules or policies that influence, however indirectly, the social and economic integration of newcomers. One purpose of this chapter is to begin to map these express and de facto dimensions of U.S. immigrant policy. In so doing, we have decomposed immigrant policy into three broad categories: (1) *targeted* policies deliberately and primarily addressed to newcomers, such as refugee social service programs; (2) legislatively or administratively set *rules of eligibility for mainstream social programs,* such as Medicaid, where eligibility is typically determined by means tests; and (3) the primarily court-made rules regarding the *rights and entitlements of non-citizens* including the right to due process, work, and political participation and to services.

By decomposing policy in this manner, we have identified a number of broad trends. First, examination of the limited number of targeted programs underscores their political fragility, the severe budget cuts they have suffered or are likely to suffer, and their limited scope. Second, our assessment gives rise to concerns that the steep reduction in targeted programs will eliminate what little public institutional capacity exists at the state and local level to plan and advocate for immigrants. Third, congressionally imposed restrictions on mainstream benefit programs have shifted many immigrant-associated costs to state and local governments and private providers. Finally, an increasingly complex maze of immigration statuses has complicated eligibility determinations and service delivery for public benefits.

In contrast to these trends toward reduced federal funding and legislatively constrained program eligibility, the federal courts have selectively expanded over the past two decades the rights of immigrants to receive public benefits and to attend public schools and receive appropriate instruction. However, the very character of litigation has meant that the policies that flow from these decisions are fashioned in a piecemeal and occasionally inconsistent manner. Further, while the rights declared may fall to newcomers, the costs typically fall to state and local governments, governments whose capacity to pay has been reduced over time.

The next section of this paper describes the trends in immigration and public policy that are shaping immigrant policy in the United States. We then attempt to outline what we take to be the express and de facto immigrant policies of the federal government.

IMMIGRANT POLICY: THE FEDERAL CONTEXT

Increased Immigration

As we indicate above, there is a disjuncture in federal policy between rising immigrant admissions and declining federal support for social programs targeted to immigrants. Immigration to the United States has risen steadily by decade since the 1930s. Over the last two decades alone, total immigration, legal and illegal, almost tripled, from 380,000 a year in the 1960s to 950,000 a year in the 1980s (see figure 9.1). Recent data reveal that annual immigration to the United States now exceeds the level of admissions during the first decade of the century, the previous peak of immigration to the United States. These inclusive immigration policies set the United States apart from virtually all nations in the western world and are especially striking given the low rate of productivity growth since the early 1970s. The trend toward increased admissions holds for those entering under a wide range of immigration statuses. For example, the 1990 Immigration Act authorizes at least a 40 percent increase, from 492,000 to 675,000 per year, in *legal* immigration—i.e., the number of immigrants admitted as permanent residents under family unification,

Figure 9.1 IMMIGRATION TO THE UNITED STATES, BY DECADE: 1821–1830
THROUGH 1981–1990

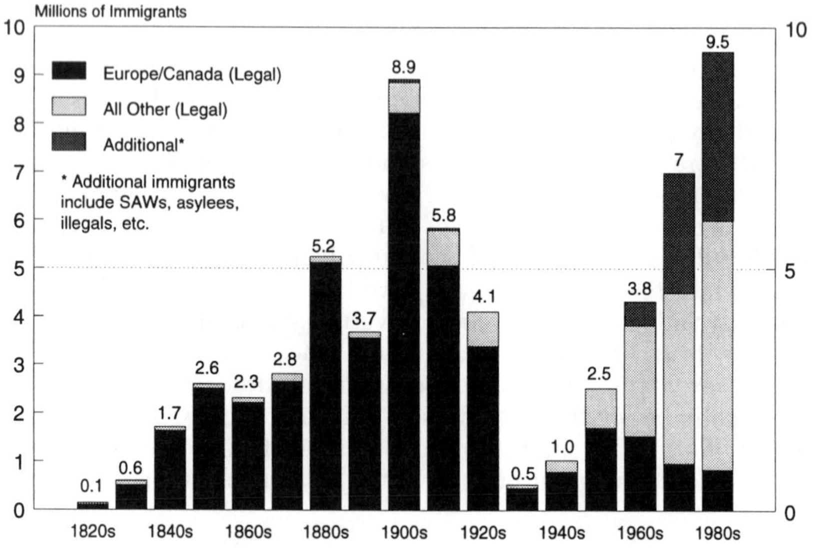

Millions of Immigrants

employment, and other criteria[3] (Fix and Passel 1991). Meanwhile, *refugee or humanitarian admissions* have doubled over the past six years, from 62,000 to the currently authorized ceiling of 121,000 for FY 1994. (Refugees are persons outside their native countries who are unable or unwilling to return because of persecution or a well-founded fear of persecution.) Expanded admissions have been authorized for many less-recognized categories of entrants. For example, the number of parolees entering for humanitarian reasons rose from 7,157 in 1984 to 21,503 in 1990, as increasing numbers of Soviets were admitted in parolee rather than refugee status.[4] All told, these figures add up to a current total level of authorized legal and humanitarian admissions exceeding 800,000 per year.

These shifts have been accompanied by other, liberalizing changes in humanitarian admissions. They include the introduction of liberalized asylum procedures, the hiring of a new corps of asylum adjudicators, and a commitment on the part of the INS to reconsider the applications of many previously denied asylum applicants.[5] Immigration policy during the past decade also included enactment of two major, targeted programs that authorized a change in status for undocumented immigrants already in the United States. The first was the grant of temporary, and later, permanent resident status to over 2.5 million aliens who legalized under the amnesty provisions of the 1986 Immigration Reform and Control Act (IRCA). Their numbers, in turn, have been added to by the family members of legalizing aliens who were in the United States before May 5, 1988 and who have received indefinite suspension of deportation under the Immigration Act of 1990. This population is estimated to be between 50,000 and 100,000. The Immigration Act of 1990 introduced the concept of safe haven into U.S. immigration law. In its first major application, an 18-month period of temporary protected status (TPS) was granted to over 170,000 Salvadorans (Immigration Act of 1990), and subsequently a one-year deferral of enforced departure was announced by the Bush Administration. The stay of deportation was further extended in late June 1992, allowing Salvadorans granted TPS to remain in the country until July 1, 1993.

Finally, the sharp recent rise in apprehensions of illegal aliens along the southern U.S. border suggests that the size of illegal immigration to the United States was, at best, only temporarily changed and, perhaps not changed at all by the IRCA employer sanctions provisions. (IRCA's employer sanctions provisions make it a civil and, in some cases, a criminal offense for employers to "knowingly" hire undocumented aliens.) (Passel, Bean, and Edmonston 1991.) The Census Bureau recently estimated the number of illegal aliens in the United States at 3.3 million, roughly the same number that was present at the time of the 1980 Census (Robinson et al. 1991, 2C). Given the level of apprehensions, it is not unreasonable to conclude that undocumented immigration contributes roughly 200,000 to 300,000 persons to the nation's population growth per year, an amount that approximates pre-IRCA levels.

One outcome of increased immigration has been the rapid growth of the immigrant population in a few states and metropolitan areas. During the 1980s, 75 percent of legal and illegal immigration was absorbed by only six states, with California becoming home to 2.3 million immigrants, or one-third of the total.[6] To the extent that newcomers impose distinct demands on the communities in which they settle, their concentration raises tough questions regarding the financing of the public services, such as schools and public hospitals, on which they rely.[7] These concentration effects are being felt, for good or ill, most forcefully in the nation's cities. As figure 9.2 indicates, in 1990, the foreign-born accounted for 60 percent of Miami's and 40 percent of Los Angeles's population. During the 1980s, the foreign-born population of Dallas and Houston doubled, while in Washington, D.C. and Boston, two cities not customarily associated

Figure 9.2 GROWTH IN FOREIGN-BORN POPULATION, SELECTED CITIES: 1980–1990

	Foreign-born Population 1980	1990	Percent Foreign-born 1990	Percent Increase 1980–1990
Dallas	54,912	125,862	12.50	129.21
Houston	155,577	290,374	17.81	86.64
Los Angeles	804,818	1,336,665	38.35	66.08
Washington, DC	40,559	58,887	9.70	45.19
San Antonio	64,876	87,549	9.35	34.95
Boston	87,056	114,597	19.95	31.64
San Francisco	192,204	246,034	33.98	28.01
Miami	186,280	214,128	59.72	14.95
Chicago	435,232	469,187	16.85	7.80

with the new immigration, it rose by 50 percent and 35 percent, respectively.

Another outcome of increased immigration is, paradoxically, increased dispersal as newcomers migrate to states or communities where immigrants have not historically settled. Here again, the fiscal impacts can be substantial, as new programs have to be created from the ground up, and few scale economies can be achieved in the adaptation of existing programs.

The fiscal and economic impacts of new immigrants may be linked both to their numbers and to the skills and education they bring with them. There is little reason to suspect that immigrants coming to the United States in the next several years will have substantially stronger skills and better educations than their predecessors. While the Immigration Act of 1990 will admit a marginally greater number of new immigrants (34,000) on employment-related grounds, the number of immigrants from the less developed traditional sending countries entering under the family unification preferences is likely to increase (Fix and Passel 1991). Moreover immigration remains a bipolar phenomenon. While roughly a quarter of newcomers enter with at least a college education, another quarter enter with less than ten years of schooling and few English language skills (see figure 9.3, and chapter 5 of this volume). Roughly half of all immigrants enter speaking English poorly or not at all (see chapter 6 of this volume). While

Figure 9.3 EDUCATION LEVELS OF MALE WORKERS: IMMIGRANTS VS. NATIVES

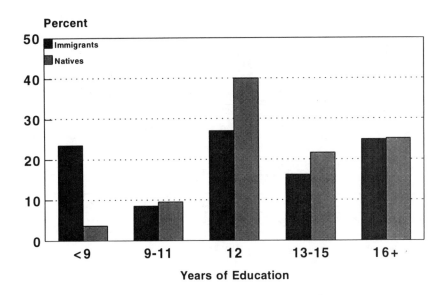

Source: Sorensen and Enchautegui (1992); derived from the 1989 Current Population Survey.

this ratio may not have changed in recent decades, the trebling of immigration rates holds powerful implications regarding the size of the nation's non-English-speaking populations. Again, these changes have their greatest impacts on the nation's cities. According to the 1990 Census, three-quarters of Miami's population spoke a language other than English in the home, as did 1.6 million of Los Angeles's 3.2 million residents. At the same time, one-half of Miami's and one-third of Los Angeles's residents reported that they were limited English proficient (LEP) (see figure 9.4).

Reduced Targeted Federal Aid to Immigrants

A second major trend is the rapidly declining funding for the targeted federal programs that, limited though they are, have been the cornerstones of our immigrant policies. To whatever extent a nascent federal

Figure 9.4 LANGUAGE CHARACTERISTICS, SELECTED CITIES: 1990

	Population 5 Years and Over	Speak Language Other Than English		Speak English Not "Very Well"*	
		Number	Percent	Number	Percent
Miami	333,063	244,044	73.27	165,065	49.56
Los Angeles	3,206,402	1,600,187	49.91	947,400	29.55
San Antonio	857,257	405,514	47.30	166,290	19.40
San Francisco	688,689	292,093	42.41	162,167	23.55
New York	6,820,456	2,793,773	40.96	1,361,746	19.97
Houston	1,495,759	458,698	30.67	229,979	15.38
Chicago	2,568,732	748,022	29.12	373,265	14.53
Boston	538,511	137,755	25.58	69,590	12.92
Dallas	926,525	205,448	22.17	103,232	11.14
Washington, DC	570,284	71,348	12.51	29,128	5.11

* Includes those who speak English "well", "not well", and "not at all"

immigrant policy was in place in the United States, its future has been jeopardized by federal budget reduction imperatives.

Clearly the most striking development has been the severe reduction in federal spending for the domestic portion of the Refugee Resettlement Program over the past decade. Total expenditures for this part of the federal refugee budget have fallen from over $7,300 per refugee in FY 1982 to roughly $2,200 per refugee in FY 1993.

The Clinton administration's projected FY 1994 budget restores some of the refugee program's funding (to $420 million). Still, total expenditures are only slightly higher than the $410 million authorized in FY 1992. The draconian cuts imposed on the program by the Bush administration had been justified because the programs had offered "benefits *unavailable* to citizens" [emphasis added] (Budget of the United States, Fiscal Year 1993, 387).[8] The irony here is programs that would be cut were specifically designed to take account of the fact that, unlike other citizens or immigrants, refugees are displaced persons fleeing persecution who are here with no resources or planning. The purpose of additional services has been to overcome these handicaps and place refugees on a more even footing with other members of U.S. society.

A second major development has been the repeated deferral of the unspent balance of the $4 billion State Legalization Impact Assistance Grants program (SLIAG).[9] The SLIAG program represented a hard-fought political compromise that made possible IRCA's enactment. The purpose of this $4 billion congressional authorization was to offset certain education, health, and public assistance costs imposed by eligible legalizing aliens' (ELAs) use of state and local services. President Clinton's FY 1994 budget has finally restored the as yet unspent $812 million in SLIAG funds to the federal budget, in large part the result of successful lobbying on the part of California. However, even if the full amount is appropriated, the program is scheduled to terminate in 1995.

At the same time, real expenditures on the only significant targeted federal education grant program aimed specifically at immigrants, the Emergency Immigrant Education Act (EIEA) Program declined 44 percent between 1985 and 1990. The program is a small one, amounting to only $30 million per year, and it provides impact aid to communities absorbing surges in immigration. The EIEA program contributed approximately $60 for every eligible immigrant child enrolled in a qualifying school district (Strang and Carlson 1991).

Finally, Title VII Bilingual Education expenditures declined 47 percent between 1980 and 1991 (see figure 9.5). This drop came during a decade in which we saw a rise in the number of children, many of them immigrants, classified as limited English proficient. While total enrollment in the nation's schools rose by 4.1 percent between 1985 and 1990, the number of students who are LEP rose by 52 percent (see figure 9.6). The recovery in spending on Title VII has been quite modest.

These trends indicate that any link between immigration and targeted federal expenditures (represented by the Refugee Settlement Program and SLIAG) is fraying as the nation's budget crisis continues more or less unabated. Beyond the areas of retrenchment noted above, we have seen efforts to privatize part or all of the Refugee Program by authorizing increased admissions of refugees who were resettled by private agencies largely at the agencies' own expense. This initiative lapsed, and a new form of privatization was proposed that would shift administration of domestic refugee programs from the states to private voluntary agencies. This Bush Administration proposal has also now lapsed. Similarly, efforts to introduce into the Immigration Act of 1990 federal reimbursement mechanisms to offset costs of providing services to legal immigrants entering under family and employment grounds were unavailing.[10] This failure, however,

Figure 9.5 TITLE VII BILINGUAL EDUCATION FUNDING: 1980–1991

Fiscal Year	Appropriation (in thousands)	Percent Change from FY 1980	Percent Change from FY 1980 Adjusted for Inflation	Budget Request (in thousands)
1980	$166,963	--	--	$173,600
1981	157,467	-5.7%	-13.7%	192,000
1982	134,372	-19.5	-32.4	139,970
1983	134,154	-19.7	-37.0	94,534
1984	135,529	-18.8	-39.9	92,034
1985	139,128	-16.7	-42.0	139,245
1986	133,284	-20.2	-46.5	139,265
1987	143,095	-14.3	-45.3	142,951
1988	146,573	-12.2	-46.7	143,095
1989	151,946	-9.0	-47.4	156,573
1990	158,530	-5.1	-47.8	157,113
1991	168,737	1.1	-46.7	175,393

Source: Congressional Research Service 1991, p. 31.

resulted largely from the effort's being widely perceived as an attempt to reduce admissions levels, and not as an attempt to assist local communities.

President Clinton's proposed FY 1994 budget included a $400 million block grant, in the form of an add-on to Medicaid, to provide additional funding for local health care systems that are "disproportionately burdened" by providing medical services to undocumented immigrants. As proposed, the funds would have been allocated to the states using the number of legalizing aliens under IRCA as a proxy for the number of illegal immigrants in the state. The proposal was not enacted and was lost amidst debate over national health care reform.

Bars to Participating in Federal Programs

In addition to reducing dramatically targeted assistance to state and local governments, Congress has barred immigrants seeking to adjust

Figure 9.6 ESTIMATED LIMITED ENGLISH PROFICIENT STUDENTS AND TOTAL ENROLLMENT: 1985–1991

	Total Enrollment	**% Change 1985–1990**	**# LEP**	**% Change 1985–1990**	**% LEP**
1985-86	39,422,051		1,491,304		3.8%
1986-87	39,753,172		1,545,553		3.9
1987-88	40,007,946		1,622,879		4.1
1988-89	40,188,690		1,834,499		4.6
1989-90	40,562,372		1,981,112		4.9
1990-91	41,026,499	4.1%	2,263,682	51.8%	5.5

Sources: U.S. Department of Education 1991; Roger Olsen 1991; U.S. Department of Education 1992.

their status from using federal public benefit programs. For example, aliens newly legalized under IRCA[11] and Salvadorans granted TPS under the Immigration Act of 1990 are denied, for the most part, federal cash assistance.[12] Further, IRCA, for the first time, explicitly authorizes states to bar ELAs from the state's own public benefits programs[13] in theory, "saving" them from having to respond to the claims of indigent ELAs. In fact, no states have taken Congress up on this offer.

Increased admissions, federal fiscal retrenchment, and the placing of new restrictions on alien use of federal benefit programs have shifted some of the costs of immigration to state and local governments. The National Governors Association—hardly a disinterested observer, to be sure—reported that reductions in federal support for refugee cash and medical assistance shifted $99.5 million in costs to the states for FY 1989, with state reimbursement for refugee welfare costs being cut from 36 to 24 months following the refugee's entry into the United States. Since that time, the period of reimbursement fell from 24 to 4 months, and in 1991 it was eliminated altogether (Vialet 1992). Commensurate increases in state and local costs accompanied these cuts. Of course, this cost-shifting is occurring in the few program areas where there have been targeted federal resources and policy. (In other program areas and for other immigrant populations, no special federal aid has been provided, so the issue of cost-shifting does not even arise.) It is not surprising that these immigration-related examples of "fend-for-yourself federalism" have contributed to a new restiveness regarding immigration and immigrants at the state level. California Governor Pete Wilson has called for the elimination of education, medical, and welfare benefits for illegal immigrants, as well as a constitutional amendment denying automatic citizenship to children born in the United States to undocumented parents.[14]

Competing Visions of Immigrants and Immigrant Policy

One explanation for simultaneously having the kind of open immigration policy and hands-off immigrant policy portrayed here may be that when taken together, the two represent a compromise between the inclusionary and exclusionary sentiments towards immigrants that have persisted throughout American history. The restrictive, exclusionary strain is embodied in what we shall term the resource preservation model, which emphasizes the costs that newcomers impose on the receiving society and justifies restrictionist and even nativist policies (Fix and Hill 1990, chapter 2). The interests of the immigrant and the community are seen as distinct from, and competitive with, one another, and the arrival of newcomers is perceived as leading to a decline in community resources. Proponents of this view believe the rights of the community should be elevated above the needs and rights of the entering alien and that deference should be shown to the power of government to exclude non-citizens. In a famous opinion that captures this perspective, Judge Benjamin Cardoza wrote:

> To disqualify aliens (from benefits) is discrimination, indeed, but not arbitrary discrimination, for the principle of exclusion is the restriction of the resources of the state to the advancement and profit of the state. Ungenerous and unwise such discrimination may be, it is not for that reason unlawful (People v. Crane 1915).

This restrictionist model of immigration predominated in American law from the late nineteenth century to the mid-1960s, when Congress struck down the quota system that had driven immigration policy. The major resulting revision of the immigration laws was infused with the rights-based doctrines of the emerging civil rights movement, and the courts began increasingly to rule in favor of immigrants and against the claims of the state (Schuck 1984).

The opposing vision of immigration, which, following Peter Schuck (1984) we shall call the *communitarian model*—emphasizes immigrants' historical contribution to the nation—their productivity and the additions to the general welfare that result from their industry and diversity. One correlate of this view is that immigrants' claims should be assessed in terms of universal rights based upon an individual's essential and equal humanity. As Schuck writes:

> I shall call these new principles "communitarian," for their central idea is that the government owes legal duties to all individuals who manage to reach America's shores, even to strangers whom it has never undertaken, and has no wish to protect.

When this vision is incorporated into policy and judicial decisions, the claims of the immigrants, including the undocumented, are weighted much more heavily vis-à-vis those of the community and its arguments for preserving resources.

These competing visions can be seen as the source not only of political but intergovernmental tensions in the area of immigration and, by extension, immigrant policy. In some instances, state and local governments, trying to restrict alien access to community resources, have come into conflict with federal law or policy. Texas's efforts to bar undocumented aliens from its school system in the early 1980s represented such a conflict. In that case, the federal courts found state efforts to preserve resources by excluding undocumented children to be unconstitutional. State actions such as these can be interpreted as efforts to close individual communities in the face of what may seem to be an apparently open and borderless state (Walzer 1983, chapter 2).

At the same time, state and local policies can be more generous than those contemplated or adopted by the federal government. For example, during the mid-1980s, Massachusetts's Department of Health adopted a broader definition of "refugee" than that adopted by the federal government as a response to the Administration's refusal to grant refugee or asylee status to Central Americans fleeing civil war in their homelands. The policy reflected the state's commitment to share community resources beyond that required, or even desired, by the federal government. Communitarian principles also motivated a number of American cities and the state of New Mexico to declare themselves sanctuaries for the undocumented.

EXPRESS AND DE FACTO IMMIGRANT POLICY

We have mapped federal immigrant policy into three broad areas. The first is our express or targeted immigrant policies—i.e., those aimed deliberately (and, hence, exclusively or largely) at newcomers. The second is the legislatively or administratively set eligibility rules for mainstream social welfare programs. The third is the rights of aliens as they have been defined by courts. The latter two represent our de facto immigrant policies.

Express Immigrant Policy: Targeted Programs

A map of the express federal immigrant policy of the United States would include at least four broad types of legislatively enacted policies:

☐ targeted policies aimed at refugees or aliens legalizing under IRCA that reimburse state or local social welfare expenditures. These policies, as embodied in the domestic assistance portion of the Refugee Act and the State Legalization Impact Assistance Grant Program (SLIAG), support a range of authorized services that might include health, public assistance, or education for eligible populations;
☐ policies designed to promote English language acquisition among elementary and secondary students and adults;
☐ impact assistance for school systems beset by rapid influxes of new immigrants; and
☐ policies intended to deter discrimination in employment against foreign-sounding or foreign-looking persons.

LIMITED NUMBER AND EXPENDITURES

When these policies are viewed in their entirety, one is struck by how few major initiatives are underway and how limited are the number of resources dedicated to them. The policies themselves are of an essentially minor and disjointed character and lack a coherent, animating goal. A generous assessment would suggest that the federal government spends roughly $300 million a year combined on the two principal English language acquisition programs cited here— bilingual education for elementary and secondary students (funded at roughly $200 million per year) and English as a Second Language (ESL) for adults ($100 million per year). Federal schools-related impact aid is negligible, amounting to only $30 million for the program under the Emergency Immigrant Education Act. That program helps offset the costs of the 700,000 students meeting the program's criteria. At the same time, the Transition Program for Refugee Children, which was to provide special educational and language services to refugee children, has gone unfunded since FY 1990 and shows no signs of reviving.[15]

As we mentioned above, the Refugee Resettlement program has been the subject of sharp, draconian cutbacks, while the remaining SLIAG funds have been deferred and perhaps lost. Indeed, with the exception of federal support for state-administered ESL instruction, spending on all the *intergovernmental* support programs cited above has declined over time. Expansion in the ESL budget can probably be explained by the fact that it falls under the broader rubric of adult education, for which federal support has doubled in recent years.[16] Indeed, ESL does not even appear as a line item in the adult education budget (Budget of the United States 1993).

LIMITED REACH

The programs cited above are also notable because they fall well short of reaching the immigrant population as a whole. The two largest programs (in terms of expenditures) have been limited to two specific groups of newcomers. SLIAG has been restricted to legalizing aliens under IRCA, and the refugee program is restricted to federally designated refugees and asylees. As a result, communities that house large numbers of legal permanent residents, the largest segment of the entering immigrant population, are not eligible for any meaningful form of impact assistance. The support for which such communities are eligible under the EIEA program is so meager and the qualifying population drawn in such a constrained fashion that the program offers little to regions with large, established immigrant populations.[17]

LIMITED COST SHARING

The targeted intergovernmental programs—the Refugee, SLIAG, language and schools programs—also differ in the share of state and local costs that they reimburse. The costs of providing legalizing aliens under IRCA with instruction in English and civics were, for all intents and purposes, fully reimbursed by SLIAG. At the same time, federal subsidies for state-administered adult education programs (the source of federal support for ESL instruction) are matched by state and local governments at a 5 to 1 ratio (Adult Education Facts 1990). Moreover, the federal government reimburses an even smaller, and declining, share (roughly 7 percent) of state and local costs of providing instruction in the area of bilingual education (Porter 1990, 224). This limited federal participation may owe to the fact that classroom instruction appropriate for non-English speakers was initially advanced not as a supplemental benefit but as a right under Title VI of the Civil Rights Act of 1964, which holds that protected minorities cannot be barred from publicly supported programs because of discrimination. Limited federal financial support explains in part the controversial character of this law and the mandate that it has carried.[18] As we point out elsewhere in this report, the share of state and local refugee resettlement costs reimbursed by the federal government has also shifted dramatically over the course of the past decade, as federal spending has fallen from roughly $7,300 per refugee in FY 1982 to $2,200 in FY 1993.

INFLEXIBILITY

Restrictions on eligibility suggest another quality of several of these programs: their general inflexibility. The liberally funded SLIAG program ($4 billion over four to seven years) was confined to offsetting the state and local health, public assistance, and education costs imposed by legalizing aliens. The program failed to take into account or permit many of the kinds of education and human capital investments (vocational training, for example) that the states, community-based organizations, and the immigrants themselves might have preferred. The U.S. Department of Health and Human Services regulations governing reimbursement of state expenditures were complex and, for some categories of spending, quite stringent. In many instances, federal reimbursement regulations forced states to change the accounting procedures used in their public health and assistance programs (Liu 1991).

Federal bilingual education requirements have also been the targets of substantial criticism through the years from state and local governments which complain of their costs and rigidity (Muller and Fix 1980). For a mix of fiscal and ideological reasons, these rules were the focus of repeated congressional and administrative initiatives through the 1980s that loosened their instructional requirements to permit a wider range of teaching styles and methods.[19]

INSTITUTIONALIZATION

The programs also vary in the degree to which they have led to the creation of separate institutions within the federal government charged with their administration. The Refugee program, bilingual education, and enforcement of IRCA's ban on discrimination have all been assigned to separate departments that are expressly identified with these objectives.[20] Other immigrant-focused activities, including ESL and SLIAG, are administered by agency or departmental staffs with other primary responsibilities and no specific program identification.[21] Organizations that are more closely identified with a program or mission may be more likely to become committed to it and to develop greater expertise within the particular field.

De Facto Immigrant Policy: Eligibility for Mainstream Social Programs

The nation's immigrant policy is defined not only by its targeted programs but also by the degree to which immigrants are made eligible for mainstream social programs. In those programs, eligibility is determined by age, income, family composition, residential location, or some combination of these and other factors. While the fundamental purpose of the mainstream social policies has not been the integration of newcomers, their value to immigrants who work in low-paying jobs or who find themselves unemployed or unemployable is substantial. Hence they constitute a key element of de facto national immigrant policy. In addition, immigrant use of mainstream public benefit programs such as Aid to Families with Dependent Children (AFDC) emerges cyclically as a highly charged political issue.

POLICIES LIMITING ACCESS TO PUBLIC PROGRAMS AND BENEFITS

While some commentators have noted that welfare rights are more broadly available to newcomers than political rights (Schuck and Smith 1985, 107), access to benefits for aliens in the United States is more constrained than in many Western European nations (Zimmermann and Calhoun 1991). The restrictive character of U.S. social policy when it comes to immigrants is not new. Beginning in the nineteenth century, immigrants' (i.e., legal permanent residents, or LPRs) use of benefits was checked by requiring that aliens applying for admission satisfy the "public charge" exclusion: that is, they had to demonstrate that they would not become paupers and go on welfare.[22] The government's current test of admissibility both for family unification and employment takes into account an immigrant's health, past and current income, education, and job skills. Congress also provides for the deportation of aliens should they become public charges within five years of admission. While in practice this ground for deportation is rarely invoked, one should not underestimate the extent to which these sanctions serve as powerful and defining symbols for entering immigrants. Immigrants are also effectively discouraged from using public services by the fact that reliance on welfare will make it far more difficult to bring relatives into the country. In addition, LPRs are effectively barred from receiving AFDC, Supplementary Security Income (SSI), and food stamps for three years following admission. This is accomplished by "deeming" or crediting the income of the immigrant's sponsor (usually a relative) to the newcomer, making it more difficult to qualify for means-tested benefits (Wheeler 1988, Part 1, 22–23).[23]

Further, beginning in 1970, immigration status began to be included explicitly as a criterion of eligibility in federal public benefits legislation. The rise of legal and illegal immigration and an expansion in the scope of the social welfare programs drove this exclusion. As a result, access by the undocumented was generally explicitly prohibited, and other, new eligibility requirements were imposed.[24]

More recently, legalizing populations under IRCA and the family unification provisions of the Immigration Act of 1990 were generally barred from all federal cash and transfer programs for five years. Significant exemptions for the blind, disabled, and aged were, however, built into the law, and Special Agricultural Workers (SAWs) were made eligible for food stamps. Along the same lines, Congress, under the Immigration Act of 1990, barred aliens awarded TPS from receiving federal cash benefits.[25] Meanwhile, IRCA mandates that states adopt the Systematic Alien Verification for Entitlement (SAVE) Program to reduce use of public benefit programs by the undocumented and other ineligible immigrants (those legalizing under IRCA, for example). This computer-based system, which operates something like a credit card verification used by merchants, is supposed to make it possible for welfare officials to verify non-citizens' immigration status at the time they apply for benefits (Zimmermann 1991).

INCLUSIVE ASPECTS OF BENEFITS POLICY

Despite these restrictions, elements of U.S. social policy remain basically inclusionary when it comes to newcomers. Perhaps the most far-reaching is the Citizenship Clause of the 14th Amendment, which states that citizenship passes by virtue of birth within the United States.[26] As a result, U.S.-born children automatically become citizens and are eligible for full participation in the social welfare system, regardless of the citizenship status of their parents. This application of the Citizenship Clause is thought by some legal scholars to represent an overly expansive interpretation of the intent of the Reconstruction-era framers of the Amendment (Schuck and Smith 1985), and constitutional amendments are periodically proposed that would deny U.S. citizenship to American-born children of illegal immigrants.[27] Other scholars, however, argue that birthright citizenship reflects the historical and contemporary importance of immigration to the United States (Brubaker 1989).

Since 1972, Congress has made some public benefits available to aliens who, while not permanent residents in fact, have strong equitable claims on the social welfare system. These aliens are considered by the federal government to be *permanently residing under color of law,* or PRUCOL (Wheeler 1988, 3–13).[28] PRUCOL's political legitimacy derives from the strong humanitarian or equitable claims for benefits of those who fall within the class. In many instances, these people entered the United States because they feared persecution in their native countries (refugees, asylees, and, in some instances, parolees). Some have been in the United States for a long time and, because of age or disability, would suffer unusual hardship if they were deported or denied public benefits.[29]

Finally, policies that extend benefits to the undocumented can be regarded as being inclusionary although they may stem from motives that are not necessarily philanthropic. For example, in 1986, Congress made undocumented immigrants who otherwise qualified for Medicaid eligible to receive selected emergency medical services under that program.[30] Similarly, the undocumented have not been excluded from the principal federal prenatal nutrition program.[31] While these policies may be inclusionary in character, their enactment stems as much from cost as humanitarian concerns. The 1986 extension of Medicaid coverage to all aliens, including the undocumented, represented a legislative response to the costs imposed on public hospitals by "anti-dumping" legislation passed a year earlier (Omnibus Budget Reconciliation Act 1986). The anti-dumping law required that hospitals taking Medicaid patients treat anyone presenting themselves with an emergency medical condition, including uninsured illegal aliens (Consolidated Omnibus Reconciliation Act of 1985).[32] By extending Medicaid to the undocumented, hospitals could be reimbursed for emergency care and substantially reduce their costs (National Health Law Program 1987, 121–122). As enacted, the provisions limited coverage to emergency assistance (defined to include labor and delivery) and not to other types of care, e.g., prenatal care, where eligibility issues were then being litigated.[33]

In sum, the basic thrust of federal policy has been to deny recently arrived immigrants, whether legal or illegal, access to most mainstream public benefit programs by deploying the public charge exclusion and the threat of deportation that it carries. This historical antipathy to immigrant welfare use has been carried forward in the bars to federal benefits use built into IRCA's legalization programs and into the Immigration Act of 1990. But the exclusion from benefits for newcomers and their families is not total. On the one hand, the U.S.-born children of immigrants in any status are deemed to be citizens and eligible for public benefits. Second, newcomers whose presence is clearly countenanced by the INS can be considered to be here under color of law and hence eligible for some federal transfer programs. Where the interests of powerful and endowed institutions become aligned with those of immigrants (as in the case of hospitals and the undocumented), barriers may also be removed. When withholding of services may lead to higher, instead of lower, costs (such as prenatal nutrition programs), access may also be permitted.

De Facto Immigrant Policy: Alien Rights

The elements of immigrant policy noted above—targeted services and benefits, the creation of immigrant-serving institutions, and eligibility for mainstream social welfare programs—are, for the most part, discretionary to government. The federal government is usually under no constitutional obligation to provide benefits such as cash transfers or employment services to aliens. The policies described above do not reflect, then, a second important dimension of the nation's de facto immigrant policy, the rights granted immigrants. These rights create entitlements for immigrants that are *not* discretionary to government. They create rights that the government or private individuals must honor. In so doing, these rights mark the limits of the power of the state to exclude aliens from the benefits or privileges enjoyed by citizens. Unlike many of the policies described above, these rights often arise out of the specific, concrete disputes that characterize litigation. They are frequently shaped by courts (rather than the legislature or the executive); and they commonly flow from constitutional doctrine and interpretation instead of political choices.[34]

We sketch below some of the rights extended to certain aliens in three broad areas. They are (1) basic constitutional rights, (2) welfare rights, and (3) political rights. The three represent a progression of sorts, with basic constitutional protections being the most broadly available to all individuals, regardless of immigration status, and political rights being the most completely reserved to citizens.

The purpose of this discussion is not to provide a catalogue of immigrant rights. Rather, we hope to illustrate how some of the most important de facto immigrant policies in the United States flow from declarations of constitutional right and not from legislative attempts to address the needs of immigrants or their host communities. We also note that some of the principles that have defined (and expanded) immigrant rights have flowed from a recognition of the federal government's superior power to regulate immigration and not from judicial solicitude for immigrant needs.

BASIC CONSTITUTIONAL RIGHTS

The rights extended to aliens, who are, by definition, not full members of U.S. society, are broadest when it comes to fundamental constitutional protections such as those extended under the Bill of Rights. These secure such rights as freedom from cruel and unusual punishment and rights to privacy, religious freedom, personal protection, personal property, and to a fair trial. Hence, all aliens, even those whose presence has been found to be unlawful, involuntary, or transitory hold the right to petition for *habeas corpus*, to a grand jury in criminal cases, not to be tried twice for the same crime, not to have to testify against themselves, and not to have their property taken without just compensation.[35] These rights parallel other constitutional guarantees such as the right to a speedy and public trial, to counsel in criminal cases, to be free of cruel and unusual punishment, and to be free of unreasonable searches and seizures.[36] These guarantees even extend to non-enumerated rights under the Bill of Rights such as the right to privacy (Aleinikoff 1990, 22).[37]

There is an important difference, though, in the rights held by those who may present themselves for entry at the border and those who have entered the country: the former enjoy none, and the latter all, of these constitutional protections.[38] As some commentators have noted, this difference provides immigrants an incentive to enter surreptitiously and the government an incentive to intercept unwanted immigrants at the border or before they have entered the country. (An example is the highly controversial interdiction in international waters and repatriation of Haitian refugees, with the result that they receive fewer procedural protections than they would in the United States.)

WELFARE AND EDUCATION RIGHTS

In the early 1970s, the states began to broadly restrict alien access to such federally funded and state-funded programs as AFDC. These restrictions coincided with perceived rising levels of illegal immigration, an expansion in the benefits offered by government, and a broadening conception of the property interest that individuals could claim in public benefits or programs (Reich 1964). Two state laws barring aliens from benefits were challenged in the landmark case *Graham v. Richardson*.[39] One law required that welfare recipients be U.S. citizens or have resided in the United States for 15 years or more; the other restricted eligibility for welfare benefits to U.S. citizens. The U.S. Supreme Court invalidated both laws, holding that the federal government had an overriding interest in matters affecting immigration and alien status, rejecting the states' argument that the restrictions were needed to conserve state resources. The court, relying in part on equal protection analysis, held that state classifications on the basis of alienage for the allocation of federal public benefits were unconstitutional (Wheeler 1988, 2–3).[40]

But while *Graham* limited *state* power to restrict federal benefits on the basis of citizenship status, a short time later, the Court ruled that *Congress* has largely unfettered power to condition federal benefits on the basis of immigration status. In *Mathews v. Diaz*,[41] the Court held that Congress had the right to restrict certain Medicare benefits to legal permanent residents who had resided in the United States for five years. *Diaz*, then, reflects the Court's greater deference to the federal government's interest in controlling immigration than to the individual immigrant's needs.

Courts have also struck down state and local efforts to discriminate on the basis of alienage in primary and secondary education. They have done so by invoking both the federal government's overriding interest in controlling immigration and by implying that a fundamental right to education exists that cannot be denied on the basis of citizenship status.

Indeed, the watershed of what might be considered the communitarian inclusionary model of judicial decision-making is the Supreme Court's decision in the landmark case of *Plyler v. Doe*.[42] In *Plyler*, the Court reversed the state of Texas's attempts to bar the undocumented children of illegal aliens from receiving a free public education. The outcome in the case turned on a number of findings: (a) the view that the children were "innocents" who should not be punished for their parents' decision to come illegally to the United States, (b) the intrinsic importance the court assigned to elementary and secondary education, and (c) the likelihood that the children would remain in the country.[43] The court was unpersuaded by the state and local governments' arguments that it needed to control its own resources, holding that it was in the best interest of the immigrants and the state of Texas to provide the children with a basic education. The court also contended that the costs to the Texas public schools would be *de minimis*.[44]

Since *Plyler*, the courts have grappled with the entitlements of both undocumented and legal aliens to post-secondary education. The most heated controversy has involved the right of the undocumented to pay in-state tuition. In California, a lower state court, following the logic of *Plyler*, has held that illegal resident aliens are entitled to attend California state colleges and pay in-state tuition.[45] However, a subsequent state court decision forcefully rejected this outcome, holding that charging the undocumented a higher rate of tuition serves a number of important state purposes. These purposes include refusing to subsidize violations of the law, conserving resources for the state's lawful residents, and avoiding the accusation that the state unlawfully harbors illegal aliens in classrooms. The court also based its decision on the claim that the parents of illegal alien students pay lower or no taxes because of a fear of deportation.[46]

POLITICAL RIGHTS

Of the rights surveyed here, political rights have been the most completely reserved to citizens. That, however, has not always been the case. In the nineteenth and early twentieth centuries, non-citizens were extended the right to vote. When Wisconsin was admitted to the Union as a state in the mid-nineteenth century, it expressly extended the right to vote to immigrants who had declared their intent to become citizens as a means of attracting migrants to the state (Rosberg 1977). Today, however, it is settled law that non-citizens have no right to vote,[47] although some state and local governments still grant the privilege in non-federal elections. In New York and Chicago, for example, all residents may vote in school board elections, regardless of legal status (DeSipio and de la Garza 1991). Along the same lines, the Constitution reserves the right to serve in federal political office (i.e., as President, representative, or senator) to citizens of the United States, but no comparable restriction applies to federal judges.

Although non-citizens have no right to vote in federal elections or to serve in federal elected office, they *are* entitled to political representation. By interpreting the Constitution to mandate that the Census count all persons in a geographic area, including the undocumented and other non-citizens, the courts have "assured indirect representation to all residents of the United States regardless of immigration status or national origin."[48] That is, each legislator should represent the same number of "persons" (versus "voters" or "citizens") as every other legislator. Here again, the fundamental right being guaranteed is not an element in a deliberate immigrant policy but is, rather, the logical extension of constitutional doctrine. This approach reflects the de facto inclusive character of U.S. immigrant policy by increasing the number of elected officials in areas with high immigrant populations. As DeSipio and de la Garza (1991, 5) have pointed out: "The implicit assumption in U.S. policy is that with indirect representation and access to formal political inclusion immigrants will be able to use the political process to obtain societal rights and benefits." It should be noted, however, that immigrants, especially undocumented immigrants, are thought to be undercounted by the Census. The refusal by the Bush administration's Secretary of Commerce to adjust the 1990 Census to reflect the Census Bureau's own estimation of the undercount limits, then, the extent of immigrants' indirect political representation.

To sum up, to a substantial degree, the contours of immigrant policy have been set by the courts as they interpret constitutional doctrine in adjudicating the rights of non-citizens. In general, the federal courts, endorsing communitarian principles, expanded the rights of immigrants through the 1970s and 1980s (Schuck 1984).

Allowing courts to serve as the de facto policymakers when it comes to immigrant policy raises some difficulties. First, some of the doctrines applied (the federal government's compelling interest in controlling immigration) have led to anomalous results, a broad right of education for undocumented children and highly restricted access to Medicare coverage for elderly permanent residents. Second, the very character of litigation—the fact that it is rooted in the specific facts of an individual case—leads to a fragmented, ad hoc style of policymaking. This is vividly illustrated by the competing rulings on whether the state of California must offer undocumented residents in-state tuition for the public higher education systems in California. Third, while increased benefits and rights may fall to immigrants as a result of litigation, in many instances, the increased costs of providing elementary and secondary education, prenatal care for the undocumented, jury trials, or bilingual instruction fall to state and local governments.

CONCLUSION

By focusing on what the immigrant policy of the United States is, this chapter may distort the world that newcomers actually encounter. U.S. immigrant policy is more remarkable for what it is not. Although federal policies are not without their inclusionary dimensions, in the main, they are not the subject of much deliberate concern. Few resources are committed to them, and those that have been are rapidly declining. The only substantial programs that have been created have been directed at subsets of the overall immigrant population and generally respond to events that have been concentrated in time, such as the 1986 legalization program. Moreover, the institutional legacy of these programs at the federal level is as limited as the programs themselves have been. For historical reasons, almost no attention is paid to the immigrant population as a whole, despite the fact that immigrants constitute an increasingly large share of the nation's total population and its workforce. Few areas of public policy, then, present the stark mismatch posed by the liberal immigration policies of the United States and its hands-off, laissez faire immigrant policies.

Given rising immigration and declining federal spending on targeted programs, what strategic policy options might be pursued in this chilly, and even hostile, political environment when it comes to newcomers? Perhaps the answer lies not in developing new targeted programs but rather in ensuring that large mainstream social welfare and education programs better serve immigrant populations.

Take, for example, the case of Chapter 1 of the Elementary and Secondary Education Act of 1965.[49] Chapter 1 provides $6.8 billion in federal funds for supplemental educational and related services to disadvantaged children. The law was enacted during the days of the Great Society and stands, along with Headstart, as the centerpiece of the federal government's commitment to providing compensatory education to disadvantaged children. The Chapter 1 program has focused largely on children living in concentrated poverty who are performing below national norms, a description that fits many immigrant children in our schools. A number of recent legal challenges,[50] as well as our own research at the Urban Institute, indicate that, despite massive changes in the demography of the nation's schools (see figure 9.5), many low-income immigrant children in inner-city schools remain unserved by Chapter 1 (Fix and Zimmermann 1993).

Chapter 1 may present one opportunity to frame a mainstream program so that it better incorporates immigrants. The implications of possible reform for increased instructional resources are substantial, to say the least. Chapter 1 expenditures are 30 times greater than federal expenditures on bilingual education, the subject of so much political combat through the years. Further, Chapter 1 is a popular program that has been shown to provide positive results and hence is likely to grow over time.[51] Change is also feasible: It appears that some progress towards serving LEP students might be made by simply eliminating legislative language that prohibits using Chapter 1 funds to meet educational needs that stem only from limited English proficiency. Finally, the opportunity to reform Chapter 1 is at hand, as the law is due to be reauthorized by Congress in 1993/1994.

President Clinton's proposal to increase dramatically the scale of worker training and retraining in the United States may present another opportunity to frame policy in a way that is responsive to a more comprehensive vision of the American population.[52] As the labor force includes more foreign-born workers, worker training and literacy programs increasingly involve instruction in ESL and other forms of language acquisition.[53] Here again, any major worker training initiative should expressly incorporate elements that contemplate the special needs of immigrant workers, such as language training and assessment of educational or vocational credentials earned abroad.

In sum, we suspect that initiatives which focus on increasing access to mainstream programs may prove more viable in the future than the targeted programs that are now the subjects of such sharp fiscal knives.

Notes

The authors thank David Rosenberg and Susan Drake for their insightful comments. Support for the research and writing of this report was provided by the Andrew W. Mellon Foundation.

1. See, for example, *The Immigration Preinspection Act of 1993* (H.R. 1153); *The Asylum Reform Act of 1993* (H.R. 1679); *The Exclusion and Asylum Reform Amend-*

ments of 1993 (H.R. 1355). Or see, "Clinton Administration Gearing Up for Effort to Strengthen Barriers to Illegal Immigration," *The Wall Street Journal,* June 29, 1993, p. A20.

2. It is important to distinguish here between immigrants admitted as legal permanent residents, who constitute the majority of annual admissions and whose arrival is, for the most part, *planned,* from immigrants admitted for humanitarian purposes: principally refugees and asylees. Because the latter are found to be escaping political persecution, their arrival is in some sense, *unplanned.*

3. These reflect admission levels in effect in 1989 and from 1995 on, respectively.

4. A parolee is defined by the Immigration and Naturalization Service (INS) to be "an alien allowed to enter the U.S. under emergency conditions or when that alien's entry is determined to be in the national interest." Parole is, in theory at least, temporary and does not constitute formal admission. However, under recent law, certain Indochinese and former Soviet parolees are now allowed to adjust to permanent resident status. See 1990 *Statistical Yearbook of the Immigration and Naturalization Service,* pps. A.1-20, A.2-7.

5. The commitment to readjudicate thousands of applications for asylum is the result of a settlement agreement entered into by the INS in *American Baptist Churches, et al. v. Thornburgh, et al.* Civ. No. C-85-3255 RFP, December 19, 1990. Stipulated Settlement Agreement, U.S. District Court of the Northern District of California.

6. The states and the share of total immigration they absorbed between 1980 and 1990 is as follows: California, 35 percent; New York, 14 percent; Texas, 9 percent; Florida, 7 percent; Illinois, 6 percent; and New Jersey, 4 percent (Fix and Passel 1991, 6).

7. In a November, 1991 report, "California's Growing Taxpayer Squeeze," The California Department of Finance noted the growth in "tax receiver" groups in the state, singling out "increases in the number of school age children, resulting from migration and a recent surge in the birth rate;" p. 1.

8. The Transition Program for Refugee Children (which reimburses costs incurred by school districts in educating refugee children) has not been funded since 1989.

9. The President's proposed budget for FY 1993 would defer $823 million to FY 1994. *Budget of the United States Government, Fiscal Year 1993.* Appendix One, p. 10.

10. See generally, Congressional Record H 8633-8692, October 2, 1990. Of special interest is a proposal by Rep. Lamar Smith (R-TX) to extend the SLIAG program through 1998 and to appropriate an additional $4 billion—a proposed amendment that was roundly defeated. (H 8681, 8682).

11. IRCA imposed a five-year disqualification from certain federal assistance programs for aliens present in the U.S. since 1982 who legalized under the law. 8 USC 1255a(h).

12. IA 90 302(a).

13. 8 USC 1255a(h). States must, however, incorporate the same exemptions (e.g., for the disabled and the aged) as does federal law.

14. Press Release, Office of Governor Pete Wilson, August 9, 1993, Sacramento, California. See, generally, Rochelle L. Stanfield, "Melting Pot Economics," *The National Journal,* Feb. 22, 1992, pp. 442–447. Federal retrenchment in the area of immigrant policy needs to be viewed within the larger context of reduced federal intergovernmental spending and the deterioration in state and local budgets that occurred in the 1980s. Between 1981 and 1989, federal aid fell as a share of local government revenue by 54 percent. (U.S. Bureau of the Census, "Governmental Revenue by Source and Level of Government 1980–81" and "Summary of Governmental Finances by Level and Type of Government: 1988–89.") State and local general funds went from a $19.8 billion surplus in 1984 to a $33.8 billion deficit in 1991. (U.S. Advisory Commission

on Intergovernmental Relations. "Estimating the Costs of Federal Mandates: Shifts in Responsibilities to State and Local Governments." Washington, D.C., April, 1992.)

15. The Refugee Assistance Extension Act of 1986 authorized the Secretary of Education (instead of the Office of Refugee Resettlement) to "make grants, and enter into contracts, for payments to projects to provide special education services (including English language training) to refugee children in elementary and secondary school where a demonstrated need has been shown." For the 1989–1990 school year, $15.8 million was made available to the states to provide education services to refugee children. The funds served 74,084 refugee children nationwide. (See Office of Refugee Resettlement, 1990.)

16. Federal funding for state-administered adult basic education (ABE) rose from $134 million in 1988 to $287 million in 1992 in real dollars. ESL is the fastest growing of three components of adult education, now representing 34 percent of all program enrollees (versus 19 percent in 1980). The Adult Education Act (PL 100-297) authorizes the State Administered Basic Grant Program, which has three parts: (1) Adult Basic Education (ABE), which provides for basic literacy services for adults whose skill levels are below the eighth-grade level; (2) Adult Secondary Education (ASE), which provides for services designed to assist students in obtaining high school equivalency; and (3) English as a Second Language (ESL), which provides language instruction for Limited English Proficient adults.

17. Assistance under EIEA is provided only to schools enrolling students who are foreign-born with less than three complete academic years in U.S. schools. To be eligible, a school district must enroll at least 500 such students, or they must represent at least 3 percent of the district's total enrollment. In FY 1989, 700,000 students met EIEA criteria; 564,000 were in 529 school districts that received funds. The remaining 136,000 (or 15 percent) were in school districts that did not receive funding because they enrolled too few students.

18. See generally, listing of most intrusive federal mandates, set out in U.S. Advisory Commission on Intergovernmental Relations, *Regulatory Federalism: Policy, Process, Impact and Reform* (1984).

19. Both the Education Amendments of 1984 (PL 98-511) and the Hawkins-Stafford Elementary and Secondary School Improvement Amendments of 1988 (PL 100-297) provided new flexibility to state, but primarily to local, governments in meeting the law's instructional requirements. See, *A Decade of Change in Regulatory Trends and Relief Strategies for the 1990s*, The U.S. Advisory Commission on Intergovernmental Relations, 1992.

20. They are, respectively, the Office of Refugee Resettlement within the Department of Health and Human Services' Administration for Families and Children; the Office of Bilingual Education and Minority Language Affairs within the Department of Education; and the Office of the Special Counsel within the Department of Justice.

21. These are the Department of Education's Office of Vocational and Adult Education and HHS's Office of Refugee Resettlement, respectively.

22. The public charge exclusion is currently codified at 8 USC 1182 (a) (15).

23. In practice, these deeming provisions are only invoked when there is some question whether the immigrant will become a public charge. If so, the sponsor is required to complete an affidavit of support.

24. For example, the buy-in provision of Medicare, which permits elderly and disabled persons who have not previously worked in covered employment to purchase hospitalization and supplemental medical insurance, is only available to legal permanent residents who have resided continuously in the United States for five years.

25. IA 90, 302 (a) 42 U.S.C. 1395, 2(a)(3). Under the terms of the Act, Salvadorans

were granted an 18-month stay of deportation and work authorization after which the need for an extension would be considered by the Attorney General.

26. The citizenship clause of the 14th Amendment states: "All persons born or naturalized in the United States and subject to the jurisdiction thereof, are citizens of the United States and of the State wherein they reside." U.S. Const. Amend. XIV. Sect. 1. The contrast to be drawn here is between nations that grant citizenship on the basis of place of birth (*ius soli*) versus those that grant it on the basis of blood relations (*ius sanguinis*).

27. See, e.g., H.R. 1191 (1993), introduced by Rep. Elton Gallegly (R-CA).

28. Four federal benefit programs use this PRUCOL formulation: SSI, AFDC, unemployment insurance compensation, and Medicaid. Seven categories of aliens are universally accepted by federal agencies as PRUCOL: refugees, asylees, conditional entrants, aliens paroled into the United States, aliens granted suspension of deportation, Cuban and Haitian entrants and applicants for registry. Other categories of aliens may or may not be eligible for public benefits depending on agency interpretation. These include aliens granted indefinite, extended, or renewable voluntary departure; aliens granted a stay of deportation and aliens in the United States with the knowledge and acquiescence of the INS. See, generally, Charles Wheeler, "Alien Eligibility for Public Benefits: Part 1 and 2; Immigration Briefings, November, 1988, pps. 3–13.

29. The courts have scrutinized the issue of alien participation in a number of cases that have defined the reach of the "color of law" (or PRUCOL) provisions written into legislation governing the nation's mainstream social welfare programs. Some of these rulings extended benefits eligibility not only to newcomers here with the clear intent of the government (refugees) but also to those here with the implied consent of the government. Thus aliens "residing in the U.S. with the knowledge and permission of the INS and whose departure the INS does not contemplate enforcing" have been classified as PRUCOL and made eligible for certain public benefits. See, *Berger v. Heckler*, 771 F.2d 1556 (2d Cir. 1985).

30. Indeed, the United States Court of Appeals for the Second Circuit recently found the fetus of an undocumented mother to be a presumptive citizen, thereby entitling the mother to prenatal care for the full term of the pregnancy, not just at the time of delivery. The court noted that there was clear evidence that such care saved the government substantial future medical costs. (See, *Lewis v. Grinker*, CA 2, No. 91-6176, January 31, 1992, reported in 5 Immigration Policy and Law, p. 1, February 7, 1992.)

31. 42 USC 1396 b(v)(3). The Supplemental Food Program for Women, Infants and Children, 42 USC 1786.

32. An emergency medical condition is defined as one that could reasonably be expected to result in: a) placing the patient's health in serious jeopardy, b) serious impairment to bodily functions, or c) dysfunction of any bodily organ or part.

33. Following the extension of emergency labor and delivery services to the undocumented, several states opted to use state funds to provide prenatal care to undocumented women, in part as a cost savings measure.

34. That is not to say, though, that the norms that influence case outcomes do not change to reflect shifts in political and social values. In the area of alien rights, for example, observers have noted that the courts departed from the restrictive, classical model of immigration policy during the 1970s and 1980s and moved towards an inclusionary communitarian model. However, the pendulum may be swinging back to a more restrictive interpretation of immigration law that defines alien rights more narrowly and, correlatively, government power to exclude aliens more broadly. This shift is reflected in such recent Supreme Court rulings as *INS v. Elias-Zacharias*. 112 S. Ct. 812 22, 1992. In *Zacharias*, the Court upheld the deportation of an asylum applicant from Guatemala who had fled to the United States to escape the consequences

of refusing to join a band of armed guerrillas who had appeared at his parents' door demanding that he join their cause. Holding that resisting conscription did not amount to a "political opinion," the Court denied Zacharias's appeal. The ruling could be interpreted to mean that persecution must be based on the *alien's* political opinion, not the persecutor's. In so doing, the Court interpreted quite literally the language of the 1980 Refugee Act that defines refugees as those fleeing political persecution on account of "race, religion, nationality, membership in a particular social group, or political opinion." [8 USC 1101(a)(42).]. See, generally Barbara Hines, "Asylum and Withholding of Deportation," *1992–93 Immigration & Nationality Law Handbook*, American Immigration Lawyers Association, 1992. p. 411, Washington, D.C.

35. See generally, T. Alexander Aleinikoff, "Citizens, Aliens, Membership and The Constitution," 7 *Constitutional Commentary*, pps. 9–34, 1990. Aleinikoff states that "Outside the immigration context, aliens present in the country—whether or not they are in legal status—are entitled to most of the constitutional protections afforded U.S. citizens. Aliens arrested for crimes in the United States receive the benefits of the fourth, fifth, sixth and eighth amendments. The equal protection clause has been read to prohibit the states from denying resident aliens public benefits and opportunities, except those identified with the exercise of the sovereign power of the state." (at p. 14). However, the Supreme Court has recently *questioned* whether the Fourth Amendment applies at all to undocumented aliens residing in the United States. *U.S. v. Verdugo-Urquidez*, 494 U.S. 259 (1990) digested in 67 Interpreter Releases 325 (Mar. 19, 1990). The Fourth Amendment declares that:

> The right of the people to be secure in their persons, houses, papers, and effects, against unreasonable searches and seizures, shall not be violated, and no Warrants shall issue, but upon probable cause . . . (U.S. Const. Amendment IV).

36. While Fourth Amendment protections are available in *criminal* proceedings, they are not equivalently available to immigrants as well as others in *civil* proceedings (where imprisonment is not available as a penalty). For example, the "exclusionary rule," which bars introduction of evidence gathered in violation of the law, applies in civil proceedings only when the purported benefits of using the evidence outweighs the costs of its introduction. This general rule has important implications, as the Supreme Court has ruled that aliens may not invoke the "exclusionary rule" in deportation hearings (which are civil in character). The Court ruled that the exclusion of illegally obtained evidence would have a great adverse impact on the INS in carrying out its job, while it would do little to deter illegal conduct on the part of INS agents. *INS v. Lopez-Mendoza*, 486 U.S. 1032 (1984), cited in Rebecca Chiao, "Fourth Amendment Limits On Immigration Law Enforcement," *Immigration Briefings*, February 1993.

37. Aleinikoff writes: "When the Court identified such [unenumerated] rights, it simply seems to assume that they apply to all persons within the territorial limits of the United States."

38. See, e.g. *Shaughnessy v. U.S. Ex. Rel. Mezei*, 345 U.S. 206 (1953) holding that aliens who are deemed not to have entered the country are not entitled to constitutional due process protections. See generally, Rebecca Chiao, "Fourth Amendment Limits on Immigration Law Enforcement," *Immigration Briefings* 93-2, February 1993.

39. 403 US 67 (1971).

40. IRCA granted states the power to discriminate in setting alien eligibility requirements for state and local financial assistance programs so long as exemptions that apply in federal law are incorporated. 8 USC 1255a(h).

41. 426 US 67 (1976).

42. 457 US 202 (1982).

43. The decision was handed down before IRCA was enacted, and it noted the uncertainty of deportation for any particular illegal alien, or what the Court referred to as "an inchoate federal permission to remain." 457 US 226 (1982).

44. 457 US 229 (1982).

45. *Leticia "A" v. Bd of Regents*, No. 588-982-5 (Ca. Sup. Ct., Alameda County, May 5, 1985).

46. *Regents of the University of California v. The Superior Court of Los Angeles County, David Paul Bradford, Real Party in Interest*, Ca. Ct. of Ap. 2d Dist. BO 51229, Nov. 28, 1990.

47. See, *Skafte v. Rorex*, 553 P.2d 830 (1976).

48. See, *Ridge v. Verity*, 715 F. Supp 1308, (1989) upholding the Census plans for counting all residents regardless of immigration status. See also *Garza v. County of Los Angeles*, No. 88-05143 (U.S. District Court, C.D. CAL. 1988); holding that, at least in California, total population may be used as the exclusive apportionment base without a requirement that the jurisdiction also balance the distribution of citizens among its election districts. See William A. Clarke and Peter A. Morrison, "Demographic Paradoxes in the Los Angeles Voting Rights Case," 15 *Evaluation Review* 714, December, 1991.

49. 20 USC 2710, et seq.

50. See, for example, *League of United Latin American Citizens et al. vs. Florida Board of Education and Florida Department of Education, et al.*, Settlement Agreement, USDC, SD, Fla. Case No. 90-1913 (1990); and *Boston Master Parents Advisory Council and Latino Parents Association v. Boston School Committee*, Civil Action No. 91-11725-Z, U.S. D.C. Mass., 1991.

51. Chapter 1 and other compensatory education expenditures have been deemed to be unusually cost-effective, returning $4.90 for every dollar spent. After declining in real terms in the first three years of the 1980s, spending on Chapter 1 rose in each of the following ten years, except one.

52. Proposals to expand worker training were advanced in Bill Clinton and Al Gore, *Putting People First, We Can All Change America*, Times Books, New York, 1992, p. 19.

53. One half of the grants issued under the Department of Education's Workplace Literacy Demonstration Grants Program in 1991 went to projects where "literacy" involved ESL instruction. "National Workplace Literacy Program, Program Year 1991 Project Abstracts," Division of Adult Education and Literacy, U.S. Department of Education.

APPENDIX 9.A
LEGAL CASES CITED

American Baptist Churches et al. v. Thornburgh et al., Civ. No. C-85-3255 RFP (Dec. 19, 1990).

Berger v. Heckler, 771 F. 2nd 1556 (2d Cir. 1985).

Boston Master Parents Advisory Council and Latino Parents Association v. Boston School Committee, Civil Action No. 91-11725-Z (U.S. D.C., Mass., 1991).

Garza v. County of Los Angeles, No. 88-05143 (U.S. D.C., Cal., 1988).

Graham v. Richardson, 403 US 67 (1971).

INS v. Elias-Zacharias, 112 S.Ct. 812/22 (1992).

INS v. Lopez-Mendoza, 486 US 1032 (1984).

League of United Latin American Citizens et al. v. Florida Board of Education and Florida Department of Education et al., No. 90-1913 (U.S. D.C., S.D., Fla., 1990).

Leticia "A" et al. v. Regents of the University of California et al., No. 588-982-5 (Super. Ct., Cal., 1985).

Lewis v. Grinker, 965 F.2d 1206 (January 31, 1992).

Matthews v. Diaz, 426 US 67 (1976).

People v. Crane, 214 NY 154, 108 NE 427 aff'd, 239 US 195 (1915).

Plyler v. Doe, 457 US 202 (1982).

Regents of the University of California v. The Superior Court of Los Angeles County, David Paul Bradford, Real Party in Interest, BO 51229 (Ct. of Appeals, Cal., 2d Dist., 1990).

Ridge v. Verity, 715 F. Supp 1308, (1989).

Shaughnessy v. U.S. Ex. Rel. Mezei, 345 US 206 (1953).

Skafte v. Rorex, 553 P.2d 830 (1976).

U.S. v. Verdugo-Urquidez, 494 US 259 (1990).

References

Aleinikoff, T. Alexander. 1990. "Citizens, Aliens, Membership and the Constitution." *Constitutional Commentary 7*, pp. 9–34.

Brubaker, William Rogers. 1989. *Immigration and the Politics of Citizenship in Europe and North America*. Lanham, Maryland: University Press of America.

The California Department of Finance. 1991. "California's Growing Taxpayer Squeeze."

Chiao, Rebecca. 1993. "Fourth Amendment Limits on Immigration Law Enforcement." In *Immigration Briefings 93-2*. February.

Clarke, William A., and Peter A. Morrison. 1991. "Demographic Paradoxes in the Los Angeles Voting Rights Case." 15 Evaluation Review 714. December.

Clinton, William J., and Al Gore. 1992. *Putting People First: We Can All Change America*. New York: Times Books.

Congressional Research Service. 1991. "U.S. Department of Education: Major Program Trends, FY 1980–1991." Washington, D.C.: Author.

DeSipio, Louis, and Rodolfo de la Garza. 1991. "Making Them Us: The Link Between Immigration Policy and Voting Rights Policy." Austin: The University of Texas.

The Division of Adult Education and Literacy. 1990. "Adult Education Program Facts—FY 1990." Washington, D.C.: U.S. Department of Education.

The Division of Adult Education and Literacy. 1991. "National Workplace Literacy Program, Program Year: 1991 Project Abstracts." Washington, D.C.: U.S. Department of Education.

The Executive Office of the President of the United States. 1993. *Budget of the United States Government: Fiscal Year 1993*. Washington, D.C.: Office of Management and Budget.

Fix, Michael, and Paul Hill. 1990. *Enforcing Employer Sanctions: Challenges and Strategies*. Washington, D.C.: RAND and The Urban Institute Press.

Fix, Michael, and Jeffrey Passel. 1991. "The Door Remains Open: Recent Immigration to the United States and a Preliminary Analysis of the Immigration Act of 1990." Washington, D.C.: The Urban Institute.

Fix, Michael, and Wendy Zimmermann. 1993. *Educating Immigrant Children: Chapter 1 in the Changing City*. Washington, D.C.: The Urban Institute Press.

Hines, Barbara. 1992. "Asylum and Withholding of Deportation." *1992–93 Immigration & Nationality Law Handbook*. Washington, D.C.: American Immigration Lawyers Association.

Liu, Lin C. 1991. "IRCA's State Legalization Impact Assistance Grants (SLIAG): Early Implementation." Washington, D.C.: RAND.

Muller, Thomas, and Michael Fix. 1980. "Federal Solicitude, Local Costs."

Regulation Magazine. Washington, D.C.: The American Enterprise Institute.

National Health Law Program. 1987. "New Developments in Health Benefits for Aliens." *Clearinghouse Review,* June.

Olsen, Roger E. W-B. 1991. "How Many Are There? Enrollment Statistics of Limited English Proficient Students in the United States." Teachers of English to Speakers of Other Languages. Alexandria, Va.

The Office of Refugee Resettlement. 1990. Report to Congress: *Refugee Resettlement Program.* January.

Passel, Jeffrey, et al. 1981. "Assessing the Impact of Undocumented Immigration to the United States." In *The Paper Curtain: Employer Sanctions' Implementation, Impact and Reform,* edited by Michael Fix. Washington, D.C.: The Urban Institute Press.

Porter, Rosalie Pedalino. 1990. *Forked Tongue.* New York: Basic Books.

Reich, Charles. 1964. "The New Property." 73 *Yale Law Journal* 733.

Robinson, J. Gregory, et al. 1991. "Estimating Coverage of the 1990 United States Census: Demographic Analysis." Washington, D.C.: U.S. Bureau of the Census. August.

Rosberg, Gerald M. 1977. "Aliens and Equal Protection: Why Not the Right to Vote?" *Michigan Law Review* 75 (1097).

Rosenthal, Donna. 1992. "Israel: The Next Exodus." *The Atlantic.* May.

Schuck, Peter. 1984. "The Transformation of Immigration Law." *Columbia Law Review* 84 (4).

Schuck, Peter, and Rogers Smith. 1985. *Citizenship Without Consent: Illegal Aliens in the American Polity.* New Haven: Yale University.

Sorensen, Elaine, and María Enchautegui. 1992. "Immigrant Male Earnings in the 1980's: Divergent Patterns by Race and Ethnicity." Washington, D.C.: The Urban Institute.

Stanfield, Rochelle L. 1992. "Melting Pot Economics." *The National Journal.* February 22.

Strang, E. William, and Elaine Carlson. 1991. "Providing Chapter 1 Services to Limited English Proficient Students." Washington, D.C.: Westat, Inc.

U.S. Advisory Commission on Intergovernmental Relations. 1992a. "Estimating the Costs of Federal Mandates: Shifts in Responsibilities to State and Local Governments." Washington, D.C. April.

————. 1992b. *A Decade of Change in Regulatory Federalism: Evaluating Regulatory Trends and Relief Strategies for the 1990's.* Washington, D.C.

————. 1984. *Regulatory Federalism: Policy, Process, Impact and Reform.* Washington, D.C.

U.S. Bureau of the Census. 1982. "Governmental Revenue by Source and Level of Government 1980–81." Washington, D.C.: U.S. Bureau of the Census.

U.S. Bureau of the Census. 1990. "Summary of Governmental Finances by

Level and Type of Government: 1988–89." Washington, D.C.: U.S. Bureau of the Census.

U.S. Department of Education. 1992. "The Condition of Bilingual Education in the Nation: A Report to Congress and the President." Washington, D.C.: U.S. GPO.

————. National Center for Education Statistics. 1991. *Digest of Education Statistics*. Washington, D.C.: U.S. GPO.

U.S. Immigration and Naturalization Service. 1984 and 1990. *Statistical Yearbook of the Immigration and Naturalization Service*. Washington, D.C.: U.S. Department of Justice.

Vialet, Joyce C. 1991. "Refugee Admissions and Resettlement Policy." *Congressional Research Service Issue Brief*. November 27.

Vialet, Joyce C. 1992. "Refugee Admissions and Resettlement Policy." *Congressional Research Service Issue Brief*. March 3.

Walzer, Michael. 1983. *Spheres of Justice: A Defense of Pluralism and Equality*. New York: Basic Books.

Wheeler, Charles, 1988. "Alien Eligibility for Public Benefits: Parts 1 and 2." *Immigration Briefings*. November.

Zimmermann, Wendy, and Charles Calhoun. 1991. "Immigrant Policies in Western Europe." Washington, D.C.: The Urban Institute. June.

Zimmermann, Wendy. 1991. "The SAVE Program: An Early Assessment." In *The Paper Curtain: Employer Sanctions' Implementation, Impact and Reform*, edited by Michael Fix. Washington, D.C.: The Urban Institute Press.

Chapter Ten

IMMIGRANT POLICY IN THE STATES: A WAVERING WELCOME

Wendy Zimmermann and Michael Fix

While immigration policy is almost exclusively the responsibility of the federal government, immigrant policy has fallen largely by default to the states. This, in turn, raises a series of questions. If immigrant policy is the province of the states, what exactly do they do, or not do, to serve immigrants? How do their policies vary across states and why? What are the implications of state immigrant policies for the integration of immigrants?

This chapter will seek to identify and describe the immigrant policies in place in two states that have historically served as hosts to substantial numbers of newcomers: Massachusetts and Texas. The story here could be described as a regression to the mean over time in policy terms. During the mid-late 1980s, Massachusetts had in place what were arguably the most activist and inclusive immigrant policies in the nation. It was Massachusetts, after all, that created the carefully named state Office for Refugees and Immigrants; that made virtually all newcomers, including those who were undocumented, eligible for public assistance benefits; and that enacted the first bilingual education law. Texas, by way of contrast, became known for trying to keep undocumented children out of elementary and secondary schools. Over time, however, the policies of the two states have grown somewhat less polar.[1] Massachusetts has grown somewhat less welcoming and its policies less generous. However, it remains a national leader in sustaining a policy focus on the special needs of newcomers. At the same time, Texas officials created a state office dedicated to immigrant-related issues, a major step in the direction of an activist immigrant policy. While the two states' approaches to integrating newcomers have converged, Massachusetts still has more inclusive immigrant policies than does Texas. These shifts between inclusiveness and exclusiveness are evidence of the constantly wavering welcome given newcomers to the United States.

This chapter addresses the states' immigrant policies by examining (a) the state characteristics relevant to immigrant policy; (b) those state efforts expressly directed to immigrants; (c) the public institutions that have been created to serve immigrants in the two states; (d) the implementation of federal programs, like the Refugee Program, directed toward newcomers; and (e) the rules and practices employed by the states in their administration of "mainstream" social welfare programs that bear on the access of immigrants to those systems.

THE CONTEXT OF STATE POLICY

A close look at the context in which each state's immigrant policy was formed reveals a great deal about why their policies varied so starkly in the 1980s and why, since then, they have undergone such significant changes.

Political Culture

Political culture has been defined as "the particular pattern of orientation to political action in which each political system is imbedded" (Elazar 1966, 79). This somewhat intangible characteristic takes on greater clarity and significance when considering the polar opposite political cultures of Massachusetts and Texas. Massachusetts's political culture could be described as activist and innovative. Texas, the "Lone Star" state, has a conservative culture that values independence or self-reliance (Fehrenbach 1983). Its political culture could be described as laissez faire or libertarian.

These cultural differences have a long history. Massachusetts's tradition of generosity toward newcomers goes back to much earlier waves of immigration. As Oscar Handlin wrote of Boston at the beginning of the nineteenth century: "Government action reflected the community's attitude towards immigrants. They were still welcome. The state had no desire to exclude foreigners or to limit their civic rights; on the contrary, during this period it relaxed some surviving restrictions" (Handlin 1969, 183). Despite the ebb and flow of the state's generosity since that time, a welcoming element has remained constant in Massachusetts's approach to newcomers.

To the extent that a state's political culture is reflected in its propensity for public spending, Massachusetts and Texas again find them-

Table 10.1 ANNUAL AVERAGE UNEMPLOYMENT RATES AND PERCENT
CHANGE: 1982–1992

Year	Texas Unemp	Annual % Change	Mass Unemp	Annual % Change
1982	6.9		7.9	
1984	5.9	− 14.5	4.8	− 30.4
1986	8.9	+ 50.8	3.8	− 2.5
1988	7.3	− 18.0	3.3	+ 3.1
1990	6.2	− 15.0	6.0	+ 50.0
1992	7.5	+ 21.0	8.5	+ 33.3

Sources: U.S. Department of Labor, Bureau of Labor Statistics, *Handbook of Labor Statistics*. Bulletin 2340, August 1989; U.S. Department of Labor, Bureau of Labor Statistics, *Geographic Profile of Employment and Unemployment*. 1990, 1991; 1992 unemployment rates are preliminary calculations from the Bureau of Labor Statistics.

selves at opposite ends of the pole. Massachusetts is one of the most generous states in terms of its public spending and social welfare programs. Its payment levels are among the highest in the nation. Texas, on the other hand, is one of the least generous states in its public spending, and its social programs are largely the result of federal action (Davidson 1990, 247–248).

Economy

Perhaps the most important driving force behind the formation of immigrant policy in the two states is their economies, which, since the 1980s, have moved in widely varying directions. Massachusetts's volatile economy played a key role in shaping state politics and policies over the past decade. The first part of the decade saw the "Massachusetts Miracle," during which per capita income between 1980 and 1987 increased by 75 percent (Osborne 1988). This dramatic economic growth gave Massachusetts the capacity to expand services and to create programs for the whole state population, including newcomers. It also created a labor shortage and contributed to a welcoming climate for immigrants who would meet the demand for labor. Since 1988, the economy has declined drastically, and the unemployment rate more than doubled between 1988 and 1992 (table 10.1), resulting in program cuts as well as cuts in state aid to local governments.[2] The full implications of this economic decline for newcomers are now apparent and have been translated into attempts to restrict eligibility, cut services, and reduce budgets for immigrant-serving institutions.

Table 10.2 EXPENDITURES, DEBT, AND TAXES PER CAPITA: FY 1990

	Texas	Massachusetts
Total expenditures per capita	$3,242	$4,598
Debt per capita	3,775	4,484
Taxes per capita	1,662	2,359

Source: U.S. Bureau of the Census, Government Finances: 1989–90, Series GF/90-5, U.S. Government Printing Office, Washington, D.C., 1991.

While Texas's economy suffered a sharp decline in the early to mid-1980s, it has since been relatively stable. Indeed, the unemployment rate dropped from 8.9 percent in 1986 to 6.2 percent in 1990. Although the fiscal problems following the collapse of the oil and banking industries could have resulted in drastic cuts in human services programs, the legislature passed a bill in 1987 to raise taxes and protect services. The state's mainstream assistance programs were already among the least generous of all states and remained so throughout the 1980s. Since the state had never made efforts to meet the special needs of immigrants, few targeted services could be cut in tough economic times. The recent, relative economic growth in Texas has allowed the state to avoid the kind of politics of scarcity experienced in Massachusetts in the late 1980s and early 1990s.

The same pattern holds true when looking at economic indicators such as expenditures, debt, and taxes per capita (table 10.2). In Fiscal Year (FY) 1990, for example, Texas spent an average of $3,242 per person, while Massachusetts spent $4,598 per person, a difference of 41 percent. At the same time, Massachusetts's debt per capita was 18 percent higher than Texas's, and its taxes per capita were 41 percent higher, reflecting Massachusetts's greater propensity to tax and spend. Again, something of a regression to the mean has taken place, as Massachusetts cut taxes in 1990, 1991, and 1992 in an attempt to revive the state economy.

Demographics

Another fact that helps to explain the disparate immigrant policies of Massachusetts and Texas is demographics—the size, growth rate and composition of each state's newcomer population. A significantly larger share of Texas's total population is made up of newcomers—refugees, legal immigrants and undocumented immigrants—than Massachusetts's (8 percent versus 5 percent). Texas, however, received a less diverse stream of immigrants in the latter half of

Table 10.3 RACIAL/ETHNIC COMPOSITION OF POPULATION: 1990

Race/Ethnicity	Massachusetts	Texas
White	89.8%	75.2%
Black	5.0	11.9
Asian	2.4	1.9
Other	2.8	11.0
Hispanic	4.8	25.5

Source: U.S. Bureau of the Census, Selected Population and Housing Characteristics for Massachusetts and for Texas, 1990; The Urban Institute, Washington, D.C. 1990. Note: The figures for white, black, Asian, and other sum to 100. Hispanics can be of any race.

the twentieth century than did Massachusetts. Massachusetts has received newcomer populations from Asia, Latin America, and the Caribbean who did not have the long-established communities within the state that the Irish and other European immigrants who settled there earlier did. Approximately one-quarter of the immigrants to Massachusetts in 1989 came from Latin America and the Caribbean, and another quarter came from Asia. Only a very small share, one-half of one percent, came from Mexico. The rest came from European and other countries (U.S. Immigration and Naturalization Service 1990). While Texas has also received a substantial flow of Asian newcomers, as refugees and as immigrants, the bulk of its newcomers still come from Latin America, with most of them from Mexico. Indeed, Texas is 25.5 percent Hispanic, while Massachusetts is 4.8 percent Hispanic (table 10.3).

At the same time, Massachusetts's Hispanic and Asian populations have been growing at a faster rate than Texas's (table 10.4). Between 1980 and 1990, Massachusetts had the third fastest-growing Hispanic

Table 10.4 SHARE OF POPULATION BY RACE/ETHNICITY AND PERCENT CHANGE: 1980 to 1990

	Massachusetts		Texas	
	% of Pop. in 1990	Percent Change 1980 to 1990	% of Pop. in 1990	Percent Change 1980 to 1990
Asian & Pacific Islanders	2.4	189.7	1.9	165.5
Hispanic	4.8	103.9	25.5	45.4
Black	5.0	35.6	11.9	18.2

Source: U.S. Bureau of the Census, Selected Population and Housing Characteristics for Massachusetts and for Texas, 1980 and 1990; The Urban Institute, Washington, D.C.; 1990.

population in the country, compared to the 23rd fastest in Texas, whose rate was nevertheless 45 percent (1990 Census). These groups clearly grew from a smaller base in Massachusetts than in Texas, presenting Massachusetts with essentially new populations with new needs. Since the majority of newcomers to Texas are Hispanic, the arrival of large numbers of newcomers may have been less visible. Hence, there may have been less of a perceived need to establish immigrant policies that addressed the needs of new population groups.

Another demographic characteristic that distinguishes the two states is the legal status of their newcomers. Texas receives a larger share of undocumented immigrants, and Massachusetts receives a higher proportional share of refugees and other legal immigrants. Texas's undocumented population is almost ten times as large as Massachusetts's, and its legalized population (immigrants who, prior to the Immigration Reform and Control Act of 1986 (IRCA), were undocumented) is about 25 times as large as Massachusetts's (table 10.5). Massachusetts's comparatively small undocumented population then, may have made it easier to politically justify programs whose beneficiaries are, for the most part, in the country with the government's consent.

In addition, labor shortages in Massachusetts, driven in part by out-migration, may have fostered a climate within which inclusive immigrant policies made sense and were politically possible. Between 1980 and 1990, Texas's population, and hence labor supply, increased both because of internal and international migration, contributing about 500,000 migrants and 600,000 immigrants, respectively (table 10.6). At the same time, Massachusetts gained about 130,000 immigrants but lost 189,000 people through out-migration. Therefore, through most of Massachusetts's prosperous 1980s, when the unemployment rate was as low as 3.2 percent, demand for labor was fueled by both growth and out-migration.

EXPRESS STATE IMMIGRANT POLICY: DIMENSIONS OF VARIATION

Perhaps the most telling aspects of a state's immigrant policy are the deliberate or express efforts the state makes to integrate immigrants. These efforts can take various forms. First, the executive branch can take initiatives to mandate planning for increased access to main-

Table 10.5 ESTIMATED 1990 NEWCOMER POPULATIONS: MASSACHUSETTS
AND TEXAS

	Massachusetts	Percent of Total	Texas	Percent of Total
Total Population	6,016,400		16,986,500	
Newcomer Population	302,300	100	1,427,500	100
	(5% of total)		(8% of total)	
Legal Permanent Residents	212,600	70	688,100	48
Refugees	39,200	13	56,200	4
ELAs (IRCA immigrants)	15,500	5	383,200	27
Undocumented (approximate)	35,000	12	300,000	21

Sources: Estimates derived in consultation with Jeffrey Passel, Director of the Urban Institute's Program for Research on Immigration Policy, from: U.S. Immigration and Naturalization Service, *Statistical Yearbook of the Immigration and Naturalization Service,* 1990, U.S. Government Printing Office, Washington, D.C., 1990; Passel, Jeff, and Karen Woodrow, "Geographic Distribution of Undocumented Immigrants: Estimates of Undocumented Aliens Counted in the 1980 Census by State," in *International Migration Review,* Vol xviii, No. 3., 1984; 1990 Census. Estimates for legal permanent residents derived from Passel and Woodrow's 1980 estimate of legal residents by subtracting 5 percent for mortality and emigration, adding immigrants admitted each year to the state (allowing for refugee adjustments and mortality and emigration), and subtracting naturalizations. Estimates for refugees, from the Office for Refugee Resettlement, include all those who entered as refugees, accounting for secondary migration. State estimates based on locally collected data are somewhat higher than these figures. For the Eligible Legalizing Alien (ELA) estimates, 10 percent of the states' total Special Agricultural Worker (SAW) approvals was subtracted, assuming that some did not live in the United States or had moved out. Similarly, 5 percent of each state's total approvals of legalization applications from immigrants who had been in the United States since before 1982 (pre '82s) was subtracted to account for mortality and emigration.

The estimates for undocumented immigrants were arrived at using a simple approximation of the 1980 Passel and Woodrow methodology. The number of foreign-born persons who entered between 1980 and 1990 was arrived at using the Census. From that number, legal permanent residents (using estimates as explained) were subtracted, 10 percent of pre-82s were added in, assuming 90 percent were counted in the 1980 Census, and refugees were subtracted, using a history of four years of conversions as an approximation of refugee status. Because the 1980 methodology resulted in a low estimate of undocumented immigrants for Texas, as borne out by the high number of legalization applicants, the final estimate of the undocumented population was increased (but may still be an underestimate). However, because the reverse occurred for Massachusetts, that estimate was decreased.

Note: These figures are rough stock estimates of the non-citizen populations residing in the two states. Legal permanent residents are those individuals residing in Massachusetts or Texas who, typically, have green cards and have not yet naturalized. Refugees are those who entered through the Refugee Program. IRCA immigrants are those who legalized their status under the Immigration Reform and Control Act of 1986.

Table 10.6 COMPONENTS OF NET MIGRATION: 1980–1990

	Massachusetts	Texas
International Migration	128,400	594,600
Net Internal Migration	− 189,000	469,600
Total Net Migration	− 60,500	1,064,200

Sources: Raw data from U.S. Bureau of the Census, and 1991, *Current Population Reports*, Series P-25, No. 1058; calculations by The Urban Institute.

stream social welfare programs or to develop programs specifically targeted at integrating immigrants, or it can take other actions that influence public attitudes toward immigrants. Second, states make choices in administering and implementing federal programs that focus on specific classes of immigrants, such as the Refugee Program. Finally, state governments may dedicate all or part of a department's institutional capacity to serving the newcomer population, or they may create new institutions specifically designed to serve newcomers.

Targeted State Initiatives

EXECUTIVE ACTIONS

It is likely that no state in recent history has adopted the kind of active, pro-immigrant policies that Massachusetts did in the mid-1980s. These included an executive order effectively barring discrimination on the basis of immigration status in the delivery of public benefits, the development in every state agency of a plan to serve refugees, and what amounted to an immigrant impact aid bill for cities.

The most far-reaching element of this inclusive immigrant policy was set out in Executive Order 257, signed in 1985 by then-Governor Michael Dukakis. It included a requirement that no state employee deny benefits to an applicant because of immigration or citizenship status, unless required to do so by federal law. The Order had the effect of making the liberal benefits that the state funded—including a generous General Relief program—available to all newcomers, including the undocumented.

Dukakis also mandated that all state agencies plan for the inclusion of refugees in their mainstream programs. This Refugee Service Plan required each state agency to conduct a needs assessment and create a plan for providing services. Dukakis's order also prohibited cooperation between the Immigration and Naturalization Service (INS) and the state and local police.

The state's inclusionary philosophy was evident in agency-level decisions. For example, the Department of Public Health defined "refugee" in a way that was broader than the federal government's definition.[3] The Department used this definition to develop and target services to a population that would not otherwise have been eligible for federal refugee benefits. Under this definition, about 1 out of every 45 Massachusetts residents is a refugee.[4] (Massachusetts Department of Public Health, Refugee Health Service Plan Review 1989.) This policy not only reflected the state's communitarian philosophy but also its independent views on foreign policy, views that were at odds with federal foreign policy in Central America during much of the 1980s. Because these changes were promulgated by executive order rather than legislation, they could be readily changed. Indeed, reversals of some of these efforts have occurred during the administration of Republican Governor William Weld.

LEGISLATIVE INITIATIVES

During the mid-1980s, the state, led by the legislature, took the unprecedented step of enacting an immigrant impact aid bill for the cities. Under the program, called Gateway Cities, the Massachusetts legislature appropriated $12.8 million in 1986 for about 30 cities and towns that were identified as having large numbers of non-English speakers (Massachusetts fiscal year 1987 budget, Sections 2 & 70, of Chapter 206 of the Acts of 1986, Acts and Resolves of Massachusetts). Gateway Cities funds, intended to defray the costs of providing services to immigrants, went to school districts, community-based organizations, and legal assistance groups. A slow start setting up the programs and the onset of fiscal difficulties in the state resulted in reduced appropriations in subsequent years. By 1991, the Division of Gateway Cities had been eliminated, along with virtually all funds to cities and towns. While a total of about $27.5 million was appropriated and $19.5 million spent between FY 1987 and 1991, only the legal assistance funds are still appropriated and spent. Once again then, we see a kind of regression to the mean, with Massachusetts moving toward a more middle-ground immigrant policy.

The state's pro-immigrant policies extend to the provision of legal services to non-citizens. Because of federal restrictions on legal services funds, (P.L. 100–459)[5] the state provided money through its Legal Assistance Corporation to pay for legal services to assist the undocumented in preparing asylum applications. State funding for these services was greatly reduced by budget cuts in the early 1990s.

BACKLASH

This extraordinary and visible activism on behalf of immigrants and refugees in Massachusetts led to a backlash in the form of efforts to exclude immigrants from programs and services. The state imposed new restrictions on legal and undocumented immigrant eligibility for the General Relief program before it was abolished altogether in 1991. Numerous initiatives were advanced to make English the official language and to restrict the instruction of bilingual education.[6] Immigrant eligibility for and use of benefits and services, particularly welfare, became a highly visible issue in the early 1990s in Massachusetts. Democratic gubernatorial candidate John Silber stated that Massachusetts had become a "welfare magnet" for Cambodians and other immigrants, a comment that received substantial publicity at the time (Worcester Telegraph & Gazette 1990). Silber went on to lose the election to Republican William Weld, but the issue of immigrants and welfare remains volatile in Massachusetts as the economy remains troubled.[7] The contrast between the Massachusetts policies of the mid-1980s and those in place in Texas could not be sharper. In Texas, neither the executive nor the legislative branch actively moved to create targeted programs for newcomers or to expand eligibility criteria for mainstream social welfare programs. Indeed, the state supported efforts to exclude the undocumented from the public schools, efforts that were forcefully rejected by the U.S. Supreme Court.[8] As in Massachusetts, numerous attempts were undertaken to make English the official language.[9]

State Administration of Targeted Federal Programs

The states' immigrant policies are also embedded in the choices they make in implementing federal programs directed toward immigrants. Some of the policies that reflect these choices include the generosity of the cash and medical benefits offered, the accessibility of those services, and the scope of a state's employment and training efforts.

THE REFUGEE PROGRAM

The largest and oldest program targeted at newcomers is the Refugee Program, which provides funds to voluntary agencies and to state

Table 10.7 REFUGEE ARRIVALS AND TOTAL FUNDS RECEIVED: 1984–1990

Year	Number of Refugees	Total Funds ($)		$ per Refugee	
		Current	Constant[a]	Current	Constant[a]
MASSACHUSETTS					
1984	2,612	16,011,533	16,011,553	6,130	6,130
1985	2,838	16,891,694	16,310,846	5,952	5,747
1986	2,326	18,172,070	17,226,990	7,813	7,406
1987	1,804	18,960,027	17,341,081	10,510	9,613
1988	2,814	17,417,382	15,297,261	6,190	5,436
1989	4,345	20,508,592	17,184,215	4,720	3,955
1990	4,655	14,749,500	11,725,119	3,169	2,519
TEXAS					
1984	5,643	13,047,832	13,047,832	2,312	2,312
1985	5,069	9,407,477	9,083,986	1,856	1,792
1986	4,362	9,773,172	9,264,896	2,241	2,124
1987	3,528	8,116,079	7,423,069	2,300	2,104
1988	2,698	7,642,061	6,711,835	2,832	2,488
1989	4,053	6,150,513	5,153,535	1,518	1,272
1990	5,704	5,184,837	4,121,688	909	723

[a]1984 constant dollars calculated using the Consumer Price Index, all items, as an inflation index.
Source: U.S. Department of Health and Human Services, Office of Refugee Resettlement, Annual Report, FY 1984 to 1990, Washington, D.C.
Note: Number of refugees admitted does not necessarily correspond to the number of refugees receiving assistance in that year.

and local governments to resettle refugees. This program has been the foundation, both financially and institutionally, for immigrant policy in the states. However, decreasing federal refugee dollars, as well as proposals to fundamentally restructure the program, have left that foundation somewhat shaken.

Between 1984 and 1990, Massachusetts and Texas, like the country as a whole, received rising numbers of refugees and fewer federal dollars (table 10.7). In 1990, Massachusetts received substantially more federal dollars per refugee than did Texas: $3,168 versus $909 (U.S. Department of Health and Human Services, Office of Refugee Resettlement). This reflects the generally higher welfare payments and Medicaid coverage in Massachusetts as well as higher refugee participation rates.

As a result of its higher payment levels and participation rates, Massachusetts was hit harder when, in 1990, the period during which the federal government reimbursed states for the full costs of providing Aid to Families with Dependent Children (AFDC) and Medicaid to refugees was decreased from 24 to 4 months.[10] The state absorbed $3.05 million in that year in costs that would have previously been covered by the federal government. At the same time, Texas's uncompensated costs were only $194,000.[11]

Secondary Migration. One would also expect that variation in benefit levels might promote secondary migration of refugees to states, such as Massachusetts, with high payment levels, leading to additional burdens on those states. In fact, throughout the 1980s, substantial internal migration of refugees (from the states in which they settled) to high welfare states took place. In 1986, Massachusetts had a net secondary in-migration of 1,170 refugees, and California had a net secondary in-migration of 7,886.[12] Texas, with its lower welfare payments had a net in-migration of −982. These states may also draw refugees for other reasons, including state-funded assistance programs that refugees can use after their period of eligibility for federal assistance runs out.

In recent years, however, the secondary migration flows have changed. In 1990, for example, Texas had greater net secondary migration, albeit only 244, than either Massachusetts or California. Consequently, this suggests that secondary migration may be responsive not only to welfare program payments but also to the availability of jobs and to other factors such as family and ethnic communities.

Proposed Private Resettlement Program (PRP). A major change proposed in 1992 for the Refugee Program would have shifted responsibility for administering much of the refugee assistance program to the voluntary agencies (VOLAGs), such as Catholic Charities, which have historically settled refugees in the United States. This change, amounting to a publicly funded, private program would have greatly reduced both funding to the states and their role in administering the Refugee Program. While the proposal did not become law, it is perhaps a harbinger of change for the future, pointing to an even more diminished state capacity in the area of immigrant policy.[13]

Accessibility of Services. The Refugee Program not only illustrates the varying levels of social welfare benefits the two states provide, it points up the difference between the two states' efforts at making services accessible to newcomers. Before the budget cuts of the early 1990s, Massachusetts had seven special units in its state welfare offices staffed with bilingual/bicultural workers and specifically designed to serve refugees. Texas, despite its slightly larger refugee

Table 10.8 REFUGEE ARRIVALS: PERCENT SOUTHEAST ASIAN AND SOVIET

	MASSACHUSETTS			TEXAS		
	Total Arrivals	% SE Asian	% Soviet	Total Arrivals	% SE Asian	% Soviet
1983	2,298	75.8	3.0	5,162	79.0	.3
1984	2,612	87.4	1.3	5,643	79.9	.3
1985	2,838	88.8	2.8	5,069	83.2	.2
1986	2,326	83.4	2.5	4,362	80.1	.2
1987	1,804	60.2	17.0	3,528	76.0	.2
1988	2,814	45.7	40.6	2,698	72.2	2.3
1989	4,345	37.9	52.3	4,053	72.8	7.0
1990	4,655	41.7	51.9	5,704	71.6	14.6

Source: Office of Refugee Resettlement, Department of Health and Human Services, Annual Reports FY 1983 to 1990, Washington, D.C.

population, had only one such unit, although it did place individual bilingual/bicultural workers in the welfare offices across the state. In Massachusetts, the Department of Mental Health has two offices serving refugees, and they are fully funded by the state. In Texas, no state dollars are spent on refugee programs besides those used to match federal cash and medical payments. The efforts by Massachusetts to meet the specific needs of immigrants can be viewed as reflecting the communitarian nature of its immigrant policies. Federal budget reductions could force their elimination, pushing Massachusetts toward a more middle-of-the-road immigrant policy.

Health Expenditures. Massachusetts also devotes a greater share of its refugee dollars to health expenditures, a difference that is driven in part by demographics and in part by public policy choices. In the early 1980s, both states' refugee populations were predominantly Southeast Asian. In the late 1980s, as the number of Soviet refugees arriving in the United States began to increase dramatically, the large, aggressive Soviet resettlement network, as well as the scientific research community in Massachusetts, drew a large number of Soviet refugees to that state. By 1990, over 50 percent of Massachusetts's incoming refugees were from the Soviet Union, while only 14.6 percent of Texas's refugees were from the Soviet Union (table 10.8).

The greater number of older and often less healthy Soviet refugees, accustomed as they were to frequent use of free health care, resulted in higher medical costs for the refugee program in Massachusetts than in Texas. Although most of the Soviets were Jews resettled through a matching grant program in which the private agency or family (rather than the government) provides cash assistance, this reliance on private agencies did not offset the higher medical costs the state has had to bear. Massachusetts's health costs are also driven up by its large number of teaching hospitals, whose cost structures tend to be comparatively high.

Employment and Training. Massachusetts has also demonstrated its activist philosophy in the way in which it has provided job training and placement services under the Refugee Program. Because of long-standing controversies over refugee welfare dependence, a central goal of the federal program has been to provide refugees with early employment. Many refugees, however, leave the jobs in which they are initially placed, resulting in an ongoing tension in the program between the goal of early employment and the placing of refugees in more durable, better-paying jobs.

Texas's refugee program has traditionally emphasized rapid job placement, whereas Massachusetts has historically placed great emphasis first on education and training and then on job placement. Texas provides primarily job placement services and only some English as a Second Language (ESL) and vocational training. Most of the latter programs have been cut as a result of decreased federal refugee funding.

Massachusetts has redesigned its employment and training program to address simultaneously the objectives of early employment and higher wages by offering additional education and training to refugees who are already employed. In the past, refugees could only receive language and employment training services if they were on welfare, which often forced them to choose between training and employment. The new program would also encourage early employment by reimbursing refugees for employment-related costs as they make the transition to a new job. Refugees would be reimbursed for such services as child care, transportation costs, and if the employer does not provide them, medical benefits. Because many refugees were hesitant to give up their cash and medical assistance for minimum wage jobs that did not provide medical benefits, state officials believe this type of assistance will increase employment. Massachusetts's new program will also incorporate comprehensive case management, delivered by private community agencies, where one case worker will coordinate all the refugee's services, including cash and medical assistance, employment and training and education. This aspect of the program is similar to the federal government's proposed private resettlement program. State officials claim these innovations will be financed through a combination of "saved" welfare dollars, careful case management, and funding by state agencies such as the Massachusetts Department of Employment and Training and the Department of Education.[14]

STATE LEGALIZATION IMPACT ASSISTANCE GRANT (SLIAG)

The other major targeted federal program administered by the states is SLIAG, which, along with the Refugee Program, is one of two cornerstones of immigrant policy within the states. Like the Refugee Program, however, it has provided fewer dollars to the states than originally promised, and because of its temporary nature, its termination threatens to diminish some of the immigrant policy capacity that has been established at the state level.

SLIAG was designed to help defray state and local costs of certain services provided to those newly legalized under IRCA. In contrast to the Refugee Program, differences between the way the two states have administered SLIAG are minimal because SLIAG is basically a reimbursement program (versus one that delivers services). Where state SLIAG programs can differ is in the kind and level of expenditures on education and anti-discrimination outreach. Both Texas and Massachusetts devoted significant funds to these services and were fairly innovative in devising ways to reach the legalizing population.

The most apparent distinction between the two states lies less in program implementation than in the impact of the termination of SLIAG funding.

The termination of SLIAG in 1994, which follows a series of delays in appropriating the funds, will hit Texas harder than Massachusetts because Texas's legalizing population is so much larger and because ELAs make up a larger share of the total newcomer population in Texas (26 percent versus 5 percent). Although Massachusetts actually receives more SLIAG dollars per ELA ($995 versus $694) because of its generally higher service costs, Texas still receives more total SLIAG dollars and will, therefore, absorb more costs that previously had been reimbursed under SLIAG.[16] This is, as we have seen, in some contrast to cutbacks in the Refugee Program, which will have a more severe impact in Massachusetts than Texas.

Both states will absorb additional costs as a result of SLIAG's termination.[17] Taken together, the cutbacks in the Refugee Program and the possible cuts in and termination of SLIAG are almost certain to eliminate much of the limited public institutional capacity that has been developed to serve immigrants.

SAVE

A third targeted federal program, the Systematic Alien Verification for Entitlements (SAVE) program, illustrates again how Massachusetts's and Texas's very different approaches to immigrant policy have converged. SAVE, which was authorized by IRCA, mandates that states verify the immigration status of applicants for certain federally funded benefits.[18] This program, which is aimed at keeping undocumented and other ineligible immigrants from receiving public assistance, reflects the exclusionary and restrictive aspects of the 1986 law. Because of SAVE's projected expense and the inaccuracies of the database, Massachusetts tried to opt out of the program by applying for a waiver from using SAVE for all the major benefit programs except unemployment compensation. At the same time, Texas originally decided to implement SAVE for all programs. In a move that suggests SAVE's cost ineffectiveness as well as, perhaps, a shift in the politics underlying Texas's immigrant policy, that state has applied for a waiver from its use in the food stamp program.

BILINGUAL EDUCATION

The most important targeted federal program that states administer in the area of education is the bilingual education program. Here, however, more similarities than differences exist between the two states. Both Texas and Massachusetts have state laws mandating bilingual education, but their approaches to providing it vary somewhat. Texas requires that schools provide bilingual education to limited English proficient (LEP) students in elementary school, while secondary school students receive ESL training, unless the school district opts to provide them bilingual education.[19] Massachusetts, which in 1971 was the first state to mandate bilingual education, provides bilingual education in grades 1 through 12.[20] In both states, most school districts provide transitional bilingual education, the most widely used bilingual program, in which LEP students are taught in their native language while they learn English. In Massachusetts, a few school districts provide two-way bilingual programs in which, for example, Spanish and English are taught in the classroom to LEP students and to English-speaking students who want to learn Spanish.

Requirements for being either a bilingual or ESL teacher are similar in both states. In Massachusetts, a bilingual teacher must pass a language and culture test, while in Texas, a bilingual teacher must get a bilingual endorsement, which usually requires 12 to 15 semester hours of university courses on bilingual education and successful completion of written and oral language tests. ESL teachers go through similar certification processes in both states.

Bilingual education has been a much-litigated issue in both states. In Massachusetts, several cases have been brought against individual school districts or the state for not providing adequate bilingual training or services.[21] In Texas, similar cases resulted in improved identification of students, an expansion in the program's scope, and better qualified teachers.[22]

Immigrant Serving Institutions and Organizations

The third and possibly most important component of a state's express immigrant policy is the existence of institutions that are aimed directly at meeting the needs of its newcomer population. Several states, including Massachusetts and Texas, have created offices for refugees and immigrants that function as the focal point for immigrant policy within the state. Like other aspects of state immigrant policy, however, the strength of these institutions varies according to changes in the state's economy and demographics as well as shifts in federal funding. Where Massachusetts and Texas were far apart on this score in the mid-1980s, they have since come closer.

Massachusetts's Office for Refugees and Immigrants was carefully named to indicate that the office exists for those groups and that it serves the needs of both refugees and immigrants. It administers both SLIAG and the Refugee Program and, more broadly, acts as an advocate for newcomers in the state. It is located within the Office of the Secretary of the Executive Office of Health and Human Services and thus has direct access to the Secretary of the department.[23]

In Texas, the SLIAG program was run within the Health and Human Services Coordinating Council, the governing body for over 20 major departments, and the Refugee Program was located within a program office of the Texas Department of Human Services. As of September 1, 1991, however, both programs were housed within the Office of Immigration and Refugee Affairs, located in the Governor's office, thus providing the office direct access to the Governor and department heads. (An effort to move the office back to the Department of Human Services by the fall of 1993 was defeated by the state legislature.)

Beyond the public agencies, other important institutions that serve immigrants are private, nonprofit advocacy and community-based organizations, including social service agencies and refugee and immigrant community self-help groups. In Massachusetts, this network is large and sophisticated and is often linked to national organizations. For example, in Massachusetts, the Immigrant and Refugee Coalition has about 50 member organizations and is staffed by at least three people. In Texas, the few important advocacy groups form a much less established and effective community. One coalition, the North Texas Immigration Coalition, is equivalent to the Immigrant and Refugee Coalition in Massachusetts but is a regional, not a statewide, organization and has only about 35 members. Although Texas is a large, diverse state and is probably better served by regional organizations, the coalition is as yet the only one of its kind in the state. The coalition has no full-time staff and has received only small foundation grants and SLIAG dollars to conduct legalization outreach.

Two factors contribute to the greater relative strength of community-based groups in Massachusetts. First, Massachusetts has more private foundations that devote resources to immigrant issues. Second, Massachusetts, unlike Texas, has more of a tradition of providing public services through private, community-based organizations.

DE FACTO IMMIGRANT POLICY: DIMENSIONS OF VARIATION

A state's de facto immigrant policy can be viewed as the access it provides newcomers to its mainstream institutions and programs (such as General Relief) and the generosity of the public benefits it provides. Two areas that have a particularly important impact on the lives of newcomers are education and public benefits.

Education

In addition to implementing the targeted bilingual education program, states shape immigrant policy in the area of education in a number of ways. These include whether they provide access to compensatory education programs in elementary and secondary schools or to institutions of higher education. State immigrant policy is also reflected in the extent to which adult education resources are used to provide ESL training.

ACCESS TO COMPENSATORY EDUCATION

Chapter 1, the federal program of compensatory education for poor, low-achieving children provides an interesting case study in how states, or more specifically schools, have adapted a mainstream program to the needs of newcomers. In Massachusetts, a lawsuit was brought against the Boston Public Schools by the Boston Latino Parents Association. The Association claimed that limited English proficient (LEP) students who were entitled to services provided under Chapter 1 were not receiving them.[24] The Boston lawsuit resulted in a consent decree in which the Boston Public Schools promised to increase the Chapter 1 resources devoted to LEP students and ensure that LEP students were proportionately served in Chapter 1. While the lawsuit appears to have resulted in a redistribution of resources, questions still remain regarding the *quality of services*. Are LEP students now receiving services that meet their specific needs? (Fix and Zimmermann 1993).

ACCESS TO HIGHER EDUCATION

Whether undocumented immigrants have access to higher education also distinguishes the two states. In keeping with Texas's laissez faire or libertarian philosophy, most public colleges and universities do not explicitly exclude or include undocumented immigrants. In Massachusetts, decisions are made on a school-by-school basis. Thus, certain community and four-year colleges have taken a hard-line stance on the issue by not permitting undocumented immigrants to be admitted, while others have expressly admitted them.

The separate but related issue of whether immigrants are considered state residents and therefore eligible for in-state tuition has been highly contested in a number of states. Because out-of-state tuition can be prohibitively expensive, the issue bears directly on access to higher education. In this case, the two states' approaches are reversed, with Texas making a determination and Massachusetts remaining silent. In Texas, the state legislature has determined that only permanent residents who have filed a declaration of intent to become citizens qualify as residents for tuition purposes.[25] In Massachusetts, state legislation is silent on the residency issue, and determinations are made by individual institutions. A sampling of major institutions in Massachusetts showed that they did not consider immigration status when establishing in-state and out-of-state tuition levels (Olivas 1986).[26] While the issue has not come under litigation in either Texas or Massachusetts, it has been litigated in other states, such as

Maryland and California.[27] In practice, then, much of the decision-making is left to the school admissions officers.

Because most immigrants arrive in this country as adults without much proficiency in English and often without much education in their native language, the efforts that a state makes to educate its adult immigrant population form a particularly important piece of its immigrant policy. The extent to which a state's adult education program serves limited English proficient adults reflects each state's changing demographics and the public policy choices each has made.

Adult education funded by the federal, state, and local governments consists of three components: adult basic education, ESL, and adult secondary education. In 1990, 43 percent of all adults served in Massachusetts's adult education program were LEP. In Texas 41 percent were LEP, despite Texas's proportionately larger adult immigrant population. While both states emphasize the ESL component of their adult education programs, overall, Massachusetts devotes a larger share of its total adult education resources to LEP students. Additionally, state funds pay for a larger portion of adult education services in Massachusetts than in Texas.

Public Assistance Programs

At the most basic level, a state's de facto immigrant policy is embedded in the generosity of the public benefits it makes available to all eligible persons, including legal permanent residents, refugees, asylees and even, in some cases, undocumented immigrants. As table 10.9 indicates, Massachusetts provides substantially higher maximum and average payments in each of the four major federal programs than does Texas.

AFDC

Although most research shows immigrants do not generally have high rates of participation in Aid to Families with Dependent Children (AFDC), for those immigrants who do participate, Massachusetts provides greater benefits than Texas (U.S. House of Representatives, Committee on Ways and Means 1991). While the amount of money required to meet the basic needs of a three-person family[28] is approximately the same (over $500 per month in both states), Massachusetts's

Table 10.9 MAINSTREAM ASSISTANCE PROGRAMS

PROGRAM	Massachusetts	Texas
Aid to Families with Dependent Children (AFDC) maximum monthly benefits for a three-person family, Jan. 1991	$539	$184
Supplemental Security Income (SSI) maximum monthly benefit for aged individual living independently, Jan. 1991	536	407
State supplement to SSI, Jan. 1991	129	None
Medicaid average expenditure per recipient, FY 1989	4,109	1,878
Unemployment Compensation maximum weekly benefit, 1991	282 – 423	224
General Relief maximum monthly benefit for an adult individual, 1991	334[a]	None

Source: U.S. House of Representatives, Committee on Ways and Means, *Overview of Entitlement Programs*, Committee Print 102-9, May 7, 1991.
[a]Massachusetts General Relief abolished in 1991.

payment equals the amount needed while Texas's payment amount is less than half of what is needed. Among all states, Massachusetts ranks 4th in AFDC payment levels and Texas ranks 48th (U.S. Department of Health and Human Services 1989, 374).[29]

From an immigrant policy perspective, one of the most salient differences between the two states is the fact that Massachusetts has had an AFDC-UP (unemployed parent) program in place for several years, making two-parent families with an unemployed parent eligible for benefits. This program is often well-suited to low-income immigrants and refugees who are typically members of two- rather than one-parent families. Until September 1990, Texas did not have such a program, and since then, it has been implemented only slowly across the state.[30] An important difference among state AFDC-UP programs lies in how states use their discretion to "credit" work experience abroad, since eligibility depends upon some prior work history. Some states, like Massachusetts, credit work abroad, while others do not.[31]

GENERAL RELIEF

Under the 1985 Executive Order issued by Michael Dukakis, undocumented immigrants were made eligible for all benefit programs, including the state's General Relief Program, unless explicitly excluded by federal statute or court precedent. This inclusionary approach to newcomer eligibility was curtailed somewhat when the General Relief Program was abolished in the Fall of 1991 and replaced by a program of Emergency Aid to the Elderly, Disabled, and Children. Still, eligibility under the new program has been extended to legal immigrants and those considered PRUCOL (permanently residing under color of law), with PRUCOL having been liberally defined to include those granted temporary protected status (TPS) and immigrants legalizing under IRCA (ELAs), two groups who have been explicitly barred from federal assistance programs.[32] The undocumented, however, who were previously eligible for General Relief under the Executive Order, are ineligible for the new program. Texas does not have a state-wide General Relief program or an emergency program equivalent to that in Massachusetts.

HEALTH CARE

Massachusetts's essentially communitarian bent is also reflected in the access to health services provided to immigrants. The state created a Division of Refugee and Immigrant Health within the Department of Public Health that addresses the special needs of the state's newcomers. The Division created, for example, a Southeast Asian Birthing and Infancy Project, offering health education, patient advocacy, and interpreter services. It also ensures that other health programs within the department provide services that are accessible to and appropriate for the state's newcomer population.[33]

Previously, under the Executive Order, all immigrants in Massachusetts, regardless of legal status, could get some medical care under the General Relief Program. Since that program was abolished, those not eligible for full Medicaid (e.g., undocumented immigrants) were left with only hospitals' provision of uncompensated care, which was paid for in part by state dollars, or emergency care under Medicaid as provided for by the Omnibus Budget Reconciliation Act of 1986.[34]

A major change in the federal Medicaid program made it one of the few federal assistance programs under which undocumented immigrants, who otherwise meet certain eligibility criteria, can receive certain services. The Omnibus Budget Reconciliation Act of 1986 allowed Medicaid coverage for treatment of an undocumented immigrant's "emergency medical condition," including labor and delivery costs.[35] However, defining what constitutes an "emergency medical condition" has been left largely to the states. Both Texas and Massachusetts have left the decision, in turn, to the medical practitioners to determine what qualifies as an emergency and how long treatment should be provided.

While Texas's health care system does not offer services aimed specifically at meeting the needs of the immigrant population, legal as well as undocumented immigrants are eligible for several of the state and local health programs. County Indigent Health Care programs, for example, provide medical assistance to people who do not qualify for other state or federal programs in counties that are not fully served by public hospitals. Other state programs require only county or state residency and do not restrict eligibility by citizenship or immigration status. Those include Maternal and Infant Health Improvement Services, which provide care to low-income pregnant women and infants, and the Primary Health Care Services Program, which provides primary health care for the poor.

CONCLUSION

In looking at Massachusetts's and Texas's immigrant policies, it is clear that Massachusetts has articulated and, to some extent, implemented immigrant policies that reflect a communitarian vision of immigrants. Through most of the 1980s, Massachusetts's strong economy, activist political culture, high levels of out-migration, and tradition of receptivity provided the perfect conditions for innovation in program planning. In fact, the rapidly improving economy of the early 1980s, the growing newcomer population, and the receptive political environment go some distance toward explaining why Massachusetts was able to develop targeted and generous immigrant policies. The Massachusetts Office for Refugees and Immigrants, the Gateway Cities program, the Department of Public Health's expanded definition of a refugee, and the Department of Public Health's Division of Refugee and Immigrant Health all illustrate the efforts Massachusetts has made to meet the needs of its newcomers. On the other hand, Texas, with its libertarian political culture, has taken few steps to promote an activist immigrant policy. Perhaps because large-scale immigration is such an accepted part of daily life in Texas and because such a large share of that flow is undocumented, it is not surprising that the state has not welcomed newcomers as Massachusetts has.

While Massachusetts may once have had an open immigrant policy and Texas a comparatively restrictive one, each has undergone significant changes in recent years, resulting in something of a regression to the mean. As a sharp economic downturn has coincided with rapid changes in Massachusetts's newcomer population, public attitudes toward immigrants have changed and what were activist and inclusionary policies have become more exclusionary. The goal of meeting immigrants' needs appears to have taken on less importance as both mainstream and targeted programs have been cut back and attempts were made to restrict newcomers' eligibility for assistance. In Texas, the creation of the Office of Immigration and Refugee Affairs has formed a foundation on which the state could build a more active and inclusive immigrant policy. Still, despite these changes, Massachusetts has maintained an element of inclusiveness and Texas an element of exclusiveness in their immigrant policies.

Immigration flows to the United States, and to Massachusetts and Texas, are reaching unprecedented levels. While many of the immigrant policies developed in Texas and Massachusetts are state and local in character, they depend on federal dollars. In this regard, the underpinnings of state immigrant policies have been the Refugee Program and SLIAG. As these federal programs are scaled down, the states lose much of their capacity to implement activist or targeted immigrant policies. With state economies as troubled as they are, states are unlikely to pick up where the federal government has left off. These trends leave the future of immigrant policy at the state and local level, skeletal though it may be, very much in doubt.

Notes

The authors thank David Rosenberg and Anne Dee Tucker for their helpful comments as well as the many people in Massachusetts and Texas who helped inform this study. Support for its research and writing was provided by the Andrew W. Mellon Foundation.

1. This report examines the immigrant policies in place in the mid- to late 1980s as well as the changes that have taken place through early 1993.

2. For example, in the 1992 budget, legislators reduced state Medicaid spending and cut about $328 million of state aid to local governments.

3. The federal definition of a refugee conforms to the definition used in the United Nations Protocol and Convention Relating to the Status of Refugees. As set out by the Refugee Act of 1980 (P.L. 96-212; 94 Stat. 102), a refugee is a person who is outside his native country and is unwilling or unable to return because of persecution or a well-founded fear of persecution on account of race, religion, nationality, membership

in a particular social group or political opinion. The Department's definition of a refugee includes individuals "who have left their home countries and have no realistic expectation of returning for fear of death or persecution." In Massachusetts, these would include primarily Haitians, Salvadorans, and Guatemalans. While the state's definition is similar to the federal definition of a refugee, it includes persons who have had refugee-like experiences but were not granted *federal* refugee status. Unlike the federal government, the Department of Public Health does not have a formal adjudication process.

4. This estimate assumes a larger number of undocumented immigrants (who would be considered refugees under the expanded definition) than is estimated in table 10.5.

5. The Departments of Commerce, Justice, and State, the Judiciary, and Related Agencies Appropriations Act, 1989, continues restrictions that bar the use of federal funds to provide legal services for or on behalf of undocumented immigrants and most other aliens not admitted for permanent residence.

6. The city of Lowell, which has a substantial refugee population, passed the state's first English Only Ordinance. Massachusetts bill H.4797, 1991, proposed making English the official language of the state. H.711, H.712, and H.713 proposed various restrictions on the instruction of bilingual education. Approximately 20 states have passed Official English legislation, including California and Florida, two states with large immigrant populations.

7. It should be noted that most research has shown that immigrants have lower welfare participation rates than comparable natives. See, for example, Marta Tienda, and Leif Jensen, "Immigration and Public Assistance Participation: Dispelling the Myth of Dependency," *Social Science Research*, Vol. 15, 1986; Sidney Weintraub and Gilberto Cardenas, "The Use of Public Services by Undocumented Aliens in Texas: A Study of State Costs and Revenues," Lyndon B. Johnson School of Public Affairs, Policy Research Project Report, No. 60, 1984. Other researchers, however, have disagreed. See George Borjas, *Friends or Strangers: The Impact of Immigrants on the U.S. Economy*, New York: Basic Books, Inc., 1990.

8. *Plyler v. Doe*, 457 U.S. 202 (1982).

9. In the 69th session of the Texas legislature HB. 2467 was introduced, in the 70th session HCR. 61 and HJR. 55 were introduced, in the 71st session HJR. 48 was introduced.

10. Beginning in 1991, federal reimbursement for the non-federal share of the categorical programs was no longer available. Refugees who do not meet the family structure eligibility requirements for AFDC or Medicaid but who are financially needy may receive refugee cash assistance (rca) and refugee medical assistance (rma), which are federally funded but administered by the states. In 1980, this assistance was available for a period of 36 months, but has since been cut back to 8 months.

11. These shortfalls vary because of Massachusetts's significantly higher payment levels, the availability of AFDC benefits to refugees in intact families who meet the means test through the AFDC-UP (unemployed parent) program (which has been available in Massachusetts but not in Texas), and the fact that the federal government covered 61 percent of Texas's AFDC costs versus 50 percent in Massachusetts. The levels of public assistance and health benefits accorded refugees mirror those provided by the state AFDC and Medicaid programs to other members of the eligible population. Massachusetts Office for Refugees and Immigrants; Texas Department of Human Services, Refugee Program.

12. The Office for Refugee Resettlement (ORR) tracks secondary migration of refugees who are receiving refugee cash and medical assistance or social services. Those refugees not receiving refugee services are not included, and many states believe this number is far larger than the number recorded by ORR.

13. The proposed plan was challenged in a lawsuit brought by several refugee and

mutual assistance agencies (MAAs) in Washington State. The suit, which alleged that ORR had not complied with the notice and comment requirements of the Administrative Procedures Act, resulted in a temporary restraining order preventing the conversion to privatization. (*Nguyen v. Sullivan*, No. C92-1867WD W.D. Wash. Dec. 22, 1992). As of early 1993, the PRP was suspended until a new director of ORR was appointed.

14. As of early 1993, the new program of employment and training is on hold pending approval from the federal government.

15. IRCA originally provided for $1 billion of SLIAG appropriations for each of the fiscal years between 1988 and 1991, with states allowed to draw unused funds for the following three years. In FY 1990 and 1991, Congress shifted $1.2 billion in SLIAG appropriations into FY 1992. In 1992, the money was again shifted to 1993. In that year, Congress only appropriated $311 million, though the remaining $812 million was appropriated in 1994.

16. Dollars per ELA were estimated by dividing the total costs accepted by the Department of Health and Human Services by the total number of ELAs in each state, as shown in table 10.5.

17. The termination of SLIAG coincides with the end of IRCA's five-year bar on many services to the legalized population, which is also likely to result in additional costs to state and local governments.

18. These benefit programs are AFDC, Medicaid, food stamps, unemployment compensation, federal housing programs, and Title IV educational assistance programs.

19. Bilingual education generally provides for some or all courses to be taught in the native language, although there is great variation in approaches to bilingual education around the country. ESL provides for the instruction of English speaking, reading, and writing skills.

20. Students typically make the transition to mainstream classes in three years.

21. *Lynn Hispanic Parent Advisory Council v. John Lawson*, Civ. Action 85-2475-K, U.S. District Court, District of Massachusetts, resulted in a consent decree agreed to in 1986; *Lowell Hispanic Parent Advisory Council v. Kouloheras*, Civ. Action 87-1968-H, U.S. District Court, District of Massachusetts, resulted in a consent decree agreed to in 1988; *Lynn Hispanic Parent Advisory Council v. Harold Reynolds*, Civ. Action 85-2575-H, ongoing.

22. *Castaneda v. Pickard*, 648 F.2d 989, 5th Cir. (1981).

23. In addition to coordinating those two programs and several smaller ones such as a citizenship education program, the Office also collects data on immigrants, monitors immigration issues, and assists in the development of community organizations. In 1990, the Office issued a report on the impacts of newcomers on the state, "Through the Golden Door: Impacts of Non-Citizen Residents on the Commonwealth," Office for Refugees and Immigrants, May 16, 1990.

24. *Boston Master Parents Advisory Council and Latino Parents Association v. School Committee, City of Boston*, Civil Action No. 91-11725-Z, U.S.D.C. Mass. (1991).

25. Texas Education Code, Sect. 54.057.

26. Mass. Gen. Laws Ann. ch. 73, Sect. 1A, 6.

27. In California, the issue of whether undocumented students should be considered state residents and allowed to pay in-state tuition has been litigated in *Leticia "A" et al. v. Regents of the University of California et al.*, No. 588-982-5 (Cal. Super. Ct., Alameda County, May 5, 1985) and *Regents of the University of California v. The Superior Court of Los Angeles County, David Paul Bradford, Real Party in Interest*, Ca. Ct. of Ap.2d Dist. BO 51229, Nov. 28, 1990. The differing results reached in the two cases have meant that undocumented immigrants are eligible for in-state tuition

in the California State University system, but not in the University of California or the community college system. In the Maryland case, *Toll v. Moreno*, 458 U.S. 1 (1982), immigrants (or children of immigrants) working in certain international organizations were allowed to establish residence for the purpose of paying in-state tuition fees.

28. Each state sets its own need standards, which are related to the number of persons in the unit receiving assistance.

29. Because of deeming requirements and the public charge exclusion, most immigrants are effectively barred from receiving AFDC and other federal benefits for three years after admission. The income of the immigrant's sponsor is "deemed" also to be the income of the immigrant, making it difficult to qualify for benefits. An immigrant must also prove that he/she will not go on welfare and become a "public charge."

30. The Family Support Act of 1988, P.L. 100-485, required all states to begin implementation of an AFDC-UP program by October 1990.

31. Massachusetts also extends its AFDC payments to additional categories of recipients, such as migrant workers with families and families affected by natural disasters, where Texas does not. Of the 23 categories of optional extensions of assistance payments, Massachusetts extended eligibility to nine, and Texas to none. See *Characteristics of State Plans for AFDC under Title IV-A of the Social Security Act*, 1989, ed., U.S. Department of Health and Human Services, p. 374.

32. PRUCOL is a term used in defining alien eligibility for certain public assistance programs. Seven categories of aliens are universally accepted by federal agencies as PRUCOL: refugees, asylees, conditional entrants, aliens paroled into the United States, aliens granted suspension of deportation, those who entered under the Cuban-Haitian entrant program, and applicants for registry. The Immigration Act of 1990 granted temporary safe haven, or temporary protected status (TPS), to Salvadorans and nationals of certain other countries. This status enabled them to reside and work legally in the United States until it was considered safe for them to return to their homeland.

33. For example, Healthy Start, which provides prenatal care and counseling to low-income mothers, employs a bilingual and bicultural staff and serves a large immigrant clientele—in part as a result of the Division's advocacy. Division staff also consulted with the state Childhood Lead Poisoning Prevention Program on adapting service delivery to reach Southeast Asian clients.

34. Massachusetts's experiment in ensuring universal care through a "pay or play" system, in which employers either paid insurance or paid into a state pool, was never fully implemented and is being eliminated.

35. Alien eligibility requirements for Medicaid are set forth in Section 1903(v) of the Social Security Act, 42 U.S.C. 1396b(v)(3). This provision was added by Section 9406 of the Omnibus Budget Reconciliation Act of 1986, Pub. L. No. 99-509.

APPENDIX 10.A
CASES CITED

Boston Master Parents Advisory Council and Latino Parents Associa-
    tion v. School Committee, City of Boston, Civ. Action 91-
    11725-Z (U.S.D.C., Mass., 1991).
Castaneda v. Pickard, 648 F.2d 989 (5th Cir., 1981).
Leticia "A" et al. v. Regents of the University of California et al.,
    No. 588-982-5 (Super. Ct., Cal., 1985).
Lowell Hispanic Parent Advisory Council v. Kouloheras, Civ. Action
    87-1968-H, (U.S.D.C., Mass., 1988).
Lynn Hispanic Parent Advisory Council v. John Lawson, Civ. Action
    85-2475-K, (U.S.D.C., Mass., 1986).
Lynn Hispanic Parent Advisory Council v. Harold Reynolds, Civ.
    Action 85-2575-H, (ongoing).
Nguyen v. Sullivan, No. C92-1867WD, (W.D., Wash., 1992).
Plyer v. Doe, 457 U.S. 202 (1982).
Regents of the University of California v. The Superior Court of Los
    Angeles County, David Paul Bradford, Real Party in Interest,
    BO 51229 (Ct. of Appeals, 2d Dist., 1990).
Toll v. Moreno, 458 U.S. 1 (1982).

References

Borjas, George. 1990. *Friends or Strangers: The Impact of Immigrants on the U.S. Economy*. New York: Basic Books, Inc.

Davidson, Chandler. 1990. *Race and Class in Texas Politics*. Princeton: Princeton University Press.

Elazar, Daniel. 1966. *American Federalism: A View from the States*. New York: Thomas Y. Crowell.

Fehrenbach, T.R. 1983. *Lone Star: A History of Texas and the Texans*. New York: American Legacy Press.

Fix, Michael, and Wendy Zimmermann. 1993. *Educating Immigrant Children: Chapter 1 in the Changing City*. Washington, D.C.: The Urban Institute Press.

Handlin, Oscar. 1969. *Boston's Immigrants: 1790–1880*. Cambridge: The Belknap Press of Harvard University.

Massachusetts Department of Public Health. 1989. *Refugee Health Service Plan Review*. August.

Massachusetts Office for Refugees and Immigrants. 1990. "Through the Golden Door: Impacts of Non-Citizen Residents on the Commonwealth." May 16.

Olivas, Michael. 1986. "*Plyer v. Doe, Toll v. Moreno*, and Postsecondary Admissions: Undocumented Adults and Enduring Disability." *Journal of Law & Education* 15(1).

Osborne, David. 1988. *Laboratories of Democracy*. Cambridge: Harvard Business School Press.

Passel, Jeffrey, and Karen Woodrow. 1984. "Geographic Distribution of Undocumented Immigrants: Estimates of Undocumented Aliens Counted in the 1980 Census by State." *International Migration Review* 18(3).

Tienda, Marta, and Leif Jensen. 1986. "Immigration and Public Assistance Participation: Dispelling the Myth of Dependency." In *Social Science Research 15*.

U.S. Bureau of the Census. 1991. *Government Finances: 1989–90*, Series GF/90-5, Washington, D.C.: U.S. Government Printing Office.

————. 1991. *Current Population Reports*, Series P-25, No. 1058. Washington, D.C.: U.S. Government Printing Office.

U.S. Department of Health and Human Services. 1989. *Characteristics of State Plans for Aid to Families with Dependent Children under Title IV-A of the Social Security Act*. Washington, D.C.: U.S. Government Printing Office.

————. Various years. Office of Refugee Resettlement, Annual Reports FY 1983–1990. Washington, D.C.: author.

U.S. Department of Labor, Bureau of Labor Statistics. 1989. *Handbook of Labor Statistics*. Washington, D.C.: U.S. Government Printing Office.

————. 1990–91. *Geographic Profile of Employment and Unemployment*. Washington, D.C.: U.S. Government Printing Office.

U.S. House of Representatives, Committee on Ways and Means. 1991. *Overview of Entitlement Programs.* Washington, D.C.: Committee Print. May 7.

U.S. Immigration and Naturalization Service. 1990. *Statistical Yearbook of the Immigration and Naturalization Service: 1990.* Washington, D.C.: U.S. Government Printing Office.

Weintraub, Sidney, and Gilberto Cardenas. 1984. "The Use of Public Services by Undocumented Aliens in Texas: A Study of State Costs and Revenues." Lyndon B. Johnson School of Public Affairs, Policy Research Project Report, No. 60.

Worcester Telegraph & Gazette. 1990. "Silber Cites 'Welfare Magnet'." January 26, 1990.

Chapter Eleven

THE FUTURE IMMIGRANT POPULATION OF THE UNITED STATES

Barry Edmonston and Jeffrey S. Passel

For four centuries, the ethnic and racial composition of the United States has been a constantly changing picture, reflecting the varying sources of immigrants as well as the different fertility and mortality of the native residents and the new immigrants. The population diversified as the immigrants had children and grandchildren and was altered by the generational composition of the residents.

The population residing in the territory of today's United States began as entirely Native American and changed in the early years of the Republic to predominantly white[1] and black residents, with some Hispanic persons residing in the Southwest. By 1800, the United States population was about 80 percent white and 20 percent black. Significant immigration during the 1800s altered the racial composition. Blacks accounted for only 10 percent of the population in 1900 and overwhelmingly resided in the South.

The most recent 30 years have witnessed another massive shift in the country of origin of U.S. immigrants. Our predominantly white society with a black minority is becoming more heterogeneous. The proportion of whites is falling, as sizable numbers of Asian and Hispanic immigrants arrive. Some new features are apparent in the present situation. The fertility of the native population is so low— below the long-run replacement level, in fact—that any racial/ethnic group that does not have significant immigration will be reduced in numbers in the coming decades. Previous periods of high immigration included large numbers of Europeans. Current immigrants are predominantly Hispanic, Caribbean, and Asian, a far cry from the overwhelmingly European movements of the 1800s and early 1900s.

The United States is once again on the eve of large ethnic transformations. In previous instances, major ethnic changes in the pattern of immigration have given rise to social disturbances, followed by periods of adaptation and integration of the immigrants (and adjustments by the U.S. society). The new phase will also likely involve disturbances and raise new questions about the identity of "Americans." For these reasons, changes in the ethnic and racial composition of the U.S. population warrant objective study. This chapter presents results from a population projection of racial/ethnic groups for the next 50 years, with some overall results shown for the next 100 years. The chapter describes the population size, growth rates, and generational composition for the Asian, black, Hispanic, white non-Hispanic, and American Indian groups of the U.S. population for 1990 to 2040.

IMPORTANCE OF INTERNATIONAL MIGRATION FOR POPULATION GROWTH

From a historical perspective, the territory now known as the United States has experienced seven waves of immigrants, each distinguished by its particular ethnicity and places of origin. The first two waves of immigrants entered the North American continent tens of thousands of years ago in apparently quite separate movements from Asia. These immigrants spread over the landscape of North, then Central, and then South America. The third major movement of immigrants consisted of the people moving north from Mexico into the Southwestern interior of what is now the United States. This third wave consisted of Spaniards and residents of the Spanish domain of Mexico. The colonization of the Eastern seaboard of the United States by settlers from England and primarily western and northern Europe provided the fourth major wave of immigrants. Black immigrants arrived as slaves in a fifth immigrant wave, particularly in the colonies in the Southern states. By the 1880s, the sources of European immigration shifted sharply, with the sixth wave of immigrants coming from the southern and eastern portions of Europe. Now, over the past three decades, the United States has experienced a seventh wave of immigrants, with immigrants coming predominantly from Asia and Latin America, the sources for the original three waves of immigrants.

Recent immigration flows have been volatile. Many new immigrant populations have entered in large numbers within a relatively short period. A high proportion of the Cuban-origin population in the United States entered during the period from 1960 to 1975. Of the Vietnamese population in the United States in 1990, most entered the United States in the period from 1975 to 1985. These groups emphasize that the movement of selected ethnic groups to the United States can be somewhat unpredictable, depending to a great extent on events in other countries.

The course of immigration is affected by several processes. First, immigration quotas are set by the U.S. government. These quotas, to a great extent, set limits on the number of immigrants from most countries. Immigration law is subject to change. Increases in immigration (such as those resulting from the Immigration Act of 1990) or decreases (such as those in the 1920s) can occur as the result of political and legislative events. They are not the outcome of purely demographic processes. Second, the entrance of illegal immigrants continues, in spite of the enhanced Border Patrol activities and stronger employer sanctions associated with the Immigration Reform and Control Act of 1986 (IRCA) (Bean, Edmonston, and Passel 1990). The future growth of the Hispanic population, especially the Mexican-origin population, derives to a considerable extent from this unmanaged source of immigration. These two processes imply that the future course of immigration to the United States, both the numbers and the sources, may be altered quite dramatically, possibly in a very short period of time.

POPULATION PROJECTIONS

Romaniuc (1990) has argued that population projections may be viewed in three ways—as predictions, simulations, and prospective analysis. Population projections as predictions may be undertaken as a statistical exercise (either as a function of statistical regularities or as a probabilistic phenomenon) or on the basis of a "law" of population (such as a logistic growth curve). Yet human population growth, especially at the national level, is neither deterministic nor purely probabilistic. Efforts to predict future population growth using a statistical apparatus are probably unavailing.

For population projections as simulations, the framework is a "conditional" projection. No attempt is made to predict the future from this perspective. Rather, assumptions are stated for basic demographic processes, and population growth is calculated dependent upon the conditions.

The purpose of population projections as prospective analysis is to examine the implications of a plausible and credible set of demographic assumptions. Plausible parameters should reflect the likely variety of future values of such key demographic input values as fertility or immigration. Credible parameters should depend on state-of-the-art research about current levels and predictions for the demographic input values. By the nature of the emphasis on analytical credibility, prospective analysis population projections are directed at the immediate future. Current demographic research provides plausible and credible parameters for intermediate-term projections for, say, 15 to 25 years. Population projections cannot, at this time, be regarded as based on credible parameters for plausible long-range forecasts.

The population projections reported in this chapter are produced from a simulation perspective. The simulations are designed to generate output on the racial/ethnic distribution of the U.S. population implied in an assumed time path of fertility, mortality, and international migration. We select demographic assumptions consistent with current observed levels for a narrow heuristic purpose—to examine the long-range demographic simulation from the assumed conditions. Given the consistency of our assumptions with current demographic conditions, however, the intermediate-term projections have a prospective character also.

The population projections presented in this chapter derive from the assumptions made. Except for arithmetic errors, the projections *must* be accurate, in a special sense, because they derive logically from the assumptions of the demographic model. Our concerns in this chapter are to explicate the new generational model used for the population projection, to develop the input data and assumptions required for the projection, and to present the basic results.

This chapter examines the future course of population change for the total population of the United States and four major constituent racial/ethnic groups: white, black, Hispanic, and Asian populations. The specific focus, in each case, is the impact of immigration and emigration on the population dynamics of each group. It should be emphasized that the racial classification in official U.S. statistics divides the population into five racial categories: white, black, Asian and Pacific Islanders, Native Americans, and other races. Persons of Hispanic origin may be included in any one of the racial groups, depending on the self-reported classifications of individuals in censuses or surveys. In practice, the Hispanic population reports itself predominantly as either white or other races;[2] virtually all persons in the "other" category are Hispanic. For our projections, we treat the Hispanic population as one of five mutually exclusive (and exhaustive) populations. It should be emphasized that the lines separating the various racial/ethnic groups are fuzzy; at the margins, classification of specific individuals may vary and be problematic.

Our projections for ethnic groups are not predictions for the future population course. Considerable uncertainty exists about the fertility and mortality dynamics for the future. We make reasonable assumptions about fertility and mortality, supported by the latest evidence about these trends, but considerable debate exists among leading researchers about the future course of these demographic processes. Furthermore, a variety of plausible courses might be examined for the future trend in immigration and emigration. The history of recent U.S. immigration suggests that a major new surge of immigration might occur from at least one or more new countries in future decades. Although we may guess that such a new immigration wave would occur, we are uncertain about its size, composition, and origins.

AN IMMIGRANT GENERATION APPROACH

Standard cohort-component population projections move a population through time by surviving the existing population under the conditions of mortality (survival of the living population at one period to the next period), fertility (births to the living population and their survival during the projection period), and migration (survival of immigrants during the projection period and survival of the population until emigration). Such population projections consider the age and sex distribution of the population, but these projections do not give explicit treatment to immigrants and their descendants.

The standard cohort-component approach has several limitations for the analysis of populations with substantial international migration. First, the basic model does not include fertility and mortality changes that occur between immigrant generations (Werner 1986). Second, the model provides inadequate specification of emigration, usually assuming either a net change in immigrants or a fixed number of emigrants (Miltenyi 1981). Finally, the standard model provides no information on such important aspects of ethnic groups as the number who are foreign-born or native-born (Tabah 1984).

The new population projections presented in this chapter distinguish the generations of the population. The projections for each racial/ethnic group consider the population characterized by four generational groups:

☐ First generation—the immigrants, or the foreign-born population;

□ Second generation—the sons and daughters of the first generation;
□ Third generation—the sons and daughters of the second generation;
□ Fourth-and-higher generation—the descendants of the third, fourth, and higher generations.

From an immigration perspective, this characterization of the population involves a foreign-born population (the first generation) and a native-born population (the second and higher generations).

A generational perspective has several advantages for examining the future population of immigrant groups. First, the generations themselves are useful numbers. The first generation speaks the language and holds many of the cultural values of the country of origin. The second generation typically grows up in households with the language of the parents' home country and many of its cultural values. Knowing the generational distribution of a racial/ethnic group, therefore, gives considerable insight into its acquisition of English language and American values. Second, a generational population projection has some methodological advantages. Generational characteristics present a more appropriate model of immigrants (who usually enter the United States as first generation foreign-born individuals) and emigrants. For example, the rate of emigration from the United States varies greatly with the number of foreign-born members of a racial/ethnic group. The model also offers the possibility for assuming that fertility and mortality rates vary by generation. Standard population projection models generally make the unreasonable assumption that childbearing patterns are the same for all generations; in other words, they assume that immigrants acquire the fertility levels of the resident population instantaneously upon arrival in the United States.

POPULATION PROJECTIONS FOR IMMIGRANT GENERATIONS

We use a modified cohort-component approach for population projections in this chapter. The initial population is characterized by age, sex, and ethnicity, as in a standard population projection. The modification used here, however, also distinguishes the population by immigrant generation, with each generation requiring assumptions about the fertility, mortality, and migration flows for age and sex groups. (See also Edmonston and Passel 1991.) The base population is moved forward in five-year intervals, with successive application of the demographic dynamics. Births are added to the population; deaths are subtracted. Net migration is either positive or negative, depending on the balance of immigration and emigration: immigrants are added and emigrants subtracted.

A Generational Perspective

Population projections are determined by the description of the base population and the assumptions made about the components of demographic dynamics (fertility, mortality, and international migration). For the population-by-generations approach, the projection is also affected by assumptions made about the generational dynamics. Values for the demographic and generational dynamics are, therefore, the important assumptions for the results and interpretation of the population projection.

In most applications, users would ordinarily like to see population projections that can be regarded as a plausible result for the future population. *Plausible*, in this context, means that the conditions for demographic dynamics could be regarded as likely for the future course of fertility, mortality, and international migration. Thus, a critical aspect of population projections is scrutiny of the assumptions made about the demographic dynamics. Later sections of this chapter review the assumptions made concerning fertility, mortality, and international migration.

Our approach assumes a relatively general model for each of the demographic processes on a generational basis. For mortality, each generation, by age and sex, experiences its own schedule of death rates, schedules that may differ by generation. Deaths in a generation reduce the numbers of that generation. For fertility, births to a generation produce an addition to the next generation.[3] Births to foreign-born immigrants (the first generation) become members of the second generation and would produce an addition to the 0–4 age group in the second generation in the next five-year interval of the population projection. In our population-by-generation approach, the highest generation is the fourth-and-higher generation. Births to the third generation and the fourth-and-higher generation would, by definition, become members of the highest generation group.

For international migration, assumptions need to be made about the generational composition of migrants. Immigrants to a population are principally foreign-born. However, a small proportion of immigrants to the United States are native-born persons who are returning to the country after residence abroad. For example, a foreign-born couple residing in the United States might have children born in the United States and, subsequently, return to the country of birth. If their children later immigrate to the United States, thus returning to the country of their birth, they would constitute the immigration of second-generation individuals. Emigrants from the United States are predominantly members of the first generation; they are persons who immigrated to the United States and then decided to return to their country of birth. A relatively small number of native-born residents, second or higher generations, also emigrate from the United States.

Population Projection Model

BASIC MODEL

The model projects a population by age, sex, and four generation groups for a period of five years. It uses survival rates by five-year age groups for each sex and generation, five-year age-specific fertility rates for each generation, and the number of migrants by age, sex, and generation during the five-year period. (Edmonston and Passel 1992b present a detailed description of the population projection by generations model.) The population projection handles four generations: the foreign-born (the first generation), the sons and daughters of the foreign-born (the second generation), the grandsons and granddaughters of the foreign-born (the third generation), and all higher-numbered generations. The basic model is implemented with a FORTRAN program called POPGEN for use on microcomputers. Results are displayed for each generation as well as for the total native-born (the second and higher generations) and the total population. Although a special procedure handles each five-year projection, the main population projection program can make projections for a time period of five to one hundred years.

The model requires the following data:

(1) initial female population in five-year age groups, by generation;
(2) initial male population in five-year age groups, by generation;
(3) five-year survival rates for females during each five-year period, by generation;
(4) five-year survival rates for males during each five-year period, by generation;
(5) annual age-specific fertility rates (for five-year age groups) for the beginning and end of each five-year period, by generation;

(6) female in- and out-migrants by five-year age groups during each five-year period, by generation;

(7) male in- and out-migrants by five-year age groups during each five-year period, by generation; and

(8) sex ratio at birth.

In addition, there are a number of parameters that control various options of the computer program and permit alternative input data (such as using Coale-Demeny model life tables instead of age-specific survival rates).

Consider a population defined with the following characteristics: P_x^t population size for age x at time t, $S_x^{t,t+5}$ rates for population age x surviving to age $x+5$ during the period from t to $t+5$, and F_x^t age-specific fertility rates for women age x at time t. Survival rates are derived from the values for person-years lived in the standard fashion, as $S_x^{t,t+5} = L_{x+5}^{t+5}/L_x^t$. We assume five-year age groups here, so the population age x represents the age group x to $x+4$.

The basic population projection model can also be expanded to include the effects of international migration. Define $I_x^{t,t+5}$ as in-migrants age x during the period t to $t+5$ and $O_x^{t,t+5}$ as out-migrants age x during the period t to $t+5$, each separate by sex. Then, the net migrants age x during the period t to $t+5$ are defined as $N_x^{t,t+5} = I_x^{t,t+5} - O_x^{t,t+5}$.

The population can also be distinguished by a generations index (and is assumed to be separate by sex). Consider now a population indexed by k generations, where $k = 1,2,3$, and 4: $k=1$ indicates the first generation, $k=2$ indicates the second, $k=3$ represents the third, and $k=4$ indicates the fourth-and-higher generations. The survival of the population alive at the beginning of the projection period, for all age groups but the last, is

$$P_{x+5,k}^{t+5} = P_{x,k}^t \, S_{x,k}^{t,t+5}$$
$$+ \frac{N_{x,k}^{t,t+5} (1 + S_{x,k}^{t,t+5}) + N_{x+5,k}^{t,t+5} (1 + S_{x+5,k}^{t,t+5})}{4} \quad (11.1)$$

and for the open-ended age category is

$$P_{x+,k}^{t+5} = P_{x+,k}^t \, S_{x+,k}^{t,t+5}$$
$$+ \frac{N_{x-5,k}^{t,t+5} (1 + S_{x-5,k}^{t,t+5}) + N_{x+,k}^{t,t+5} (1 + S_{x+,k}^{t,t+5})}{4} \quad (11.2)$$

where $S_{x,k}^{t,t+5}$ represents the survival values for the kth generation and $N_{x,k}^{t,t+5}$ indicates the number of net migrants for the kth generation.

In general, the number of immigrants by generation, $I_{x,k}^{t,t+5}$, is non-zero for the first generation $(k=1)$ and zero for the second and higher generations $(k=2,3,4)$; immigrants are generally not native-born persons. On the other hand, this model makes apparent that emigrants by generation, $O_{x,k}^{t,t+5}$, may have non-zero values for all generations. Hence, observed values of net migrants by generation, $N_{x,k}^{t,t+5}$, are usually positive for the first generation (representing net immigration of the foreign-born) and typically negative for the second and higher generations (indicating some emigration and negligible immigration of the native-born).

In a female-dominant model,[4] a mother in the kth generation would produce an offspring in the $k+1$st generation. Since it is logically impossible for a mother to give birth to a *foreign-born* child in the United States, the population aged 0–4 for the *first generation* would derive solely from immigration:

$$P_{0,1}^{t+5} = \frac{N_{0,1}^{t,t+5} (1 + S_{0,1}^{t,t+5})}{4} \tag{11.3}$$

separate for each sex. The population aged 0–4 years for the *second and third generations* result from births to mothers in the first and second generation, respectively, plus the effect of net migration:

$$P_{0,k}^{t+5} = B_k^{t,t+5} \frac{S_{b,k-1}^{t,t+5} + S_{b,k}^{t,t+5}}{2} + \frac{N_{0,k}^{t,t+5} (1 + S_{b,k}^{t,t+5})}{4} \tag{11.4}$$

for $k=2,3$ and for each sex separately, where the sex ratio at birth is needed to calculate the number of male and female births. The population aged 0–4 years in the *fourth-and-higher generation* results from births to third generation mothers plus fourth-and-higher-generation mothers along with the effects of net migration:

$$P_{0,4}^{t+5} = B_3^{t,t+5} \frac{S_{0,3}^{t,t+5} + S_{0,4}^{t,t+5}}{2} + B_4^{t,t+5} S_{0,4}^{t,t+5}$$
$$+ \frac{N_{0,4}^{t,t+5} (1 + S_{0,4}^{t,t+5})}{4} \tag{11.5}$$

for each sex separately, where total births during the period are obtained using equation (6). The total number of births in the kth generation for the female-dominant model is calculated as:

$$B_k^{t,t+5} = 2.5 \sum_{x=15}^{45} P_{x,k-1}^t (F_{x,k-1}^t$$
$$+ S_{x,k-1}^{t,t+5} F_{x,k-1}^{t+5}) + B_{I,k}^{t,t+5} \tag{11.6}$$

We would ordinarily assume that births to net immigrants during the period, $B_{I,k}^{t,t+5}$, would be non-zero only for the second generation.

MIXED GENERATION MODEL

The female-dominant model does *not* correspond to the generational classifications used in most U.S. censuses or surveys. The population is usually classified in censuses by the most recent immigrant ancestor. Thus, the second generation is normally designated as the "native-born population of foreign or *mixed* parentage." An individual in the second generation, so defined, could thus have a native-born mother. More generally, a kth generation female might marry a male of a different immigrant generation and their offspring would not necessarily be the $k+1$st generation. If a third generation woman were to produce an offspring in union with a first generation man, the child would report ancestry relative to the father (the most recent immigrant generation of the parents) and would indicate second generation ancestry. Because some females marry males with a lower order immigrant generation than themselves, the observed generational composition of births (and the resulting population aged 0–4 years) is always a lower order than implied by a female-dominant model.

The female-dominant model can be modified to make it correspond to the most recent ancestor definition used in virtually all data collection methods. We first assume that births to kth generation mothers are still derived by equation (11.6), but are assigned to their own generations in a different manner. Consider a matrix $G_{k,m}$ which indicates the proportion of births in the mth generation ($m=1,2,3,4$) born to women in the kth generation, subject to the condition $\sum_{k=1}^{4} G_{k,m} = 1.0$ for $k=1,2,3$, and 4. In the female-dominant model, $G_{1,2} = G_{2,3} = G_{3,4} = G_{4,4} = 1.0$, and all other cells in the G matrix are zero. A model incorporating the G matrix, where mothers of the kth generation produce births in the mth generation is:

$$P_{0,m}^{t+5} = \sum_{k=1}^{4} \left[G_{k,m} \left(B_k^{t,t+5} \frac{S_{b,k}^{t,t+5} + S_{b,k+1}^{t,t+5}}{2} \right) \right]$$

$$+ \frac{N_{0,m}^{t,t+5} (1 + S_{b,m}^{t,t+5})}{4} \tag{11.7}$$

for $m=1,2,3,4$ and separate by sex. The empirical challenge, in this case, is to estimate the intergenerational birth matrix, $G_{k,m}$. We describe a procedure used to estimate the intergenerational birth matrix for racial/ethnic groups in the United States later in the next section.

Assumptions for the Population Projections

BASE POPULATION

The base date for our projections is April 1, 1990, the date for the 1990 U.S. Census of Population. The population total for each racial/ethnic group is taken from the census. Estimates of the age-sex distribution and generational distributions (the native-born population and the second, third, and fourth-and-higher generations) were developed by fitting the basic "projection" model to the series of twentieth century censuses. (See Passel and Edmonston 1992, and chapter 2, this volume, for a description of the procedures used.) Five racial/ethnic groups are used in the projection: black, Hispanic, Asian and Pacific Islanders, white non-Hispanic, and American Indian.[5] The groups are mutually exclusive and derived from the basic 1990 Census data.

FERTILITY ASSUMPTIONS

Age-specific fertility rates for the white and black population were estimated using recent fertility data from the National Center for Health Statistics (NCHS) (1992, Table 4). Rates for the Hispanic and Asian population were taken from analysis of the June 1986 and 1988 Current Population Survey (CPS) special fertility supplements, prepared by the U.S. Bureau of the Census. The CPS data also provide fertility estimates for the foreign-born and native-born population by ethnicity. We assumed that the foreign-born population corresponded to the first generation. We assumed that the native-born population corresponded to the third and fourth generations. Age-specific fertility rates for the second generation were obtained by taking the average of the first and third generation values. Age-specific fertility rates for the fourth-and-higher generation were assumed to be the same as the third generation.

The overall total fertility rate (TFR) of U.S. women hovered around 1.7 to 1.8 births per woman for much of the 1970s and 1980s. In recent years, the TFR has increased, reaching a level of about 2 in 1990. We assume that the long-term trend of the total fertility rate is toward 1.9 (Preston 1991, 23–30). We assume that the native-born population for each racial/ethnic group achieves a 1.9 level in the year 2020, but we assume that foreign-born fertility remains higher than this level. The fertility levels for this projection, by generation for major racial/ethnic groups, are given in table 11.1.

MORTALITY ASSUMPTIONS

We calculate age- and sex-specific mortality rates for the white and black population using NCHS sources. We assume that mortality for Hispanic and Asian populations is the same as white mortality. We assume that the mortality does not vary across generations.

The projections incorporate the mortality forecasts of Lee and Carter (1990) and assume that mortality will decline at a faster pace than in forecasts done by the U.S. Bureau of the Census (1989) or Social Security Administration (Trustees of OASDI 1990). Moreover, we assume that sex differences in mortality will narrow, as an increasing proportion of males stop smoking. Although we assume mortality improvements for all racial/ethnic groups, we do not assume that all groups will have the same life expectancy at birth at some future date. The assumed values of life expectancy at birth for the projection by sex, race/ethnicity, and year are given in table 11.2.

IMMIGRATION ASSUMPTIONS

The age and sex of immigrants are assumed to continue to have the distribution observed in recent years. We assume that ultimate immigration will be at a level of about 1,125,000 annually, including 855,000 legal immigrants, 200,000 net undocumented immigrants, and a net gain of 70,000 from Puerto Rico and other civilian immigration. These assumptions are compatible with recent immigration levels, given the changes specified in the Immigration Act of 1990 (Fix and Passel 1991). More detailed data on the immigration assumptions are shown in table 11.3.

EMIGRATION ASSUMPTIONS

The emigration assumptions for the projection are specified as an ultimate rate of departure of the foreign-born population. This assumption translates to a level of about 175,000 annually. Taking immigration and emigration into account, the population projection assumes net immigration of about 900,000 in 1990, which gradually increases to 950,000 per year in 2005. Data on the emigration assumptions for the population projection are also given in table 11.3.

Table 11.1 FERTILITY ASSUMPTIONS, FOR 1990 BASELINE AND 2020: TOTAL FERTILITY RATES BY RACIAL/ETHNIC GROUP AND GENERATION

Population Group and Region of Origin	1990 Baseline			2020 Ultimate		
	Immigrant	Native		Immigrant	Native	
	First Generation	Second Generation	Third + Generations	First Generation	Second Generation	Third + Generations
White, non-Hispanic Europe, Canada, Australia, New Zealand	1.9	1.9	1.9	1.9	1.9	1.9
Asian Asia, except Western Asia	2.3	2.0	1.8	2.0	1.9	1.9
Black Africa and parts of the Caribbean	2.1	2.1	2.1	2.0	1.9	1.9
Hispanic Mexico, Central and South America	2.7	2.1	2.0	2.3	2.0	1.9

Table 11.2 MORTALITY ASSUMPTIONS, FOR 1990 BASELINE AND 2040: LIFE
EXPECTANCY AT BIRTH BY RACIAL/ETHNIC GROUP

	1990 Baseline			2040 Ultimate		
Population Group	Both Sexes	Male	Female	Both Sexes	Male	Female
White, non-Hispanic	76.7	73.3	80.0	81.6	78.5	84.6
Asian	76.7	73.3	80.0	81.6	78.5	84.6
Black	70.7	67.0	75.0	75.9	72.4	79.4
Hispanic	75.3	73.0	79.9	81.6	78.5	84.6

Notes:
1. White female life expectancy at birth in 2040 is derived by quadratic interpolation
from 2010, 2030, and 2050 forecasts of Lee and Carter (1990). The figure for females
(84.6 years) can be compared to the U.S. Bureau of the Census (1989) low mortality
forecast of life expectancy at birth of 87.1 years. The Lee and Carter forecast is favored
by Preston (1991) in a review of the assumptions of current U.S. population projections.
2. White male life expectancy at birth is assumed to decrease to 4.0 years less than
the white female level in 2090. This assumes that the 6.7-year difference in life
expectancy at birth between females and males decreases steadily during the next
century, primarily as a result of diminishing sex differences in cigarette smoking. We
calculate the male life expectancy at birth in 2040 by interpolating the sex difference
and then subtracting it from the estimated life expectancy at birth for females. The
figure for males (78.5 years) can be compared to the U.S. Bureau of the Census's (1989)
low mortality forecast of life expectancy at birth of 80.8 years.
3. Asian and Hispanic life expectancy at birth is assumed to be the same as the white
population. U.S. Bureau of the Census (1992) assumes much lower mortality for Asians
than for whites but approximately equal mortality for Hispanics and non-Hispanic
whites.
4. Life expectancy at birth for the black population is assumed to follow the U.S.
Bureau of the Census (1989) middle mortality assumption through the year 2015 and
then to increase at the same rate of increase as the white population. We assume no
decrease in the sex differences in life expectancy at birth for the black population.
The figure for both sexes combined (75.9 years) can be compared to the middle
mortality forecast of life expectancy at birth from the U.S. Bureau of the Census of
78.7 years (1989 projection) and 76.6 years (1992 projection).

INTERGENERATIONAL BIRTH MATRIX

The population projection model requires information about the
probability that a birth to a kth generation mother gives rise to an
mth generation child. The fertility assumptions for the model determine the overall chances of having a child; the intergenerational
birth matrix, therefore, affects the generational distribution of births,
not the fertility process itself.

Data are lacking on childbearing by parental generation, for both
parents, for racial/ethnic groups in the United States. We use data
from the 1989 CPS to make estimates of this matrix, examining the

Table 11.3 INTERNATIONAL MIGRATION ASSUMPTIONS, FOR 1990 BASELINE AND 2005: IMMIGRATION AND EMIGRATION
BY RACIAL/ETHNIC GROUP
(numbers in thousands)

Population Group	1990 Baseline			2005 Ultimate			Percent of **NET** in 2005
	Net Immigration	Immig.	Emig.	Net Immigration	Immig.	Emig.	
Total	900.0	1,070.0	170.0	950.0	1,125.0	175.0	100
White, non-Hispanic	125.3	171.2	45.9	132.7	180.0	47.3	14
Asian	288.7	321.0	32.3	304.3	337.5	33.2	32
Black	105.8	117.7	11.9	111.5	123.7	12.2	12
Hispanic	380.2	460.1	79.9	401.5	483.8	82.3	42

Table 11.4 U.S. POPULATION FOR RACIAL/ETHNIC GROUPS: 1990–2090
(All figures rounded independently. Populations in millions.)

Year	All Races	White Non-Hispanic	Asian	Black	Hispanic	American Indian
Population						
1990	248.8	187.1	7.3	30.0	22.4	2.0
2000	276.8	198.4	12.0	34.1	30.3	2.1
2010	299.4	204.2	17.1	37.4	38.6	2.1
2020	320.5	208.4	22.7	40.2	47.1	2.2
2030	340.1	211.1	28.5	42.5	55.8	2.2
2040	355.5	210.5	34.5	44.1	64.2	2.2
2050	369.4	209.1	40.6	45.2	72.4	2.1
2060	385.8	209.8	46.8	46.4	80.7	2.1
2070	402.7	211.0	53.1	47.6	89.1	2.0
2080	419.1	211.6	59.5	48.5	97.4	2.0
2090	436.7	213.2	66.0	49.6	106.1	1.9
Percentage						
1990	100.0	75.2	2.9	12.1	9.0	0.8
2000	100.0	71.7	4.3	12.3	10.9	0.8
2010	100.0	68.2	5.7	12.5	12.9	0.7
2020	100.0	65.0	7.1	12.5	14.7	0.7
2030	100.0	62.1	8.4	12.5	16.4	0.6
2040	100.0	59.2	9.7	12.4	18.1	0.6
2050	100.0	56.6	11.0	12.2	19.6	0.6
2060	100.0	54.4	12.1	12.0	20.9	0.5
2070	100.0	52.4	13.2	11.8	22.1	0.5
2080	100.0	50.5	14.2	11.6	23.3	0.5
2090	100.0	48.8	15.1	11.3	24.3	0.4

Beginning with an annual net immigration of 900,000 in 1990, table 11.4 and figure 11.1 indicate that the 1990 U.S. population of 249 million will grow to numbers approaching 350 million in the mid-2030s, will reach 356 million in 2040, and will continue growing to 437 million in 2090.[6] Thus, the level of immigration and emigration assumed in these projections avoids any population decline in the next 100 years. Even with continued immigration, the rate of population growth of the United States will slacken (table 11.5). The U.S. population will grow at an average annual rate of 1.1 percent from 1990 to 2000. This rate will gradually diminish, reaching a level of 0.4 percent within the next 50 years. Although the population would continue to grow for a few decades even without immigration, these

generational status of the population for young cohorts i
black, Hispanic, and white non-Hispanic populatioː
adopted an iterative procedure to develop estimates that
patterns for both the CPS data and the known overal,
births. This procedure produces approximate estimates 1
generational birth matrix. We estimate, for example, tŀ
third generation Hispanic mothers are distributed apprɗ
30 percent in the second generation, 20 percent in the tl
tion, and 50 percent in the fourth-and-higher generatioŗ

Our current analysis of intergenerational births is ɹ
Analysis of the 1989 CPS data suggests that the interg
birth matrix is affected by the existing generational disˤ
males and females. In a population with a high proportiɑ
grants, the chances are greater that a native-born person n
a foreign-born person and produce a child with a more re
grant generation. Populations with few immigrants, oŗ
hand, would have an intergenerational birth matrix that m
resembles the female-dominant perspective.

For the population projections presented here, we aʂ
each racial/ethnic group has an intergenerational birth mat
that is estimated from 1989 CPS data for the particular ra
group. Over time, we assume that the matrix changes, deɲ
the generational distribution of males and females in the ɼ
at the beginning of the projection period. For detailed diʂ
the empirical modeling of the intergenerational birth n
Edmonston and Passel (1992b). Detailed results for these ɹ
projections are available in four volumes (Edmonston a
1992a), which present information separately for the Asi
Hispanic, and white non-Hispanic populations.

RESULTS FROM IMMIGRANT POPULATION PROJE

Even without immigration but with the maintenance of
low fertility levels, the U.S. population would continue to g
the next 20 years. The current momentum of population ʂ
the result of a younger age distribution—provides a cushion
30 million more people in the next decades, even if imn
were to cease. A population projection with no immigratio
indicate a U.S. population peaking at about 288 million in ʑ
then slowly declining (not shown in the tables).

Figure 11.1 U.S. POPULATION BY RACIAL/ETHNIC GROUP: 1950–2040

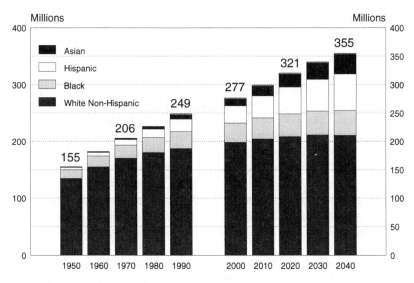

Source: Table 11.4.

Table 11.5 AVERAGE ANNUAL RATE OF POPULATION GROWTH FOR RACIAL/
ETHNIC GROUPS, BY DECADE: 1990–2040
(expressed as average annual percent growth)

Year	All Races	White Non-Hispanic	Asian	Black	Hispanic
1990–2000	1.1	0.6	5.0	1.3	3.0
2000–2010	0.8	0.3	3.6	0.9	2.4
2010–2020	0.7	0.2	2.8	0.7	2.0
2020–2030	0.6	0.1	2.3	0.6	1.7
2030–2040	0.4	0.0	1.9	0.4	1.4

results suggest the prospect for moderate growth for the next five decades and beyond.

Racial/Ethnic Composition

What are the implications of these population dynamics for the racial/ethnic composition of the population? If immigration were zero, then the future racial/ethnic composition would be determined solely by fertility and mortality differentials in the present population. Thus, even with no immigration, the racial/ethnic composition would not remain static. The resident population composition provides the fixed component, the stock, for the effects of immigration.

The immigrant component plays the central role in determining the future racial/ethnic size and composition of the U.S. population. The effect of immigration on population growth has two aspects. First, the level of immigration matters. The number of immigrants has a direct effect on population growth, with each new immigrant adding one new person to a racial/ethnic group. Second, the reproductive value of the immigrants affects the population by adding descendants. The reproductive value of immigrants is, in turn, determined by the immigrants' ages and their fertility level. A young immigrant with high fertility will add the most descendants, while an old or low-fertility immigrant will add few descendants. Hence, the future growth of racial/ethnic groups is the product of several interacting factors.

According to the 1990 Census, 75 percent of the population is white non-Hispanic. The "minority" population—i.e., the remaining one-quarter of the population—is 12 percent black, 9 percent Hispanic, 3 percent Asian, and about 1 percent American Indian. Future trends in immigration and differential fertility and mortality levels will lead to major changes in these proportions (see table 11.4 and figure 11.2).

WHITE NON-HISPANIC POPULATION

The white non-Hispanic group will increase its numbers from 187 million to a peak of 211 million in 2030, where it will stabilize. Within the next 50 years, this group will become relatively less numerous and drop from 75 percent of the total population to less than 60 percent in 2040. The annual rate of population growth of the white non-Hispanic population will drop considerably during the next decades, as shown in table 11.5, from a rate of 0.6 percent in the 1990s to a very slightly negative rate in the 2030s.

The components of population change for the white non-Hispanic population are presented in the top panel of table 11.6. With a crude birth rate (CBR) of 15 per 1,000 and a crude death rate (CDR) of 9 per 1,000, the annual rate of natural increase (RNI) during 1990–1995 is 6 per 1,000. As the age structure increasingly becomes older, the CBR will decline, the CDR will increase, and the annual RNI will gradually decrease and become negative in the late 2020s. The net

Figure 11.2 RACIAL/ETHNIC COMPOSITION OF THE UNITED STATES:
1950–2040

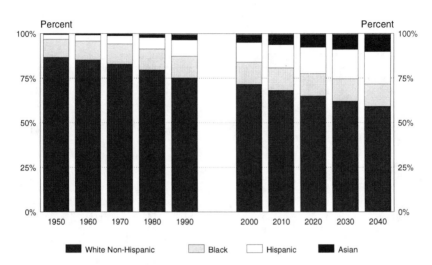

Source: Table 11.4.

immigration rate (NIR) during the 50-year period is only 1 per 1,000 for the white non-Hispanic population, however, and does not contribute much to population growth. As a result, the annual population growth rate (which equals the rate of natural increase plus the net immigration rate) becomes negative by the end of the 50-year projection period. Results not shown here indicate that the long-term population change for the white non-Hispanic population will stabilize with a rate of natural increase of -1 per 1,000, a net immigration rate of 1 per 1,000, and an annual growth rate of zero. The population size for long-term stabilization is about 211 million, under the assumed conditions of fertility, mortality, and migration.

BLACK POPULATION

Over the next 50 years, the black population will increase substantially, from 30 million to 44 million (again assuming the current level and composition of immigration), but the black proportion of the total population will experience little relative change. It will increase only slightly, from 12.1 percent in 1990 to 12.4 percent in 2040. The growth rate of the black population will drop from an annual rate of

Table 11.6 COMPONENTS OF POPULATION CHANGE FOR RACIAL/ETHNIC
GROUPS, FOR SELECTED FIVE-YEAR PERIODS: 1990–2040
(rates per 1,000 population)

Population and Measure	Five-Year Period					
	1990–1995	2000–2005	2010–2015	2020–2025	2030–2035	2040–2045
White, non-Hispanic						
CBR	15	12	11	12	11	11
CDR	9	10	10	11	12	12
RNI	6	3	1	1	−1	−2
NIR	1	1	1	1	1	1
GR	7	3	2	2	0	−1
Asian						
CBR	21	18	16	16	15	14
CDR	4	4	5	6	6	7
RNI	17	13	11	10	9	8
NIR	38	25	18	14	11	9
GR	54	38	29	24	20	17
Black						
CBR	19	16	14	14	13	12
CDR	8	8	9	10	11	12
RNI	11	8	5	4	2	1
NIR	3	2	2	2	2	2
GR	14	10	7	6	4	3
Hispanic						
CBR	21	19	17	16	15	14
CDR	4	5	5	6	7	7
RNI	17	14	12	10	8	7
NIR	15	12	9	8	7	6
GR	32	26	21	18	15	12

Notes: All components of population change are shown to the nearest digit, per 1,000.
Rates may not add because of rounding.

The abbreviations for the rates are:
- CBR—crude birth rate, per 1,000 mid-period population
- CDR—crude death rate, per 1,000 mid-period population
- RNI—rate of natural increase, per 1,000 mid-period population, or the crude birth rate minus the crude death rate
- NIR—net immigration rate, the number of net immigration per 1,000 mid-period populatin
- GR—population growth rate, per 1,000 mid-period population, or the rate of natural increase plus the net immigration rate

1.3 percent in the 1990s to 0.4 percent in the 2030s. Compared to the white non-Hispanic population, the current age distribution of the black population is more favorable for a higher rate of natural increase, a CBR of 19 per 1,000 and a CDR of 8 per 1,000 produces an annual rate of natural increase of 11 per 1,000 in the early 1990s. When this rate is coupled with a net immigration rate of 3 per 1,000 during 1990–1995, the black population would have an annual growth rate of 14 per 1,000. The CBR and the CDR will converge at about 12 per 1,000 during the next 50 years, yielding an annual RNI of 1 per 1,000 in the early 2040s. A positive net immigration rate of 2 per 1,000 will also help to ensure a small annual growth rate by the end of the 50-year projection period.

ASIAN POPULATION

Two groups are likely to experience substantial growth during the next half-century: Asians and Hispanics. The Asian population will grow at rates exceeding 1 percent for the next 50 years, increasing from 7 million in 1990 to 35 million in 2040, under the conditions of this projection. These gains would increase the proportion of Asians in the population from 3 percent in 1990 to 10 percent in 2040.

Fueled by recent heavy immigration, the current age structure of the Asian population is relatively young, with a predominance of younger adults and children and comparatively few elderly. As a result, the CBR is high (21 per 1,000), the CDR is low (4 per 1,000), and the RNI is 17 per 1,000. Large-scale immigration, a net immigration rate of 38 per 1,000, produces a high rate of population growth— 54 per thousand or 5.4 percent per year. The RNI of the Asian population will diminish during the next five decades, as the age structure becomes older and the CBR and CDR converge. The net immigration *rate* will also diminish because, even though the annual number of immigrants is assumed to be constant from 2005 to 2040 in this projection, immigrants will decrease as a proportion of the resident Asian population. However, this projection shows that a relatively high rate of population growth will continue for the Asian population during the next 50 years, with annual rates of population growth of 1.7 percent existing even at the end of the 50-year period.

HISPANIC POPULATION

The Hispanic population—assumed to have the largest share of immigration, in part because of its predominant share of illegal immigration—will grow substantially over the next 50 years. The Hispanic population would increase from 22 million in 1990, or 9 percent of the total population, to 30 million in 2000. Growth would continue uninterrupted for the five decades of the projection, at which time Hispanics would number 64 million and constitute 18 percent of the population. The Hispanic population will pass the black population to become the largest minority group in the nation shortly before 2010, under these assumptions.

The annual rate of population growth of the Hispanic population would exceed 1 percent throughout the next 50 years, declining from a rate of 3.0 percent in the 1990s to 1.4 percent in the 2030s. Like the Asian population, the current Hispanic population is also relatively young. With a CBR of 21 per 1,000 and a CDR of 4 per 1,000 during 1990–1995, the annual RNI for Hispanics is 17 per 1,000. Combined with a net immigration of 15 per 1,000, the resulting annual growth rate is 32 per 1,000. The CBR will decrease, and the CDR will increase during the next five decades, producing a lower level of natural increase over time. The net immigration rate for the Hispanic population will also gradually decrease during the next 50 years as the size of the Hispanic population becomes larger. As a result, the annual rate of population growth will decline from 32 per 1,000 in the early 1990s to 12 per 1,000 in the early 2040s. This annual growth rate would still exceed the current growth rate for the white non-Hispanic population.

This description of the future racial/ethnic composition of the U.S. population reflects a continuation of the current high levels of immigration and the racial/ethnic composition of that immigration. Serious questions are raised about the reality of these assumptions (such as constant levels of immigration) over a 50-year period, to say nothing of the 100-year scenarios. We stress the use of these projections as a simulation representing the long-run implication of plausible current trends.

Generational Composition

Generational patterns vary greatly between the major racial/ethnic groups. Table 11.7 and figure 11.3 present results for the numbers and distribution of generations for the white non-Hispanic, Asian, black, Hispanic, American Indian, and total population. The Asian population has grown rapidly during the past two decades because of its large number of immigrants. Continued heavy immigration will maintain the rapid increase of the first generation Asian population

Table 11.7 U.S. POPULATION BY GENERATION, FOR RACIAL/ETHNIC GROUPS:
1990–2040
(populations in millions)

Race and Year	Total	Foreign-Born	Total Native	Native Population		
				Second Generation	Third Generation	Fourth + Generations
All Races				*Population*		
1990	248.8	21.3	227.5	24.2	31.5	171.8
2000	276.8	28.4	248.4	26.8	30.4	191.2
2010	299.4	35.2	264.2	30.3	29.3	204.7
2020	320.5	41.4	279.1	34.8	28.6	215.7
2030	340.1	46.5	293.6	40.1	28.8	224.8
2040	355.5	50.4	305.1	45.7	29.6	229.8
				Percent Distribution		
1990	100.0	8.6	91.4	9.7	12.6	69.1
2000	100.0	10.2	89.8	9.7	11.0	69.1
2010	100.0	11.8	88.2	10.1	9.8	68.3
2020	100.0	12.9	87.1	10.9	8.9	67.3
2030	100.0	13.7	86.3	11.8	8.5	66.1
2040	100.0	14.2	85.8	12.9	8.3	64.6
White Non-Hispanic				*Population*		
1990	187.1	5.9	181.2	15.9	27.6	137.7
2000	198.4	6.3	192.1	13.3	25.6	153.2
2010	204.2	6.8	197.4	11.0	23.1	163.3
2020	208.4	7.3	201.0	9.6	20.0	171.4
2030	211.1	7.8	203.3	8.9	16.4	178.0
2040	210.5	8.3	202.2	8.5	13.0	180.7
				Percent Distribution		
1990	100.0	3.2	96.8	8.5	14.7	73.6
2000	100.0	3.2	96.8	6.7	12.9	77.2
2010	100.0	3.3	96.7	5.4	11.3	80.0
2020	100.0	3.5	96.5	4.6	9.6	82.3
2030	100.0	3.7	96.3	4.2	7.8	84.3
2040	100.0	3.9	96.1	4.0	6.2	85.9
Asian				*Population*		
1990	7.3	4.8	2.4	1.6	0.5	0.4
2000	12.0	7.8	4.2	3.1	0.6	0.5
2010	17.1	10.6	6.6	5.1	0.8	0.6
2020	22.7	13.2	9.5	7.5	1.3	0.7
2030	28.5	15.3	13.2	10.0	2.3	0.9
2040	34.5	17.1	17.5	12.7	3.6	1.1
				Percent Distribution		
1990	100.0	66.3	33.7	21.6	6.9	5.1
2000	100.0	64.8	35.2	26.2	5.0	4.0
2010	100.0	61.7	38.3	30.0	4.8	3.5
2020	100.0	58.0	42.0	32.9	5.9	3.2
2030	100.0	53.8	46.2	35.1	8.1	3.1
2040	100.0	49.4	50.6	36.8	10.5	3.3

continued

Table 11.7 U.S. POPULATION BY GENERATION, FOR RACIAL/ETHNIC GROUPS:
1990–2040
(populations in millions) (continued)

Race and Year	Total	Foreign-Born	Total Native	Native Population Second Generation	Third Generation	Fourth + Generations
Black				*Population*		
1990	30.0	1.4	28.6	0.7	0.3	27.7
2000	34.1	2.1	32.0	1.1	0.3	30.5
2010	37.4	2.7	34.7	1.6	0.4	32.6
2020	40.2	3.3	36.9	2.1	0.7	34.0
2030	42.5	3.8	38.7	2.7	1.0	35.0
2040	44.1	4.1	40.0	3.2	1.4	35.4
				Percent Distribution		
1990	100.0	4.6	95.4	2.3	0.9	92.2
2000	100.0	6.1	93.9	3.3	0.9	89.7
2010	100.0	7.3	92.7	4.3	1.2	87.2
2020	100.0	8.3	91.7	5.3	1.7	84.7
2030	100.0	8.9	91.1	6.3	2.4	82.4
2040	100.0	9.4	90.6	7.3	3.2	80.2
Hispanic				*Population*		
1990	22.4	9.1	13.2	6.1	3.1	4.0
2000	30.3	12.2	18.1	9.3	3.8	4.9
2010	38.6	15.1	23.5	12.6	4.9	6.0
2020	47.1	17.6	29.5	15.6	6.6	7.3
2030	55.8	19.5	36.2	18.5	9.0	8.7
2040	64.2	20.9	43.3	21.3	11.6	10.4
				Percent Distribution		
1990	100.0	40.9	59.1	27.2	14.0	17.9
2000	100.0	40.4	59.6	30.7	12.7	16.3
2010	100.0	39.1	60.9	32.6	12.7	15.6
2020	100.0	37.3	62.7	33.1	14.1	15.6
2030	100.0	35.0	65.0	33.2	16.2	15.6
2040	100.0	32.6	67.4	33.1	18.1	16.2
American Indian				*Population*		
1990	2.0	0.0	2.0	0.0	0.0	2.0
2000	2.1	0.0	2.1	0.0	0.0	2.1
2010	2.1	0.0	2.1	0.0	0.0	2.1
2020	2.2	0.0	2.2	0.0	0.0	2.2
2030	2.2	0.0	2.2	0.0	0.0	2.2
2040	2.2	0.0	2.2	0.0	0.0	2.2
				Percent Distribution		
1990	100.0	0.0	100.0	0.0	0.0	100.0
2000	100.0	0.0	100.0	0.0	0.0	100.0
2010	100.0	0.0	100.0	0.0	0.0	100.0
2020	100.0	0.0	100.0	0.0	0.0	100.0
2030	100.0	0.0	100.0	0.0	0.0	100.0
2040	100.0	0.0	100.0	0.0	0.0	100.0

Figure 11.3 RACIAL/ETHNIC GROUPS BY GENERATION: 1990–2090

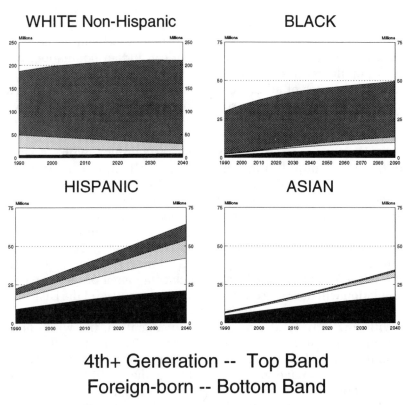

WHITE Non-Hispanic

BLACK

HISPANIC

ASIAN

4th+ Generation -- Top Band
Foreign-born -- Bottom Band

Source: Table 11.7. Note scale of White Non-Hispanic.

during the next several decades, and the first generation Asian population will grow from 4.8 million in 1990 to 17.1 million in 2040. The second generation will also increase substantially from 1.6 million in 1990 to 12.7 million in 2040. The first and second generations of the population are called the "foreign stock" of the population by demographers. The foreign-stock population (immigrants and their sons and daughters) includes the people who are most likely to be non-English speakers and to retain cultural values and behaviors from their country of origin. The foreign stock of the Asian population was 88 percent in 1990 and, it decreases only slightly to 86 percent in 2040. It requires no additional emphasis, it seems, to note that the Asian population will continue to be an overwhelmingly immigrant group during the next 50 years.

The black population will continue to be a predominantly native-born population, with a very high proportion of its population in the fourth-and-greater generation. The fourth-and-higher generations of the black population presently constitute 92 percent of the total black population. Except for the American Indian population, the black population has the longest average generational residence in the United States of all racial/ethnic groups. The black population is now experiencing the first substantial immigration in the past two centuries, with about 120,000 immigrants arriving from Africa and the Caribbean annually.

The Hispanic population now numbers 22 million, with a sizable foreign-stock population. Immigration will support continued increases in the first generation, with births increasing the numbers in the second and third generations during the next 50 years. The first generation population will more than double, from 9.1 million in 1990 to 20.9 million in 2040; the second generation will more than triple, from 6.1 million in 1990 to 21.3 million in 2040; and the third generation will almost quadruple, from 3.1 million in 1990 to 11.6 million in 2040. The foreign-stock component of the Hispanic population will decrease only slightly as a percentage of the Hispanic population, from 68 percent in 1990 to 66 percent in 2040.

With low fertility and modest net immigration, the white non-Hispanic population is projected to peak in 2030 and then fluctuate around a level of about 211 million. The generational distribution for the white population will also change; there will be a decrease in the proportion of second and third generation members, predominantly the descendants of previous waves of immigrants. The proportion of fourth-and-greater generation will increase steadily, growing from 138 million in 1990 to 181 million in 2040. With these numerical shifts in the generations, the white non-Hispanic population will become more dominantly fourth-and-higher generation, increasing from 74 percent in 1990 to 86 percent in 2040. By 2030, the white population will have roughly the same proportion in the fourth-and-higher generation as the black population. Thereafter, the white population will have a higher proportion in the fourth-and-higher generation than any of the other major racial/ethnic groups.

The racial/ethnic populations in the United States will follow two main patterns over the next five decades. The Asian and Hispanic population will remain predominantly immigrant-centered for the next 50 years. Over one-half of their population groups will be immigrants and sons and daughters of immigrants. The black and white

Table 11.8 ALTERNATIVE PROJECTIONS OF THE U.S. POPULATION, BY RACE/
ETHNICITY: 2000–2040
(populations in millions)

Year and Projection	Total	White Total	White Non-Hispanic	Asian	Black	Hispanic	Other
2000							
Census	274.8	224.6	196.7	12.3	35.5	30.6	2.4
PRB	279.1	230.6	200.3	12.1	36.4	30.3	—
UI	276.8	228.7	198.4	12.0	34.1	30.3	2.1
2020							
Census	322.6	250.6	206.2	23.1	45.7	49.0	3.2
PRB	316.9	252.2	205.6	20.3	44.4	46.6	—
UI	320.5	255.5	208.4	22.7	40.2	47.1	2.2
2040							
Census	364.3	268.8	205.6	35.0	56.4	69.8	4.1
PRB	333.3	257.2	196.9	27.8	48.4	60.3	—
UI	355.5	274.7	210.5	34.5	44.1	64.2	2.2

Sources: Census—U.S. Bureau of the Census (1992). Figures in the table are derived from the middle series of the projections. PRB—Population Reference Bureau (Bouvier and Davis 1982). Figures in the table are from the PRB projection series with an assumed one million immigrants annually. The total white numbers are the sum of the Hispanic and white non-Hispanic populations. The PRB projections include the Asian and Other Races in a combined number. UI—Urban Institute. The figures are from table 11.4. For comparative purposes, the white total is shown as the sum of Hispanic and white non-Hispanic populations.

population will continue to have members primarily in the fourth-and-greater generation.

Comparison with Other Population Projections

Two other groups have recently prepared population projections for racial/ethnic groups of the U.S. population. The U.S. Bureau of the Census (1992) prepared projections for racial/ethnic groups comparable to those presented here; these projections supplanted earlier projections (U.S. Bureau of the Census 1986, 1989). Another group, the Population Reference Bureau (Bouvier and Davis 1982), prepared projections for Asian and Other Races, black, Hispanic, and white non-Hispanic groups.[7] Population projection results from the U.S. Bureau of the Census and the Population Reference Bureau (PRB) are presented in table 11.8 along with our projections.

It should be noted that the PRB projection was completed several years ago and uses the 1980 Census for a base year. Our projections use the 1990 Census as the base year and take advantage of more recent information on the volume of immigration and the racial/ethnic composition of immigrants. The Census Bureau projections use more detailed information from the 1990 Census and assume no future changes in fertility or immigration beyond 1990. Compared with the other two projections, our work assumes intermediate levels of mortality and fertility overall but with some substantial racial/ethnic differences. The impact of different demographic assumptions plays out over time in the various groups. In general, our projections fall between the other two, but the three sets of projections give a similar picture for the U.S. population 30 to 50 years hence, a larger and growing population with significantly higher minority populations, especially Asian and Hispanic.

Noting the racial/ethnic composition in 2040 for the three population projections, we see that the Asian population is virtually identical in our projections and the Census Bureau's. Our 2040 projections for the black population are somewhat lower than PRB's and much lower than the Census Bureau's. These differences reflect the respective assumptions about future levels of fertility.

All three projections show that the Hispanic population will almost triple by 2040. The projections diverge from ours by less than ± 10 percent, a rather small difference when the projection horizon and growth rate are taken into account. Finally, our projections assume slightly higher immigration and higher fertility for the white non-Hispanic population than the two other projections. The white non-Hispanic population in our projections in 2040 is projected to exceed the Bureau of the Census's figure by about 5 million and the PRB figure by 13 million.

CONCLUSIONS

To any casual observer, it should be obvious that the composition of U.S. society is undergoing considerable change. Our demographic analysis confirms this trend and presents evidence about future trends. The statistical evidence tells only part of the story. That the white non-Hispanic proportion in the population will decline in future years seems certain. Both the Asian and Hispanic populations will grow, both numerically and proportionately. Blacks will increase their numbers, but their proportion will remain similar in the future.

Hispanics will increase to a number exceeding that of blacks by about 2010.[8]

But how will these new immigrant groups adjust to U.S. society? The contribution of immigration within each racial/ethnic group provides data to alert us to potential issues and difficulties. As table 11.7 shows, over one-half of Asian and Hispanic residents will consist of first generation (foreign-born) or second generation (sons and daughters of immigrants) persons for the next half century. On the other hand, the black population, which currently is primarily fourth-and-higher generation, will experience its first sizable immigration in over two centuries.

Both the size and the relative recency of the movements of people from Asian and Latin American countries suggest that the integration process will take some time to be accomplished if immigration levels remain high in future years. Thus, in considering the impact of immigration on the future population of the United States, the issue of the time of entry and what it means for adaptation is important.

One noteworthy limitation in the model presents itself in this chapter. Our model, like standard population projection models of racial/ethnic groups makes a crucial (and debatable) assumption of perfect endogamy for the group for the projection period. These models assume nonoverlapping racial/ethnic groups—that is, all individuals are members of only one racial/ethnic group, and they marry members of the same group and produce single-ancestry children. This is a false assumption for most immigrant groups, so such projections give a questionable picture of the future population dynamics. Considerable exogamy exists for most racial/ethnic groups in the United States, and ethnic exogamy varies significantly by generation.

We have completed some preliminary work that considers the impact of exogamy on racial/ethnic populations characterized by single and mixed ancestry (Edmonston and Passel 1993). Single ancestry means that both parents are of the same ethnicity, and their offspring would be single-ancestry children. Mixed ancestry means either that the parents are of different ancestries or that one or both of the parents are of mixed ancestry. Taking this approach, we assume that a mixed-ancestry person can never produce a single-ancestry offspring. In our initial work, we use a probability of ethnic endogamy for each generation, separate for each racial/ethnic group, with the probability of endogamy assumed to be constant for all ages of a generation.

Our preliminary work assumes that ethnic endogamy in the population projection does not affect the survivorship function and that mortality conditions are the same for single- and mixed-ancestry persons. It is less clear, however, what should be the impact of international migration on the single- and mixed-ancestry groups. For the initial work, we assume that immigrants are single-ancestry and that emigrants, by generation, have ancestry characteristics similar to the resident population. We also assume that the U.S. population in 1990 is entirely single ancestry.

The fertility function varies, however, for the single- and mixed-ancestry groups in our initial formulation. Only single-ancestry mothers give birth to single-ancestry offspring. Yet the birth function for the mixed-ancestry population includes those women who are mixed-ancestry plus those women who are single-ancestry but marry someone of a different ethnic group.

Using exogamy rates similar to those reported for U.S. racial/ethnic groups in the 1980s, we find that the mixed-ancestry population would increase from zero in 1990 (the baseline assumption) to 31.4 million, or 9 percent of the total population, in 2040 (Edmonston and Passel 1993). The large group of individuals of mixed ancestry would have an important impact on the size of the U.S. minority population (American Indian, Asian American, black, and Hispanic). If only single-ancestry minority persons reported themselves as minority, the population would be 37 percent minority in 2040. With a mixed-ancestry minority population of 7 percent in 2040, however, a much greater minority population is a possibility. If all persons with minority ancestry were to report themselves as minority, then the minority population in 2040 would increase to over 44 percent.[9]

Current assumptions of no intermarriage between racial/ethnic groups is clearly too restrictive for thinking about future demographic trends for race and ethnic groups in the United States. Preliminary analysis suggests that a substantial increase will occur in the proportion of persons of mixed ancestry, particularly for individuals who will have an American Indian, Asian, or Hispanic ancestor. A critical research task is to understand trends in intermarriage and how individuals of mixed ancestry report their racial/ethnic origins and to devise improved census and survey questions that include mixed-ancestry categories.

We do not claim to know what the future will bring to the U.S. population. There is always a danger when interpreting population projection numbers of accepting them as a statement of fact. We have expressed caveats in many places about the assumptions made for these projections. We have emphasized that they are simulations based on "what would happen under these stated assumptions."

They are not predictions about the future. The future depends, in fact, on future demographic behavior.

We can use these projections to give us some idea about the direction in population trends. Under currently low fertility, immigration will need to continue at a substantial level to avoid population decline. With continued immigration at current levels and composition, the principal conclusion of this study is that the racial/ethnic composition of the nation will be substantially altered over the next century.

Fertility and immigration are the basic mechanisms through which populations are regenerated. These regeneration processes not only add numbers to the population, ensuring demographic continuity in the face of departures through death and emigration, they also change the character of the population. At the national level, fertility and immigration change the character of the population in terms of the age and sex structure, socioeconomic composition, cultural makeup, and regional distribution. At the individual level, these processes change the patterns of relationships among people: the size and composition of families and kin networks as well as types and characteristics of relationships with other social networks both within and beyond the family and community. The main difference between fertility and immigration is that the process of socialization into the receiving society is more complete when the new arrivals are infants born to resident families. Because of their previous socialization in another society, immigrants contribute a greater element of newness or difference. Immigration brings the "outside in" to U.S. society, promoting a link to another country, community, and family.

The immigration issue, from a population policy perspective, is how many members are to be added to U.S. society and by what means. A related question is how the benefits and costs of new immigrants are distributed among existing residents. How should the society distribute the costs and benefits of additional children between the immigrant families and the larger community? Similarly, how are the costs and benefits of immigration to be distributed between the immigrants themselves and their sponsoring families, on the one hand, and the receiving community, city, or state, on the other hand? How much effort do receiving communities need to expend to help the new arrivals adapt? Equally important, how much does the receiving community need to adapt itself to the presence of the new arrivals? These are fundamental policy questions to address.

This chapter deals with the demographic effects of immigration. We have observed that immigration, even at moderate levels, can make a substantial difference to future population size and growth. Regarding other demographic parameters, we have seen that immigration has a major impact on the racial/ethnic composition of the U.S. population, with striking differences for the generational composition of racial/ethnic groups.

We conclude this discussion of immigration policy by admitting that it is very hard to make a policy argument based on demographic issues alone. Population, by itself, is a fairly neutral variable in a society's welfare. Advantages and disadvantages obtain to both larger numbers and smaller numbers. The value placed on population size and growth also depends upon which considerations are given priority (more space for parks or more power in the world community, for instance). No doubt questions of technology and innovation are more important than population size in promoting social welfare. Nonetheless, it is hard to avoid the impression that numbers do count in questions of welfare and that, in general, the United States is not suffering from the moderate population increases derived from current immigration.

One important social consideration deserves final attention. Current immigrants are changing the racial/ethnic composition of the United States. The policy implications of this change are not clear. The proportion of the population that can be classified as minority (under current definitions) is increasing, almost entirely as a result of immigration. Several chapters in this volume demonstrate that the recently arrived immigrants from Asia and Latin America are suffering disadvantages. Clearly, the new immigrant groups that arrived in the 1980s and 1990s have not been able to take full advantage of their human resources.

These observations are not meant to imply that the arrival of new immigrants should be controlled. It is unusual for a society to be completely open to the arrival of racial and ethnic groups that are different from the resident groups. The recent U.S. experience with non-discrimination in immigrant selection—which has opened the door to increased immigration from Asia, Latin America and the Caribbean, and Africa—has been reasonably successful. In addition, the U.S. commitment to non-discrimination in immigration is a key element for winning political support in the international community for immigration as well as other international policies. While U.S. immigration policy has been that immigrants should be selected without regard to national origin, other chapters in this volume suggest that immigrants need to be aware that they will need to adjust to a new language and to new social structures in order to take effective part in their newly adopted home country.

Notes

This manuscript is a revision of a paper presented at a conference entitled "Immigration and Ethnicity" at the Urban Institute, Washington, D.C., June 17–18, 1991.

1. In most contexts within this chapter, the term "white" is used interchangeably with "white, non-Hispanic." When the term refers to all whites including those of Hispanic origin, it will be noted.

2. Reports of "other races" includes individuals who do not choose a specific race category from the list supplied but write-in such responses as "Mexican," for example.

3. The discussion here assumes that generation membership of the parents is unique— that is, either both parents always have the same generation or only the mother's generation is considered. We discuss mixed generational models in a later section.

4. We use *female-dominant* here to mean the model derives the generational characteristics of children from the mother. In other words, the generational membership of the father has no relevance for the offspring in the female-dominant perspective.

5. The American Indian projections were made assuming zero net immigration. Projections were done with simple growth assumptions. We project the 1990 population assuming a diminishing annual rate of population growth and no net change in the number of persons reporting themselves as American Indian. This latter assumption is contrary to recent trends (Passel 1992).

6. Table 11.4 includes projection results for 100 years. We concentrate our exposition, however, on the next 50 years (1990 to 2040), a period over which we consider the projections to be more credible.

7. Bouvier (1991) has prepared more recent projections, but the published materials do not provide sufficiently detailed tabular results for comparison. In this recent work, Bouvier assumes a constant 950,000 net immigration per year as compared with our assumption of 900,000 per year in 1990, increasing to 950,000 per year in 2005. The assumed racial/ethnic composition of immigrants differs for Bouvier's and our projections.

Both projections assume an overall long-term total fertility rate of 1.9. Our work assumes generational differences in fertility, but similar levels for the native-born population of all racial/ethnic groups. Bouvier assumes higher fertility for the Asian, black, and Hispanic populations and lower fertility for the white non-Hispanic population. Our life expectancy assumptions are higher than those of Bouvier who acknowledges a "conservative" assumption of modest mortality improvements.

8. Indeed, under current trends, the Asian population would exceed the black population by 2070.

9. The largest relative impact of exogamy is on the future Hispanic populations. With a continuation of current intermarriage patterns, the Hispanic population could vary from 51 million to 78 million in 2040, depending on how mixed-ancestry individuals choose to identify (Edmonston and Passel 1993). The baseline, presented here for this group, is 64 million in 2040.

References

Bean, Frank D., Barry Edmonston, and Jeffrey S. Passel. 1990. *Undocumented Migration to the United States: IRCA and the Experience of the 1980s*. Washington, D.C.: The Urban Institute Press.

Bouvier, Leon F. 1991. *Peaceful Invasions: Immigration and Changing America*. Washington, D.C.: Center for Immigration Studies.

Bouvier, Leon F., and Cary B. Davis. 1982. "The Future Racial Composition of the United States." Manuscript Copy. Washington, D.C.: Population Reference Bureau.

Edmonston, Barry, and Jeffrey S. Passel. 1991. "Generational Population Projections for Ethnic Groups." *Proceedings of the Social Statistics Section of the American Statistical Association*. Washington, D.C.: American Statistical Association.

———. 1992a. *Population Projections for the United States, 1990–2090*. In four volumes: Asian, Black, Hispanic, and White Non-Hispanic Population. Washington, D.C.: The Urban Institute.

———. 1992b. "Immigration and Immigrant Generations in Population Projections." *International Journal of Forecasting* 8: 459–476.

———. 1993. "Exogamy and Race/Ethnic Ancestry in U.S. Population Projections." Paper presented at the 1993 Winter Conference of the American Statistical Association, Fort Lauderdale, Florida, January 3–5.

Fix, Michael, and Jeffrey S. Passel. 1991. "The Door Remains Open: Recent Immigration to the United States and a Preliminary Analysis of the Immigration Act of 1990." Program for Research on Immigration Policy, Policy Discussion Paper PRIP-UI-14. Washington, D.C.: The Urban Institute. January.

Lee, Ronald, and Lawrence Carter. 1990. "Modeling and Forecasting U.S. Mortality." Paper presented to the annual meeting of the Population Association of America, Toronto, Canada.

Miltenyi, K. 1981. "Population Projections: Problems and Solutions. Report of the Workshop on Population Projections, Budapest, Hungary, March 1980." Department of Technical Co-operation for Development. New York, NY: United Nations.

National Center for Health Statistics. 1992. "Advance Report of Final Natality Statistics, 1990." *Monthly Vital Statistics Report* 41 (9, Supplement).

Passel, Jeffrey S. 1992. "The Growing American Indian Population, 1960–1990: Beyond Demography." Paper presented at the annual meetings of the American Statistical Association, Boston, Massachusetts, August 9–13.

Passel, Jeffrey S., and Barry Edmonston. 1992. "Methodology for Estimating the Population of the United States by Race and Generation: 1900–1990." Unpublished memorandum. Washington, D.C.: The Urban Institute. May.

Preston, Samuel H. 1991. "Demographic Change in the United States, 1970–2050." Working Paper Series 91-1. Pension Research Council. Philadelphia, Pennsylvania: The Wharton School, University of Pennsylvania.

Romaniuc, Anatole. 1990. "Population Projection as Prediction, Simulation, and Prospective Analysis." *Population Bulletin of the United Nations* 29: 16–31.

Tabah, L. 1984. "Population Projections: Methodology of the United Nations. Papers of the United Nations Ad Hoc Expert Group on Demographic Projections, United Nations Headquarters, 16–19 November 1981." *Population Studies* 83. Department of International Economic and Social Affairs. New York, NY: United Nations.

Trustees of Old Age and Survivors Insurance and Disability Insurance Trust Funds (OASDI). 1990. "1990 Annual Report of the Federal Old-Age and Survivors Insurance and Disability Trust Funds." 101st Cong. 2d sess. House Ways and Means Committee. Washington, D.C.: U.S. Government Printing Office.

Werner, B. 1986. "Family Building Intentions of Different Generations of Women: Results from the General Household Survey, 1979–83." *Population Trends* 44 (Summer): 17–23.

U.S. Bureau of the Census. 1986. "Projections of the Hispanic Population: 1983 to 2080." *Current Population Reports,* Series P-25, No. 995. Washington, D.C.: U.S. Government Printing Office.

_____. 1989. "Projections of the Population of the United States, by Age, Sex, and Race: 1988 to 2080," by Gregory K. Spencer. *Current Population Reports,* Series P-25, No. 1018. Washington, D.C.: U.S. Government Printing Office.

_____. 1992. "Population Projections of the United States, by Age, Sex, Race, and Hispanic Origin: 1992 to 2050," by Jennifer Cheeseman Day. *Current Population Reports,* Series P25-1092. Washington, D.C.: U.S. Government Printing Office.

ABOUT THE EDITORS

Barry Edmonston is study director of the Panel on Census Requirements for the Year 2000 and Beyond, a three-year study conducted by the Committee on National Statistics of the National Academy of Sciences. Prior to joining the National Academy of Sciences, he was a senior research associate at the Urban Institute, where he completed the work for this volume. His demographic research has dealt with population distribution, early childhood mortality, models of human reproduction and family formation, and international migration. Recent publications include "Immigration and Immigrant Generations in Population Projections" in the *International Journal of Forecasting* (November 1992) and "Immigration and Ethnicity in National Population Projections" in the *Proceedings of the International Population Conference, Montreal, 1993*, volume 2.

Jeffrey S. Passel is the director of the Urban Institute's Program for Research on Immigration Policy, a program aimed at providing analysis and research to inform the nation's immigration and immigrant policies. Prior to joining the Urban Institute in 1989, Dr. Passel directed the Census Bureau's program of population estimates and projections and its research on demographic methods for measuring census undercount. His own research at the Urban Institute has focused on the demography of immigration, particularly the measurement of illegal immigration, and the impacts and integration of immigrants into American society. His interests also include measuring and defining racial/ethnic groups in the U.S. Recent publications include: an edited volume, *Undocumented Migration to the United States: IRCA and the Experience of the 1980s* (with Frank D. Bean and Barry Edmonston), *The Coverage of Population in the United States* (with Robert Fay and J. Gregory Robinson), and several articles on illegal immigration and population projections.

Frank D. Bean is Ashbel Smith Professor of sociology and director of graduate training programs, Population Research Center, at the University of Texas at Austin. A demographer with specializations in international migration, fertility, the demography of racial and ethnic groups, and population policy, his recent books include *Undocumented Migration to the United States: IRCA and the Experience of the 1980s* (edited with Barry Edmonston and Jeffrey S. Passel) and *The Hispanic Population of the United States* (with Marta Tienda).

Ruth R. Berg is a doctoral candidate in demography and sociology at the University of Texas at Austin. Her interests include the demography of U.S. racial/ethnic groups and the sociology of fertility. She is currently completing her dissertation, which deals with intermarriage and fertility among African Americans, Mexican Americans, and non-Hispanic whites in the United States.

Jorge Chapa is an associate professor at the Lyndon B. Johnson School of Public Affairs. He is the author of many publications and the co-author of *The Burden of Support* (Stanford University Press, 1988). Dr. Chapa has studied and written about a range of Latino issues, and has focused on the policy implications of demographic, economic, educational, and intergenerational trends.

María E. Enchautegui is a senior research associate at the Urban Institute. Since joining the Institute in 1991, she has conducted research in the area of economic impacts of immigration, Hispanic poverty, and ethnic labor markets. Her research has been published in *Economic Development and Cultural Change, International Migration Review*, and *Eastern Economic Journal*.

Angelo Falcon, a co-principal investigator of the Latino National Political Survey, is president and founder of the Institute for Puerto Rican Policy, a nonprofit and nonpartisan policy center based in New York City. In 1984, he created the National Puerto Rican Opinion Survey (NPROS), the longest running continuous survey of Puerto Rican leadership opinion in the United States. He has published in *New Community* and the *Hispanic Journal of the Behavioral Sciences*. He recently co-edited the volume, *The "Puerto Rican Exception": Persistent Poverty and the Conservative Social Policy of Linda Chavez* (1992).

Michael Fix directs the Urban Institute's Immigrant Policy Program. Recent works include: *Educating Immigrant Children: Chapter 1 in the Changing City* (with Wendy Zimmermann); *Clear and Convincing Evidence: Measurement of Discrimination in America* (co-editor with Raymond Struyk); and *The Paper Curtain: Employer Sanctions' Implementation, Impact, and Reform* (editor).

F. Chris Garcia is a co-principal investigator of the Latino National Political Survey, and is a professor of political science at the University of New Mexico. His research and teaching interests are in the areas of American and Hispanic politics, public opinion, political socialization, campaigns and elections, and education policy. He is author of many articles and chapters on these and other topics as well as author or editor of several books including *The Political Socialization of Chicano Children* (1973); *La Causa Politica* (1974); *New Mexico Government* (1976, revised 1981); *The Chicano Political Experience* (1977); and *Latinos and the Political System* (1988).

John Garcia, a co-principal investigator of the Latino National Political Survey, is an associate professor of political science at the University of Arizona, where he is department head. During 1978–1980, he was involved in the National Chicano Survey, the first national probability survey of Mexican-origin populations in the United States. His published works are found in a wide variety of social science journals, and as book chapters in collections that deal with ethnic politics, local government, and public policy.

Rodolfo O. de la Garza is Mike Hogg Professor of community affairs in the department of government at the University of Texas at Austin. The principal investigator of the Latino National Political Survey, he also initiated and directed four other major studies of Latino politics: *From Rhetoric to Reality: Latinos in the 1988 Election* (Westview, 1992); *Latino Voices: Mexican, Puerto Rican, and Cuban Perspectives on American Politics* (Westview, 1992); *Barrio Ballots: Latino Politics in the 1990 Elections* (Westview, 1994); and *Do Latino Votes Count? Latinos in the 1992 Elections.* He has published extensively on Mexican-American politics, Latino politics, and U.S.-Mexican relations.

Sharon M. Lee is associate professor of sociology at the University of Richmond. She was previously at the National University of Singapore, as a faculty member in the Department of Sociology, and at Cornell University, as a visiting fellow with the Southeast Asia Program and a visiting assistant professor in the Department of Rural Sociology. Her research interests are race and ethnicity, immigration and immigrant adaptation, and poverty. Recent publications include "Racial Classifications in the U.S. Census, 1890 to 1990" in *Ethnic and Racial Studies* (January 1993) and "Poverty in the U.S. Asian Population" in *Social Science Quarterly* (September 1994).

Kristin E. Neuman is a doctoral candidate at the University of Chicago. Her research interests focus on Mexican migration to the United States, U.S. immigration law and policy, contemporary Mexican culture, and the effects of divorce on children in the United States. After six months of fieldwork in Mexico and California, she is writing her dissertation on the integration of Mexican immigrants in the United States, using a combination of quantitative and qualitative methods.

Elaine Sorensen is a senior research associate at the Urban Institute. Her recent research in the immigration area has focused on the earnings trends of Mexican-origin males in the 1980s. Previously, she analyzed the impact of immigrants on the earnings and employment of native workers. This latter work was published in a book titled *Immigrant Categories and the U.S. Job Market: Do They Make a Difference?* (Urban Institute Press, 1993).

Kathryn A. Sowards is a doctoral candidate in demography and sociology at the University of Texas at Austin. Her research interests include the demography of inequality and the sociology of health and reproduction. Her dissertation focuses on the changing epidemiology of infant death among Mexican-origin and Anglo teenage mothers in San Antonio, Texas. She has published previously on the effects of racial classification schemes on the measurement of child mortality in Brazil.

Gillian Stevens is associate professor of sociology at the University of Illinois at Urbana-Champaign. Her research field is social demography. Her most recent publications have focused on ethnic and ethnolinguistic populations in the United States.

Marta Tienda is professor of sociology at the University of Chicago and coauthor of *The Hispanic Population of the United States*. Currently she is studying ethnic variation in the school-to-work transition (with V. Joseph Hotz), the dynamics of minority underemployment (with Franklin Wilson and Larry Wu), and contextual determinants of minority educational achievement (with Ross M. Stolzenberg). Tienda is editor of the *American Journal of Sociology*.

Wendy Zimmermann is a research associate at the Urban Institute, where she has conducted research on immigration and immigrant policy and on employment discrimination. Her most recent publications include *Educating Immigrant Children: Chapter 1 in the Changing City* (with Michael Fix).